COLLECTIVES IN THE SPANISH REVOLUTION

Gaston Leval

Translated from the French by Vernon Richards

Collectives in the Spanish Revolution
Gaston Leval
Translated from the French by Vernon Richards
This edition © 2018 PM Press

ISBN: 978–1–62963–447–0
Library of Congress Control Number: 2017942919

Cover by John Yates / www.stealworks.com
Interior design by briandesign

10 9 8 7 6 5 4 3 2 1

PM Press
PO Box 23912
Oakland, CA 94623
www.pmpress.org

Printed in the USA by the Employee Owners of Thomson-Shore in Dexter,
Michigan.
www.thomsonshore.com

CONTENTS

PREFACE TO THE 2018 EDITION

Collectives in the Spanish Revolution can only deal in any detail with some of the self-managed collectives that were established in Republican Spain during the struggle against Franco, for, as the author points out, there were 400 agricultural collectives in Aragón, 900 in Levante, and 300 in Castile. In addition, the whole of industry in Catalonia and 70 per cent in Levante was collectivised.

Leval's study brings together two aspects that are generally difficult to unite—analysis and testimony—but, and in part owing to this method of presentation, the reader's interest is held throughout the book. He visited the towns and villages of revolutionary Spain where, soon after July 19, 1936, people had opted to live a libertarian communist lifestyle almost without precedent in all history, collectivising the land, factories and workshops, and the social services.

He paints a serene but not uncritical picture of the role of the countless rank-and-file activists of "the idea" who had long discussed the possibilities of a self-managed economic and social system that was truly communal and anti-authoritarian:

> It is clear, the social revolution which took place then did not stem from a decision by the leading organisms of the C.N.T. or from the slogans launched by the militants and agitators who were in the public limelight. . . . It occurred spontaneously, naturally, not (and let us avoid demagogy) because "the people" in general had suddenly become capable of performing miracles . . . but because, and it is worth repeating, among those people there was a large minority who were active, strong, guided by an ideal which has been continuing

through the years a struggle started [more than half a century earlier] in Bakunin's time (p. 80).

This raises the question: were the collectivisations enforced at the point of a gun, as argued by a number of bourgeois historians?

In fact, in most villages collectivisations occurred after the major landowners had fled to the Francoist zone: usually, assemblies were held at which it was decided to expropriate the landowners' land and machinery and share their own for the common good; teams were formed to carry out the necessary tasks, each electing recallable delegates to a village assembly. Leval writes that in Aragón, where the libertarian militias were numerous, their role was minimal if not negative inasmuch as they lived, in part, at the expense of the collectives. As he describes it, they "lived on the fringes of the task of social transformation being carried out," although Durruti, realising their importance, did send some of his men, skilled organisers not armed troops, to help the collectives. All the energy, however, came from the local militants who took initiatives "with a tactical skill often quite outstanding" (p. 91).

Other chapters make fascinating reading: "The Socialisation of Medicine," "The Charters," "Rubi," "Lerida," etc. The agricultural, industrial and social service industries are all explained with their own peculiar aspects, and their development traced within the overall scheme of self-management.

A number of points deserve separate study, such as the problem of the relationship of individuals to their work in a new society: "Obviously some would have preferred to stay in bed, but it was impossible for them to cheat" (p. 117); "there was no place in the rules for the demand for personal freedom or for the autonomy of the individual" (p. 125); "Building operatives were working with enthusiasm. They had started off by applying the eight-hour day, but the peasants pointed out they worked a twelve-hour day" (p. 146 and also pp. 211, 212, 304).

Some of the author's comments are well off track: "his Slavonic psychology, his generous Russian nature" (p. 18 on Bakunin, but Lenin too was a Russian), "preaching the libertarian gospel" (p. 47), "the Good News" (p. 56), but fortunately they are few and make no difference to the essence of Leval's story.

More curious, however, is Leval's position: "convinced very soon that the anti-fascists would end by losing the war" (p. 68), he dedicated himself to collecting together the results of this unique experiment for posterity. There are contemporary articles written by Leval: "I had to make an effort to give them confidence and offered them words of hope" (p. 112). We cannot but underline Leval's patronising hypocrisy in this matter—a sort of tourist's eye view of the attempts to live of the condemned. What was there to do? Leval seems to be trying to be a historian first and anarchist second, overlooking that it is always one and the same struggle: "Posterity is us, just later on."

There are, in fact, two faces to Leval. In one chapter entitled "Political Collaboration" he writes, "This excursion in the corridors of power was negative" (p. 324). But while he was in Spain, during the Civil War, that was not Leval's opinion at all. On arrival he published an article in *Solidaridad Obrera* (November 27, 1936, p. 8) entitled "Discipline: A Condition of Victory"; in February 1937 he took part in a meeting with Mariano R. Vázquez (a strong supporter of CNT participation in the government) and again in France in November 1937, in *Le Libertaire,* he pleaded for a moratorium on the anarchist programme for the duration of the war.

Leval also published articles of a practical nature, such as: "The Small Proprietor and the Small Business," "Our Programme for Reconstruction," "Let Us Establish Co-operatives," (*Solidaridad Obrera*, December 12, 1936, p. 4; December 27, 1936, p. 10; March 2, 1937, p. 6). His stand in support of the pro-governmental section of the CNT is important. Before the war Leval was better known for his books on social reconstruction, written in the spirit of Peter Kropotkin's *The Conquest of Bread* but adapted to the epoch. Many of the collectivists knew Leval from these writings and had he defended at the time the position he takes in *Collectives* then the opposition to the political sidetracking that was going on could well have been far greater.

Interesting too is that the translator and publisher of the original 1975 English-language edition, Vernon Richards, fails to point out this evolution in Leval's thinking. It would also have been useful to know that Sam Dolgoff, author of *The Anarchist Collectives: Workers' Self-Management in the Spanish Revolution, 1936–1939,* took his texts from the 1952 Italian edition of Leval's book, with variations. (The figures, for example, given in the chapter on the socialisation of medicine are different from Richards' translation. Are they typographical errors by Dolgoff or forgetfulness on the part of Richards?) Other texts, in particular "The Characteristics of the Libertarian Collectives," an excellent résumé of the nineteen points of the main aspects of self-management, as well as the section of the 1948 Italian pamphlet *L'attivita sindicale nella transformazione sociale* that deals with industry, should have been included in the 1975 edition but for some reason Leval and Richards chose not to do so.

Collectives in the Spanish Revolution demonstrates clearly that the working class are perfectly capable of running farms, factories, workshops, and health and public services without bosses or managers dictating to them. It proves that anarchist methods of organising, with decisions made from the bottom up, can work effectively in large-scale industry involving the coordination of many thousands of workers in many hundreds of places of work across numerous different cities and towns, as well as broad rural areas. The Spanish Revolution also gives us an insight into the creative and constructive power of ordinary people once they have some control over their lives. The Spanish working class not only kept production going throughout the war but in many cases managed to achieve increases in output. They improved working conditions and created new techniques and processes in their workplaces. They created, out of nothing, an arms industry without which the war against fascism could not have been fought. The Revolution also showed that without the competition bred by capitalism, industry can be run in a much more rational manner. Finally it demonstrated how the organised working class inspired by a great ideal has the power to transform society.

Stuart Christie
January 2018

INTRODUCTION

The only constructive, valid, important achievement during the Civil War was in fact that of the Revolution, on the fringe of power. The industrial collectivisations, the socialisation of agriculture, the syndicalisations of social services, all that, which made it possible to hold out for nearly three years and without which Franco would have triumphed in a matter of weeks, was the achievement of those who created, organised without concerning themselves with ministries and ministers.

Gaston Leval, *Collectives in the Spanish Revolution*

1

More than eight decades ago revolutionary Spain implemented a massive model of worker-controlled agriculture, industry and public services based on libertarian communism and collectives in the midst of the Civil War. Workers had to do so under the threat posed by Francoist troops, the Communist persecution of anarchists,[1] the active boycott of the most conservative policies established by the Spanish Second Republic,[2] and the scarcity brought about by the conflict. The experiment only lasted for a brief time in the Republican zone, but the world is still fascinated

---

1 "The brigade led by the communist Lister was soon to abandon the front to go and destroy 'manu militari' almost all the Aragonese Collectives, including that of Binefar and its canton" (p. 121).

2 "It was not an easy matter to assert themselves so as to avoid friction among the anti-Francoist sectors. For the socialist, republican, and communist politicians actively sought to prevent our success, even to restoring the old order or maintaining what was left of it" (p. 239).

by this classless and self-governed society erected by the people for the people. One of the most privileged witnesses of these collectives was Gaston Leval.

This volume represents the results of his experience and research. *Collectives in the Spanish Revolution* aims to chronicle the Spanish collectives established after the Frente Popular's victory in February 1936, with a particular focus on those created in the immediate aftermath. It also can be conceived as a critical libertarian history of both the Second Spanish Republic (1931–1939) and the Civil War (1936–1939). In his own words, "What he presents is therefore a collection of materials for a general history of the Spanish revolution which he is not entirely without hope of writing himself one day if he can return to a Spain freed from the Franco regime" (p. 69). It should, however, be made clear from the outset that the book was not conceived as a guide for collectivising applicable uncritically to all countries and times. As we shall see below, not everything and everyone was praiseworthy in the collectives: "While praising and proclaiming the constructive achievements of the Spanish libertarian revolution, this writer recognises that it was not without its failures nor was it perfect" (p. 353).

2

For those who do not know him, Gaston Leval (né Pierre Robert Piller) was born in 1895 in Paris. He fled to Spain in 1915 after defecting with the intention of refusing to fight in the First World War.[3] He had encountered anarchist ideas in his youth while in France. He carried out several jobs in Barcelona, Valencia, and Saragossa and collaborated with countless national and international anarchist periodicals. His anarchist militancy brought him into conflict with the authorities; resulting in his incarceration in both Valencia and Barcelona.[4] Once released, he joined the National Confederation of Labour (CNT) and was part of a

---

3   "The present writer arrived in Barcelona in June 1915" (p. 54).
4   Miguel Íñiguez and Juan Gómez Perín, *Esbozo de una enciclopedia histórica del anarquismo español* (Madrid: Fundación de Estudios Libertarios Anselmo Lorenzo, 2001), p. 52.

CNT delegation (together with Andrés Nin, Jesús Ibáñez, Joaquín Maurín, and Hilario Arlandis) that attended the Third International Conference in Moscow (1921).[5] This conference influenced both his life and ideology. One year later, the CNT held a national conference of unions in Saragossa, and the conference's participants rejected the CNT's adherence to the principles of the Third International Conference.[6] After spending time as an itinerant photographer Leval settled in Corunna, northwestern Spain, and become a teacher at the CNT-sponsored rationalist school. He remained there until the Primo de Rivera dictatorship (1923–1930) closed the school in 1923. In search of a better life Leval and his wife boarded a ship to Uruguay as stowaways. Unfortunately, Leval did not find it. His time spent in Latin America included three years of extreme misery in Argentina, where his daughter died as the family could not afford medical assistance. He worked with the Argentine Regional Workers' Federation (FORA) but, due to the popularity of Bolshevism, the union's membership continued to shrink until it was eventually disbanded in 1930.[7]

The author returned to Spain in 1936 and in 1937—feeling that the war was going to destroy all the agrarian and industrial collectives—he embarked on an eight-month tour around the majority of those collectives in order to record the impressive work done by the people (not exclusively CNT members) on a self-organised basis.[8]

---

5 Manuel Buenacasa, *El movimiento obrero español, 1886–1926: historia y crítica* (Madrid: Ediciones Júcar, 1977).

6 Xavier Paniagua, "La visió de Gastón Leval de la Rússia soviética el 1921," *Recerques*, no. 3, pp. 199–224.

7 Yaacov Oved, "The Rise and Fall of Anarcho Communism in Argentina," in Tzvi Medin and Raanan Rein, eds., *Society and Identity in Argentina: The European Context* (Tel Aviv: Tel Aviv University, 1997).

8 "The author, who had previously lived and struggled in Spain, was domiciled in South America when the civil war broke out. Having to travel illegally, he could only manage to return and disembark in Gibraltar in November. Convinced very soon that the anti-fascists would end by losing the war, and being aware of the importance of the social experiment that had been under taken by his comrades, he had only one thought: to promote by his propaganda the intensification and spread of this experiment to the preparation of which he had contributed for so long, and to record the results for the future" (p. 68).

Following the defeat of the Revolution he was exiled: first in France (1938)—where he was imprisoned but managed to escape—then he spent two years in Belgium and subsequently returned to France where he was granted an amnesty. In this country he founded and edited *Cahiers de l'humanisme libertaire: revue mensuelle d'études sociologiques* (1955–1976). He died in 1978 in Saint-Cloud (near Paris), having spent his final years in France among Spanish anarchist refugees and the new approaches to libertarian communism that came from the revolutionary movements of May 1968.[9]

From an intellectual point of view, Leval, like the majority of anarchist writers, was not a systematic thinker. He is best described by combining the labels "anarchist historian"[10] and "militant." As he pointed out in *Collectives in the Spanish Revolution*: "This he did to the extent that the circumstances allowed, and though with a long delay due to the ups and downs of his life as a militant, presents the result of his personal enquiry which was facilitated not only by his direct enquiries in the Syndicates' factories, and village collectives, but also by the spontaneous contribution of documents made to him by fraternal comrades with whom he maintained contact in his search for materials" (pp. 68–69).

Despite these problems, Leval felt duty-bound to write his book. First of all, because the creators of the collectives were mainly workers and peasants, that is, they created history with their tools and physical labour but were hopeless using the written word. To put it simply, the protagonists of history were so busy taking action that they had neither the opportunity nor the capability of leaving a written record of their collectives. Therefore, someone had to collect their stories and experiences, and that became Leval's undertaking. Second, after Franco's victory in 1939 the protagonists of the collectives were executed or went into exile in the bellicose context

9   Miguel Íñiguez and Juan Gómez Perín, *Esbozo de una enciclopedia histórica del anarquismo español* (Madrid: Fundación de Estudios Libertarios Anselmo Lorenzo, 2001), p. 482.

10 See Matthew S. Adams, "The Possibilities of Anarchist History: Rethinking the Canon and Writing History," *Anarchist Developments in Cultural Studies* 1 (2013): pp. 33–63.

of the beginning of the Second World War (1939–1945). The book was a "now-or-never" endeavour. Ultimately, as mentioned above, we could question the veracity and academic qualities of this book coming from a militant "anarchist historian." Luis A. Fernandez, among many others, argues that whenever possible, academics (and mainly militants) should "be there" exercising what he calls "participant observation."[11] In other words, it is important to be present in situations which raise issues of concern to the public interest or knowledge because one can understand firsthand what one has studied for years in the abstract. In this regard, Leval "was there" but only sometimes.[12] As already mentioned, he stayed in Spain between 1936 and 1938,[13] during which he completed an eight-month tour around the agrarian and industrial collectives.

Then what were his historical sources for writing this book? To begin with, he admitted: "The facts we are reproducing were not obtained on the spot. They are based on the testimony of militants who took part in this constructive task and who explained it to the author in discussions he had with them after Franco's triumph" (p. 307). These testimonies were obtained mainly through interviews[14] but also through numerous letters where workers and

---

11 Randal Amster, Abraham De Leon, Luis A. Fernandez, Anthony J. Nocella II & Deric Shannon (eds.), *Contemporary Anarchist Studies: An Introductory Anthology of Anarchy in the Academy* (London: Routledge, 2009), 95.

12 The author confirmed this idea when mentions that the origin of the book came "In the first place, from my own first-hand observations . . ." (p. 91). In other part of the book he commented, "This writer was present at a number of these assemblies in Aragon . . ." (p. 206). Similarly, he managed to write the book using his memories, something that we could deduce from the beginning of the first chapter, "if my memory serves me well" (p. 17).

13 ". . . his imprisonment in France in June 1938, did not allow him to carry his studies further" (p. 69).

14 "So the parties decided not to collaborate any longer in the practical tasks of a municipal nature, or within the jurisdiction of the Council. Our comrades had therefore to take over the most important duties: food supplies, public works, industry and agriculture. They were so successful that the organisers with whom I discussed these achievements fifteen years later had tears in their eyes in recalling that lost Paradise" (p. 300).

peasants provided him with a firsthand account of the collectives.[15] Next, Leval stressed the need to support his findings on collectives by studying "journals propagating the ideal . . . openly or clandestinely" (p. 27), and his book mentioned *Solidaridad Obrera, CNT, Tierra y Libertad, El Productor, Campo Libre, Cultura y Acción, Acracia, Tiempos Nuevos, La Revista Blanca, Orto* and *Estudios*, among many other examples. Finally, Leval's book drank from classical sources of the notion of libertarian communism. From an international perspective, he draws upon the works of the following writers—not necessarily anarchist or libertarian—for explaining the theoretical framework of the collectives: Plato, John Ball (1338–1381), Thomas More (1478–1535), Thomas Müntzer (1489–1525), Francis Bacon (1561–1626), Tommaso Campanella (1568–1639), Jean Meslier (1664–1729), Sylvain Maréchal (1750–1803), Jacques Roux (1752–1794), Jean-Baptiste Joseph Fourier (1768–1830), Robert Owen (1771–1858), Étienne Cabet (1788–1856), Constantin Pecqueur (1801–1887), Pierre-Joseph Proudhon (1809–1865), Louis Blanc (1811–1882), Mikhail Bakunin (1814–1876) and his Italian disciples (Emilio Covelli, Carlo Cafiero, Andrea Costa, Carlo Gambuzzi, Errico Malatesta,[16] Saverio Friscia and Giuseppe Fanelli), Giovanni Morelli (1816–1891), Élisée Reclus (1830–1905),[17] Peter Kropotkin (1842–1921), Max Nettlau (1865–1944), Pierre Besnard (1886–1947), but also Friedrich Engels (1820–1895) and even Karl Marx (1818–1883). From a Spanish perspective, Leval highlights in his book the relevance of Spanish theoreticians such as Francesc Pi i Margall (1824–1901), Anselmo Lorenzo (1841–1914), Rafael Farga i Pellicer (1844–1890), Joaquin Costa (1846–1911), Adolfo Posada y (1860–1944), Ricardo Mella (1861–1925), Federico Urales (1864–1942), Isaac Puente (1896–1936), Higinio Noja Ruiz (1896–1972),

---

15 "Less than two months after its constitution, I received a letter from the secretary of the Collective of Jativa which I feel deserves to be quoted in full" (p. 170).

16 Errico Malatesta, *Life and Ideas: The Anarchist Writings of Errico Malatesta* (Oakland: PM Press, 2015).

17 Élisée Reclus, *Anarchy, Geography, Modernity: Selected Writings of Elisée Reclus* (Oakland: PM Press, 2013).

and Diego Abad de Santillán (1897–1983).[18] That said, Leval, unlike most traditional libertarian communist authors, proclaimed not an idealistic or utopian approach to the Spanish collectives but a scientific or pragmatic one,[19] that is: "For the first time in the history of world anarchism, in turn D. A. de Santillan, Higinio Noja Ruiz, Gaston Leval dealt with these problems, not in the form of utopias and imaginary anticipations, but basing themselves on the concrete reality of the economy of the country, in the light of the statistics concerning industrial and agricultural production, the problem of raw materials, power, and international exchanges, public services, etc." (pp. 37–38).

3

In effect, the book avoids any utopianism and embraces the socio-economic achievements of the Spanish libertarian revolution during the years 1936–1939. Nevertheless, "the author considers it essential to present a picture, however brief, of the political conditions in which these experiments were undertaken and carried out, so that certain facts may be understood more clearly" (p. 321). In this sense, it has to be said that during its first days the Second Spanish Republic was euphorically considered by many a panacea[20] powerful enough to resolve the five main problems that encumbered Spain for over a century: *latifundism* (agriculture dominated by privately owned large estates), clerical domination of the State, illiteracy,[21] exploitation of the proletariat, and centralism. It soon became clear that the Republic was nothing more than a reformist

---

18 Diego Abad de Santillán, *El organismo económico de la revolución* (Madrid: Zero, 1978).

19 H. L. Osgood, "Scientific Anarchism," *Political Science Quarterly* 4, no. 1 (1889): pp. 1–36.

20 "And the Spanish people were hungry for bread and for land. For those who had voted Republican with republican feelings and hopes, Republic was synonymous with true freedom, true equality, true fraternity; it implied, above all else, the disappearance of social injustice and poverty" (p. 66).

21 "Let us not forget that at that time Spain had a population of 18 million 65% of whom were illiterate" (p. 44).

political regime[22] perpetuating the same problems and promoting repression.[23] As reported by Leval, these remaining unfulfilled promises ignited the agrarian and industrial workers, that is: "Faced with the slowness in applying agrarian reform, peasants began to work on their own account, invading collectively those estates which the large *terratenientes* (landowners) kept uncultivated—and which, one must admit, were generally of very poor quality" (p. 65). During the elections in 1936, the fear of another right-wing victory led to the creation of the coalition Frente Popular. It consisted of political parties and trade unions, including Izquierda Republicana (Republican Left), the PSOE (Spanish Socialist Workers' Party), the PCE (Communist Party of Spain), the POUM (Workers' Party of Marxist Unification) and the ERC (Republican Left of Catalonia). The CNT (with over one million members)[24] decided not to boycott Frente Popular, since it promised amnesty for all political prisoners. The coalition won and the amnesty happened. This absurd coalition started to fall apart because each group began to follow its own interests. The CNT tried to establish the libertarian communism that it had defended since its congress in 1936 in Saragossa. During July, with such an unstable situation, a part of the army rebelled against the Republic. The CNT declared a general strike in response and started to implement tactics of the urban guerrilla that had a revolutionary character. These events marked the

---

22 "In these conditions the new regime could not establish itself solidly except by undertaking bold social reforms which would have weakened the army, the Church and the old caciquism which was still master in almost all the provinces. But the reforms envisaged, and those achieved by the left socialists and republicans who were the government during the first two years (1931–1933), could only appear bold and very important to the jurists, professors, lawyers, journalists and professional politicians who comprised a majority of the members in the Cortes (the parliament). They meant nothing or very nearly nothing, for the people as a whole" (p. 65).

23 "But the repression was let loose. Spanish law allowed for—and never ceased to do so even during the Republic which on the contrary, intensified the repressive legislation—internment both of common law criminals, even if they had served their sentence, and political opponents, especially militant workers considered to be subversives or constituting a danger to public order" (p. 55).

24 George Woodcock, *Anarchism: A History of Libertarian Ideas and Movements* (Harmondsworth: Penguin, 1986), p. 323.

beginnings of the Civil War. The anarcho-syndicalists controlled the main Spanish cities, including Barcelona—"the capital of Spanish anarchism"—and organised life by means of the collectivisation of factories, transport, and health system.

During the Civil War, four anarchists became ministers of Francisco Largo Caballero's socialist government. As C. M. Lorenzo argued,[25] Joan Peiró Belis (Minister of the Industry), Federica Montseny (the first woman to be a cabinet minister of a Western European country), Juan García Oliver (Minister of Justice) and Juan López Sánchez (Minister of Commerce) joined the ranks of other anarchists who had previously acted as directors, mayors, and even military commanders, especially in Catalonia. For Leval this was a fundamental mistake because "we had only four ministers out of 16 in the Valencia government; we were constantly put in a minority position by the other sectors in a coalition against us" (p. 81). The guiding slogan for betraying anti-state anarchist principles was: "If the war is lost, so will be the revolution and the fascist steamroller that flattened a part of Europe will also destroy Spain"; in a quite manipulative fashion CNT leaders presented the collaboration with the Republican government as an act of participatory internal democracy and as something that was decided in several assemblies.[26] For the leaders, the Revolution was of secondary importance, whereas for the collectivists the Revolution had nothing to do with politics or leaderships;[27] the official political rule was to prioritise the creation of a united front against fascism.

---

25 César M. Lorenzo, *Los anarquistas españoles y el poder: 1868–1969* (Paris: Ruedo Ibérico, 1972), pp. 191–204.

26 "We could be told that that collaboration had been ratified by the assemblies, plenums and congresses of our movement. But in fact what happened was that, drowned by the bursts of eloquence of our interminable *speechifiers*, the delegates of the provinces, the small towns and villages approved of the ministerial collaboration because they were overwhelmed by a situation that was presented to them in the most sombre colours, and lacked information and oratorical abilities to refute the promises, the unverifiable explanations, the arguments the validity of which they were not in a position to check" (p. 81).

27 "They did not feel tied by the political manoeuvres, and they were right, for not only would we have lost the war anyway, but the magnificent experiment of the Spanish Revolution would not have taken place" (p. 81).

Yet Largo Caballero hoped that with such political burdens, the anarchists would abandon spontaneous struggles in the streets and demonstrate the discipline necessary to be given weapons. This implied the dissolution of anarchist militia in order to join the professional army dominated by the minor—albeit powerful—PCE, which CNT eventually refused to do. In May 1937, the communists betrayed the Revolution in Barcelona by directly attacking the libertarian movement, assassinating their own comrades and assaulting the Telefónica Building, where the anarchists were barricaded. The struggle continued in the streets, and the militias of CNT, FAI, FIJL, and POUM were declared by the communist as fascist elements. On top of that, on July 18, 1936, Generalissimo Francisco Franco (1892–1975) proclaimed a military insurrection. Franco halted the dreams of Spanish socialists, republicans, communists, anarchists, nationalists and progressives for more than thirty-six years. Unsurprisingly, therefore, Leval reached the conclusion that if Franco had not won the war, "the [collective] movement would have developed well beyond this." (p. 182).

4

In any case, the key element is that before Franco's victory in 1939 the principles of the Revolution had spread throughout Spain. The Revolution aimed at the destruction of any form of official, repressive and bureaucratic government. The enemy was any type of authoritarianism based on systematic centralisation, civil servants, intermediaries and speculators or, in other words, "[those] who considered themselves a class apart" (p. 285), that is, all counter-revolutionary forces. Given that political power is nothing more than an expression and instrument of the economic exploitation of the poor by the dominant classes, if the working class take over the means of production by expropriation and self-management, classist social fabric would collapse. Against this classist society, libertarian communism proposed mainly two things: the creation of a classless society and to make this society function properly by means of federalism and free association. As stated by Saint-Simon and later paraphrased by Engels: "The government of people will be replaced by the administration of things."[28] In the light of the above, Buenaventura Durruti's speech at the CNT-FAI meeting (1936) became paradigmatic, where he delivered the famous words: "We carry a new world here, in our hearts. That world is growing in this minute." Leval witnessed these words in action and in *Collectives in the Spanish Revolution* he describes the revolutionary process mainly as a clash of civilisations between two Spains:[29] the old Spain rooted in medieval values, privileges, and classism represented by the trinity of the *caciques* (municipal mayors), the priests, and the civil guard; and a new Spain based on libertarian communism and on values such as responsibility, a new humanism built around the notions of brotherhood and human solidarity,[30] education and culture. A society, in essence, based on "social justice, of work organised jointly, of a real brotherhood resulting from the egalitarian enjoyment of goods and services" (p. 36). This list of nuances within the new Spain was rounded off by elements such as a common creative effort, mutual aid, respect for individual initiatives, the notion of carrying out revolution without leaders,[31] the implementation of public health, the promotion of money discontinuance (or at least promoting local currencies and ration cards), and the concept of the economy at the service of all and controlled by the people. After all, in this nascent Spain, the economy was not the dominant subject but rather an important one among many

---

28 Henri Saint-Simon and Ghiţa Ionescu, *The Political Thought of Saint-Simon* (Oxford: Oxford University Press, 1976).

29 "The revolution had created a new civilisation" (p. 143).

30 "Here, the basic inspiration is in the first place an ideal of brotherhood. It is above all a question of extending to all the peoples, to all the inhabitants of the world, the practice of human solidarity" (p. 23).

31 "It is clear, the social revolution which took place then did not stem from a decision by the leading organisms of the C.N.T. or from the slogans launched by the militants and agitators who were in the public limelight but who rarely lived up to expectations. It occurred spontaneously, naturally, not (and let us avoid demagogy) because 'the people' in general had suddenly become capable of performing miracles, thanks to a revolutionary vision which suddenly inspired them, but because, and it is worth repeating, among those people there was a large minority, who were active, strong, guided by an ideal which had been continuing through the years a struggle started in Bakunin's time and that of the First International" (p. 80).

others. Then, we can say without any intention of producing in the reader a mental picture of the Revolution as something created by decrees, it is therefore hardly surprising that the CNT's political agenda for setting the Revolution in motion focused firstly on abolishing private property in the means of production. The CNT's Saragossa Congress (May 1936) proclaimed libertarian communism: "The free commune is to confiscate whatever was formerly possessed by the bourgeoisie in the way of provisions, clothing, footwear, raw materials, work tools, etc. Such tools and raw materials pass into the hands of the producers so that the latter may administer them directly in the interests of the collective. Firstly, the communes will see to it that all the inhabitants of each district are housed with as many amenities as possible, with specific attention being guaranteed to health and education."[32]

The organisation of this society with no private property, authority or state was determined by individual and social pacts, that is, by free agreements concluded between the various groups that composed the society. Consequently, for CNT the three pillars of this new revolutionary society were: "individual, commune and federation."[33] Although for some traditional anarchists—for example, Pierre-Joseph Proudhon (1809–1865) and Ricardo Mella (1861–1925)—the families were the first groups of moral order. The second pillar was the communes (the autonomous municipalities and the collectives). The third pillar of the new society was the federation. CNT's Congress described it as follows: "So we proceed from the individual to the collective, guaranteeing all individual rights, thereby maintaining the principle of liberty."[34] And later on: "Federations are to deliberate over major problems affecting a county or province and all communes are to be represented at their reunions and assemblies, thereby enabling their delegates to convey the democratic viewpoint of their respective communes."[35] The final

32 Quoted from: José Peirats, *The CNT in the Spanish Revolution, Vol. 1* (Oakland: PM Press, 2013), p. 103.

33 Peirats, *The CNT in the Spanish Revolution*, p. 104.

34 Peirats, *The CNT in the Spanish Revolution*, p. 105.

35 Peirats, *The CNT in the Spanish Revolution*, p. 106.

pillar above the federation is the confederation: "So the starting point is the individual, moving on through the commune, to the federation and right on up finally to the confederation."[36] Each of these pillars was managed through general assemblies: "Assemblies are to be summoned as often as required by communal interests, upon the request of members of the communal council or according to the wishes of the inhabitants of each commune."[37] The direct consequence of this organisation system was a radical democratic framework of decision-making where everyone participated in the res publica, or the public administration of the collective. Leval referred to this stating that "the assembly is sovereign and its agreements are law" (p. 220).

Furthermore, special mention should be made of the inclusion of women in the revolutionary processes. For the CNT's Saragossa Congress this was a *conditio sine qua non* for a successful revolution: "The first step in the libertarian revolution consists of ensuring that all human beings, without distinction of sex, are economically independent. Thus it is understood that both sexes are to enjoy equality of rights and duties alike and the economic inferiority between man and woman will thereby disappear."[38]

Nevertheless, the latter was too briefly displayed in *Collectives in the Spanish Revolution*. Leval describes women's roles as crucial for the collectives but not in a very revolutionary way, for example, stating: "Most of the young girls were not paid specially to come and work there, since their basic needs were guaranteed by the family wage based on the number of members in the household. . . . We were in the world of human solidarity" (p. 100). Later on, he describes the organisation of one collective in Graus (Huesca) in these terms: "Two experienced women were responsible for seeing that the place was kept clean and for preparing meals in the huge kitchen which previously was only used by the wealthy owners for a few weeks in the year" (pp. 103–4). However, every collective was organised differently. For example, in Fraga (also Huesca) people

36 Peirats, *The CNT in the Spanish Revolution*, p. 106.
37 Peirats, *The CNT in the Spanish Revolution*, p. 105.
38 Peirats, *The CNT in the Spanish Revolution*, p. 107.

covered the issue of wage equality between women and men without hesitation and concluded: "Working women were paid at exactly the same rate as men" (p. 109).[39] Obviously, Leval confirmed that what he found in the collectives was far removed from CNT principles. This represented a large, underutilised opportunity. In parallel to this, one of the best accounts of women in Spanish collectives was written by Martha Ackelsberg. Ackelsberg presents the extent to which women's liberation struggled with not just the economic issue of participating in revolutionary activities for avoiding economic domination but also with the long-standing cultural issues embedded in the Spanish patriarchal imaginary. The latter is what the organisation Mujeres Libres (Free Women) tried to resolve by implementing education reforms, literacy programmes, training opportunities for women, sexual education, combating macho stereotypes against women, and significant changes in mentality within the spheres of politics, economy, religion and family. Ackelsberg also details the process of an almost forced empowerment experienced by Spanish women in the majority of collectives given that men were in the front, and consequently those militants and soldiers were unable to deal with agriculture or industrial activities.[40] Similarly, in an original contribution to the literature, Leval's account of the collectives—contained in this book—situates the seeds of this revolution precisely in the education system:

> The yearning for culture, the intense desire to spread education were one of the mainsprings and one of the major objectives of the Revolution. Thus every Collective created one or two schools as promptly as it set about its first economic initiatives. The family wage and the new ethic made it possible for all children to attend school. In their sphere of influence the Spanish Collectives gave the coup de grace to illiteracy in record time. The magnitude of the achievement can be

---

39 Another example can be found in an Alicante collective: "Wages were 10 pesetas a day for men and women" (p. 310).

40 Martha A. Ackelsberg, "Models of Revolution: Rural Women and Anarchist Collectivisation in Civil War Spain," *Journal of Peasant Studies* 20, no. 3 (1993): pp. 367–88.

gauged if one bears in mind that in the Spanish countryside in 1936, 60% of the people were illiterate (p. 158).

These rates of illiteracy can be explained in part by the country's economic poverty, but another reason could be that in the old Spain education was very expensive, and in the hands of the institution that had been the most ideologically and economically powerful entity in Spain since the fifteenth century, that is, the Catholic Church. In other words, only the children of the wealthy could afford to pursue an education. The long-term legacy of these injustices was addressed at length both in the collectives and at the CNT Saragossa Congress.[41] Moreover, these education projects were aimed not only at the young (attendance at school was meant to be compulsory up to the age of fourteen) but everyone. Each collective was equipped with *Ateneos* (athenaeums),[42] libraries and library-schools where men and women had "all the means for comfort and the cultivation of the mind" (p. 136). Having said all of this, we must keep in mind that people on the ground took the CNT's proposals further.

5

Under these circumstances, in the past two decades the achievements of the collectivisation process in Spain have been rejected in some historiographies. One of the most extreme cases is that of

---

41 "Firstly there will have to be a vigorous and systematic assault upon illiteracy. It is an obligation of restorative social justice incumbent upon the revolution that learning be restored to those who have been dispossessed of it, since just as capitalism has appropriated and arrogated society's wealth to itself, so the cities have appropriated and arrogated learning and education for themselves. . . . Our immediate task is to organise elementary education among the illiterate population, consisting of, say, reading, writing, arithmetic, physical culture, hygiene, the historical processes of evolution and revolution, some theory regarding the non-existence of god, etc." Peirats, *The CNT in the Spanish Revolution*, p. 108.

42 "Yet in Barcelona there were four workers' centres called 'Ateneos' because they each had a library, tables at which one could sit and read, and where lectures were given. The movement of anarchist groups acted in agreement with the C.N.T." Peirats, *The CNT in the Spanish Revolution*, p. 54.

Michael Seidman.[43] For Seidman, the majority of historians have inclined towards the production of a "largely apologetic literature" on the agrarian collectives. In his work, he describes this literature as merely "propaganda" and an "idealistic picture." Similarly, Seidman links the collectivisation process to a forced—and sometimes violent—imposition of the libertarian agenda. He outlines an overall picture based on selfishness, hoarding, localism, inflation, sexism, debauchery, laziness, indiscipline, looting, discrimination (against gypsies, the elderly, and soldiers) which, in summary, was a failed social experiment because its internal problems not because of outside forces or a context of wartime economy. Seidman's arguments are academically impeccable although biased against anarchists and supported mainly on testimonies coming from CNT, FAI and UGT leaders—in comparison to Leval's book, which is based on grassroots collectivists—and revisionist historians such as Stanley Payne.

Despite Seidman's obvious dislike for collectivisations, he is forced to acknowledge that in Aragon "*only* 40% of the land of the region was expropriated,"[44] that "collectivization occurred both spontaneously and unwillingly," and that even if some pressure was put on peasants and landowners for the collectivising process, "in comparison with the Soviet precedent—where a powerful state forced, literally at gunpoint, peasants to combine—Spanish collectivization appears largely to have been spontaneous and voluntary."[45] In addition, he criticises collectives for their selfishness and lack of solidarity but, at the same time, points out that in a wartime economy context "[t]he shortage of trucks led to the abandonment of food shipments destined for troops defending Madrid. The same insufficiency made it difficult to collect milk for dairy production." Later on he writes that troops were very much responsible for the food shortage: "Towns hid what they possessed and the knowledge of it for fear that Republican police or soldiers . . .

---

43 Michael Seidman, "Agrarian Collectives during the Spanish Revolution and Civil War," *European History Quarterly* 30, no. 2 (2000): pp. 209–35.

44 Seidman, "Agrarian Collectives," p. 211 (italics are mine).

45 Seidman, "Agrarian Collectives," p. 212.

would confiscate it. The fear was not unrealistic since, as has been seen, police and soldiers sometimes did 'abusively' take what they wanted."[46] Moreover, his study hints unjustly that peasants and workers were allergic to hard work. Nonetheless, the author himself assumes that "[t]he civil war created what may have been the first significant scarcity of hands in the history of modern Spanish agriculture. Many men had been conscripted into the army."[47] Yet, in spite of this negative outlook, Seidman ended by recognising that collectives "may have been productive locally."[48]

Lastly, it seems curious to note the paradox of acknowledging that none of Seidman's critiques are original compared to Gaston Leval's self-criticism which appears in *Collectives in the Spanish Revolution*. Based on Leval's proposed definition: "Collectivism—a term widely and spontaneously adopted—presupposed the disappearance of all the small, medium and, above all, the large, private properties; the small properties voluntarily, the rest by force, and their integration in a vast system of public ownership and work in common" (pp. 76–77) we can see the extent to which this was an "imposed" procedure. Nevertheless, Leval's diagnosis of the partial failures of the collectives starts by pointing out the low quality of the land in Spain: "Thus in fact the land available for cultivation each year was only 28% of the total area" (p. 59). In such geographical conditions it was very hard to run viable agriculture in a collectivised economy, particularly if we remember that 60% of the Spanish population were peasants who did not own the land they worked.

The second element of his criticism was the repressive nature of the Republic and its direct sabotage over the collectives. A good illustration of the gap that existed between the government and the people is the crime that happened in the village of Casas Viejas (Cadiz)[49] in January 1933, where 25 people—one of whom was the coal merchant Francisco Cruz, more commonly known

---

46 Seidman, "Agrarian Collectives," p. 222.
47 Seidman, "Agrarian Collectives," p. 225.
48 Seidman, "Agrarian Collectives," p. 217.
49 Both Spanish and English versions of the book refer erroneously to Casas Viejas as a village of Extremadura.

as "Seisdedos"—were burnt alive by the Republican Civil Guards. The motive for the attack was the proclamation of libertarian communism in Andalusia. The Civil Guards had an effect contrary to what they desired: rather than silencing the anarchists, they elevated the humble peasants to the status of martyrs, ignited libertarianism in a number of areas (mostly in Asturias, Aragon, Barcelona, and Levante), and produced radical discontents towards the Second Republic, and towards those CNT leaders who became ministers.

The third reason why collectives did not develop further, according to Leval, was because of the July 19, 1936, fascist attack on the Republic and the subsequent recruitment of soldiers and militiamen (and some women) for the war. Everybody and every resource were mobilised to stop fascist triumph: "The war came first" (p. 75). It was against this background that the communist attacks on the collectives began.[50]

Leval's fourth critique describes a number of different elements named under the label of "human weaknesses" (p. 120) such as individual selfishness, lack of training, individual hoarding of some products (primarily tobacco),[51] some opposition to collectivism, the ideological diversity of the collectivists (mainly anarchists, communists, socialists, republicans and UGT members), the differences between rural-city mentalities, the wrong notion of federalism and nationalism coming from Proudhon and Pi y Margall[52] based on the division of the country in tiny pieces[53] rather than devolving a Bakunin federalism on the basis of the notion of "unity" and "the universal association of all local associations through freedom"

---

50 "The Communist attack which took place shortly afterwards was to prevent the general application of this project. Having to retire within themselves, greatly reduced in numbers by the destruction they had suffered, the Collectives were, as a result, condemned to a precarious existence" (p. 197).

51 "I was told there were abuses and for some articles the demand far exceeded supplies" (p. 132).

52 "Just as for the land cultivation, or the running of workshops and factories, the dispersal of forces represented an enormous loss of energy, an irrational use of human labour, machinery and raw materials, a useless duplication of efforts" (p. 259).

53 Michael Bakunin, *Bakunin on Anarchism* (New York: Vintage Books, 1971), pp. 120–75.

(p. 19). Notwithstanding the previous criticism, ultimately, even if the collectives did not achieve amazing economic figures, what Leval says is that collectivism was not all about initiating a revolution in the production of goods but mainly a humanist revolution: "One should never forget that moral reasons have at least as much as material reasons, inspired and supported the activities of the Syndicates founded and activated by the Spanish libertarians" (p. 280).

Pedro García-Guirao
January 2018

FOREWORD

This is not yet another book about the Civil War, and its author is not yet another academic jumping on the Spanish band wagon. The book is about what Burnett Bolloten in the opening paragraph of *his* remarkable book[1] calls "a far reaching social revolution more profound in some respects than the Bolshevik revolution in its early stages".

The author, Gaston Leval, at eighty is still earning his living in the printing industry, lives in Paris, though as a war-resister in 1914-18, and French nationalism being what it is, spent most of his adult life in exile. It was in 1915, during World War I, that he sought refuge in Spain, and became involved in the Spanish workers revolutionary movement. His deep interest in economic questions and in new forms of organisation stems from that period. In 1921 he, a Frenchman, was one of the Spanish delegation to the Congress of the Red International of Trade Unions in Moscow and, unlike some of his colleagues, returned disillusioned with the way events were developing in Russia.

When Primo de Rivera's dictatorship was established in 1923 Leval sought refuge in Argentina, since France was still closed to him and remained so until an amnesty was granted in the heady "liberation" days after World War II to the rebels of the first holocaust. Leval returned to Spain via Gibraltar at the end

1 *The Grand Camouflage*, London, 1961.

of 1936 and, realising that the revolution, politically speaking, had been lost and that it was doubtful whether Franco's armies could be defeated militarily, felt that the most useful thing he could do was to participate in the social revolution which was growing in spite of the military reverses and the resurgence of State power in the Republican zone. And at the same time he resolved to record for posterity what ordinary people, left to their own devices, did when large landowners or factory owners who sympathised with Franco fled; when local government which was controlled by the priest, the business men, the landowners and contractors, collapsed with their departure; when central government without the force that matters—the military—issued orders, threatened or cajoled, and was too unimaginative to realise that its power had been Franco and the Army, and too puffed up with political pride to realise that its only hope was with the people.

What happened in the half of Spain free from occupation in the months following the military uprising *is unique in the annals of contemporary social history.* Yet the collectives are still largely unknown, or written-off as failures, or denounced as authoritarian systems imposed by the anarchist militia, and it is significant that their detractors have at no time made a serious effort to examine the considerable material available on the subject.

As Burnett Bolloten indicates by copious references in his chapter on "The Revolution in the Countryside", there is much printed material on the subject of the collectives which has still to be studied and analysed, though it is true that the material consists mainly of articles by journalists, some by sociologists, and much of it hurriedly observed and therefore superficial. This will become even more apparent now that the unabridged translation of Leval's major study of the collectives can be used as a yardstick to assess the value of works by professional historians and sociologists, some of which, Franz Borkenau's *Spanish Cockpit* for example, have become "classics". I have no intention of attempting such a task here, but as an example of what I mean the reader should compare Leval's report on the Aragon town of Fraga (pp. 104-112) with Borkenau's. Apart from the fact that Borkenau only spent a day in Fraga, he makes great play of the executions and terror that he was told (by a peasant in a bar) had taken place there, from which his conclusions are that the anarchist nucleus "under the influence of the Durruti militia column, had helped to kill an enormous number of people in the village, but they had achieved nothing else". How much Dr. Borkenau must have seen in his visit can be gauged by the fact that he refers to Fraga as "a village [which] has only a thousand inhabitants", whereas it was and is a town with a population of 8,000!

Professor Hugh Thomas who only "discovered" the collectives some years after publishing his notorious history of the Spanish Civil War, in an essay on *Anarchist Agrarian Collectives in the Spanish Civil War*[2] writes:

"The most complete series of accounts of the life of the collectives appears in the anarchist press, and this is far from complete and not unprejudiced. The anarchist writers, Peirats and Gaston Leval . . . gathered information on the activities of a number of collectives, but the details they give extend to an apparently arbitrarily chosen selection of about eighty collectives out of what appears to be about 1,500 in all. Much of even their information comes from newspapers at the time . . .".[3]

The reader of Leval's work will be able to distinguish quite clearly between the author's direct observations, information subsequently received or gleaned from documents and other reports, for in the course of the narrative he is at pains to make the distinctions. Nor have the collectives described been "arbitrarily chosen" as Prof. Thomas asserts, but on the contrary since for space reasons Leval could use only a part of his material he made a careful selection which gives the reader an opportunity to acquaint himself with the many forms assumed by the collectives. And it is surely one of the most interesting and important aspects of this unique experiment in living that, having sprung from the people and not created from above it manifested itself in so many different ways, reflecting local

2 *The Republic & the Civil War in Spain,* ed. Raymond Carr, London, 1971.
3 This latter objection is a curious one considering that Prof. Thomas was in his rompers at the time of the Spanish Civil War and must have therefore relied even more than Leval on printed sources for the material to fill his own 600 page "history". This has not prevented it, alas, from being considered the standard history.

conditions, both geographical and economic, as well as the political backgrounds of the workers and peasants themselves.

*

Some critics of the collectives (and it is significant that the most determined among them were the Spanish Stalinists who were at the same time paying lip-service to the "achievements" of the Collective Farms in Russia!) have declared that they were created by anarchist force of arms. Though Leval does not devote a chapter to this very important question, he does make pointed comments on the subject in the course of his narrative which I find convincing. Had the collectives in Aragon been imposed by anarchist "terror" would one not expect a 100% membership? Yet in Fraga, according to Leval "the Collective of agricultural workers and herdsmen comprised 700 families—half the agricultural population". And Mintz[4] concludes that collectivists represented 35% of the town's population of 8,000, and that so far as his research went it revealed a maximum of 180,000 collectivists out of a population of 433,000 inhabitants in that part of Aragon unoccupied by Franco's forces. Leval readily acknowledges that the presence of the CNT-FAI militias in Aragon "favoured indirectly these constructive achievements by preventing active resistance by the supporters of the bourgeois republic and of fascism". But then who, in the first place, had undermined the status quo if not the officer class in rebellion against the duly elected government? In the circumstances only an academic could be shocked at acts of violence by the people or the militia against those who for generations had been the local oppressors, and exploiters deriving their wealth from ownership of land which belonged by right to the community?

Leval's conclusions on the role of the "libertarian troops" in the development of the Aragon collectives are that they were on the whole negative (p. 91) for they "lived on the fringe of the task of social transformation that was being carried out". And the reasons he gives are themselves of profound significance for all revolutionaries who recognise, albeit reluctantly, that at some stage in the age long struggle against privilege, violence will be used by the powers that be which will have to be overcome if

4 ——in *l'Autogestion dans l'Espagne Révolutionnaire*, Paris, 1970.

the revolution is to have any hope of success. Leval writes:

"From my own first-hand observations, they [the libertarian troops] lived on the fringe of the task of social transformation that was being carried out. A military world—even if libertarian —and a civilian world. A military spirit with its own pre-occupations and, to some extent, withdrawn into itself, generally indifferent to whatever was not life in the Front Line."

There were exceptions but very few. "Most of the soldiers, often Catalans, came from industrial areas, lived alongside Aragon villages without interesting themselves in them—even when they were billeted in the villages." Last, but not least, the negative economic aspect of the "military presence", for the Collectives "supplied provisions without payment for these troops who had to be adequately fed, since the government did nothing for them".

Mintz in a documented chapter on "How Collectivisation was brought about", in which the question 'Forced or spontaneous Collectivisation?' is paramount, confirms Leval's conclusions but then in *his* conclusions goes on to make a distinction between the troops recruited outside the region, who "in our opinion, organised the localities on the basis of a war economy for their victualling rather than being really concerned with social reforms" and "the Aragonese anarchists who being familiar with local politics, took advantage of the situation without abusing their advantage, and succeeded in putting their ideas into practice with the approval of the majority of the peasants".[5]

Leval makes a further telling point against the forced collec-tivisation argument when he contrasts the case of Aragon where admittedly "the armed presence of our men contributed to the liberation of the population from a traditional past which would have limited its effort far too much" with other regions such as the Levante where "in spite of the existence of legal authorities and non-libertarian military forces, the revolution took place there as well".

However discredited Stalinism may appear to be today the fact remains that the Stalinist lies and interpretation of the Spanish Civil War still prevail, presumably because it suits the political prejudices of those historians who are currently interpreting it. It would indeed be an invaluable piece of anarchist research to

5 *Ibid* (p. 69).

answer in depth the question 'How were the collectivisations brought about?' not simply in order to silence the critics who are not concerned with the truth anyway, but because the conclusions would help to enrich and refine anarchist theory about the means by which our ends may be achieved.

*

On the other hand those seeking to prove either to themselves or, if they are propagandists, to their political opponents, that Spain in 1936 was anarchy in action will find it difficult to use Leval as their bible for though he refers in some detail to a number of outstanding examples of workers' initiative and self-management in industry he does not hesitate to declare that in his opinion the achievements on the whole, from an anarchist (or libertarian, to use the term he prefers) point of view, cannot be compared with those in the countryside. There collectivisation was "genuine socialisation" whereas in industry it was "a workers' neo-capitalism, a self-management straddling capitalism and socialism" (p. 227).

Nevertheless consider some examples of the rich harvest of *anarchistic* attitudes and solutions that emerge from Leval's account of this great social experiment.

Firstly: Almost all the collectives came into existence through the initiative of the people who worked in them and not from government nor even the municipal councils.

Secondly: When the landed estates were seized there was no question of dividing them up into strips for distribution among the landless workers (which was the basis of socialist Land Reform). Instead the land workers organised themselves into working parties to cultivate it to the best advantage for the community as a whole.

Thirdly: In the affluent society of the 1970s the term "collective" has been used more or less indiscriminately (mainly by middle-class radicals) to describe what at most are consumer-cooperatives or community-living projects. It is significant to note, for it may be one of the reasons for the success of the Spanish agricultural collectives, that no attempt was made to interfere with the existing family pattern or to encourage communal living, though the Collective invariably made itself financially responsible both for ensuring that all members had adequate accommodation and for keeping it in good repair. The collectives were based on *the community of work* and in so doing were echoing the Spanish Internationalists who declared in their Manifesto of 1872: "We want work to be the basis on which society rests".

Fourthly: Economic equality was in the forefront of all collective enterprises. Apart from the attempts at abolishing money, which might appear to have been more frequent than they in fact were thanks to the popular journalists in search of an "unusual" story what is significant is that whatever the currency used—local or national, *carnets* or *libretas*—what the Collectives abolished were differentials. When this could not be done (mostly where technicians and professionals were involved) the differential was however reduced to a minimum but not viewed as a permanent situation.

Fifthly: The initiative taken to provide education not only for children but for adults as well cannot be simply explained away by the fact that Spain had one of the highest illiteracy rates in Europe to overcome. As Leval shows again and again in his invaluable *Preamble*, literacy and education loom large in the history of the Spanish workers revolutionary movement (not only in the words of the first Manifesto in 1872: "We want for all individuals of both sexes a complete education in science, industry and the Arts . . .") but also in the (Ferrer) schools and *Ateneos* they organised before 1936. The revolutionary publications issued (p. 27) are further evidence, by their number, their quality and large circulation, that the Word was at least as powerful a weapon in the struggle as that of Direct Action.

Sixthly: Besides giving many examples of how the Collectivists organised their own local medical services, Leval deals with the Socialisation of Medicine (pp. 264-278) and in special detail with the achievements of the Syndicate for Sanitary Services in Catalonia which was constituted in September 1936 "and organised according to the libertarian and industrial norms of the Syndicates of the C.N.T." and had a membership of more than 7,000. But what is remarkable bearing in mind the current struggles in the National Health Service in this country, *is the composition of the Syndicate*: "1,020 doctors, 3,206 male nurses, 330 midwives, 633 dentists, 71 specialists in diathermy, 10 unspecified specialists, 153 pharmacists, 633 assistant pharmacists, 335 preparers of dressings, an unspecified number of masseurs, and 220 veterinary surgeons."

This was Spain 1936, *sin gobierno* (without government) but with a new spirit.

Seventhly: Anarchists have always maintained that a revolutionary situation releases creative energies among people who in normal times would neither call themselves anarchists nor be militant propagandists. Many of the Collectives, in Castile and the Levante for instance, seem to confirm that this potential-goodwill-waiting-to-be-released really does exist, and such a conclusion should be of considerable encouragement to all who are engaged in anarchist propaganda.

These are but a few of the anarchistic situations and solutions which were experienced by a very large number of people for periods varying from only a few weeks to nearly three years, depending almost entirely on the ability of the "popular army" to stem the advance of Franco's forces. It is important for once to underline the fact that the social experiments carried out in Spain during those momentous years involved not just hundreds, or thousands, but *some millions* of people. We will probably never know exactly how many. According to Leval, in Aragon, the Levante and Castile there was a total of 1,600 agricultural Collectives. In Catalonia all industry and public services were collectivised, in the Levante 70% of industry, and in Castile only a part of industry. In his introduction to the French edition he suggests that between 5 and 7 million people were either directly or indirectly involved. Frank Mintz estimates the figure of those directly involved in industry at 1.5 million though he points out that no official statistics were available. For the agricultural Collectives the figures he gives for July 1937 are of a minimum of 800 Collectives with a minimum of 400,000 collectivists but notes that by the end of 1938 though the number of Collectives had increased to 1,015 the collectivists had dropped to 230,000.[6] What nobody will be able to deny is that the scale on which the collectivist enterprises operated in Spain was such as to silence once for all those critics who argue that self-management along anarchistic lines is possible on a small scale but quite impractical when applied to large enterprises and urban concentrations.

In a world where relations in industry between management

6 *Ibid* (p. 148). These figures appears to be too low as well as confusing. See further reference to them in the Bibliographical Notes.

and worker, and in the public services between workers and government, become daily more strained, not simply over money but over the growing demand by more and more workers to be responsible for and in control of the organisation of the work they do, surely the Spanish experiment of 1936 is of more than academic interest. Such experiments are never exactly repeated, not even in a Spain which has been freed from the military dictatorship. They don't have to be. Their importance for us now is in showing what ordinary people, land- and industrial workers, technicians, and professionals of goodwill, can do when the State machine collapses even for a brief moment and the people are left to their own devices. The result is not chaos but cooperation, the discovery that for most of us life is richer and happier when we practise mutual aid than when we engage in the power and status struggle which invariably leads to permanent bitterness for the many and a doubtful "happiness" for the few.

FEBRUARY 1975   VERNON RICHARDS.

PART ONE
Preamble

CHAPTER I

THE IDEAL

"Now I can die, I have seen my ideal realised." This was said to me in one of the Levante Collectives, if my memory serves me well, by one of the men who had struggled throughout their lives for the triumph of social justice, economic equality, and for human liberty and brotherhood.

His ideal was libertarian communism, or anarchy. But the use of this latter word carries with it the risk in all languages of distorting in people's minds what the great savant and humanist, Elisée Reclus, defined as "the noblest concept of order". More especially because very often, and it was the case in France, the anarchists seem to have done their utmost to agree with their enemies, and to justify the negative and nihilistic interpretation which one already finds in such and such an order or edict of Philip the Fair in France. It is therefore to betray the meaning of what the old militant, who had struggled so long and had suffered so much, and who probably was shot by one of Franco's firing squads, was saying to me, thus to stick to the simple expression of a word so widely interpreted. Let us therefore look into the matter more deeply.

In his pamphlet *El Ideal Anarquista* Ricardo Mella, who was the most genuine and original thinker of Spanish anarchism, gave the following definition of this ideal: "Liberty as the basis, equality as the means, fraternity as the ends". Let us bear this well in mind: the ultimate goal, the crowning glory was fraternity, in which freedom would be at the same time both a basis and a consequence, for can there be fraternity without liberty; but equally can one deprive one's brother of liberty?

Besides, these concepts had not penetrated into Spain with the much debated and debatable word anarchy. In his book *El Proletariado Militante,* to which one must continually return, Anselmo Lorenzo, who after Mella was the most qualified thinker among Spanish anarchists, recounts how these ideas had been revealed to him, first by reading some of Proudhon's books before 1870, among them *De la Capacité Politique des Classes Ouvrières* which had been translated by Pi y Margall.[1] These books, and the articles published by Pi y Margall himself in his journal *La Discusíon* had demonstrated to him the reality of the social problem, whereas other men were struggling for a republic which could not be other than bourgeois, and they affiliated themselves with the Carbonaro movement or with some other European secret society.

It was at that time that the Bakuninist influence penetrated into Spain. Its bearer was a distinguished fighter, the Italian Giuseppe Fanelli, a former Garibaldian combatant, later an Independent Liberal Deputy, who having met Bakunin, presumably at the time of his stay in Florence, was to subscribe to his social ideas.

Bakunin defended and propagated socialism. At that time, the word anarchy was for him synonymous with disorder, chaos, delinquency. He also founded in Geneva, with friends, including some intellectuals of the first order,[2] the International Alliance of Socialist Democracy. He had known Proudhon during his stay in Paris, during the years 1844-1848.[3] As with Proudhon, Bakunin's socialism was anti-statist. It satisfied his Slavonic psychology, his generous Russian nature, his cosmic view of things, and the broad human philosophy based on experimental science which he constructed for himself. His thought matured during the twelve years he spent in detention in the fortress, in prison and in Siberian deportation. The behaviour of the authoritarian and dictatorial Marx during this long and painful period only strengthened his suspicion and aversion to dictatorship, even when called popular.

1 Philosopher and apostle of republican federalism who was—not for long—one of the Presidents of the first Spanish Republic (1873-74).
2 Not only the Reclus brothers, but men such as James Guillaume, Jules Guesde, Victor Dave, Alfred Naquet, belonged to the Alliance.
3 Deported from France by Guizot in 1847, he returned there when the revolution of February 1848 took place.

So when, in 1869, Fanelli expounded the doctrine of the Alliance to the new friends he had made in Madrid and in Barcelona, he was able to refer to the seven Articles of the programme of that secret organisation, written in the hand of its founder:

"The Alliance declares itself atheistic; it demands the political, economic, and social equality of members of both sexes" . . .

"The land, working tools, as well as all wealth, by becoming the collective property of the whole of society, cannot be used other than by the workers, that is to say by the agricultural and industrial associations."

"It demands for all children of both sexes, from the moment they are born, equality of the means for development, that is to say maintenance and education to all levels in science, industry and the Arts" . . .

"It recognizes that all political and authoritarian States that exist now will have to be submerged in the universal union of free federations both agricultural and industrial" . . .

"It not being possible to find a definitive and real solution to the social question other than on the basis of the international solidarity of workers of all countries, the *Alliance* rejects all policies based on so-called patriotism and on the rivalries between nations" . . .

"It demands the universal association of all local associations through freedom."

In this programme Bakunin went further than Proudhon, for example, on women's equality of rights—he had already done so, among others in his *Revolutionary Catechism;* he went further than Marx in his vision of a new society constructed on an international basis of workers' economic organisations. For the Statutes of the International don't go so far, they do not imply a clear technique of social reorganisation at the same time as a political doctrine (which was to leave the way open to many surprises and lead to the capture of Parliament and of the State).

But it is surprising to see with what alacrity and ease, with what precision, the two nuclei—in Madrid and Barcelona— assimilated and spread the fundamental doctrine of the Alliance.

For, a year later, on June 19, 1870, the first congress of the Spanish section of the First International was held in Barcelona at the Teatro Circo Barcelonés.

That congress, at which 40,000 workers were represented out of a population of 18 million inhabitants, was characterised by the seriousness and profundity of the discussions, the problems studied and the resolutions passed. The need to have done with the domination of capital and the exploitation of man by man; the establishment of a tactic which belonged to the working class independently of the political parties; the need to prepare oneself to take over from the bourgeois society through the workers' associations, was developed at length. And from the beginning the ways of applying the ideal called for the elaboration of directives which one finds in the resolution relative to the *organisation of the workers*:

"1. In every locality workers of each trade will be organised in specialised sections; in addition a general section will be established which will include all workers engaged in trades that are not yet included in special sections: it will be a section of different trades.

"2. All sections of trades from the same locality will federate and organise a solidary cooperation applied also to matters of mutual aid, education,[4] etc., which are of great interest to the workers.

"3. Sections of the same trade belonging to different localities will federate to constitute resistance and solidarity within their occupation.

"4. Local federations will federate to constitute the Spanish Regional Federation which will be represented by a Federal Council elected by the congresses.

"5. All the trade sections, local federations, trade federations, as well as the Regional Federation will govern themselves on the basis of their own rules worked out at their congresses.

"6. All the workers represented by the workers' congresses will decide, through the intermediary of their delegates, as to the methods of action and development of our organisation."

Certainly the fundamental postulates of the ideal were the work of Bakunin and were brought there by Fanelli. But here one finds a vast organisational concept and a creative initiative going beyond all that had hitherto been done in Europe, indicating to what a degree the ideal was understood and assimilated. In this complex and complete structure principles guided action,

4 Note the importance attached right from the beginning to schooling, and which continued up until 1936-39.

but the action to follow was to guide and complement the principles. On the other hand we find ourselves confronted by an innovatory spirit, an active will and an ethical sense, which in one bound went beyond the limits of syndical corporatism. One was not only thinking of creating an organisation with a professional character but one that was also humanist and social in the broad sense of the word. Even while an effective weapon of struggle for the immediate future against the class enemy was being forged, the foundations were being laid of a new society.

Already, what later was to be called the vertical organisation constituted on the basis of national federations, completes the horizontal organisation. At the same time, the local federations set up in the somewhat less important centres, where different craft unions existed, bring together and federate the latter for common struggles. In France, this happened thirty years later in the form of the *bourses de travail* (labour exchanges) and to achieve this it was necessary that Fernand Pelloutier, who came from the petite bourgeoisie, should become its advocate.

But the ideal also appears in other resolutions that were adopted, and other tasks are envisaged for the immediate future —though often the bitterness of the social struggle prevented the application of the decisions reached. At that same congress, the question of cooperatives was also taken up. For men who envisaged the radical transformation of society in a very short time, the cooperatives might have appeared as a dangerous setback. But though they still did not know of the programme of the Rochdale Pioneers, the worker delegates at the Barcelona congress found commonsense and well balanced solutions to this problem. Paragraph 3 of the resolution on which they had voted stipulated that:

"When circumstances demand it, cooperation in production must favour the production of goods for immediate consumption by the workers, but we take it to task when it does not extend, in fact, its solidarity to the large workers' organisations."

Nevertheless, the principle of universal solidarity, extended to all the exploited seems specially practicable through consumer cooperation, "the only one which not only can be applied in all cases and in all circumstances, but which must also provide the rudiments and the means for the general development of all those workers whose cultural backwardness makes new ideas difficult to comprehend".

Finally, the sixth and last paragraph stipulates that "alongside consumer cooperatism and complementary to it, one can place cooperatives for mutual aid and *public instruction*" (my italics).

One must point out that we are talking about June, 1870. At that time Marx's book *Das Kapital* was still unknown as was the Communist Manifesto, and the Paris Commune was not to explode until the following year. Federalist and libertarian socialism in Spain was therefore to develop by the impulse of its own strength. In one stroke, the ideal was stated in general terms and what was later to be called French revolutionary syndicalism was formulated after that period.

But what was elaborated in those historic days was to be added to in the congresses that followed in the next decade. Thus in the following year the conference of the organisation comprising the "Spanish Regional Section of the First International" goes further in clarifying these questions. The most able of the militants had been to Switzerland to establish contact with Bakunin who inspired their action thanks to a constructive mind and to organisational gifts embracing life on a world scale. But they added their own ideas to his. In the interests of the immediate struggle, of working class resistance and for the organisation of the new society, Spain was organically divided into five regions by the delegates: North, South, East, West and Central. As had been decided the previous year, the local and national trades federations were founded. A form of cooperation, also by trades, was outlined in order to be able to facilitate and to control this part of general activity. On September 1, 1871, after a week of discussions on various subjects, a declaration of principles against republicanism as the political, but not social, enemy of the monarchical regime was approved:

"Seeing that the true meaning of the word 'Republic' is 'the public thing', that is what belongs to the collectivity and involves the collective property;

"That 'democracy' means the free exercise of individual rights, which is not practicable except under Anarchy, that is to say by the abolition of the political and juridical States in the place of which it will be necessary to constitute workers' States[5] the functions of which will be simply economic;

"That man's rights cannot be subjected to laws for they are

5 The word State here has been used in the sense of nation, as one will readily see from what follows.

indefeasible and unalienable;

"That in consequence the Federation must simply have an economic character;

"The Conference of the workers of the Spanish region of the Workers International gathered in Valencia declares: "That the true democratic and federal republic is the collective property, Anarchy and the economic Federation, that is to say the free universal federation of free associations of agricultural and industrial workers, formula which it adopts in its entirety."

One cannot but admire the richness of this thinking, which has never been improved on by any working class movement since it was first formulated. It took the French working class movement thirty-five years to get as far as the Amiens Charter, which is far inferior both in its theoretical and doctrinal content, in the breadth of the constructive horizons on the practical side, as well as in that sense of universality and internationalism which raises spirits and guides actions. Here, the basic inspiration is in the first place an ideal of brotherhood. It is above all a question of extending to all the peoples, to all the inhabitants of the world, the practice of human solidarity.

In the following year—1872—the International was declared illegal by the Madrid government in spite of its brilliant defence made in the Cortes by Nicolas Salmeron, a noble figure and eminent republican jurist. In Italy the government was to take the same steps. In France, where the Le Chapelier law still prevailed, courts continued to condemn Internationalists to heavy terms of imprisonment. But whereas the Italian Internationalists, guided by Malatesta, Covelli, Andrea Costa, Carlo Cafiero and other young enthusiasts from the bourgeoisie, welcomed this measure which they believed would hasten the revolution, and launched out in wild insurrectional attempts which provoked the complete dissolution of the movement, the Spanish militants did not lose sight of the objectives of a constructive nature and of the immediate organic action which stems from it. They began by confirming the positive aspirations in a Manifesto addressed to public opinion by the Federal Council of the Spanish Section of the First International:

"We want justice to be achieved in all human relations;

"We want the abolition of all social classes and their fusion into a single class of free, honest and cultured producers;

"We want work to be the basis on which society rests; that

the world be converted into one immense federation of free working class local collectives which, by federating among themselves, will constitute a completely autonomous local federation; that the local federations in one canton will constitute the cantonal federation, that the various cantonal federations in a region will constitute the regional federation and finally that all the regional federations of the world will constitute the large international federation.

"We want the instruments of work, the land, the mines, the shipyards, the merchant navy, the railways, factories, machines, etc. . . . having become the property of the whole of society, should not be utilised except by the workers Collectives who will make them produce directly and within which the worker will receive the full produce of his work;[6]

"We want for all individuals of both sexes a complete education in science, industry and the Arts[7] so that intellectual inequalities, almost entirely imaginary, will disappear, and that the distinctive effects of the division of labour should not recur; one will then secure the unique, but positive, advantages from that economic force by the production of that which is destined to satisfy human needs;

"We believe that by the organisation of society in a vast federation of workers Collectives based on work, all authoritarian powers will disappear, converting themselves into simple administrators of the collective interests, and that the spirit of nationality and patriotism, so antagonistic to union and solidarity among men, will be obliterated before the great fatherland of work, which is the whole world.

"Such is the socialism that is proclaimed by the International of which the two fundamental affirmations are: collectivism in economics and anarchy as a political principle. Collectivism, that is the common property in the instruments of work, their use by the workers' Collectives which use them to produce directly, and individual ownership of the whole product of each person's labour. Anarchy, or the abolition of governments, that is to say their conversion into the simple administrators of collective interests."

Do not these last paragraphs remind one of Proudhon's formula:

6 It will be seen later that the formula of the right of the worker to the full product of his labour will give way, with the introduction of the communist principle, to a more generous approach to things.
7 Clearly a Bakunian phrase.

"The workshop will make the government disappear"? Or better perhaps that of Saint-Simon: "To replace the government of men by the administration of things"?

Still in the year 1872, the Spanish Section of the First International continued to clarify principles and the means for realising them. A new massive contribution came from the Saragossa congress just before it was declared illegal. The moral level of the matters dealt with, the resolutions that were passed, often prevailed by far over economic problems and solutions, the whole generally interpenetrating for the first time in the working class movement. The subjects dealt with included the fate of woman "whose emancipation is intimately linked to the problem of property", the sections of consumers' cooperatives, the consumer committees organised by workers' sections of resistance and by a specialised Cooperative Federation. A long report, worthy of a jurist, indicates how much, and in what detail, the authors had studied the problem of property. But above all the report on "Integral teaching" holds our attention for it was the first time that this subject gave rise to such a profound analysis.

It is amazing to find, in the first place, the combined scientific considerations, and the enumeration in order of importance of the relations between the biological development of the child and that of the physiological faculties which were then being propounded. One is tempted to say that since then none of the great masters of pedagogy has gone further. In fact, this report was the work of an intellectual won over to the workers and with whom he collaborated, but how praiseworthy of those metal workers, masons, printers, labourers, weavers, stevedores, to support the launching of pedagogic ideas half a century in advance of their time!

Viewed as a whole their constructive spirit was exceptional. We can find confirmation of it in the third Resolution approved at the Congress of St. Imier, held on the 15th and 16th September, 1872. That congress brought together those sections of the International which would not bow to the dictates of Marx and to the dissolution of that Association as the answer to the protests of the majority of the sections against the fraudulent expulsion of Bakunin, James Guillaume and the Jura Federation.[8]

8 Not only was the pretext for expulsion false but Bakunin had not been warned of what was being hatched. He was absent and a number of the delegates who voted in the manner desired by Marx were in possession of false mandates.

Among the questions on the Agenda, was one on the subject of "The organisation of work, statistics". The report presented had been obviously written by Bakunin, and ended with these words:

"The Commission proposes to nominate a Commission which will have to present a project to the next Congress for the universal organisation of resistance, and complete tables of statistics of work from which this struggle will seek its inspiration. It recommends the Spanish section as the best up to now."

The following year, and though, as we have seen, the Spanish Federation was declared illegal, the figures show that there were 162 local federations and a further 62 in the course of formation. A year later, according to the Belgian historian Laveleye, the number of members reached 300,000, which in our view is excessive, and probably refers to the influence exercised by the Spanish Section of the International. Then, when the movement became clandestine because of the persecutions, its numbers decreased. Nevertheless, in 1876 a Conference of cantonal federations once again enumerates the principles which have to be applied at the time of revolution:

"1. The localities where the members of the International may triumph as a result of the International movement will declare themselves free and independent and released from the national structure.[9]

2. Each locality will immediately declare that what is enclosed within its boundaries belongs to it, that nothing belongs to any individual, to anybody, apart from furniture, clothing and other objects for personal use.

5. The organisation of the federation of popular forces of all the federations, cantons, and of all countries.

8. The local councils will subdivide into as many commissions as are considered necessary: defence, subsistence, administration, work, education, cantoral and federal relations, etc. . . .

9. Dissolution of all the organs of the existing State; destruction and burning of all title deeds and *rente* certificates, mortgages, financial securities, recognizances, etc. . . .; seizure and concentration of all gold reserves and paper money, jewellery and precious stones found in the locality; centralisation of all consumer goods and partial concentration of tools and

9 It refers to the political structure of the State, to construct a different structure, as we shall see in due course.

machines in utilizable workshops.

11. Cantonal and regional congresses will take over the management, through special commissions, of all that cannot be done by individual communes; cantonal and regional defence, the organisation of public services, the merchant navy, railways, Posts and Telegraphs, etc.; nomination of delegates from the region to the general Congress and in other regions."

Clearly, the problems went on being studied in the theoretical sense, without preventing the movement from achieving great material strength. At that time "wild-cat" strikes took place in the countryside, particularly in Levante and Andalusia. Depending on the regions and provinces in which the governors, delegates and representatives of the central power had the right to suspend constitutional guarantees, to close down premises, to arrest and deport administratively whoever they chose to pick on; where the police resorted to torture, where unemployment was rife, where "agitators" and their families were reduced to such a state of penury that a pair of canvas shoes was often a luxury, journals propaganding the ideal appeared openly or clandestinely.

Who will ever know how many? Let us take an example. In the small town of Corunna (on the coast to the north of Portugal), alone, where the number of inhabitants increased from 30,000 to 60,000 between 1874 and 1923, four libertarian communist or anarchist, and of course also syndicalist, weeklies appeared in succession during those years: *La Bandera Roja, La Emancipación, El Corsario, La Lucha Obrera.* Later, after a prolonged period of repression, there were another five: *Germinal, La Emancipación, La Voz del Obrero, Tierra* and *Solidaridad Obrera* (the present writer has contributed to the two latter journals).

It would be impossible, unless one had the archives of the Ministry of the Interior at one's disposal, to list all the publications that appeared between 1870 and 1936. But let us quote the figures we know for the year 1936—and probably the list is not complete:—two dailies: *Solidaridad Obrera,* organ of the C.N.T., which appeared in Barcelona with a circulation of between 40,000 and 50,000, and *C.N.T.,* the Madrid organ of the same organisation with an average circulation of 30,000. Among the periodicals—about ten in all—the veteran of the Spanish anarchist press, *Tierra y Libertad,* published in Barcelona with a circulation of 20,000; *Vida Obrera* was published in Gijon (Asturias); *El*

Productor appeared in Seville; *Cultura y Accion* in Saragossa.

But that is not all, for in addition there were the Reviews. There was *Tiempos Nuevos* in Barcelona with a circulation of 15,000; *La Revista Blanca*, with a minimum circulation of 5,000; *Esfuerzo*, also published in Barcelona and with the same circulation; in Valencia *Orto* had a similar circulation, but above all there was *Estudios*, with an average circulation of 65,000 copies which at times reached 75,000.

In all these publications the same objectives were continually put forward. Whereas in other countries, and during periods of struggle, stress was only laid on criticism, the single immediate demand, the denunciation of the ills of society, often with curses, the directing and constructive ideas were here continually recalled. Even during a period of illegality, *El Municipio Libre*, a journal published in Malaga, could publish the following in its May or June issue of 1880:

"We want the constitution of free communes, independent from any centralising tie, with no other union than that which stems from federal pacts freely agreed to and always subject to repeal by the contracting communes.

"The appropriation by the communes of the land, the instruments of work of which the full right of use has been granted to the agricultural and industrial Collectives.

"The recognition of the social rights of individuals of both sexes who contribute to production.

"Complete education, and application of all the moral and physical means of development to the education of children.

"A municipal system guaranteeing in full the rights of the individual.

"Organisation of work allowing to each worker the enjoyment of the whole product of his labour.

"Advances to be made in all activities which will allow mankind to take advantage of all inventions and progress, the fruits of man's genius."

Most certainly some objections on details can be levelled at the ideas on economic organisation, so long as one puts oneself in the context of the period, and takes into account, for instance, the economic structures of Andalusia and other regions. But what matters are the broad outlines, the ever-present constructive spirit, which means that the errors of anticipation can be quickly corrected when the time comes.[10] And one should bear in mind this constant return to "complete education". It has been possible to write, and with justice, that Joaquin Costa, the great republican leader and sociologist, an inspired autodidact, who did so much to raise the cultural level of the Spanish people, and made free education one of the major planks of his struggle, had been preceded by those libertarian workers and peasants whose material existence was so dull but whose spirit was so illumined.

The period of illegality begun in 1872-73 passed, and after nine years during which innumerable struggles were engaged, the syndical organisation, once more nationally linked, held a congress in Barcelona. At the end of the discussions a *Manifesto* was drafted for the Spanish people. Exaggerations apart, the same ideal was recalled with the same insistence:

"We the workers who are the true craftsmen in society, its creative and vital force, who through our material and intellectual efforts[11] are building towns and villages; who work on the land and extract from its bowels the most precious products; who build ships which cross the seas transporting the wealth that we produce; who build the railways which link the most isolated regions; who lay cables at the bottom of the ocean which make it possible for the Old World to communicate with the New; who tunnel the mountains, build aqueducts and dig canals; those of us who take part in all that mankind produces with our bare hands . . . as a result of a terrible contradiction, do not enjoy its riches. Why? Because the power of Capital and of the bourgeoisie reduces our sweat to a commodity which is deemed a wage rate and carries the seal of slavery and is the source from which stem all the evils which oppress us."

Once again one sees how the problem of social classes is clearly posed: Here now, is the statement of the methods of struggle and the ends to be attained.

"Our organisation, which is entirely economic, distinguishes itself from all the political bourgeois and workers' parties; it is opposed

10 This was verified in fact during the revolution; some libertarians had remained at the stage of the free, autarchic commune; they easily rectified.
11 It is noteworthy that the proletarian attitude did not exclude a criterion which gave to intellectual workers a place in the struggle.

to them all because all those parties organised themselves to win political power, whereas we organise ourselves to destroy all existing political States and to replace them by a FREE FEDERATION OF FREE ASSOCIATIONS OF FREE WORKERS."

A further commentary is necessary. The preceding paragraph is clearly aimed at international Marxism and naturally at Marx who had led his supporters along the road of Parliamentarianism and the State, by submitting at the Congress of The Hague (September 1872) a resolution declaring that "the conquest of political power is the primary duty of the proletariat". The political polemic between the two schools of socialism began in Spain. It has continued to spread and to grow ever since.

The Manifesto then stressed the internationalism, the universality of the objectives pursued and the vision of the future:

"The social problem is not only national, but concerns workers in both worlds, for the cornering of raw materials, the introduction of machines, the division of labour, the concentration of Capital, bank transactions and financial speculations, the development of the means of communication—are so many economic forces that have favoured the full rise of the bourgeoisie and its exclusive domination of social interests."

Even the relatively uninformed reader will observe that the drafters of this document had read Proudhon, and especially *Qu'est ce que la Proprieté?* and the *Contradictions Economiques*. But he will also observe that these workers, some of whom— Ricardo Mella, Anselmo Lorenzo, Rafael Farga, Pellicer, Federico Urales—in analysing the structure of capitalism and its development with an extraordinarily profound knowledge, had attained to the level of sociologists.[12]

This progress and development which were pursued whenever the situation was favourable were on several occasions referred to by Peter Kropotkin who, in the journal *Le Revolté* which he had founded and which was the only anarchist journal then extant in the French language, wrote in an editorial (November 12, 1881) that the workers' movement was reviving "with a new vitality in Europe". Then, referring to Spain:

"But it is above all in Spain that at the moment there is an important development. After having brooded for the past eight years as the fire under the cinders, it has just appeared

12 Ricardo Mella a worker in the hat-making industry was to become a mining engineer.

openly with the latest congress in Barcelona at which 140 workers' organisations were represented by 136 delegates. Not just sections of seven or eight members who have been drawn together in a district by pure chance, but sections of workers in the same trade, whose members know each other intimately and meet every day, who are inspired with the same hopes and who share a common enemy in the boss, and a common objective—that of casting off the yoke of Capital; in a word, a real *organisation*.

"We look through the issues of *La Revista Social*, a newspaper produced by the workers themselves and each one informs us both of the creation of new trade sections, the support of existing groups and the federation of groups formerly isolated. In reading the bulletin of the Spanish movement we feel ourselves carried back to the best times of the International with just this difference: more sharpness in the aspirations, a clearer conception of the struggle to be waged, and a more revolutionary outlook among the grouping as a whole.

"A comparison comes immediately to mind: the comparison between the movement which exists in Spain with that which exists in France all to the advantage of Spain and all to the disadvantage of France."

After other considerations Kropotkin stresses the difference between the two countries:

"Faithful to the anarchist traditions of the International these intelligent, active, restless men will not keep to themselves to pursue *their* narrow ends; they remain in the working class, they struggle with it and for it. They bring their energy to the workers' organisation and work to build up a force which will crush Capital on the day of the revolution: the revolutionary trade association. Trade sections, federations of all the trades of the locality, the region, and combat groups independent of all trades but above all socialists.[13] That is how they constitute the cadres of the revolutionary army . . .

"We could not do less than advise the French workers to take up again, as their Spanish brothers have done, the traditions of the International, to organise themselves outside all political parties by inscribing on their banner solidarity *in the struggle against Capital*."

13 Note that the word *socialist* was still used by Kropotkin at the time.

We would like to comment on this commentary. We note in the first place that it needed, at the time, a Russian to publish in Geneva the only anarchist paper in the French language, the French anarchists being neither numerous enough nor enterprising enough to do so themselves; whereas in Spain . . . This difference is most significant.

Furthermore, for the French workers it was not a question of returning to the traditions of the First International, for the simple reason that it had never existed in France as an organised movement, and that the few local sections which managed to form themselves were relentlessly persecuted, whereas in Spain the movement had a few years to establish, and to learn how to organise, itself.

Then also it lacked a Bakunin. In spite of all his qualities Kropotkin could not exercise this influence, this fascination, which were characteristic of the great fighter who was also a great thinker and organiser. He lacked that gift of human, personal attraction and understanding, which made it possible for a peasant or a labourer to feel uninhibited when talking with Bakunin who because of, or in spite of, being a hereditary "lord" understood the common man and knew how to put himself at his level.

All this explains why Kropotkin, though in favour of workers' militancy and organisation, could not exert an influence over his comrades comparable with that of Bakunin. Furthermore, at the time, the Italian movement, because of the impatience and clumsiness of its outstanding personalities was reduced almost to a skeletal state; and likewise the Swiss Jura Federation.

It also explains why the French anarchist movement was organised on the basis of groups of "seven or eight members who have been fortuitously brought together in a district" pursuing "their petty ends" and abandoning the great tasks of social transformation.

In June of the following year Kropotkin returned to the Spanish example. But without effect. It required the disastrous terrorist activity of the so-called "heroic" period, and a kind of internal disintegration as a result of numerous deviations, for some anarchists to decide, from about 1895 onwards, to enter the syndicates where they introduced not only the practice of violence, as Georges Sorel wrote of it, but a body of doctrine of which the main elements were adopted by the school of revolutionary syndicalism.

But let us return to Spain. Years have passed and in 1887 a

congress was held and a Manifesto issued which was reproduced in the newspaper *El Productor*.[14] In it we read:

"We declare for anarchy (no-government) and we aspire to a socio-economic system in which, by agreeing on the interests and the reciprocity of rights and duties everybody will be free, all will contribute to production and will enjoy the maximum of happiness, which consists in that the products consumed are the fruits of the labour of each one, without exploitation, and consequently without the curses of a single exploited worker.

"The land must have no master, any more than the air and the light, or the underground riches, or the forests, or all that is not the fruit of men's work.

"Science cannot have a master, any more than can the means of production which are the result and application of scientific knowledge.

"The Land, Science, the machines of heavy industry, have not been created by their custodians, but are created either by causes independent of Man's will, or by the applied work of all men . . .

"Social unity is fundamentally the producer . . . The first social group is the group of producers in the same line of work. The basic contract is made between the producer and the respective group of producers of the same line.

"The groups of producers from a particular locality establish a contract—by which they constitute an entity facilitating exchange, credit, education, health and the local police; and they conclude contracts with other localities for credit and for exchange in a wider sphere, such as communications, general and reciprocal public services . . .

"The land, the mines, the railways and in general all the means of production, of transport and exchange are conceded for full right of use to the workers' collectives. The final goal of the revolution is:

"The dissolution of the State.

"The expropriation of the owners of the common inheritance of the world.

"The organisation of society on the basis of the work of those who can produce; the rational distribution of the products

14 In the 1890s the editors of *El Productor* were engaged in a polemic with their counterparts on *Temps Nouveaux* (successor to *La Révolte* on the usefulness of activity within the workers' movement. The *Temps Nouveaux* denied that it was useful.

C

of labour; help for those who are not yet qualified to work or who are no longer able to; the integral physical and scientific education of future producers . . .

"For these reasons the congress, which considers the Spanish Regional Federation as a free grouping in which workers can resolve all special cases by common initiative whenever unanimous action is necessary, recognises the freedom of individuals and of the collectives so that they may develop according to the special conditions that regulate the life of each one of us . . ."

Such declarations, such programmes, to which are often added complementary conceptions or initiatives, indicate that the constructive preoccupations remain always in the forefront. And underlying these preoccupations there is invariably a fundamental doctrinal basis which inspires plans and projects. In that last Manifesto what remains is the collectivist concept proposed by Bakunin and modified by the Proudhonian mutualist concept of which the distinguishing feature is the formula of the contract.

But in the same period there was an important development, which showed that lively minds were at work. Up to that time, following the collectivist doctrine and, as we have seen on different occasions, each producer had to enjoy "the whole product of his labour". Naturally, this formula had as its aim to destroy every vestige of the exploitation of man by man; but a new problem had been posed by the communist school of anarchism—and in fact was posed implicitly in the constructive conceptions of Bakunin: many members of society were not qualified to work, so far as a productive contribution was concerned. Society was therefore obliged to keep them and to do so there was nothing for it but to deduct whatever was necessary from that part which, according to the principle maintained until then, belonged to the producers. The latter would not therefore be able to "enjoy the whole product of their labour". The formula which more and more commanded attention was that of true communism "to each according to his needs, from each according to his ability", which Louis Blanc had advocated and which Proudhon attacked partly on the ground that it was conceived in the form of State communism, and partly also because he rejected instinctively, one could almost say with all his being, what he called "the community". We are now assenting to a morality of complete solidarity, which was to find its practical expression in the Collectives of 1936-1939.

At the instance of Marx and Engels, who sent Lafargue to combat on the spot the Spanish Internationalists who would not submit to their directives, another syndicalist organisation, which was Marxist and reformist, was set up (its founders were seven in number and all lived in Madrid). But it did not present either the moral strength that philosophical and social convictions based on a broad humanism give, or the characteristics of will and historic activity that spring from the ideal incorporated with action. In Spain, anarchism, or rather let us call it anti-authoritarian socialist federalism, preceded authoritarian State socialism, thus turning to advantage the time gained. But because of the influence it exerted on minds it was also better able to win over people: for not only did anarchism reject authority outside the individual, it also influenced society by its cultural activity spread among the masses. Let us not forget that in 1882 *La Revista Social*, edited by Luis de Oteiza, had a circulation of 20,000 and was probably the journal most read in Spain. Furthermore, in the history of international anarchism we do not know of a cultural manifestation to compare with that of the *Segundo Certamen Socialista*[15] and it is probably worthwhile underlining, once again, how easy it was for the Spanish anarchists to look upon themselves as one of the schools of socialism. In France such an attitude would have been judged and condemned as an unforgivable heresy . . .

One will understand even better the importance achieved by this movement when one knows that in 1903 in Madrid, *Tierra y Libertad* which, as we have already pointed out, was to become the traditional journal of Spanish anarchism, became a daily newspaper under the editorship of Abelardo Saavedra.[16]

In the following years one observes a kind of irresolution in the thinking of Spanish anarchism, which had previously been lucid and unambiguous. For unfortunately French anarchism, so out of sympathy with Proudhon and Bakunin, exerted an

15 *The Second Socialist Contest*, called a "contest" because rewards were given according to the value of the works.
16 A talented journalist from the petit bourgeoisie who rallied to the side of the people; an excellent speaker who could have made his career among the privileged classes and who until his death was a paragon of devotion to the cause which he had adopted. When I met him in 1917 he had already suffered imprisonment on twenty-two occasions.

influence which was intellectually and spiritually restrictive. Its late entry into the syndicalist movement brought with it only a part of the militants. The custom of small groups, which Kropotkin deplored, had established itself only too well. It is true that there was much talk about making the revolution, but this was seen as the apotheosis of the General Social Upheaval, romanticized to the point where Jean Grave and Charles Malato had to polemicise with their own comrades for whom all organisation was necessarily authoritarian and threatened the rights of the individual. Then, as the revolution was long in coming about matters of secondary importance were taken up. Individualism appeared, with its Stirnerite demands more or less ably interpreted by the "self"; the revolt became purely negative, when it did not change course in quest of various marginal hobby-horses such as vegetarianism, naturism, aestheticism, Nietzschean exaltation, etc.

France enjoyed an immense prestige in Spain. It was from France that many new ideas had been introduced or reintroduced, such as republicanism, socialism and anarchism. Before long the French anarchist deviations were to be imported by a number of Spanish anarchists.[17]

These novelties became confused with those of a form of anarchist communism which rejected union activity and the broad organic anticipation of the future by the Spanish anarchists. But on the one hand the very intensity of the Spanish problem limited these fantasies. And on the other the natural social feeling and the spirit of solidarity so strongly present in the Spaniard's nature were too powerful for such a movement to founder in these human follies. Furthermore the existence of the anarchist groups did not prevent, in the first place, social activity, and in the second, syndical action from fomenting this almost mystical dynamic of history which drives people to big dreams and big actions.

The ideal dwells deep in the Spanish soul. For the ordinary militant it is not a question of philosophical abstractions but of social justice, of work organised jointly, of a real brotherhood resulting from the equalitarian enjoyment of goods and services.

17 Exile in France, during the periods of repression or of prolonged unemployment which obliged people to seek their bread on the other side of the Pyrenees, favoured the making of contact with the numerous little groups where long hair, sandals and the loosely tied bow were the widespread hallmark of the superior individuality of each one.

The humblest anarchist peasant knows this, partly undoubtedly because his lot is so difficult that he cannot indulge in chimeras when the social question is at stake. And the congress at the Comedia theatre, held in Madrid in 1919, confirms what has always been: the aim of the C.N.T. is libertarian communism; to achieve it, it was decided to transform the traditional craft syndicates into industrial syndicates[18] in order the better to guarantee the management of the new economy. A situation which was to be ratified after ten years of civil and military dictatorship by the Congress of Saragossa in 1936, which marks a new departure in our syndical organisation.

Let us say so bluntly: the Resolution of a constructive order voted by the delegates in a situation which was felt to be pre-revolutionary was inferior to those that had been voted at previous congresses. But the unceasing repetition of the ends and means, the will for constructive activities by the syndicates, the local, cantonal, regional, national federations, of their cohesion, the idea of communal activities, of widespread instruction, of large scale workshops to replace the decrepit ones in which craftsmen and small contractors were so badly recompensed for their work, all this had remained impressed in the minds of the rank and file militants, and all those who, until then, had given themselves heart and soul to the triumph of the ideal. And it is surprising to see how, though the texts were unknown to the generation that made the revolution, the resolutions of the congresses of 1870, 1871, 1872, 1882 and others were applied, often to the letter, in the agrarian collectives and in the unions industrial achievements of 1936-1939.

It should be pointed out, in conclusion, that during the five years of the republic (from 1931 to 1936) many studies were published which sought to prepare the way for the constructive realisations of the revolution. For the first time in the history of world anarchism, in turn D. A. de Santillan, Higinio Noja Ruiz, Gaston Leval dealt with these problems, not in the form of utopias and imaginary anticipations, but basing themselves on the concrete reality of the economy of the country, in the light of the statistics concerning industrial and agricultural production, the problem of raw materials, power, and international

18 Unfortunately under the influence of eloquent demagogues, the congress rejected the constitution of federations of industries which were so necessary. It was only started in 1931 and this delay made itself felt during the revolution.

exchanges, public services, etc. . . . Other, but less documented, studies such as the one by Dr. Isaac Puente with the title *El Communismo Libertario* and other essays of lesser importance appeared at the same time. And five or six books translated from the French were by economists such as Cornelissen, by militant revolutionary syndicalist theoreticians such as Pierre Besnard, and less dogmatic sociologists such as Sebastien Faure. All the foregoing, and in addition many other books and numerous pamphlets issued by at least three publishing enterprises, contributed to preparing the majority of militants for the tasks that lay ahead.

The ideals pursued by the Spanish anarchist-communists are the same as those followed and propagated by the greatest minds from Plato and perhaps some of the Stoics, right up to our own times. The Spanish revolution achieved what the early Christians were asking, what in the XIVth Century the Jacquerie in France and the English peasants led by John Ball struggled for, and those in Germany whom Thomas Münzer was to lead two centuries later, as well as the English Levellers led by Everard and Winstanley, the Moraves brothers, disciples of Jean Huss. That which Thomas More foresaw in his *Utopia,* and Francis Bacon, and Campanella in *La Città del Sole* and the priest Jean Meslier in his famous *Testament* (too often ignored) and Morelli in his *Naufrage des Iles Flottantes,* and Mably who like Morelli inspired the noblest minds in the American Revolution, and the *enragés* of the French Revolution of whom Jacques Roux, the "red priest" was one. And the army of thinkers and reformers of the XIXth Century and of the first thirty years of the present. It is, in world history, the first attempt to apply the dream of all that was best in mankind. It succeeded in achieving, in many cases completely, the finest ideal conceived by the human mind and this will be its permanent glory.

CHAPTER II

THE MEN AND THE STRUGGLES

For most of those who deal with social history, with the revolutionary achievements or possibilities, it is almost exclusively in the industrial areas and among the industrial proletariat that research has to be directed. The agrarian regions and the land workers are discarded straightaway. What is more, the social class of small peasants is inevitably deemed to be counter-revolutionary, above all by Marxist "science" according to which the conditions of existence and the techniques of work condemned their users to being the pillars of reaction, or its incarnation. Marx insisted on this "law" of history, even affirming that the struggle between the town and the country had been one of the main aspects of the class war.

It is true that in this matter, the peasants have lagged behind the townsmen on many occasions. Nevertheless, nothing is absolute and events show that one cannot claim to be able to contain the development of the life of peoples within hermetic formulae. Spain is a case in point. In fact, if it is true that the anti-statist collectivist socialism conceived by Bakunin appeared in 1869 in Madrid and Barcelona, it was soon to extend to the exclusively agricultural areas and also to the towns whose economy was linked to the general activities of agriculture. In fact the social and socialist-anarchist movement spread to the North, above all in Catalonia, the most industrialised region, and in the South to Andalusia, a region in which agriculture dominates and occupies almost all the South from the Atlantic south of Portugal to the

Levante region on the Mediterranean coast.

It was in these two regions that before the revolution, and for a long time, most propaganda journals, magazines and pamphlets were sold, and where social activity and sustained struggles have been among the most intensive.

One can give a number of explanations. Firstly psychological, for the Andalusian is perhaps among Spaniards the most opposed to orders emanating from outside, to the tutelage of the State and to the authority represented by the lawyer or the functionary. Secondly economic, for the structure of agrarian property in the form of *cortijos*, very large farms, often covering thousands of hectares, which employed locally and on a permanent basis a large number of workers who were miserably paid, predisposed the workers to agree among themselves over resistance and facilitated their grouping. Those who knew that period recount how in the evenings, labourers and harvesters, worn out by the day's work, would gather in the barn where they slept and there, in the small light of the solitary lantern, the one among them who could read would acquaint his comrades with the contents of the revolutionary papers published in Barcelona or in the Andalusian towns. Thus were the ideas spread.

This does not explain everything, however. For as one will see later it was in certain provinces, most often among the small landowners who were able to engage in the struggle more freely thanks to their economic independence, that our most tenacious, most heroic and able militants were to be found.

Furthermore, if hunger, unemployment and endemic poverty were factors and causes of the social war, other factors motivated the supporters in their efforts for social renewal. We return to the characteristics of human nature. Abelardo Saavedra recounted to us how, when Francisco Ferrer undertook to spread the new education under the form of *escuelas modernas* (modern schools) he had in that huge area of Andalusia alone—he himself was born in Seville—started 148 small schools. Ferrer supplied the money and equipment, while Abelardo Saavedra organised. But he had to find means of support and the teachers locally. The workers' syndicates supplied them. Almost always the teachers were young self-taught militant workers, who buckled to these new tasks and with success.

The same happened outside Andalusia. In 1919-1920 I visited in the Levante area, especially in the province of Valencia, several of these schools where they carried on as best they could the work of the martyr of Montjuich.[1] They existed above all in what we might call small rural towns. The resources previously supplied by Ferrer being no longer available, the local syndicate which included workers from all trades, or the local federation where there were several syndicates, brought funds deducted from the dues received. Often, the school became the main, almost mystical, objective of the workers' association. And I have known peasants who would deprive themselves of tobacco, their only luxury, in order to hand over each month a *duro*—five pesetas—to support the school which was by then called "rationalist".

One could write moving pages on the struggle waged locally around and over these achievements in which moral character predominated. For naturally they came into conflict with the active hostility of the caciques, the large landowners, masters of local life, who ganged up with the priest, the civil guard, and sometimes the chemist and the doctor too. Often, applying an ancient custom, the unofficial teacher would be arrested, and deported on foot, handcuffed and walking between two mounted civil guards toward the distant regions where he would live under surveillance. Almost always, the most educated militant in the locality would take his place. Then almost always it would be his turn to experience deportation. And another worker or peasant would replace him, who would also go, from prison to prison, to the distant provinces. Sometimes the authorities succeeded in closing the school. With a determined syndicate there were cases where the pupils would leave for the mountains each morning with their most recently improvised teacher, where he would get them to read, teaching them by writing words and figures in the air, or natural history by direct observation.

What I have just written only portrays one of the aspects of the social struggles which, it goes without saying, applied to existing conditions of life, but which were also inseparable from a higher objective. It is true that these struggles assumed many forms, such as demonstrations against the State, which so often aroused the peasants of France, Italy and Central Europe against the tax collectors in the times of the great kings and emperors; but to them was added a class war which at the time was more bitter than it had ever been.

Using information drawn from reliable sources and going back

---

1 Montjuich, fortress of Barcelona where Ferrer was executed by firing squad in 1909.

to a particularly troubled period, we will enumerate facts which will allow the reader to grasp the importance of the social struggle engaged in by the disinherited of Spain in revolt. They only refer to a very limited period but the intensity of the events they describe allows one to appreciate the acuteness of the general situation. They do not give an idea of the widespread nature of the general strikes, in Andalusia above all, during the latter part of the 19th Century which brought everything to a standstill in the towns, villages and countryside, where shepherds abandoned their flocks on the mountains, the wet nurses handed over their charges to their aristocratic mothers, domestic staff joined in with industrial wage earners. Nevertheless, what follows, and which started ten years after the birth of the Spanish libertarian movement, will allow us the better to understand the meaning of that social struggle.

The Year 1879—Execution, by garrotting, of the anarchist peasant Oliva, sentenced for social reasons—presumably for having made an attempt against a cacique. Dissolution of workers' societies in Tarragona (Catalonia) and of a cooperative in the village of Olivera (province of Cadiz). In Valencia a strike of farmers and share-croppers who refuse to pay the landowners. Intervention by the civil guard, many arrests, proclamations by the strikers affixed to trees, 75 peasant strikers are deported, though unconvicted, to the Marianne Islands (archipelago of the Philippines, which were Spanish colonies at the time). In Arcos de la Frontera (province of Cadiz), in Granada, Ronda, Jean— all in Andalusia—demonstrations of strikers demanding work and bread. Numerous arrests. In many places, the populace raids the bakers' and butchers' shops.

In June and July, burning of the harvest, in the vineyards, forests, and grain fields as well as in the barns of the large landowners of Castile, Estremadura, the Valencia region and above all in Andalusia, where the fires blaze for the whole of the month of August. A man named Moncasi is executed for an attempt on the life of a master. He is followed by Francisco Otero Gonzalez, who fired two shots unsuccessfully against a rich man.

1880—Gangs sack churches and tax collectors' offices, hold to ransom a number of rich people in the provinces of Tarragona, Toledo, Ciudad Real (the latter two in the very heart of New-Castile). Agitation in Andalusia. According to the *Revista Social*, 4,566 allotments were seized and sold by the collectors of taxes.

Later a further 51,854 were seized but not sold because of a shortage of buyers. In the early months of 1880, 39,000 more allotments suffer the same fate.

In May and June, fire raising involving small farmhouses and vineyards of the large landowners takes place in the region of Jerez, in Andalusia. In that town, 13 militants have been held in custody for twenty-three months charged with incendiarism which had occurred in Arcos; two of them, Manuel Alvarez and José Campos Rodriguez, die. A bomb explodes in front of the mayor's house in Coruña (in Galicia).

In the province of Huelva (Andalusia) destruction of the flocks by the strikers, and of tree plantations. A dozen or more uprisings against tax collector's agents in various parts of the country (Valls, Arriate, Orense, in Galicia; Almodovar, province of Ciudad Real, etc.).

Still in 1880, fires are started in the countryside of the province of Cordoba. Thousands of hectares of cereals, including 84 belonging to the Duke of Alba, are destroyed. Once again the homes of the rich are set on fire. Misery is driving the people to despair. The liberal newspaper *El Siglo* declares: "We prefer to withdraw into private life, as we are convinced that the triumphant revolution in Spain would immediately be captured by all the demagogic elements in the country." A grenade explodes in the Jesuit convent in Gandia (province of Valencia). The inmates move into the house of the Duke of Pastraña, but it is set on fire by the revolutionaries.

On August 3rd, the three people responsible for a derailment and attack on a train near the Alcazar, in Castile, are executed by firing squad. On the 17th, four sentenced to death are executed in Berzocana, one in Riazza on the 19th, and another in Marchena: ten executions in ten days. An underground journal appears, *El Municipio Libre,* which is distributed in the towns and countryside. The house of the collector of taxes in Requeña (province of Valencia) is stormed and the accounts books with some of the archives from the municipality are burned in the public Square. The army intervenes, the people face up to them. In the town of Alcoy, province of Valencia[2] the Jesuits are obliged to leave, faced with the hostile attitude of the people. Militants are arrested in Malaga where the clandestine print shop for the *Municipio Libre* is discovered.

2 See later the achievements of Alcoy during the revolution of 1936-1939.

1881—From 24th-26th September, a congress of *comarcal* (cantonal) federations is held in Barcelona. By their very structure, many of these federations are based on land workers grouped into the syndical organisations. Two hundred sections are represented, 136 delegates attend. With only 8 votes against, a resolution is accepted declaring their goal as collectivist anarchism. The dissenters subscribe to Marxist State Socialism.

1882—National Congress (referred to as Regional since the libertarians consider Spain as a *region* of the International) held in Seville; 212 delegates. 10 Regions organically constituted; 218 local federations, 633 syndical sections and 49,711 members. The latter figure is made up as follows: Western Andalusia 17,021 members, Eastern Andalusia 13,026; Aragon 689; Catalonia 13,181; Old Castile 1,036, New Castile 515; Murcia 265; Galicia 847; Basque country 710; Valencia 2,355. These figures are much lower than the number of people who were active in the social struggles.

Let us also underline the efforts, in some cases extraordinary, that are implied by the presence of so many delegates, a great number of whom had to travel on foot, or cross Spain under unbelievably bad conditions.

Let us note too that at this congress, it was decided, some thirty years before Francisco Ferrer undertook the task which cost him his life, to establish schools which were under the aegis neither of the Church nor of the State.

Still in Andalusia, the Local Federation of Seville, where at the time social life was bound up with agrarian activities, consisted of 53 syndical sections and 6,000 members. Immediately after the Seville congresses, seven new local federations are organised in the province, and 19 sections affiliate to the Andalusian regional federation. Each issue of the journal *El Trabajo* (Work) which ' appears in Malaga announces the formation of a score of syndical sections which land workers join in large numbers. Of the circulation of 18,000 copies of *La Revista Social* 8,000 were sold in Andalusia alone. Let us not forget that at that time Spain had a population of 18 million 65% of whom were illiterate. One should add that about 20 regional congresses had preceded the Seville congress in order to study the Agenda and to decide upon the motions to be submitted for it.

1883—*La Revista Social* announces that at Marchena, a worker earns from 2 to 3 "reales" (1 "real" = a quarter of a peseta) a day. There are 30,000 unemployed in the Andalusian countryside; the federation helps 3,500 of them (there is therefore a practical mutual aid limited only by available resources). The government "closes libraries and workers' schools".

But the violent, desperate character of the social struggle has provoked the constitution of a secret society, *La Mano Negra* (The Black Hand). More than 400 people are arrested, accused of belonging to it. Militants from the province of Valencia are deported to the Mariannes Islands. Soon 2,000 workers are charged with belonging to the mysterious organisation; terror reigns. The local federations dissolve, house searches take place throughout most of the country, social crimes are committed, the civil guard carries out searches night and day, arrests, imprisons, tortures. A large scale trial is being mounted in Montilla (province of Cadiz-Andalusia). In the library-school in La Linea (province of Cadiz) the civil guard seize furniture, tables, books, equipment, etc.

In May the first trial of the *Mano Negra* starts. The Advocate General demands thirty death sentences. Five of the wretches sentenced will be executed. The police make out they have discovered a new secret organisation and arrest twenty of its members.

1885-1886-1887—In Coruña (Galicia) an uprising of peasants against the city toll. Books, papers, registers are committed to the flames. The troops open fire, the insurrection lasts two days. The peasants of Canollas,[3] in the province of Barcelona, refuse to pay taxes, a hundred men armed with sticks oblige the collector to withdraw. According to the libertarian journal *El Obrero* (The Worker) in December 1886 alone the State seized 75 farms in Jodar, 32,000 in the province of Logroño, 4,000 in the Balearics, for non-payment of taxes. In Onteniente, province of Valencia, the people storm the town hall with the battle cry of "Down with Taxes!" and burn all book-keeping documents. It is estimated that from 1880-1886 the Finance Ministry seized by order of the courts 99,931 rural and urban properties. Since the Restoration, in thirteen years, the figure was to reach 999,000.[4]

The number of seizures was enormous, but we cannot check the exact figure retrospectively. Nevertheless in May 1887 it is announced that in the region of Alcañiz (province of Teruel) 3,000

3 The name of this place must have been mis-spelt.
4 The struggle against the Inland Revenue explains in part, probably, the hostility of the Spanish people for the State.

farms must be sold for non-payment of taxes. New and widespread disturbances are announced in various places against the city tolls, and the civil guard reply by firing on the demonstrators, killing and wounding some. Arrests take place throughout Andalusia to counteract the campaign for the Chicago Martyrs. In Grazanela (province of Cadiz) 24 men and 6 women are imprisoned. In many small towns (for instance in Rio Tinto, province of Huelva, Andalusia) there is active solidarity between the factory workers' movement and that of the miners. Desperate poverty in numerous villages and small towns in Andalusia. In La Loja (province of Granada), Ecija, Los Arcos, Sanlucar, Grazamela, the mayors telegraph to the Madrid government asking for help and troops. The Portuguese newspaper *Grito de Provo* announces 414,565 confiscations of property (without specifying in what period of time), of which 63,562 in the province of Cuenca (New Castile), 73,395 in the province of Saragossa. The peasants of Old Castile emigrate in large numbers.

What we have just enumerated, and which is necessarily incomplete so far as it concerns the social struggle during this period of twelve years, allows one to judge the intensity of the battles waged by the people in all the regions of Spain—with the probable exception of the Basque country.

Other factors complete the explanation of the behaviour of the people of the countryside, and one would be wrong to judge their attitude simply by the desperate uprising to which we have just referred. Certainly the struggle was punctuated with periods of inactivity, when the forces of repression got the upper hand and drove the peasants' syndicates into illegality for whole years, and when the majority were overtaken by a feeling of resignation. But the libertarian militants were always there as a ferment, as a leaven. They continued to influence through action or by propaganda, the circulation of newspapers and journals, the creation of libraries, even to support of the local section of the republican party when one existed. They gave proof of a will, a stoicism, and heroism often staggering. In their hundreds they experienced—and often for long periods—prison, banishment to the penal islands, deportation, exile, boycott by the caciques and by their administrators, blacklisting by the bosses, by tradesmen refusing to give credit, by innumerable

persecutions. But this struggle hardened men, and forged powerful wills. We have said, and will see increasingly, that often
the small proprietors who enjoyed a certain material independence,
could act and struggle with greater effect than the wage earners.
It is these small, independent libertarian proprietors who contributed most during the years 1915-1920 to the rebirth of the
libertarian movement even in the town of Valencia, where,
under the monarchy, republicanism had captured the opposition.
On Sunday mornings, abandoning their tasks, they came down
from the villages and the mountain districts, or from the Huerta,
to collaborate with those in the town who were exerting themselves to re-establish the forces that had been swept away by the
repressions. They were the supporters, the principal artisans of
this revival.

*

It was in the region of the Levante that I came to know
Narciso Poimireau[5] who lived in the village of Pedralva, in
the mountainous and poor region of the province of Valencia
where he owned some land and figured amongst the well-to-do
of the area. And yet, Narciso Poimireau, tall, spare, with a
heart of gold and an illumined mind, was the agitator *par
excellence* in the canton of Liria, which possibly provides the
most interesting social history of the region of the Levante.

He worked in his fields, and at night would leave on foot
in order not to tire his mule who like himself had to work
the next day—crossing the rocky paths, going from one village
to the next, preaching the libertarian gospel, and organising
the peasants. He had realised on some of his assets and maintained
a rationalist school at which his daughter was the teacher. At
the same time as struggling against the rich exploiters he carried
on the struggle against the priest. He also spoke at meetings; but
within our movement because of his moral rectitude he was
in the region the inspirer and thoughtful guide, who calmed
the outbursts of anger and opposed manifestations of hatred.

When Franco's troops took over, his local adversaries who,
after all, had not been pursued by him during the anti-Franco
period, arrested him. There was no news of him for some
time, then one day the authorities summoned the inhabitants

5 The name is more French than Spanish. Narciso Poimireau was a
distant descendant of those peasants about whom Taine speaks and
who, ruined by the extortions of Louis XIV's tax collector, driven
by misery, had to emigrate to Spain.

to the village square. And before them, holding him up to ridicule, they paraded a cart on which there was a large wooden cage. In the cage was Narciso Poimireau locked up like Don Quixote on his pitiful return and subjected to the mockery of the public summarily assembled. "But the people did not make fun of me; they looked at me with sorrow, and Franco's men got nothing for their pains," he told my informant from his prison cell. Narciso Poimireau was shot by the Francoists.

*

Let us turn to the northern part of Aragon, and to another of those exceptional men who compel admiration. His name is Juan Ric, and he is still alive somewhere in France. He lived in Binéfar in the province of Huesca, and owned 15 hectares (37 acres) of good irrigated land—a small fortune— and raised and sold some hundred sheep a year, owned two mules and, with his wife, looked after a grocer's shop which belonged to her. At the same time he was the principal activist in the local and cantonal libertarian syndicalist movement.

Always driving himself with an inexhaustible vitality, he was on a number of occasions pursued for subversive activities. Following a premature uprising in December 1934 in which some civil guards had been killed in the struggle, he found himself condemned twice to a life sentence (which at that time meant thirty-three years in prison) with a further fifteen years added. In all some eighty-two years; Ric no longer remembers exactly how many. He came out of prison with the amnesty of 1936, and of course immediately resumed the struggle. And naturally a few months later he was in the forefront of the anti-francoist counter-offensive. It was also obvious that I should find him, ever active and smiling, as the prime mover in the collectivist organisation of the canton of Binefar, which will be described in a later chapter. He had to cross to the other side of the Pyrenees at the time of the Franco advance, experienced the French concentration camps,[6] and later that of Dachau where he was taken by the Hitler police and from which he came out

---

6 Those concentration camps over which hardly anyone was aroused at the time, were guarded by the *garde mobile* and the Senegalese sharpshooters. Hundreds of refugees died there. Ric managed to escape and took part in the struggle against the Nazi forces in the Rouergue region and, informed against by communists (this is not the only example), he was arrested and sent to Dachau from where he eventually emerged weighing 35 kilos (79 lbs.).

alive by a miracle, and is ready tomorrow if he can return to Binefar (where the local inhabitants refused to buy his fields which the francoists had put up for auction) to begin again the experiment of an egalitarian and libertarian collectivity with the same enthusiasm, the same willingness, the same illumined faith.

How many more rich, exciting biographies could be written of exceptional men, of revolutionary libertarians, peasants, small proprietors and salaried workers, stubborn believers in the revolution because they were believers in justice and love! I have in front of me a short account that one such man drafted at my request, and who was the key figure in the peasant struggles in Navalmoral de la Mata, a small town of 7,500 inhabitants in the province of Caceres, in Estremadura. He was twice condemned to death, gravely wounded in the battles against the francoist forces, spent eighteen years in convict prisons, and if he had the strength and the opportunity he too, I am sure, would be ready to resume the struggles which I will now summarise. But this unknown hero, modest and humble, feels it necessary to pay homage to another modest and unknown hero, before writing about himself. This is what he says:

"Before I start talking about myself I want to speak of Alfonso Gonzalez, the oldest militant of Navalmoral. He was the father of all us anarchists, had been imprisoned many times, twice sentenced to death, arrested by the francoists on 22 July, 1936 and set free in 1942; he was rearrested in 1944 because he was acting as the liaison agent for the guerrillas in the region, was condemned to a convict prison and locked up in the penitentiary of Ocana. He served his sentence and returned; at the age of 84 the authorities expelled him from Navalmoral. He spent six months in the village of Talavuela, and returned to Navalmoral where he died six months later. By a will made before a notary he demanded a civil burial. The authorities sought to ignore his wishes but the notary succeeded in getting the old fighter's wishes respected. A breach was made in the wall of the cemetery so that the passage of the body along the paths blessed by God and the priests should not contaminate other tombs, and he was buried in an isolated corner."

And now, summarised, what concerns the writer of these lines, Ambrosio Marcos, himself:

"The liberal opposition, which represented an important step in Navalmoral, appeared, during the years of the monarchy

D

towards the end of the last century, in the persons of eminent republicans who left behind them pleasant memories among the people. One of them founded a large public library where were to be found all the books on general culture as well as those dealing with the social problem, and therefore also books of anarchist sociology, so numerous in Spain. This is not at all surprising, for certain republican currents of thought maintained fraternal relations with the workers' revolutionary movement in the anti-monarchist opposition. Social conflicts arose in the form of agrarian strikes, struggles against the large landowners. We have no details, but at the beginning of the century, there is talk of the *Mano Negra* (The Black Hand) which caused such terror that mothers threatened their children with it! It replaced the devil."

In 1905, the people of Navalmoral rose to defend the liberal mayor who had just been elected, and against whom the Marquis of Comillas, who was reputed to be the richest man in Spain, possessing estates within the jurisdiction of Navalmoral as well as in many other regions, applied his veto. A company of Civil Guards hastened there with rifles and light artillery, to give support to the local forces; after skirmishes it ended with their withdrawal and a triumphant people. In the years that followed there are records of demonstrations against the high cost of living. In 1916 a local workers' Federation was founded, which supported the General Union of Workers (U.G.T. —socialist and reformist). But there were some libertarian militants on the spot who, a year later, won over this Federation to the National Confederation of Labour (C.N.T.). The usual social conflicts took place. In late 1923 Primo de Rivera established his dictatorship. The syndicates were closed, as happened in many other towns and regions of Spain where social agitation was intense. There then emerged that kind of genius for clandestinity which has already been noted. The union movement continued in spite of the closing of the syndicates, the members paid their dues, met in the fields (in other parts it might be in the woods or the mountains). As the law did not forbid the constitution of work groups, nor even of certain forms of association, the carters organised themselves into a work collective. At the height of the repression, they went beyond the wage system. Workers in other trades did likewise.[7]

7 Ambrosio Marcos does not tell us which.

Primo de Rivera abandoned power in November 1930. The Syndicate is immediately reconstituted. In one month it boasts a membership of 1,500. The peasants join in their turn. Soon there are 400, some landless, the others possessing only a few *ares* (1 *are* = 120 square yards) of "secano" (dry lands). Ambrosio Marcos concerned himself with the agricultural friendly society which had been founded by Catholic militants or socially neutral people. Himself a landowner, and aided by other workers and peasants, he has an influence on the members and wins them over to the struggle for the land, and in January 1931 the field workers and the poor peasants take possession of the estates of the Marquis de Comillas and of other very large owners of these properties which had always remained uncultivated and which they have always wanted. In great numbers they set about clearing and digging and sowing. The Civil Guard intervene, the workers appear to give in, withdraw with their animals, their carts and their tools; the Civil Guard remain in occupation, triumphant. But instead of returning home, the peasants go to the other side of the village, on another estate, where they resume the same kind of work. The women and children bring them drinks and food and then remain on the roads to warn of the arrival of the enemy, who in the end get tired of this game of hide-and-seek and leave to the peasants the fruits of their occupation.

In April 1931 the Republic was proclaimed. The new authorities did what their predecessors of the monarchy did not. A trial against the peasants lasted for six months. They were condemned to pay compensation for the use of the land but did not. Come July, they gather the harvest. The winter (1931-32) comes. The landowners want repossession of their property, the peasants resist. The Civil Guard intervene armed with rifles, but again beat a retreat.

On a spring day a caravan of 500 labourers took to the road leading to the fields. A regular ants' nest of humans set to work. The incident caused a sensation, the Madrid newspapers reported it, journalists and photographers turned up for on the spot reports. In other regions, peasants invaded the uncultivated estates, and the Civil Guard, now republican, began to open fire. But not in Navalmoral de la Mata for the time being because, in Ambrosio Marcos' words, "they are afraid of us". Come 1933, The collective work on the estates continues, but relations are more and more tense. There were continuous conflicts between the big *terratenientes*, the caciques or their administrators backed by the armed forces on the one hand, and the peasants and the workers' syndicates on the other. In March 1933, eight of the most active militants, which of course included Ambrosio Marcos, were secretly arrested during the night. The order had been given to apply to them the *ley de fuga*.[8] But within an hour the news was known, the telephone mobilised, and the whole population was in the streets, and all the approach roads blocked to prevent the arrival of the detainees at the provincial prison of Caceres. The authorities arranged for the itinerary of the cars to be changed, and no one dared to apply the *ley de fuga*, and at three in the morning our comrades arrived safe and sound at their proper destination. But at daybreak in Navalmoral, not only were all the roads still cut off; the Town Hall was taken by assault, the local authorities were taken hostage by the peasants and workers, salaried or otherwise.

The detainees were not released, as the authorities wanted to destroy the expropriation movement at all costs. But their places were taken by other militants and the struggle in Navalmoral de la Mata continued.

A strike by the casual workers in May and August at the time of the harvest hits the medium sized landowners. The republican government authorities, a different lot from the apostolic figures of republicanism in its early days, intervene. But the movement extends to the neighbouring villages, to Peralta de la Mata, a village of no importance in which our organisation had 500 members, to Valdeuncar with 200, to Josandilla de la Vera, to Villanueva de la Vera. And it even wins over the nearby Castilian province of Plasencia which had slumbered for centuries.

In December 1933, as a reaction against the electoral triumph of the right wing parties, the C.N.T. sought to call for a national general strike which in the event proved to be a tactical error. In Olivia de Plasencia, the Town Hall was taken by storm, but it was in Navalmoral that the attack was seen to be the most powerful of all. For three days the people were masters of the town. Battle was engaged, and the Civil Guard managed in

8 Under this law the police, the Civil Guard or others had the right to fire on any detainee who might attempt to escape whilst being transferred to the prefecture, to prison or transportation. The Civil Guard, specialists in such matters, murdered militants in this way with the pretext that they had attempted to escape.

the end to oblige the C.N.T. to beat a retreat.

Thirty-five militants, most of them peasants, appeared before the Courts and were sentenced to terms of hard labour. They emerged from prison when the leftist Popular Front, triumphant at the elections of February 1936, granted an amnesty. In the meantime, the peasants of Navalmoral de la Mata, faced by the superior strength of the adversary, had lost some of the ground it had won. But they had also won some rights of land usufruct. Ambrosio Marcos modestly sums up the results of this epic, which alas ended with the triumph of the francoist forces who soon after their attack on July 19, 1936 made their victorious appearance:

"One can say, so far as the organisation of agriculture is concerned, that our Collectives were not the integral application of libertarian communism,[9] but that if we take into account the circumstances, there was not a single failure. This is what is most important, for every failure results in a setback and sows confusion in our midst. We had to prove that our ideas were practical and our programme could be realised. In spite of the authorities and the landowners, the first attempt at cultivation in common was carried out. The least fortunate were helped, the strongest helped the weak. Some workers became peasants in order to take part in this new enterprise. People in other districts were helped. When the strike of Duro-Felguera[10] took place in the Asturias, a truck-full of chick peas and many sacks of potatoes were sent to the strikers, as well as money. The strikers at the Central Telephone Exchange were similarly helped by us, and there were other acts of solidarity."

*

We have so far only given a brief account—limited in time and geographically speaking—of the intensity of the social struggle in the peasant and agricultural areas. But in spite of its intensity, sometimes savage, it was possibly surpassed by the struggle that was waged in the towns. In the first place, especially in Andalusia, town and country often acted together, the social conflicts intermingling. But in the industrial zones, and especially in Catalonia, the movement very quickly spread and with a

9 This statement is debatable, as will be seen by what follows. But the libertarian rank and file militants always wanted *to go further.*
10 A miners' strike which was full of dramatic incidents, as most of them were.

vigour which was quite exceptional. From the beginning of the century, Catalonia was responsible for 70% of Spain's industry. The use of water power from the Pyrenees, the permanent contact with France, the broad access to the Mediterranean, the contribution of Franco-Belgian capital and local human initiative, resulted in this region, which lacked raw materials, developing in time a manufacturing industry that acquired considerable importance.

The conditions were therefore brought together for the creation of workers' syndicates which had already appeared in the first half of the 19th century (as was also the case in Italy), so much so that in 1840 there existed not only resistance societies of workers, but also craft federations which, as that of the weavers, extended throughout the region, and that of the three steam industries which, when federated, could be compared by Anselmo Lorenzo to the Trades Unions in England.

And from 1870 onwards the anarchist syndical movement was a revolutionary school, free from interferences, in which the most important workers' organisations were responsible for their own destiny. Partial and general strikes, sabotage, public demonstrations, meetings, struggle against strike-breakers (they existed too), imprisonment, transportation, trials, uprisings, lock-outs, some *attentats* . . .

The present writer arrived in Barcelona in June 1915. At that time, the Spanish National Confederation of Labour (C.N.T.) which had been founded four years earlier, was going through a difficult period. Meetings against World War I organised by our comrades were attracting fewer supporters than were the Republicans' calling for Spain's participation alongside the Allies. Yet in Barcelona there were four workers' centres called "Ateneos" because they each had a library, tables at which one could sit and read, and where lectures were given. The movement of anarchist groups acted in agreement with the C.N.T.

But then came the Russian Revolution, the influence of which spread to the West, raising so many hopes. Suddenly the membership of the syndicates grew, strikes increased, the social struggle was intensified, always with the confrontation of power between the workers' organisation and that of the employers. It was at that time that our weekly, *Solidaridad Obrera,* of which Francisco Ferrer had been among the founders, became a daily. Two years later (in 1919) we had six dailies with the same title (in Barcelona, Bilbao, Saragossa, Madrid, Valencia and Seville) and about a dozen weeklies which appeared in different regions of Spain. To these one must add magazines such as *Paginas Libres,* an excellent publication edited by Dr. Pedro Vallina in Seville.

In the Andalusian countryside the harvest went up in flames, but in the towns, in Catalonia and in Aragon and in some industrial centres in the North of Spain, strike followed strike.

The most important of these has come to be known in the social history of Spain as the strike of *La Canadiense* (the Canadian), which broke out in Lerida, some 90 miles south of Barcelona. This Canadian Company was building a large dam which would have made possible the building of a big electricity generating station. Some workers were dismissed and their comrades immediately came out on a solidarity strike, and in view of the resistance put up by the Company the movement first spread throughout the province, but then to the other three Catalan provinces. There has rarely been a general strike which was more complete, more uncompromising or more impressive. Not only the workshops and factories, but all means of communication came to a halt. Workers' power made the law in the streets. Only doctors could freely circulate. Cafes, hotels, restaurants, all were closed. At night Barcelona had a complete blackout. That strike, which lasted from February 5 up to March 20, 1919 was an extraordinary battle waged against the employers and the authorities.

But the repression was let loose. Spanish law allowed for —and never ceased to do so even during the Republic which, on the contrary, intensified the repressive legislation—internment both of common law criminals, even if they had served their sentence, and political opponents, especially militant workers considered to be subversives or constituting a danger to public order.

This gave the political authorities possibilities of taking action which they used in full measure. In the years from 1920 to 1924, there were times when the internees could be counted in thousands. Not only was the "Model Prison" of Barcelona bursting its sides but internees had to be housed in the monumental Arenas, and boats were loaded with them in the outer harbour, as had been done in France after the Commune using pontoons. Whoever lived through those intensive turbulent days cannot forget.

But that was not all. So long as Spain had colonies, the enemies of the regime were transported as were the Communards to New Caledonia. At the time of the *Canadiense* strike, apart from the Isle of Fernando Po the only other available island was Mahon in the Mediterranean. It was not enough, so they had recourse to deportation in Spain itself. Convoys were formed of prisoners chained in pairs and all linked to a common rope. It was for this reason that these convoys were called *cuerdas de deportados*. Thus groups of 30, 40, 50 would be taken on the highways, escorted by mounted Civil Guards, ever ready to use the Mauser rifle with which each man in the polished cocked hat was armed. It was a case of relegating these revolutionary workers to the more isolated regions, 300, 400 miles and more distant, in order to cut them off from contact with the masses. But when men are possessed of an ideal these measures are of no avail. In the event the *cuerdas de deportados* produced the opposite results to those intended.

All along the route, the sight of the deportees aroused sympathy, generosity, solidarity. The announcement of the arrival or the passage of a *cuerda* swept through the villages, and even before the convoy had reached the first houses voices were raised crying out: *"Los presos!* The prisoners!"

And the doors of the houses would open and the women, children and old folk would come out offering them bunches of grapes, bread, melons, while the men came down from the fields bringing tobacco. It was a collective offering which the Civil Guard could not do otherwise than accept.

And as in those most backward regions to which they were sent our comrades joined in working in the fields and were able to communicate more advanced technical ideas, and teach the children to read, the result was that the Good News penetrated into the socially most backward areas of the countryside.

However, the forms the repression took did not end there. In Barcelona, at the end of 1919, an employers' lockout was declared in all industries, in order to break the syndical movement once and for all. It lasted seven weeks. But though the workers' organisation emerged from it much weakened, it was not destroyed. So the government suspended constitutional guarantees (a course it had often resorted to in the past and to which it would have recourse frequently in the future) and our movement was made illegal. The "workers' centres" were closed as well as the *Ateneos*. And the witch-hunt against the C.N.T. began.

How many were murdered, shot down in the streets of

Barcelona? I have before me a list, which is not complete, but which includes 101 names. Among them men of the quality of a Salvador Segui, a manual worker, self educated and an outstanding speaker; of an Evelio Boal, our finest union organiser, and many others, some of whom were my friends. Some gravely wounded survived only by a miracle, as in the case of Angel Pestaña, who received a shot in the throat and another in a lung as he was coming out of the station in the small town of Manresa where he was to give a lecture. When he came out of hospital he straightway went and delivered the lecture announced two months earlier.

CHAPTER III

MATERIALS FOR A REVOLUTION

For an area of 505,000 sq. kilometres including the Mediterranean and Atlantic islands (Balearic and Canary) Spain had a population of 24 to 25 million inhabitants on July 19, 1936 when the francoist attack was launched, which is 48 to the square kilometre.[1]

The low population density could lead one to believe that in this predominantly agricultural country economic resources would ensure the well-being of the population. But the wealth of a country, even when viewed from the agrarian angle only, is not just dependent on its size. Lucas Gonzalez Mallada, Spain's most eminent geologist, who was also an excellent geographer, classified as follows the economic value of the land—and his conclusions are as valid as ever:

10% bare rocks

40% really bad land

40% mediocre land[2]

10% land which gives us the impression of living in a paradise.

These natural conditions are confirmed by other basic statistics which dispel any illusions one might have. Of the 50 million hectares an average of 20 million were cultivated; the remainder were more or less unproductive, and only suitable for grazing sheep or goats. In addition, out of the 20 million hectares suitable for cultivation, 6 million hectares on average were

1 The corresponding density for the United Kingdom which in 1938 had a population almost double that of Spain was approximately 200 per sq. km. [Translator]

2 The "mediocre" land in Spain is similar to the "bad" land in France.

always allowed to lie fallow so that the land could renew itself under the system known as *año y vez* (one year out of two). Thus in fact the land available for cultivation each year was only 28% of the total area.

The orographic situation worsens the statistics already quoted. The average altitude is 660m (2166 ft.) which, according to the geographer Gonzalo de Reparaz is only exceeded in Europe by Switzerland. In the Centre the Castilian plateau covers 300,000 sq. kilometres and its average height is 2625 ft. To the North the mountain range of the Pyrenees predominates on the Spanish side and occupies 55,000 sq. kilometres (a tenth of the area of France). There are in Spain 292 peaks in the 1000-2000m range, 92 from 2000 to 3000m, and 26 from 3000-3500m. This mountainous relief map influences in no small way the climate, which in turn conditions the agriculture. Furthermore, the direction of the Sierras, which cut and clip the peninsula in all directions, interrupts and often deflects beneficial rains into the wrong direction. Thus it is not only the winter, with the low temperatures that are typical of all high altitudes and which militate against living conditions; but also the summer with its droughts. All these conditions give point to the much quoted remark that "Africa begins at the Pyrenees".

Take the map of Spain: in the North continuing along the mountain range of the Pyrenees, one meets the Cantabrian mountains parallel to, and 50 km. distant from, the Atlantic coast with peaks at 9000 ft., forming a screen to the passage of clouds which the winds are blowing from the sea. Consequently it rains a great deal in the Asturias, as well as in the Basque country in the province of Santander and as far as Galicia, to the north of Portugal. In all that region there is a recorded annual rainfall of from 1200 to 1800mm.

But on the other side of the Asturian mountains, on the Castilian plateau, the granary of Spain, the average rainfall is no more than 500mm, and in vast regions of the Ebro basin, the principal river of Spain, fed by the waters that come down from the Pyrenees, often less than 300mm of rain is recorded annually. However these statistics alone do not give a true picture of the reality. For, in general the porous nature of the soil and the intensity of the sun account for losses due to seepage and evaporation of up to 80% of the atmospheric precipitations.

Sometimes it is even worse: such as the combined geographic-economic conditions of what Gonzalo de Reparaz defines as the *tragico sudeste* (the tragic South-East). Over about 500 km. from Gibraltar to Murcia there are rainless years. The same writer points out that Spain is the only European country which experiences this phenomenon on such a vast scale.[3]

The dryness of the soil is therefore a commonplace in the basin of the Ebro, which covers 5 million hectares, that is a tenth part of the country; "the deserts alternate with the oases, but the former prevail; the Iberian steppe which extends along the whole length of that river is the largest in Europe".

One must mention other steppes, and first of all that of the Mancha which begins at the gates of Madrid and reaches Cartagena. In all, 40% of the land surface of Spain consists of steppes.

The *Huerta* of Valencia, the market gardens of Murcia and of Granada extolled by the poets are no more than islands which blind some romantic travellers to the realities. Thus the average yields of wheat (the most important crop at the time) was of the order of 9 quintals per hectare, very occasionally 10 and more often 8, compared with from 16 to 18 in France (a ten year average in both cases) from unirrigated land, and of 22 quintals in Germany and in England. The highest averages in Spain from irrigated land produced from 16 to 18 quintals which remains the yield to this day, whereas in France without irrigation the average harvest today is in the region of 32-35 quintals.[4]

We have taken wheat as an example because it constituted the basis of, and the major crop in, Spanish agriculture. For other crops the situation was the same except for potatoes, where the average yield was comparable with that of other European countries, but these were grown on irrigated land. The importance of sheep flocks (18-20 million animals) and of olive groves[5] is unassailable proof of the problems of Spanish agriculture: throughout the Mediterranean periphery the sheep and the olive tree are an indication of poor lands and scant yields.

✳

A long time ago, when I undertook to make a serious study

---

3 The lowest rainfall areas in the United Kingdom average not less than 550mm annually. But at the other extreme, in parts of Scotland and Wales average rainfall can be as high as 2,500mm on the Lowlands and 4.300mm in the Highlands. [Translator]

4 At present the average yield in Spain is of 9-11 quintals of wheat. On an average it would seem that the increase has been of 1 quintal per hectare in 30 years.

5 In 1936, calculated in pesetas, the return on an hectare of olive trees was worth a third of that from an hectare of wheat.

of the Spanish economy, I thought at first, faced with the disappointing agricultural balance sheet, that for historic, political and religious reasons which had dominated the economic life of Spain, especially after the expulsion of the Moors, the country had taken and pursued a road which was contrary to its natural potential. Spain according to some writers *es la bodega mas rica del mundo*—possessed the richest underground resources in the world. The grounds for this optimism, which other, better informed, specialists did not share, were that there was coal, iron, lead, tin, copper, zinc, mercury, silver and wolfram. To all appearances these were grounds for setting up industries the general effect of which would be to change the economic character of the country. But if one studied the serious reports on the subject published by geographers, geologists, hydraulic engineers and even the official technical offices, it was clear that the various minerals and metals existed only in small quantities, and apart from mercury—the economic importance of which was infinitesimal compared to the national product—could not offer optimistic prospects.

Spanish mines have been exploited by the Phoenicians, the Carthaginians, the Romans, the Arabs, the British, even by the Spaniards. They were not inexhaustible and they are now, generally speaking and, with the exception of those supplying iron ore (the reserves of which are not of great importance), more or less exhausted. In 1936 Spain only supplied less than $\frac{1}{2}$% of the world's copper; the Rio Tinto mines were no longer profitable and for some time the company had been transferring its capital to other parts of the world. Lead? Its market value in 1933 amounted to $21\frac{3}{4}$ million pesetas, and would be approximately the same in 1936. But to put this in perspective it should be compared with the average wheat crop then valued at 10,000 million pesetas.

Coal and iron are, and were even more so at the time, basic to industry. Well, Spain produced on average 7 million tons of mediocre coal. Even today when under government pressure production has been raised to between 11 and 12 million tons, it is estimated that the "potential" reserves guarantee supplies of coal and lignite for about 140 years . . . on condition that production is not increased. But, on the present basis of necessary consumption for an average industrial development, these reserves would not last more than about 40 years.

Spain is no better off so far as iron ore is concerned. Even on the basis of the unsubstantiated "potential" reserves, and average consumption per inhabitant in France, she would have sufficient reserves to last 40 years. And one should not overlook the fact that the population is increasing by 300,000 a year and has already reached 33 million.

Let us dispel other illusions on one point concerning agriculture. Many people with neither the time nor very often the inclination to be seriously informed, believe in the miracle of irrigation. Unfortunately this hope has no foundation. The volume of water carried by the streams and rivers of Spain is a limiting factor to development: about 50,000 million cubic metres a year,[6] whereas the Rhone on its own, at the level of Avignon, carries 60,000 million. Seeing that one cannot completely dry up all the streams in Spain, that anyway some of them, those which flow towards the Atlantic, cannot be utilised, for there is already too much rain in those regions,[7] the most optimistic calculations allow one to foresee the possibility of irrigating at most 5 million hectares; just a tenth of the country. Of these 5 million, at least 2 million are already irrigated.

Following the departure of the Moors who had in the Levante increased the *acequias* (narrow and ditch-like pipe systems) more dams were constructed than many observers imagine. Primo de Rivera himself and Franco have put into practise some kind of hydraulic policy that had been advocated by Joaquin Costa. The trouble often was that after having built many artificial reservoirs it was realised that not enough water was getting there to fill them, and that in many cases it was necessary to replace the hydraulic production of electricity with thermal power.

*

Such was the natural cause of social poverty of the Spanish people in 1936; such is the cause of the continued emigration which we are witnessing to this day. But there is another which, because it is man made can be corrected by Man, and it is to this that the Spanish Revolution directed its efforts.

The problem of land ownership is of capital importance in Spain. It appeared in two basic forms: the *latifundia* (large

6 The Miño which flows through Galicia and borders on Portugal is in importance the second river of Spain in terms of its flow. But as there is already too much rain in the region of its source, the waters are not used.

7 The Miño is such a case.

estates) and the *minifundia* (small properties). There are very many small proprietors in Spain: the figures in the cadastral survey dated December 31, 1959 accounted for 5,989,637. An enormous proportion of the present total population. But to begin with, most of the plots are of *secano*, that is dry lands, which because of their unproductivity are at the present time driving the peasant masses towards the towns where they are packed in the *ciudades miseras*, the shanty towns.

In 1936 only a partial census of the land and its owners had been made. But the figures available gave a sufficiently clear picture of the terrible social reality which we will have many occasions to observe in the chapters that follow.

Out of a total of 1,023,000 proprietors, 845,000 could not produce the equivalent of one peseta a day from their land—and bread then cost on average 0.60-0.70 peseta a kilo. They had to work as day labourers, as shepherds for the rich, as roadmen, or go to look for or "steal" wood in the neglected forests, avoiding arrest by the Civil Guards though not always succeeding, traversing 5, 10, 15 kilometres and more, driving their donkey ahead of them, to go and resell to more fortunate people than themselves the product of their "theft". Or again they would go to work in the town, for some periods of the year as labourers.

The second category consisted of 160,000 medium sized proprietors, who lived independently and frugally.

The third was of the large landowners. They comprised only 2.04% of the census total but possessed 67.15% of the cultivated lands. Their estates covered from 100 to more than 5,000 hectares.

It is not difficult to understand the extent of peasant poverty. To start with the peasants represented more than 60% of the population in Spain. To believe that this mass of humanity would put up with and be indefinitely resigned to its lamentable fate, showed a lack of understanding. For the Spanish people are not among those who resign themselves servilely. In past times Andalusians, Extremeños, Galicians, Asturians, Basques, Castilians emigrated in large numbers to Central and Southern America to seek there the means of existence and they still continue to emigrate—especially in Europe. But throughout its history, whether it was for a just or unjust cause, the Spanish people have been combative and adventurous. They slumbered for a long time after the traumatic experience caused by the expulsion of the Moors, by Catholic dominion and the consequences of the conquest of America, but in the end they woke up with their spirit and character, capable of courage; with, also, that mystical background which predisposes them to struggle for noble causes, for themselves and for others, with a spiritual drive which is almost cosmic;[8] and this capital of human dignity which allows them to accept under duress authoritarian interference and to rebel against it when they can; and then also with a sense of solidarity and equality which leaves its mark as much on the morale of the Barcelona worker as on that of the Andalusian peasant.

These two factors, social poverty and individual dignity, linked to collective solidarity, predisposed a large section of the population to accept libertarian ideas.

*

In 1936, two revolutionary organizations embodied these ideas: the National Confederation of Labour (C.N.T.) and the Anarchist Federation of Iberia (F.A.I.). The former was composed of regional federations which in their turn were integrated by *comarcales* (cantonal) and local federations; these latter remind one of the French *Bourses du Travail*, but were more structured, more interdependent and owed absolutely nothing to governmental charity. In 1936, the C.N.T. had a million members. That figure is the more important when one bears in mind that the population at the time was between 24 and 25 million people.

The C.N.T.'s aim, as specified in its declaration of principles, was libertarian communism. It was the exclusive work of the anarchists who struggled in the syndicalist and purely ideological fields, and who were the organisers, propagandists and theoreticians.

With the proclamation of the Second Republic on April 14, 1931, the advance towards a grave social crisis appeared inevitable. From its birth the life of the new political regime was hazardous. The monarchy had only been routed thanks to the part played by the C.N.T., and by the anarchists who were active outside this organisation (but it was above all the C.N.T. which mattered and that was producing a million votes). Among the forces which had declared themselves against the royal family and had contributed to its overthrow, were the employed industrial workers and peasants who also supported the socialist party

---

8 Keyserling wrote that after the Russian people, the Spaniards of all the people in Europe were the ones who possessed the greatest reserve of spiritual strength.

and the General Union of Workers (U.G.T.), or who normally voted socialist, which made up another million votes. Finally came the communists, anyway numerically very weak, the federalist republicans, enemies of a jacobin and centralist republic, and regional, separatist forces such as those predominating in Catalonia and the Basque country.

On the other side, the Right still included considerable forces. Monarchists, dyed in the wool conservatives, reactionaries, dominant in the still slumbering provinces, traditional clerical forces. Of the votes cast, those from true republicans must have represented about a quarter of the total. So much so that Count Romanones, leader of the liberal monarchist party and the most intelligent in this sector, could sum up the situation with the humorous comment: "I can clearly see a republic, but I do not see any republicans."

In these conditions the new regime could not establish itself solidly except by undertaking bold social reforms which would have weakened the army, the Church and the old caciquism which was still master in almost all the provinces. But the reforms envisaged, and those achieved by the left socialists and republicans who were the government during the first two years (1931-1933), could only appear bold and very important to the jurists, professors, lawyers, journalists and professional politicians who comprised a majority of the members in the Cortes (the parliament). They meant nothing or very nearly nothing, for the people as a whole. If before the Republic the normal diet for many peasants and workers consisted mainly of chick peas with oil, with the Republic it continued to be chick peas with oil, and those who went around in slippers could no more buy shoes with the coming of the Republic than before it.

And the Spanish people were hungry for bread and for land. For those who had voted Republican with republican feelings and hopes, Republic was synonymous with true freedom, true equality, true fraternity; it implied, above all else, the disappearance of social injustice and poverty.

Faced with the slowness in applying agrarian reform, peasants began to work on their own account, invading collectively those estates which the large *terratenientes* kept uncultivated—and which, one must admit, were generally of very poor quality. Consequently, by order of the government, the Civil Guard which served the Republic as it had served the Monarchy, would intervene. In the first two years of the pseudo-socialist republic, 109 peasants from

Estremadura, Andalusia, Aragon and Castile were murdered in the name of republican legality. The tragedy of Casas Viejas, in Estremadura, where the poorest of the poor families would make repayments at the rate of a penny a month for clothes bought on credit; where many peasant women wore the same skirt for the whole of their lives (this could also be seen in Galicia) being content to reverse it on Sundays—this tragedy, we were saying, aroused the indignation of the population.[9]

The second period was the consequence of the first. Disgusted and shocked, the majority of the people voted for the conservative "republicans", that is to say for the Rightists who had had the chance to criticise their opponents and to promise to do better. But their triumph implied a dangerous retreat, and the Asturian miners launched a formidable insurrection against the coming to power of those who, visibly and legally, were opening the road to fascism. Too localised, due to a lack of previous agreement with similar forces in the other regions, the insurrection was implacably crushed.

If what has been called the *bienio negro* (the two black years) was no more disastrous than the so-called liberal *bienio* that preceded it, it was equally harsh, and when insurrectional attempts, were made, especially in Catalonia and Andalusia, repression was raised to the level of permanent government practice. The two years passed without the slightest improvement in the standard of living of the masses. Furthermore, the economic crisis which started in the United States and had spread to Europe, struck at Spain too where there were some 700,000 unemployed at least a half of whom were to be found among the industrial workers. Unemployment relief was then unknown. At the same time the number of prisoners—sentenced at summary trials or held without trial—reached a total of 30,000, the overwhelming majority of them belonging to the C.N.T. and the F.A.I.[10]

Faced with the promises of the parties relegated to the opposition, republican workers began again to hope. Once more the non-

9 All the family of one Seisdedos (thus called because he had six fingers on one hand) were murdered: fourteen (or sixteen) people in all because he had refused to allow the seizure of his few possessions by order of the tax collector.

10 The first parliament had voted a *ley de vagos,* a law against "vagrants" and set up camps for them. Those who were interned in these camps were unemployed, workers without work who were more or less demonstrators. It was also the workers who exposed the incompetence of the regime. The creative imagination of the government *of the Left* did not go any further.

political leftists, forgetting their grievances felt a mutual bond of solidarity and aligned themselves with the parties. And when the elections took place in February 1936, the *Frente Popular* that had been set up won the day.

But it was not an easy victory. Once again to avoid the greater evil, the members of the C.N.T., who did not meanwhile forget their principles of direct action, voted in order to deny fascism legal access to power. But in spite of this reinforcement the Leftist bloc secured 4,540,000 votes against the Rightists 4,300,000; it only needed a shift of 150,000 votes for the admirers of Mussolini and Hitler to have triumphed. An additional fact to bear in mind was that there were six political parties of the Right, six of the Centre and six of the Left; a total of 18. This was not a guarantee of soundness.

By the application of a dishonest electoral law, the Rightist bloc only secured 181 seats whilst its Leftist opponents got 281. And from that moment, the vanquished set in motion preparations for the *coup d'état*. Everybody was aware of it. Reports were received at the War Ministry and by the Ministry of the Interior. The Left press, especially the libertarian press, exposed the conspiracy and the secret meetings between high ranking officers of the army and navy who had not resigned, though the first government had invited them to do so if they were not in agreement with the Republic.

The Madrid government did nothing to deal with the ever increasing threat. It could have armed the people, disbanded the army, arrested or dismissed the conspiring generals. It did not budge, being satisfied with energetic declarations. And when the rebellious army attacked, a good number of the republican governors went over to the enemy and helped him very effectively to arrest the most militant anti-fascists.

In the circumstances, it was the anarchists, aided in Barcelona, it must be said, by the Assault Guards,[11] who succeeded in forcing the withdrawal of the eleven infantry regiments which the military governor, Goded, had launched against the city. The same happened in Malaga. In the other regions rank and file Madrid socialists, Catalan *Cenetistas* (C.N.Ters) and anarchists, liberal separatists from the Basque country, very few republicans even among the Catalans, all fighting, in many cases without

---

11 Special police force organized by the Republic, and which had until that moment shown itself to be particularly ferocious where the anarchists were concerned.

arms, obliged Franco and his generals to engage in battle for nearly three years before being finally victorious.

*

It was in the course of these three years that the social experiment to which this book bears witness took place. This experiment was entirely the work of the libertarian movement, especially of the C.N.T. whose militants, accustomed to practical problems in syndical organisation, were able to create very rapidly, in collaboration with the masses, the new forms of social organisation which we will be describing. Even when men belonging to other political tendencies also organised similar enterprises, they did no more than imitate our comrades' example. It was the libertarians who brought the basic ideas, the social principles and proposed the new forms of organisation based on non-governmental federalism directly controlled. The Spanish revolution was the work of the people, realised by the people, but especially by the libertarians, who came from the people, who were at the heart of the people and of the syndical organisations.

On the other hand our comrades' success would have been impossible if the libertarian concepts had not satisfied the innermost psychology, if not of all, then at least of a great proportion of workers, operatives and peasants. Particularly if among the latter in Aragon, Castile, the Levante, Andalusia and Estremadura, natural sociability, a spirit which was at the same time individual and collective, had not allowed for these unique achievements in the history of mankind.

The author, who had previously lived and struggled in Spain, was domiciled in South America when the civil war broke out. Having to travel illegally, he could only manage to return and disembark in Gibraltar in November. Convinced very soon that the anti-fascists would end by losing the war, and being aware of the importance of the social experiment that had been undertaken by his comrades, he had only one thought: to promote by his propaganda the intensification and spread of this experiment to the preparation of which he had contributed for so long, and to record the results for the future.

This he did to the extent that the circumstances allowed, and though with a long delay due to the ups and downs of his life as a militant, presents the result of his personal enquiry which was facilitated not only by his direct enquiries in the

Syndicates, factories, and village Collectives, but also by the spontaneous contribution of documents made to him by fraternal comrades with whom he maintained contact in his search for materials.

He has no pretension of presenting a general history of the Spanish revolution, even viewed simply from the constructive point of view; for this was much greater than this book might lead one to believe. Particularly where the Agrarian Collectives are concerned he regrets that, on the one hand, the triumph of the Stalinists who were their implacable enemies, and on the other his imprisonment in France in June 1938, did not allow him to carry his studies further.

What he presents is therefore a collection of materials for a general history of the Spanish revolution which he is not entirely without hope of writing himself one day if he can return to a Spain freed from the Franco regime.

CHAPTER IV

A REVOLUTIONARY SITUATION

When on July 19, 1936 the fascist attack was unleashed the reply to it was centred entirely on resistance to the insurgent army, against the threat which not only put the legal government in jeopardy, but the very existence of the forces of the Left and Centre, as well as the quite relative, but nevertheless tangible, freedoms that were represented by the Republic.

Already on the eve of the military uprising the C.N.T. had called for a general strike and almost everywhere this call had been followed. It was not a case of social revolution, of the proclamation of libertarian communism as had been attempted prematurely in other circumstances. The offensive was not being taken against capitalist society, the State, the parties and the defenders of established order; one was confronting fascism. As we have seen, in Catalonia and particularly in Barcelona, it was above all the forces of the C.N.T. and of the F.A.I. supported by the Assault Guards who forced back the infantry regiments which had been sent onto the streets by their officers on the orders of the military commander in charge.

Firstly, to prevent the triumph of fascism; for if they won the struggle, it would be the end of the republicans of the different tendencies, the Prieto and Caballero socialists, Catalanists of the Left wing (the more numerous) but even those of the Right, threatened because of their separatism, of liberals and Basque autonomists, communists, of U.G.T. and C.N.T. members. Solidarity was established spontaneously in varying degrees, depending on the town, village, or region. In Madrid, socialists, U.G.Ters, republicans, libertarian groups and C.N.T. syndicates collectively took by assault the barracks from which danger might come and arrested notorious fascists, and then dispatched forces to reconquer those localities that had fallen into the hands of the enemy, entrenched themselves and halted General Mola's troops in the Sierra de Guadarrama which Napoleon's army had had such difficulty in crossing.

In fact, there was no official resistance for the government had broken down. Ministers made energetic speeches on the radio, made gestures in a vacuum, ran round in circles for they no longer had any organised forces, or military machinery at their disposal, not even a bureaucratic organisation in working condition. The officer corps, most of the artillery and airforce had gone over to the mutineers; what remained of the army lacked unity and hesitated, the non-commissioned officers who did not follow the fascists inspired no more confidence than the four or five generals who remained faithful to the regime, and of whom no one was sure whether they too would change sides at any moment. A government, a ministry, are created to command an organisational whole which functions properly and according to the rules. All this was missing.

Yes, resistance was in the streets, and for that very reason the government was not in command of it. Political power had been shifted, and the men who had just struck a blow to halt fascism paid scant attention to official orders, for the ministers, who on the eve of the uprising had proved themselves so unworthy of their tasks, had lost most of their credibility. In any case, they had lost it entirely so far as the libertarian masses were concerned, who reproached the politicians of the Left, and not without reason, of having done nothing to ward off the threat they had bombastically denounced.

Still, in Catalonia, which enjoyed an autonomous status, the situation took on a special aspect. The day after the triumph over the military forces and the capture of the barracks at a cost of so many lives, Companys, president of the Catalan government, requested the C.N.T. and F.A.I. to send a delegation for an important meeting. When he had the delegates before him he made the following little speech:

"Without you, the fascists would have won in Catalonia. You, the anarchists, have saved Catalonia and I am grateful to you; but you have also earned the right to take over the control of public life. We are therefore ready to withdraw and to leave you in charge of the situation."*

Garcia Oliver, one of the most prominent anarchists, who gave this account of the interview, replied that it was out of the question; the hour was too grave, anti-fascist unity had to be maintained. Companys would have to remain at the head of the Catalan government and assume full responsibility for the situation.[1]

But in fact the Catalan government was more nominal than real. The dominant power was well and truly in the syndicates of the C.N.T. and to a much lesser degree in the F.A.I. The resistance militias were improvised, action groups of men wearing red and black arm bands replaced the Republican police which stood aside; revolutionary order was being established not only in Barcelona, but in all the towns of Catalonia. It even happened that in many places, such as in Igualada, Granollers, Gerona, the local political parties, composed of Left Catalanists, socialists, federalist republicans, as well as, sometimes, republicans of the Centre in Manuel Azana's party, and libertarians of the C.N.T., would meet as a single group within the municipality, and the new communal authorities, free from ties with the Catalan government, and more so with the Central government (which soon moved from Madrid to Valencia) constituted a local management bloc. Life thus assumed an almost autonomous communal character.

The melting away of the republican State was even more marked in Aragon. Cut off from Castile in the West, where the francoist forces were dominant and threatening, bordering in the North along the Pyrenees with France, and to the East with Catalonia which exerted no political pressure on it, this region was only in contact with the zone where the central government was seeking to dominate along what remained of the common boundaries to the South and South-East of the province of Teruel. Now, that province had been left to its own devices. This ensured

---

Translator's note: This is in fact only a summary of part of what Companys said.

1 In fact the deeper reasons for Garcia Oliver's attitude were others. He expressed them in conversations with comrades. "What would I have done with the power? I was in no way prepared for what was implied, the situation was such that I could not but fail." And it was quite true. Garcia Oliver like all the more or less demagogic orators of the F.A.I. was quite ignorant of the steps that had to be taken to direct the life, industry and provisioning of a city like Barcelona. The same could be said of Federica Montseny. This did not stop them from becoming ministers of the Republic. It was easier than organising a Collective.

almost complete independence for Aragon.[2]

The civil war thus created a revolutionary situation, for even in the provinces of the Levante which were not yet being threatened, the determining influence exerted by the popular forces which were inspired by the C.N.T. and the F.A.I., was upsetting public organisation. In many cases the united strength of the other parties could surpass the numerical strength of these two organisations, but their personnel were not the men for the situation. The absence of directives and official institutions paralysed them whereas it facilitated the initiatives of the men who made the revolutionary struggle the basic motive for their historic activity. Very often, for this very reason, even when in village committees or municipal councils the C.N.T. was in a minority, it was quite as decisive, our men knowing what they wanted and coming up with solutions where the others could only argue, raising problems for the others as well as for themselves.

Of new problems there were many, often big and always urgent problems. In the first place that of local defence against attacks launched from nearby villages or from neighbouring towns, the threat of a potential fifth column or forces gathered in the mountains. In Aragon, every village or small town had on the spot to face the francoist army which, after having taken the provincial capitals of Saragossa and Huesca,[3] was advancing on Catalonia. To halt the invaders and then to drive them back as far away as possible: some places were taken, retaken, sometimes lost again and yet again retaken. In other cases the population after liquidating local fascism, sent their available forces (most often they were civilians armed only with shotguns) to help those who were resisting or taking the offensive elsewhere. All this required a spontaneous yet real organisation in spite of inevitable shortcomings. Then the militias would arrive, also improvised, sent by Catalonia and composed for the most part of members of the C.N.T. which suffered heavy losses of

2 A similar situation had arisen in the Asturias and in those parts of Andalusia and Estremadura which the francoists did not conquer immediately. In the Basque country the autonomous government had the situation under control for, among other reasons, the libertarian movement of the C.N.T. did not have significant strength there, or at least, it was not comparable.

3 Teruel had at first remained in some kind of no-man's land. In order to seize control for themselves, the Republican authorities in Valencia had sent a force of Civil Guards which turned on our forces, destroyed them and handed over the town to the fascists.

militants, often the best ones.

At other levels, and for other reasons, the need for a new organisation representing a logistics apparatus, even improvised, made itself felt immediately. In Aragon, those mayors who stayed at their posts or the councillors who undertook their civic responsibilities were the rare exceptions. Terrified, outflanked, unsuited to the struggle, or in sympathy with the fascists, almost all stood down or disappeared. By contrast, in many cases militants of the C.N.T. would appear with the advance guard and often took control of the situation. Once the struggle was over—in the rearguard it was of short duration—a general organisation in the villages had to be improvised and coordination essential to local life established. There again, in the overwhelming majority of cases the same men took the necessary steps. Their experience as union organisers predisposed them to undertaking the tasks of local administration. They were used to public meetings, responsible committees, administrative boards, and the role of coordinators. It is not surprising therefore that in most cases, if not in all, where the local authorities had disappeared, they should have called all the inhabitants of the village to a public meeting in the public square or in the municipal buildings (just as previously they would call members of the syndicate to a meeting of workers) in order to examine the situation with them and to decide what should be done. And everywhere, in those villages of Aragon abandoned by the authorities, they appointed not another municipal council based on the political parties but an administrative *Comité* instructed to take in hand the responsibilities of public life.

This was decided either by a majority vote or by unanimous agreement, and it is not surprising that in general men known for their dynamism, so needed at that moment, were chosen. They also included, but in smaller numbers, and often on the insistence of C.N.T. militants themselves, militants of the U.G.T., occasionally Left republicans who in their personal conduct had not always followed the party directives, and still attributed to republicanism the social content which it advocated in the past.

But this variety of loyalties did not imply the setting up of fundamentally political authorities. Without hampering themselves with grand definitions, and inspired by the standards which the movement had always advocated, our comrades proposed a new structure for all aspects of collective life. For them, who had struggled so hard and suffered against social inequality and for an equally social justice, since the Republic had collapsed, the occasion presented itself to instal a new regime and a new way of life. And instead of reconstructing along the old lines they proposed a natural and functional structure in accordance with the local situation considered as a whole.

The war came first but the lives of each and all, the problems of general consumption, agricultural production and all activities indispensable to collective life were also important. It would therefore be decided to nominate someone to be responsible for directing or coordinating agricultural work; it was followed by the problem of stock rearing[4] for which another delegate was given the task of preparing a return, of dealing with overall supervision and the rapid increase in the production of butcher's meat. Then followed the small local industries the continued existence of which had to be assured, and also if possible expanded. At the same time immediate steps were taken to deal with public instruction, a permanent concern in our movement in view of the scandalous level of illiteracy. Then the public services; health, planning, roads, and the organisation of barter and food supplies. The various delegates composed the *Comité*.[5] Sometimes, depending on the importance of the localities, the same comrade would have two functions. More often than not these men would be working in the fields or workshops and only one of them would be available during the day to deal with urgent matters.

It goes without saying that this revolution was accompanied by another quite as fundamental, in the distribution of consumer goods, not only as a consequence of the new needs created by the war, but also by the new social ethic that was manifesting itself. All along in the Aragonese villages—and it started very soon in the region of the Levante—the struggle against fascism seemed incompatible with the capitalist order and its inequalities. Thus, in subsequent meetings of the villages, often even in the first, the family wage was established which equalised the means of existence for all the inhabitants, men, women and children.

Local finances were soon under the control of the elected *Comité*, which sequestrated any funds found in the local branches

4 In Spain the raising of livestock is considered as separate from what is referred to as agriculture.
5 One encounters here the practical application of almost all the measures and the forms of organisation advocated in the programme that we summarised in the chapter on *The Ideal*. One could not however affirm that this transition from theory to practice was conscious.

of banks, sometimes issuing a receipt, or in the homes of the rich who generally had decamped. In some cases local currency, based on the nominal value of the peseta, was printed, as well as food vouchers and to which we will refer in due course. In others, all money was entirely abolished and a Rationing Table drawn up and applicable to everybody. The important point was that equality of the means of existence was emerging, and from one day to the next a social revolution was being achieved almost without upheaval.

In order the better to ensure free consumption, or to avoid both waste and possible hoarding, the *Comité* took over control of distribution. In some cases the shopkeepers themselves were entrusted with the job or collaborated. In others, commerce disappeared as such, and there were created one or more depots and municipal warehouses, generally referred to as cooperatives, in which often former professional distributors were put in charge. Sometimes, out of a feeling of humanity, small shopkeepers who, after all, harmed nobody were left to go on selling their remaining stocks at controlled prices. Once the stocks were exhausted they joined the Collective.

One should remember that the Francoist uprising took place on July 19. By then the corn was ripe and the departure of the large *terratenientes* (most of whom lived in their town houses) or their administrators—almost always local despots dominating a large section of the peasantry—carried with it the abandonment and loss of the crop. The question of the harvest therefore presented itself immediately after the general administrative takeover.

And in agreement with the delegates for agriculture, the prime movers among the peasants called a conference of their comrades. Machines and equipment found on the large estates—the only ones to possess machines—were requisitioned as well as the beasts of burden, and the men and women reapers who so often were still cutting the corn with scythes. The corn was cut, the sheaves made and gathered, and the harvest stored in improvised communal barns. Wheat, potatoes, sugar beet, vegetables, fruit, meat became collective assets placed under the responsibility of the local *Comité* nominated by everybody.

Nevertheless, collectivisation in the full sense of the word had not yet been achieved. Taking over the usurped property was not enough. Collectivism—a term widely and spontaneously adopted

—presupposed the disappearance of all the small, medium and, above all, the large, private properties; the small properties voluntarily, the rest by force, and their integration in a vast system of public ownership and work in common. This was not done everywhere in a uniform manner.

Whereas in Aragon, 80% of the cultivated land belonged to the large landowners, in other regions, such as the Levante and above all in Catalonia, small holdings very often predominated or played an important role in the villages which had a very diversified horticulture. Though our best comrades were often smallholders, and though in many cases the other smallholders joined the Collectives with enthusiasm and even organised them, it was a fact that in the region of the Levante (provinces of Castellon de la Plana, Valencia, Murcia, Alicante and Albacete) difficulties unknown in Aragon emerged. In the first place, because at that time many inhabitants of the region imagined themselves protected from the fascist danger by the distance that separated them from the front line, and by the superiority of republican armament (official demagogy deceived the people to the very end). Secondly because the various political parties had not disappeared; after a brief moment of panic they had recovered at the same time as the central government was consolidating itself and organising its bureaucracy and police. If the government's transfer to Valencia freed the Central region from its pressures, and facilitated the emergence of the Castilian Collectives, it increased the possibilities in the Levante of an anti-socialisation resistance not only among the parties but also from the bourgeoisie, the petty traders, and peasants who were attached to their property.

The act of expropriation was therefore directed against the large estates the owners of which were either fascists—which made things easier—or were considered as such. In any case, the large estates could not be openly defended, at least in the first period, by what was left of the local authorities. The cultivation of the orange tree, which is one of the features of the Levante, demands heavy outgoings; so much so that almost all the orange-groves belonged to large, often public, Companies and, sometimes, included jurisdiction over many villages. On a small scale, the same situation often obtained in the much smaller rice-growing zone. The seizure of these large estates was justified at that time when the political and the social were interdependent, for the need to disarm economic fascism completed its political and military disarmament. And in one way or another the revolution was establishing itself.

It did so using other means too. Still in the Levante, our comrades not wishing to provoke clashes with other anti-fascist sectors since the struggle against the common enemy remained in the forefront, had to take initiatives which the republicans, socialists, and other respecters of the Law were demonstrably unable to do. In the villages, more numerous than in Aragon for the soil and the climate made possible a more intensive cultivation and a denser population, in the small agro-industrial towns of from 10-20 thousand inhabitants, provisioning was paralysed or decreased in an alarming manner because the middlemen, doubtful of the morrow and often of the outcome of the war, hesitated at parting with their money and even at selling the goods that they had in stock (thoughts of speculation certainly influenced some of them). In addition, for others who were supporters of fascism, it was a kind of passive resistance. There was fairly soon a growing shortage of groceries, haberdashery, sanitary goods, fertilisers, selected seeds, tools, some foodstuffs and this was beginning to upset daily life. So, faced with the inertia of the other sectors, our comrades who, almost everywhere, had gone into the municipal councils where they increased the number of motions and the initiatives, succeeded in having original measures adopted. Often, thanks to them, the municipality organised provisioning centres which reduced the ascendancy of private business and set in motion distributive socialisation. Then, rapidly, the same municipality undertook to buy from the peasants, still reluctant, the products of their labour, for which they were paid at a higher rate than they received from the normal middlemen or wholesalers. Finally, a stage which had become complementary, integral Collectives, though incomplete in relation to the local population as a whole, appeared in due course and developed.

*

As to industrial production in small towns and large cities, the situation often reminded one of that created by small commerce and agriculture. The small bosses, the artisans employing up to four workers often hesitated as to what they should do, not daring to risk their meagre financial resources. So our syndicates would intervene, recommending or demanding as the case might be, that production be continued.

But inevitably new steps were rapidly taken. It is true that in general the Catalan industrial bourgeoisie was anti-francoist, if for no other reason that that Franco, a son of Galicia and a Spanish nationalist, was anti-Catalanist, and that for the Catalans his triumph would mean the end of regional autonomy won with difficulty, and the suppression of political rights as well as linguistic privileges. But it is probable that between these dangers and those represented by the revolutionary forces advocating libertarian communism and expropriation of the bosses, the former evil soon appeared to them as the lesser. Thus the interruption of work as a result of the closure of factories and workshops on the morrow of the defeat inflicted on the armed forces could quite rightly be viewed as an indirect contribution to the insurgent fascists' cause. Poverty, already symbolised by unemployment, a problem to which the Republic had been incapable of offering any solution, was to increase and would be one of the most potent factors of disorder from which the enemy would profit. Work had to continue therefore, and to make sure of it control committees were set up in every industrial enterprise on the initiative of the C.N.T. or of its militants acting spontaneously, to supervise all aspects of production.

That was the first step. But another reason, fully justified, obliged them to take another, and in some industries to take both almost at the same time. It was necessary to create without delay an armaments industry to supply a still mobile front 160 miles from Barcelona and 32 miles beyond the boundaries of Catalonia, and which could get closer with dire consequences to Catalonia (the terrain was an easy one over most of its area). We have seen that, once the armed forces employed by the fascists, without being themselves fascists (consisting often of ordinary soldiers) had been driven back at the barracks of Barcelona, militias had been organised which immediately set off for Aragon. To do this it was necessary to get the trains moving again. The railway workers' Syndicate undertook to do so without hesitation. At the same time the metal workers' syndicate first called for a return to work (which had been stopped by the general strike) and then refused, as did the other syndicates, to accept the reduction in working hours proposed by the Catalan government; finally it instructed the workshops to blind lorries and vans so that they could be despatched to the combat areas.[6]

6 They were called tanks. Poor tanks, it is true, and how inadequate, against which bullets perhaps ricocheted but not so shells, but, in any case, they gave a feeling of security to those who left for the fronts.

And it was thus that in the name of the measures necessary to ensure victory, a fair number of industrial enterprises were expropriated, their owners treated as real or potential fascists, which was true in a very large number of cases. In the medium sized enterprises, matters did not stop there, for by an irreversible development systematically carried out, the Control Committee changed into a management *Comité*, where the boss no longer figured as such, but as a technician when he had the necessary qualifications.

It is clear, the social revolution which took place then did not stem from a decision by the leading organisms of the C.N.T. or from the slogans launched by the militants and agitators who were in the public limelight but who rarely lived up to expectations. It occurred spontaneously, naturally, not (and let us avoid demagogy) because "the people" in general had suddenly become capable of performing miracles, thanks to a revolutionary vision which suddenly inspired them, but because, and it is worth repeating, among those people there was a large minority, who were active, strong, guided by an ideal which had been continuing through the years a struggle started in Bakunin's time and that of the First International;[7] for in countless places were to be found men, combatants, who for decades had been pursuing constructive objectives, gifted as they were with a creative initiative and a practical sense which were indispensable for local adaptation and whose spirit of innovation constituted a powerful leaven, capable of coming up with conclusive solutions at the required time.

*

The situation was therefore revolutionary both by reason of the will of the people as well as by reason of the forces in action. And this obliges us before entering more deeply into the exposition of the directions and the development of the new achievements, to refute some statements concerning these basic factors in the situation.

In the first place we refer to the contradictory situation resulting from the political participation of our movement in the central government, and in the regional Catalan government.

7 There is no yardstick between the numerical importance of the Spanish libertarian forces in 1936 and those of the Bolsheviks in 1917. Neither as to the existing aptitudes of those forces in the field of production, work, and creative activities. The Bolsheviks were in all some 200,000 to 250,000 in a population of 140 million.

"Since you collaborate with the government," the anti-fascists opposed to the Collectives have many times repeated, "you don't have to act outside governmental legality."

Theoretically the argument seemed logical. In fact things were much less simple. Firstly, we had only four ministers out of 16 in the Valencia government; we were constantly put in a minority position by the other sectors in a coalition against us, and the key ministers—Finance and War for instance—were filled by members of that coalition. It would have been too clever and too easy to constrain us to revolutionary passivity in return for an illusory concession at governmental level. And certainly, too often, our ministers tended to be only too ready to accept such a state of affairs.

We could be told that that collaboration had been ratified by the assemblies, plenums and congresses of our movement. But in fact what happened was that, drowned by the bursts of eloquence of our interminable speechifiers, the delegates of the provinces, the small towns and villages approved of the ministerial collaboration because they were overwhelmed by a situation that was presented to them in the most sombre colours, and lacked information and oratorical abilities to refute the promises, the unverifiable explanations, the arguments the validity of which they were not in a position to check. But once back in their towns and villages, they continued to build the new society. They did not feel tied by the political manoeuvres, and they were right, for not only would we have lost the war anyway, but the magnificent experiment of the Spanish Revolution would not have taken place.

But some of our adversaries, in particular the Stalinists, made play with another argument which they always use wherever they happen to be, so long as they are not powerful enough to take charge of a situation: the time for the revolution had not yet come, unity among the anti-fascist forces had to be maintained in order to defeat Franco. By expropriating the industrialists, landowners, bosses, shareholders, the *terratenientes*, one ran the risk of driving them into the enemy camp.

No doubt this happened on a very small scale. But so long as the situation is not yet ripe for them to seize control of it, the Stalinists will always say that the initiatives of its partners who do not submit to their control are premature, as well as counter-revolutionary. On the other hand does one believe that without socialisation the chances of victory would have been

[81]

F

greater? If so, it is to overlook the realities of the situation.

Firstly the hostility of the dispossessed bosses did not in any way diminish the combative enthusiasm of the workers and peasants who made up the army of militiamen. We have seen that in general the members of the bourgeoisie and of the political parties remained passive or acted as in a vacuum when faced with a situation which was beyond them. The struggle having been transferred from Parliament and the polling booths onto the streets, the reply to the fascist attack could not but adjust itself to the new circumstances and follow the path that it took. If one had had to wait for the triumph of the official organisation duly formed, francoism would have triumphed in a year, perhaps even in three months.[8]

8 At the other extreme was Trotsky. He reproached us for not having swept away all the forces, parties, bourgeois and reformist socialist formations, of not taking power to continue the war as the Bolsheviks had done in Russia. One had to be blinded by his prejudice to confuse two quite dissimilar situations. It only needs a modicum of commonsense to realise that is was quite impossible for us to wage at the same time a war against Franco and in the rearguard a second war against the other antifascist sectors who would not have allowed themselves to have been wiped out so easily. It would have been a nonsense and a crime. The war of movement which favoured the forces of the Red Army in Russia could not be repeated in Spain where the enemy soon seized heavy industrial and war production centres and where military forces and high ranking officers such as came from tzarism were not available; and they included war specialists such as General Brassilof, one of the glories of the Russian Army, and Toutkatchevsky who was without a doubt the No. 1 strategist of the Red Army when Stalin ordered him to be shot.

PART TWO

Agrarian Socialisation

CHAPTER V

THE ARAGON FEDERATION
OF COLLECTIVES

On February 14 and 15, 1937 the Constitutive Congress of the Aragon Federation of Collectives took place in Caspe, a small town in the province of Saragossa which had been freed of the fascists by forces coming from Catalonia.[1] Twenty-four cantonal federations were represented. The list is as follows: Federation of the Canton of Angués, Alfambra, Aïnsa, Alcoriza, Alcañiz, Albalate de Cinca, Barbastro, Benabarre, Caspe, Enjulve, Escucha, Graus, Grañen, Lecera, Monzón, Muniesa, Mas de las Matas, Mora de Rubielos, Puebla de Hijar, Pina de Ebro, Pancrudo, Sástago, Tardienta, Valderrobres. Each of these *comarcal* (cantonal) federations represented from 3 to 36 villages of greater or lesser importance. We have the complete list of these villages, totalling 275. The number of member families was 141,430. But at the time, collectivism was a reality and in full swing. So much so that very soon after many more collectives added their names to this first list.

Furthermore, the existing ones witnessed a rapid increase in their resources. For example at that congress the canton of Mas de las Matas comprised 19 villages of which only the head village was completely collectivised, but at a plenum held three months later the other 18 were too. The canton of Angues accounted for 36 collectives at the Congress of Caspe, whereas

---

1 A preparatory meeting, at which this constitutive congress had been decided on, had taken place at Binefar; representatives of the Collectives already in existence had attended in large numbers.

at the following plenum the number had risen to 70. In the same period, the number of federated collectives in the canton of Barbastro had gone up from 31 to 58. The development was so rapid that in the time needed to print the latest statistics, those figures had been exceeded.

It is worth pointing out that this movement was expanding rapidly in spite of the difficulties created by the war: in some cases, such as Grañen, Aïnsa, Pina de Ebro, the Front was only a few miles away, and large numbers of our militants were engaged in the armed forces. One cannot but admire the sense of organisation and solidarity shown by the Aragon libertarian collectives from the beginning.

The following are the practical decisions that were taken at the end of the discussions, the range of which can well be imagined:

(1) Abolition of money within the Collectives and the constitution of a common fund by a general contribution of goods and financial resources for use in exchanges with other regions and countries. A ration book to be issued which will be valid for all collectivists.[2]

(2) The examination of the structures of organisation gave rise to what constituted an innovation, by assigning the most important role to the communal organisation: "We accept the communal organisation because it makes it easier for us to supervise activities as a whole in the villages."

Then the traditional geographic-administrative limits were modified on the basis of the needs of the revolution and the logic of a social economy opposed to the arbitrary and capricious carving up by the historic State.

(3) The text adopted on this subject specified that: "In constituting the cantonal federations, as well as the regional Federation, it will be necessary to eliminate the traditional limits between the villages themselves; on the other hand, all working tools will be held in common and raw materials put at the disposal of Collectives requiring them, without any kind of discrimination."

This intercollective and intercommunal solidarity—for each collective included, if not the whole village, at least the major part of each village—was completed by other practical decisions:

"In Collectives with a surplus of labour which they cannot use at certain times of the year for agricultural work, the Com-

2 See chapter "Collectivist Accounting".

mittee of the Cantonal Federations will come to an agreement to send those comrades wherever there is need of their services."

Thus while maintaining the spirit and practice of federalism, which imply an internal liberty and the autonomy of management, one immediately goes beyond the spirit of turning in on one's self, or the autarchic vision of organisation stemming from a narrow concept of communalism. But is this not the practical and almost automatic consequence of concepts and practices of syndical organisation guiding, often unconsciously, the organisers of the collectives?

We now pass on to the projects of development and improvement in agriculture. The resolution recommends, as a first step, the organisation of experimental farms and nurseries in order to improve on the one hand the livestock—sheep, pigs and cattle—and on the other vegetable varieties by plant breeding and seed selection. In every district, the resolution declares, it will be necessary to reserve for such experiments "at the very least a strip of land for the purpose of acclimatizing new forms of arboricolous cultivation".

Later a project was worked out to divide the territory of Aragon into three zones where huge areas would be reserved for the production of seeds for the Collectives in general "even if they did not belong to the zone reserved for their production"; that is, even if they are not in Aragon. Thus having risen above the communalist mentality, the next thing was to overcome the regionalist spirit, considered as a very important step forward by those who know how the Spanish mentality has remained attached to the traditions of regionalism. In this connection, creative practice almost always goes beyond a type of theoretical literature which was a little too widely distributed.

The Resolution suggests: "Take for example potatoes. The seed has to be produced in Upper-Aragon and then delivered to the Collectives in the other zones, for this plant is more able to resist virus diseases in the mountainous areas than in the lowlands where the climate is damp and warm."

The three large sectors into which Aragon is specially divided "will exchange their seeds according to the needs, and on the basis of the results of research at the experimental stations which must work in complete harmony and under the direction of technicians carrying out all the research deemed necessary."

We have thus reached a planning concept of agrarian economy and there was no practical reason why it should stop at potatoes.

[85]

One can easily envisage the meeting of technicians from the different zones comparing notes on their respective experiments and drawing lessons the more useful by reason of the fact that there were no clashes of interest to prevent the generalizing of the most efficient methods of work.

The third big theme on the agenda was that of the position to be adopted towards the small landowners who refused to enter the Collectives. A Study Commission had been nominated. It consisted of F. Fernandez of the Canton of Angues, Julio Ayoro of Montono, R. Castro of Alforque, R. Bayo of Gudar, E. Aguilar of Pina, and M. Miro of Ballobar. By six votes to one the following Resolution was proposed by the Commission—and adopted by the majority:

(1) The small landowners who wish to remain outside the Collective must therefore consider themselves able to be self-sufficient by their own work; they will therefore not be able to benefit from the services of the Collective. Nevertheless their right to act in this way will be respected on condition that they do not interfere with the interests of the Collective.

(2) All agrarian or urban properties as well as the assets of fascists which have been seized, will be held in usufruct by the workers' organisations that existed at the time of the seizure, on condition that those organisations accept the Collective.

(3) All the estates of landowners which had hitherto been worked by farmers or share-croppers will be transferred to the Collective.

(4) Any smallholder who has remained outside the Collective will only retain as much land as he can cultivate by his own efforts; the employment of workers is absolutely forbidden.

To counteract the spirit of individual property typical of the smallholders, their property will not be entered in the cadastral register."

This latter measure is reminiscent of the procedure suggested by Bakunin regarding the attitude to be adopted by the revolution towards the small landowners. One had to avoid a violent expropriation, and the solution of the problem seemed to him to lie in "the suppression of the right of inheritance". He came back to it on many occasions in his writings. And in *The Conquest of Bread* Kropotkin wrote that not only would the revolution not dispossess the small landowners who slaved to cultivate land that had been acquired by such efforts, but would send its young people to help them reap the corn and bring home the harvest. Though not formulated in specific terms, this concept was generally shared by the international libertarian movement in general.

As one will be seeing on many occasions, not only was the right of small landowners respected but in practice conciliatory and even fraternal feelings were shown to them.

The fourth point in the Agenda was the formulation of a general Rule which stipulated the general directives of the Aragon collectives, the text of which is as follows:

(1) Under the title Federation of Agrarian Collectives an Association is constituted in Aragon the object of which is to defend the interests of workers comprising these Collectives.

(2) The task of this Federation will consist in the following:

(a) To spread far and wide the benefits deriving from collectivism based on the application of mutual aid.

(b) To supervise the experimental farms and trial stations which will be organised in the most suitable localities.

(c) To encourage the preparation of the most gifted young people by the organisation of specialised technical schools.

(d) To organise a corps of technicians who will study the way to achieve a more efficient use of labour in the different branches of agriculture.

(e) To seek means for establishing and improving methods of exchange outside the region.

(f) To organise exchanges on an international scale, thanks to the establishment of statistics relating to the production surpluses of the region; a Resistance Fund will be set up to provide for the needs of federated Collectives, always through close collaboration with the regional Council of Aragon.

On the subject of public education, the Federation will undertake to:

(a) Supply the Collectives with all the rudiments for encouraging leisure and the development of the cultural interests of everybody.

(b) Organise lectures which will make a contribution to the general education of the peasantry, as well as cinema and theatre evenings, outings, excursions and all possible kinds of propaganda and cultural activities.

(3) It is also necessary to set up in each Collective stock rearing centres directed to the selection of more suitable breeds in order to achieve better returns than hitherto . . . Such activities must be supervised by qualified technicians . . . On the other hand all farming must include agriculture and stock-rearing . . .

Various plans for experimental farms are available to the Collectives."

Such were the Resolutions adopted by the constitutive Congress of the Aragon Federation of Collectives on the most important problems.[3] One must draw attention to the rejection of any kind of money system, and this corresponded to what one could call libertarian communist orthodoxy; on the adoption of the Ration Book, described as the "family ration book"; and that the calculation on which distribution was based was the official currency, the peseta. The intention was to allow the unification, and to facilitate the levelling of social relations, among the inhabitants of the three Aragon provinces, where living conditions were determined by the laws of nature which in that mountainous region often varied from one region to another, from the simple to the complex, by the extreme differences in climate and the irrigation of the land. Nevertheless, the generalisation of the egalitarian levelling up, which corresponded to the spirit of general solidarity, could not be realised because of the attack by the Stalinist armed forces in August 1937, which prevented many other projects from being put into operation.

It is important to note, however, that even though these resolutions constitute a coherent whole that includes the principal aspects of social life, they are but a pale reflection of what actually took place in Aragon. To fully appreciate what was achieved it was necessary to traverse the three provinces, be present at the creative effort of the collectivists in the villages, on the land, in the workshops, the municipal or communal distributive warehouses, and to talk to the men who were to be found full of confidence, buoyed up by enthusiasm, and smiling both at the present and the future.

*

The final Resolution adopted by the Caspe Congress had a political content. Faced by the virtual absence of governmental authorities in Aragon, and with a view to preventing an attack by the Valencia government, the libertarian militants conceived the idea of setting up a Defence Council which would replace the provincial Governor who represented the central government, and prevent or postpone government intervention in the region for as long as possible.

3 We have cut the text where it was simply repetitious.

But it goes without saying that this government could not tolerate the existence of an autonomous administration. Thus it published a first decree according to which municipal councils had to be set up everywhere in accordance with established legal norms. Since the Collectives had often replaced the municipalities, or had, as it were, merged with them, these reconstituted organisms encroached on those which the revolution had set up.

On the other hand, this reconstitution provoked the resurrection of the political parties which had nothing to do with the Collectives—no more, anyway, than other revolutionary tendencies established as autonomous movements: the Collective had become the embodiment of the natural and general organisation of the population as a whole. Nevertheless, after July 19 and in many places, though the parties had been dismantled (mainly because, in most cases they had effaced themselves), their local branches either reappeared timidly, or were making efforts to reorganise.

In isolation their members exerted no influence; united they could not jeopardise the Collectives while creating however a kind of nuisance opposition. And the radical republicans of the Right and Left (those that still remained), the social democrats (at least the official ones), some sections of the local *Poumistas*,[4] the Communists as well as the anti-collectivist smallholders, attempted to set up a force which in most cases sought government support (*Poumistas* excepted), and might have created difficulties.

In the event, and in spite of this situation, many members of the political parties threw in their lot with the Collectives. But the resurrection of the official municipal councils, strictly political in the past, would allow a degree of penetration or pressure from the government since, according to the law, the municipal councils had to obey orders emanating from the Ministry of the Interior.

Faced with this counter attack, a defence tactic had to be improvised. And the Congress of Caspe adopted the following Resolution:

"Considering that the municipal councils perform a different role from that of the Collectives;

"That these councils are legally constituted organisms in which all the anti-fascist organisations collaborate and of which the highest representation is the Council of Aragon;

"That the administrative committees of the Collectives exercise

4 Members of the P.O.U.M., the Workers' Party of Marxist Unification with Trotskyist tendencies.

a different function from that of the municipal councils;

"That the Syndicates are called upon to nominate and control the comrades who will represent the C.N.T. in those two kinds of organisms;

"That there cannot exist any opposition between the management of the Collectives and that of the municipal councils;

"That the one and the other are interdependent with the Syndical organisation, so long as the latter takes part in the constitution of the councils of the Collectives, the municipal councils will maintain fraternal relations through the spokesmen of the C.N.T."

The C.N.T. and its syndicates, a traditional combative force, were being thus reintroduced into the political field, and with the Collectives would make it possible to guard against the disadvantages resulting from the re-establishment of the municipal councils. And by means of these three organs—since our comrades were entering the municipal councils as well—the libertarian movement gave great flexibility to its creative activity. The support of the Aragon Council, an organ which had become semi-official, was, at least for the time being, an additional factor to that flexibility.

Opponents of the Collectives, especially the Stalinists, old and new, often state that the Collectives in Aragon were imposed by our militias, most of whom had come from Catalonia to check the enemy's advance, which they succeeded in doing for two years at the price of heavy losses.[5]

It is true that the presence of these forces, against which the other parties had nothing with which to oppose them, favoured indirectly these constructive achievements by preventing active resistance by the supporters of the bourgeois republic and of fascism. But in the first place, if the other parties did not act in this manner, it is simply because they lacked combatant forces, not only coming from Catalonia but, above all, in Aragon. For, even without this rapport of forces, our movement would have played the leading role in its own right. It must be continually repeated *the situation had become revolutionary* due to the francoist uprising coupled with the insolvency of the republican govern-

5 By July 1937, our losses had included 20,000 killed without having succeeded in retaking the small town of Huesca with a population of 18,000.

ment. In such a situation, it was the most important revolutionary elements that had to play the outstanding role because of their superiority and the support they received from the masses. Without the quality of the men, of the militant cadres who seized the initiative and adapted themselves to the circumstances with a tactical skill often quite outstanding, almost nothing would have been done. Perhaps, in spite of the peasants' hunger for land, the large estates would have been only partially seized, and without far reaching constructive imagination, because of a lack of clear ideological guidance. The armed presence of our men contributed to the liberation of the population from a traditional past which would have limited its effort far too much; that is all.

But that presence is far from explaining everything. Other regions bear witness that in spite of the existence of legal authorities and non-libertarian military forces, the revolution took place there as well. It was in the Levante, as we shall see, that the Collectives were most numerous and of the greatest importance. It was, for instance, in Valencia, capital of the Levante, that the government established itself with its bureaucracy and extensive policing forces. And in Castile, where at the beginning republicans, socialists and communists predominated, peasant Collectives were created and developed, and generally speaking, became perhaps more powerful than in Aragon.

In going into things in greater depth, I feel able to say that, contrary to the statements which attribute the setting up and development of the Aragon Collectives to the presence of specifically libertarian troops, they did not play a positive role in this historic event. In the first place, from my own first-hand observations, they lived on the fringe of the task of social transformation that was being carried out. A military world—even if libertarian —and a civilian world. A military spirit with its own pre-occupations and, to some extent, withdrawn into itself, generally indifferent to whatever was not life in the Front Line. There were exceptions in which relations were established between civilians and militiamen; they involved a very minor number of people. Most of the soldiers, often Catalans, came from industrial areas, lived alongside Aragon villages without interesting themselves in them —even when they were billeted in the villages.

As to the new organisation of life, production and exchanges, the military presence was more negative than positive. On the one hand the Collectives supplied provisions without payment for these troops who had to be adequately fed, since the government did nothing for them. On the other hand a goodly number of the youngest and strongest *maños*[6] had been called up and so taken away from their work in the fields and workshops. All in all, and from the strictly economic point of view, the Collectives would have benefited from there not being sections of the armed forces in the region. But it is true that in that case the fascists would have advanced.

1. Graus

Graus[7] is situated in the north of the province of Huesca in a region less suited to socialised agricultural production than the villages we visited further South. The topography of the land is the principal reason. Here one is in the heart of the Spanish Pyrenees, in the middle of the thinly wooded forests where the rocks are more numerous than the trees. Fields are rare, and cultivated areas small. Cultivations rise in irregular terraces among the rocky and chaotic formations. One reaches Graus by passes where machines cannot penetrate. There is no shortage of water; streams, springs, rivers and torrents abound. But soil is sparse. Erosion carried it away in centuries past. Thus the villages are lost in the greyish masses, with their small populations and dreary homes, which do not always reach the hundred mark; one also finds them on the heights, dominating the minute valleys, and surrounded by enormous jagged boulders in the midst of which they resemble nests.

In the more isolated places where life is so peaceful, progress penetrates with difficulty. Long established traditions hold sway, and minds are slow. New ideas hardly penetrated the high mountains of Aragon, as in all mountainous regions untraversed by living arteries. The restricted outlook on social life, the withdrawal into oneself, predisposed few of the inhabitants to a broad collectivist experience, which did not exclude however, and especially in this region, either loyalty or a regal hospitality.

By June 1937, of the 43 villages comprising the canton of Graus, Capella, Campo, Vesian, Pelatua, Benasque, Bocamorta, Puebla de Castro, Torres del Obispo, Puebla de Fantova, Laguares

---

6 The popular name given in Spain to the Aragonese.
7 Pronounced Graooss.

were 50% collectivised. The organisation which I had the time to study most carefully was that of Graus. This cantonal village of 2,600 inhabitants which gives the appearance of a small town, is situated on the banks of the Esera, the river of Spain with, I was told, the most constant flow, rising in France and feeding the immense barrage of the canal of Aragon and Catalonia.

Also surrounded by high mountains and well watered, Graus is situated at the intersection of many roads. It therefore became a relatively important commercial centre and the spirit of enterprise resulted in the creation of numerous small businesses to satisfy the needs of the surrounding country. In July 1936 40 per cent of the inhabitants earned their living from commerce; and industry and agriculture shared equally the remaining 60 per cent.

One fifth of the cultivated land was irrigated, and used for growing vegetables. On the dry lands cereals, grapes, olives and almonds were the main crops. But in that year throughout North Aragon the almonds had failed following a heavy frost on one night, whilst more to the south, the grapes in the canton of Binefar had been destroyed by a thunderstorm lasting an hour.

40 per cent of the irrigated land belonged to two proprietors. Another 40 per cent was more equitably divided, but the poor harvest obliged the average peasant (and one can guess at the fate of the really impoverished ones) to obtain a third or even a half of his income by work other than on the land. They took jobs in local industry, or as casual labourers on the land of the wealthy. Or again they would go to other regions on seasonal work. In the industrial jobs, wages ranged from 6 pesetas for labourers to 8 for builders and mechanics. But an accurate assessment showed that, bearing in mind that unemployment was rife, builders averaged 5 pesetas a day. As for the labourers . . .

During the early thirties the young emigrated and went to live in Catalonia or in France; about one fifth of the young girls left to find jobs as domestic servants in the towns. The tradesmen and the small industrialists did not live any better. For a long time their debts had exceeded their total assets.

As soon as the antifascists, advised by our comrades, had taken the situation in hand, they set about the social changes which we are about to enumerate.

One has seen that the living conditions of the various sections of the population were very different. A day-labourer working in the fields earned a half of a mechanic's wages. The first thing to be done therefore was to establish the family wage which assured to all an equal right to the means of life. At the beginning this wage was paid by vouchers. At the end of a month, tickets which were divided into points were issued. Later, the relative commercial importance of Graus, its situation on busy roads, brought back the use of the peseta, the official money maintained throughout most of Spain, as the general standard of values; then the *Comité* issued its own local small coinage.

Trade was at first controlled but was soon socialised. Individual transactions were replaced by collective ones. A "Food Cooperative" was set up where all the goods found in the small shops were concentrated. Then a second cooperative[8] for cloth and haberdashery was opened and replaced 23 of the 25 specialised shops—for just two were retained. There were also 25 to 30 grocers' shops which were transformed into two large collective stores. One shoe shop was retained out of three; the two hardware shops were merged into one; and of the six bakeries and bread stores four disappeared and one bakehouse (instead of three) proved to be sufficient.

The process of reorganisation and technical improvement went hand in hand with that of the collectivisation of the land and industry. In Graus as in many other places in Aragon, the application of socialism started with the organisation of the agrarian Collective. Faced with the gravity of the situation, the revolutionary *Comité* dealt first with the most important and urgent needs. The harvest had to be gathered, the land cultivated and sown and maximum returns obtained from reduced efforts, seeing how many young men had been taken away by the demands of war. By the efforts of comrades of the U.G.T. and C.N.T., the old swing-ploughs drawn by a donkey were discarded, the strongest ranking animals were rounded up and set to work with the best ploughs on the land from which the boundary hedges had been grubbed up. The land was then sown with corn. The agrarian Collective was constituted on October 16, 1936 barely three months after the fascist attack. On the same day, the means of transport were officially collectivised though they had been in fact almost from the beginning. Other new steps were decided upon, in accordance with suggestions made by the two syndicates—the one socialist, the other libertarian. The

8 As in most cases, the name cooperative was given to what were communal stores.

socialisation of the printing industry was decided on on November 24.[9] It was followed two days later by that of the shoe shops and bakers.

On December 1st it was the turn of the businessmen, doctors, chemists, blacksmiths, and locksmiths. On December 11th, that of the cabinet makers and carpenters. Gradually all the social activities entered the new organism.

The Resolution voted by the agricultural workers allows one to get a clearer picture of the basic outlines and general principles of the collectivisations that followed, since in all cases their principles were more or less the same. This is the text:

"Agricultural workers, meeting in Graus on 16 October, 1936 resolve as follows:

1. They join the general Community of all trades;

2. All the members join the Community of their free will; they are expected to bring their tools;

3. All the land of comrades entering the Community must be handed over to increase the common wealth;

4. When agricultural workers have no work to do, it is obligatory that they help in other trades which might have need of their labour;

5. An inventory in duplicate will be made of the land and chattels that have been brought to the Collectivity; one copy will be given to the owner of those properties and the other will remain in the hands of the Collective.

6. If for unforeseeable reasons the Collective were to be dissolved, each comrade will have the indisputable right to the land and goods he had brought to the Collective;

7. Members will nominate, at their meeting, the administrative Commission for their trade;

8. When agricultural workers have reached agreement on this latter point, they will have to nominate an administrative Commission composed of a chairman, treasurer, a secretary and three members;

9. This agrarian Collective will maintain direct relations with the communal Bank of all the assembled trades, which will be set up by the liaison *Comité;*

10. Workers who come to work collectively will receive the following wages: for families of three people or less,[10] six pesetas

---

9 The person who undertook the task was a well organised, young employer.

10 The limit was afterwards set at two persons.

a day; those consisting of more than three people will receive an additional peseta a day for each of them;

11. The wage can be modified according to the circumstances and at the suggestion of the administrative Commission of all the assembled trades;[11]

12. Workers whose relatives do not belong to the Collective will receive wages to be established by the *Comité*;[12]

13. The expulsion of a member of the Collective will have to be decided by the central Commission of all the trades, to which the agricultural section also belongs;

14. The members of the Collective undertake to work as many hours as the administrative Commission, in agreement with the local central Commission, will consider necessary, and it is vital that they should work with interest and enthusiasm.

Duly informed and in full agreement, the agricultural workers take cognizance of this Resolution."

This document as all the others of a similar nature—only in Alcorisa will one find an exception to the rule—was drafted by peasants who were not literate persons, and even made frequent spelling mistakes; one could also object to clumsiness in the drafting of the text, or to ambiguities in the terms used. Nevertheless the essential tasks are defined and practice would clarify and sharpen the thinking.

As a contribution to this clarification, it should be said that no collectivisation was carried out independently of the will of the people concerned. As to the collectivist revolutionary *Comité*, which is not always called by the same name in different texts, its function was restricted to calling to a meeting—and only after previous agreement with the militants best informed on the problems and activities—each section of the producers which decided, with complete independence, to collectivise. Once having joined the Collective, that section was no longer autonomous.[13] The revolutionary *Comité* was soon transformed into a *Comité de enlace* (liaison Committee) which managed or coordinated everything. It disappeared in January 1937 with the reestablishment

---

11 It will be noted that the peasant Collective is not separated from, but always united with, "all the assembled trades".

12 There were in Aragon, and in other regions, many cases where young boys and girls left their family, which had remained individualist, in order to join the Collective.

13 Though the right to secede remained. But in fact isolation was impossible.

of the municipal Council as required by the government.

Again, complete harmony existed between the two workers' organisations, U.G.T. and C.N.T., who agreed to nominate four councillors each, and that the president, whose role was that of mayor, should be a republican worker chosen by a general assembly of all the inhabitants of the village. Impartiality and unity were thus secured.

But the mayor was only a figurehead; he simply applied the decisions taken by the majority of the municipal Council which had to represent the Central government, to call up conscripts for the war, furnish identity documents, establish rationing for all the inhabitants of the village, individualists and collectivists. The Collective was only answerable to itself. The municipal Council intervened neither in its activities nor in its administration —and it was also true for all the Collectives in general. It supervised 90 per cent of production (only in agriculture were there still individualists) and all the means of transport, distribution and exchanges. Of the eight comrades who comprised it, six were at the head of the section of which they were most qualified. The following was the classification established for each delegate:

Education and Public Health which included everything connected with cultural life, not least the theatre, cinema (there was one in Graus which when required was used as a hall for meetings). The same section also extended to matters concerning sport and public health in general;

Work and Statistics which dealt with the classification and allocation of workers, remuneration and the general census;

Provisioning (commerce, coal supplies, chemical fertilisers, warehouses, depots and distribution);

Transport and Communications (lorries and trucks, cars, waggons, taxis, garages, Posts and Telegraphs);

Industry (factories, workshops, electricity, water, building works).

The remaining two comrades, one from the C.N.T., the other from the U.G.T., were in charge of the general secretariat; they were also entrusted with propaganda.

In the industrial organisation, each workshop nominated a delegate worker who maintained the necessary permanent relations with the secretary for the industry.

Each industrial speciality had its own accounts kept by the general Accounting Section where I was shown the master Account Book from which I was able to note the most important sections existing at the time. This list gave a fairly complete picture of the non-agricultural activities of the locality and of the general organisation: drinking water, the manufacture of goat-skin bottles, carpentry, mattress making, cinematography, cartwright's workshops, flour milling, photography, silk spinning, chocolate making, sausage making, liqueur distilling, electricity, oil-store, haberdashery, hotels and cafés, forges, linen drapery, gypsum kilns, bakeries, hairdressing establishments, laundry, tailors collectives, soap making, paint shop, tile works, tin-shop, cycle repairs, dressmaking workshop, sewing machine workshop, assembly and printing shops, dairy-farm, building materials.

Thus all was supervised and coordinated. Just as for distribution, organisation for production was rationalised. For this reason the Collective brought together in one building the small undertakings which bottled wine, which made lemonade, soda water, beers and liqueurs. Consequently the work was carried out properly, under more hygienic conditions for both the producers and consumers.

The Collective also installed a mill for the production of olive oil using modern techniques, with the result that the waste material could be used for making soap; one industry stemming from the other. Among purchases one also observed two 8-ton lorries, made available to the whole village, and a weighbridge of 20 ton capacity, which allowed Graus for the first time in its history to control the movement of goods arriving and leaving the village. In addition, two electric washing machines were acquired —one for the hospital, the other for the local collectivised hotels.

Needless to say, agriculture did not stand still so far as output was concerned. In view of the small proportion of cultivable land, the irrigated area only increased by 5 per cent and of the dry lands by 10 per cent, but the removal of the old property boundaries allowed for some to be reclaimed from useless hedges and paths. The land was also more rationally cultivated; and the headlands were all cultivated; production of potatoes was increased by 50 per cent, which made it possible to use three-quarters of the production in exchange for goods coming from Catalonia. And by a better use of tools and equipment, fertilisers and human effort, more lucerne was available for the livestock, and a doubling of sugar beet for human consumption. Furthermore, making good use of even the smallest patches of land, about 400 selected fruit trees were planted.

The Collective bought a modern threshing machine, modern

ploughs and seed drills, a powerful tractor, a reaper-binder, a vine spraying machine, a ridge plough. The use of all these mechanical aids, to which must be added those supplied by the chemical industry, make it easy to understand why the productivity of the Collectivised land was 50 per cent higher than that of the individualist farmers, and that the latter ended by joining in the common effort.

Before July 1936, the rearing of livestock had been neglected in Graus. But due to the force of circumstances this too commercial locality had to change some of its activities. For instance, the rearing of sheep was intensified by the purchase of 310 sheep as the beginning of a larger flock that could graze on the mountain slopes. But better still, I visited two *granjas* (farms) which gave a fine impression of the creative urge. Farm no. 1 was assigned to the rearing of pigs. It was constructed far from the village, on a site surrounded by trees and fields where the Collective was intending to establish a paddock for rearing fowls. At the time of my visit one of the two sections of the building had been completed. It was constructed with solid materials: stone walls, concrete floors, with ample room and well lighted and aerated. In twenty-two divisions, 162 pigs were housed according to age and breed. A central alleyway separated the two rows of stalls. The walls were whitewashed and everything swilled down daily, including the pigs when considered necessary. Work was almost completed on a large outside pen which would then allow the pigs to take the air and sun daily.

On the upper floor of the building which was as solidly constructed though not as high, reserve stores of pig food were kept, and a large cistern into which water was pumped by motor. Outside, specially dug furrow drains took the liquid manure and solid wastes to pits where, after any necessary treatment, these were sprayed onto the surrounding fields.

The breeding sows were housed separately, and in peace. Once all the building work was complete, the Collective expected to increase its production by at least 400 more pigs than Graus normally produced. The increase would be even greater bearing in mind the improved strains and the feeding methods.

The project for a huge fowl rearing complex not far from this pig-farm should not lead one to believe that when I visited Graus and studied what was going on, everything still had to be done in this domain. The *granja* no. 2 was proof of it. It had been organised from the first days. A plan had been prepared on the basis of the most recent experiments. In a surprisingly short time, considering that only human labour was available, on one site five two-storey buildings were put up and on the other one building with seven sub-divisions. Rearing was then started, using what was at hand. They used Leghorns, Prats, the latter an excellent and too little known Catalan breed, and hundreds of laying hens. Eggs were reserved for the Collective though some families owned a small back yard. There was also a large number of ducks, geese and goslings, for whom a pool was being laid out. Furthermore, young turkeys and sixty pairs of breeding rabbits were the beginnings of greater things to come.

In June 1937, 1,500 chicks had been hatched and another 800 were on the way in seven hatcheries, five of which had been bought in Catalonia, one had been donated and the seventh had been built on the site.

The standards of construction and the hygienic conditions of the building were excellent. The chicks were reared according to the highest standards: dried milk, cod liver oil—they lacked nothing.

But let us return to the non-agricultural activities. In what was the corset factory some thirty women were at work making shirts and trousers for the militiamen. Most of the young girls were not paid specially to come and work there, since their basic needs were guaranteed by the family wage based on the number of members in the household. Nevertheless they came in two groups, one in the morning, the other in the afternoon; and they worked as hard as anybody. We were in the world of human solidarity.

Let us now examine a little more closely the new conditions of existence. We have seen from the Resolution of the agricultural workers that a couple received six pesetas a day, that an extra peseta was added for every additional person on the principle that the more people there were in a family proportionately less would be the cost of living per person. The increase was uniform; thus a family of eight persons received 14 pesetas, a sum they had never seen before in their lives, for no special grants had been available for large families. Then as economic conditions improved the family wage for large families was increased by 15 per cent. Furthermore, there was no rent to pay, housing being looked upon as a public service; the price of gas and water had been halved, and medical services and prescriptions were free, both these services having been socialised.

One should add that there was no unemployment, *and as in all the Collectives*, wages were paid in full for fifty-two weeks of the year for, as one of the organisers in Graus put it to me, "one must eat every day".

On the other hand the cost of clothing coming from Catalonia and foodstuffs from other regions had increased by 30 per cent.

If one wants to make comparisons, then let us take a family of five (which is the average for Spain) consisting of mother and father and three children or two children and one grandparent; in other words a family in which there is a single breadwinner. And if we take the highest wage ruling at the time, that of a mechanic and assuming he is always in employment, then his 8 pesetas a day, a good wage for a Spanish village, makes 200 pesetas a month based on 25 days' work. Under the Collectives' family wage those five people would receive (including the 15 per cent increase) 310.50 pesetas a month. Bearing in mind the increases that took place in certain prices, the difference was not as large as might appear at first sight. However, it did offer a considerable advantage. Furthermore, as we have seen, that family did not pay rent, which, with medical costs and prescription charges, was calculated at 70 pesetas a month. That supplemented the wages as did also the plot of land available to each family to cultivate what they wished on it for their own use. It was also supplemented by the selected seeds, and fertilisers distributed free, and by the animals kept in the back yard. And it rose very much more for the builders, and builders' labourers working out of doors, and farm labourers who used to get paid four pesetas a day for six months of the year . . . Under the Collectives system it was no longer necessary to go elsewhere to look for work, and young girls stopped going to France or Catalonia to work as domestics.

One can therefore say that in general the standard of living rose by from 50 to 100 per cent in a few months, that the productive capital increased in an astonishing manner during a war and when a part of the labour force, mainly the youngest and most active, was at the Front. The miracle was made possible not only because the work was carried out with a collective enthusiasm that was praiseworthy, but also thanks to economy in the use of labour and the means of production. One must bear in mind that some 40 per cent of the population had previously been engaged in commerce, and realise that a better distribution of activities made it possible there, as elsewhere, to free a labour force until then virtually parasitic and employ it on work which benefited everybody.

*

The whole economic machine—production, exchanges, means of transport, distribution—was in the hands of twelve employees, who kept separate books and card-index files for each activity. Day by day, everything was recorded and allocated: turnover and reserves of consumer goods and raw materials, cost prices and selling prices, summarised income and outgoings, profit or loss noted for each enterprise or activity.

And as ever, the spirit of solidarity was present, not only between the Collective and each of its components, but between the different branches of the economy. The losses incurred by a particular branch, considered useful and necessary, were made up by the profits earned by another branch. Take, for instance, the hairdressing section. The shops kept open all day and operated at a loss. On the other hand drivers' activities were profitable, as was that for the production of alcohol for medical and industrial purposes. So these surpluses were used in part to compensate the deficit on the hairdressing establishments. It was also by this juggling between the sections, that pharmaceutical products were bought for everybody and machines for the peasants.

The Graus Collective gave other examples of solidarity. It gave shelter to 224 refugees who had to flee their villages before the fascist advance. Of this number only about twenty were in a position to work and 145 went to the Front. Twenty-five families whose breadwinners were sick or disabled received their family wage.

In spite of all these expenses a number of quite ambitious public works were undertaken. Five kilometres of roads were tarred, a 700 metre irrigation channel was widened by 40 cm and deepened by 25 cm for better irrigation of the land and to increase its driving power. Another channel was extended by 600 metres. Then there was the wide, winding path that led to a spring until then forbidden to inhabitants of the village. The story is worth recounting.

*

This spring discharged in the depression of a large estate which its owner divided into parcels and let for rent. This jealous cantankerous man refused to allow people to go and drink the water because to reach it they had to take a path which crossed a hedge skirting a field and a small forest which were his property. Even his tenant farmers on hot days could not use it to slake their thirst. Nevertheless, quite frequently, and understandably, people disobeyed the owner's injunctions. So the chap had his way by having the orifice of the spring sealed off.

But the revolution changed the roles. Among the measures taken by the Revolutionary *Comité*, to the great joy of so many people, was the expropriation of the estate of that stiff-necked egoist and also the public enjoyment of the forbidden spring. It was decided to build, even through the hedges, a fine winding path down to the sparkling water; and the former proprietor had to take part in the work with those who had been his tenant farmers. When all was completed, and with that love which water arouses in Spain—and in so many other countries! —a marble plaque was placed above the sparkling jet. What I read, in golden letters, was: "The Spring of Freedom, 19 July 1936".

*

As everywhere else, Graus also gave high priority to education. The most striking achievement, due largely to a man inspired by his task and by his convictions, was an Art School which was used during the day by primary school pupils and in the evenings by young workers. Drawing, painting, sculpture (or its study), choral societies (which must have already existed as they were to be found throughout Spain); the mind was being cultivated and the soul of man and of the child was raised through Art.

At the time of my visit, eighty small refugees from the francoist zone had been housed in a fine property, which had of course been seized by the Collective, situated several miles from the village. Five teachers, three of them women, were taking classes in the shade of the large trees. In the main building, beds of every kind, which had been provided by the people of Graus, furnished the rooms. Two experienced women were responsible for seeing that the place was kept clean and for preparing meals in the huge kitchen which previously was only used by the wealthy owners for a few weeks in the year. Food, furniture, linen, staff wages, all were provided by Graus.

The situation was splendid with its woods descending towards the river, its park, swimming pool and varied outbuildings. The children were visibly happy. They had obviously never had such a wonderful time in their lives. It was the intention of the U.G.T. and C.N.T. to eventually establish a permanent colony there so that all the children of Graus could take it in turns to go there to learn and to play in the open air and the sunshine.

*

I will end with a final impression, a last recollection which always takes me back to the past I lived through.

It was in Graus that I saw proclaimed at first on the facades in all the streets most strikingly and intensively, the joy of effort and of the new order. All the places of work, all the workshops, depots, goods stores, carried on their facades wooden boards of different sizes painted red and black, on which one read according to their classification in the collective machinery of production: Communal Linen Drapery No. 1 and No. 2; Communal Joinery No. 3, No. 4 and No. 5; Tailors' Collective No. 1, No. 2, No. 3 and No. 4; Bakers' Collective, Cartwrights' Collective, Cobblers' Collective, etc. . . . It was a hymn, a proclamation by each and all, an explosion of confidence and happiness.

All this was destroyed by a Brigade led by the Stalinist general Lister and then by Franco.

It all remains vivid within me and will remain as long as I am able to recall things and men.

2. Fraga

On the bank of the Cinca river, which races down from the Pyrenees to plunge into the Ebro, Fraga, situated on a hillock, rises up with its very old houses appearing to be leaning on each other as would ailing blind people; one gets the impression that they will all crumble together.

There is no shortage of land, and Fraga's 8,000 inhabitants should have enjoyed a happy life. The municipal boundaries comprise 48,000 hectares of which, however, only 30,000 can be cultivated; the remainder is steppe which is more or less useless.[14]

In addition one is faced with the misdeeds of private landed property and of the historic thefts which, more often than not, go back to the time of the Christian reconquest at the expense of the Arab world: the rich owned 10,000 hectares used as a game preserve.

Nevertheless, the ancient municipal rights prevailed—at least in principle. Theoretically the Commune was the master of 35,000 hectares and only granted the right of usufruct whether for agriculture, stock rearing or for hunting. Stock-rearing being an important source of revenue, uncultivated land (for the custom was to sow a crop one year out of two or even three because of the poor soil) had to be automatically ceded to graziers whose herds in feeding themselves spread much needed manure on the land.

But privilege violated legality, and the owners, a small minority, had in fact the rights of ownership (one can imagine what must have been their influence on the municipal council), and were the masters of life at local level. Nevertheless it is only right to point out that the inhabitants of Fraga in general enjoyed a higher standard of living than that of most people in other towns and villages in Aragon.

The Local Syndicate of the C.N.T., which included all trades, had been established in 1918. It was dissolved by the dictatorship of Primo de Rivera in 1924 as a result of which our comrades started the cultural Association "Aurora" which carried on the propagation of our ideas. When the Republic was proclaimed in 1931, the Syndicate was reconstituted, then closed down by the new regime from which one had expected something better. It was necessary to return to the "Aurora" cultural Association which, stronger than in the past, built premises where it set up a "rationalist" school. When the Leftists triumphed at the February 1936 elections, the Local Syndicate was reorganised for the third time and soon had 500 members who were agreed on the principles of the C.N.T.; the Syndicate would in all probability have been closed down for a third time had the fascist movement not come and in spite of itself obliged them, to push ahead . . . only to destroy everything in the end.

From the early days of August 1936, that is a fortnight after the uprising of the Rightists, the Collective began to be formed.

14 See chapter on "Materials for a Revolution" for the views of the geographer Gonzalo de Reparaz on the steppes of the Ebro basin.

But even though our comrades were at the same time the leaven and the principal actors in this enterprise others kneaded the dough with them. I saw in the socialised administration of Fraga, working alongside seasoned libertarians were middle class republicans, professional administrators, collaborating with enthusiasm at the chosen tasks. The delegate for food supplies belonged to the Left Republican party, whose leader was Manuel Azaña, more Jacobin than socialist. The breadth of his views, his intelligence and his impeccable Castilian kept you spellbound by his conversation. When I asked him whether in the event of our winning the war he would or would not return to his party and leave the Collective, he replied with that ring in his voice which is a characteristic of the Aragonese: "I cannot say for sure what I will do then, but what I can say is that now I am for what is being done here."

Then he showed me the index cards which referred to the administrative section he was in charge of, with an enthusiasm which matched mine. And this gave me once again the opportunity to see how the community of interests of all sections of activity was the great general rule.

Undoubtedly a communal tradition inspired the organisational structure in Fraga where the municipality played an important role. The local council was the continuation of the revolutionary *Comité* in action from the first weeks following the July uprising. It was this *Comité* that took over the management of all aspects of daily life, based on the normal tasks undertaken: agriculture, livestock, industry, distribution, health, social assistance, public works, school organisation. There was one councillor for each. All were nominated by the workers concerned, with the exception of the Councillor for provisioning and distribution who was designated by a gathering of representatives of all the local activities, for it involved problems concerning all the inhabitants, both collectivists and non-collectivists without distinction.

But whilst being linked to this coordinated whole, each trade had its own organisation, corresponding to its tasks, needs and preferences. Being responsible for its work each trade organised it in its own way. Thus the Collective of agricultural workers and herdsmen which comprised 700 families—half the agricultural population—was divided into 51 groups of which 20 were involved in intensive cultivation and 31 in non-intensive, where cereal farming prevailed. Each group nominated a manager and they met every Saturday to decide upon the tasks to be undertaken. The Communal Councillor of Agriculture attended this very large section in order to harmonise the activity of the growers, stock-rearers and the individualist peasants.

At the time of my visits, the herdsmen were rearing and minding 6,000 breeding ewes, 4,000 lambs, 150 cows,[15] 600 goats and 2,000 pigs. Almost all the livestock had previously belonged to the large landowners and they employed the herdsmen and shepherds who were continuing to work, but for the benefit of the whole population.

Each flock had two or three shepherds, one of whom was nominated by his comrades as their representative. The representatives also met every Saturday, with the Councillor for Agriculture being present at their meetings where the grazing sites were decided upon, arrangements made for the different herds, the importance of a breeding programme based on the consumers' needs, and exchanges on questions such as upkeep of stables, slaughtering arrangements, etc. . . .

Thus the work was carried on in a rational manner. Land, pastures, and irrigation when needed were used systematically. And the results were visible. The animals were slaughtered when they were in the right condition. One no longer saw 50 sheep grazing where 200 could be accommodated nor 100 vying with each other for grass which could barely feed 40.[16] Ewes that formerly would have been prematurely sold were now being kept in sufficient numbers for breeding. For the same purpose a suitable number of selected sows and cows were retained. Collective piggeries, cowsheds and stables for the mules employed on the land were built *outside Fraga*. Favoured by being able to use some 10,000 hectares previously reserved for hunting, the increase in livestock was rapid, and would have been even more remarkable had not the Collectives in Aragon undertaken to keep the front line fighters supplied with virtuality all their food without payment. Even so it was estimated at the time that if the municipalist Collective of Fraga were allowed unhampered development the

15 The number of cows was not high; in most of Spain there is a shortage of pasture. There were about 3,600,000 head of cattle in 1936 compared with 15,000,000 in France.
16 Already at that time the Collective of Fraga carried the system of "rotational pastures", which was used in the Inn Valley in Austria and which was more or less unknown in France. The system consisted in dividing up the pasture into strips and by grazing them in rotation allowing the grass to grow by the time the first strip is again grazed, and was obviously easier to apply over the large areas belonging to the Collective.

herds would double in two years as well as showing a notable improvement in the quality of the stock.

∗

Now let us pass on to non-agricultural activities. The other trades comprised a general Syndicate with 30 sections; including the farmers and shepherds there were at the time of my visit, 950 members. Those sections were not therefore important in themselves and in many cases one can hardly talk of industry: three sawyers, three farriers, thirty-two building workers, nine plasterers, twenty-eight tailors and the same number of dress-makers . . . In the relations between producers and consumers, whoever needed a suit would contact the tailors' delegate, anyone needing repairs to his house would approach the building workers' delegate; to shoe his horse the individualist would go to the delegate of the farriers or the blacksmiths. Prices were fixed, and determined by a joint meeting of the general delegate for labour, the municipal council's technician for industry, representatives of the producing section and many members of the consuming public; they come to a decision based on the cost of raw materials, the work involved, general expenses and the resources of the collectivists. I noted the following scale for furniture: a double wooden bed 130 pesetas, a single bed 70 pesetas; a simple cupboard with mirror 270 pesetas; a dining room table 50 pesetas, with extension 70 pesetas; a folding kitchen table with drawers 25 pesetas, without 20 pesetas; a child's bed 40 pesetas. The quality of the raw materials was specified in writing.

The buyer paid the delegate who handed the money to the Labour Councillor. The check on the actual payment was effected by means of a counterfoil book with receipts in duplicate, one of which was handed to the buyer, the other to the councillor. The stub remained under the control of the delegate of the producing Collective. Thus it was a simple matter to check, and there was no possibility of double dealing.

As in all the Collectives, the different sections were not, so far as accounts went, autonomous or independent. They constituted a whole the separate parts of which were interdependent and practised mutual aid through the general machinery. Here too, building workers who were without work would go to help the land workers and when necessary the opposite would happen. And all the wages were the same, paid in local money established by the Council of the Commune.

A single collectivist producer received 40 pesetas a week. A couple 45 and so on to a maximum of 70 pesetas for a family of ten people, following the general consensus that the larger the family unit, the lower the cost of living per person. Where there were two producers in a family the weekly family wage was slightly higher at 50 pesetas for a family of three, to 85 for ten people. Working women were paid at exactly the same rate as men.

To make a complete break with the past, the word wage was dropped and replaced by the word "credit".

The individualists some 750 families in all though the numbers were decreasing all the time sowed, cultivated and raised their animals for their own needs. But through the intermediary of the Collective, their activities were coordinated with the general plan of work. The agricultural delegate attended their meetings and in a friendly manner would advise them on the best things to grow and on how to improve quality. The same delegate would purchase their products, on the basis of the price scale established by the Syndicate which those individualists who wished could join and of which, anyway, not even all collectivists were members. And this resulted in a quite remarkable freedom of movement which was a characteristic of the Levante Collectives as we shall see later.

The foregoing indicates that distribution was also completely socialised, so that even the individualists were collectivists where this aspect of social life was concerned. The food councillor was responsible for barter arrangements with Catalonia,[17] the Levante and other parts of Aragon. With the knowledge of what stocks of wheat or the quantities of meat, wool and hides, would be available at any given moment, he could in advance make offers for barter based on the established scale of prices. An alternative practice which was tending to become more widespread was to use the Aragon Council (which was controlled by the libertarians) as go between in these exchanges for it was successful in obtaining for the agrarian areas large quantities of the things they most needed from the areas with industrial surpluses such as machinery, fertilisers, petrol, lorries, textiles, groceries, etc.

At the beginning a system of vouchers was used instead of

17 Fraga is situated on the boundary between Catalonia and Aragon, in the centre of a steppe almost desert and which overwhelms the traveller who crosses it on foot.

money. But what was successful in one place was not necessarily successful in another. There was no misuse in Colanda, Rubielo de Mora and elsewhere. There was however in Fraga, so I was told (though my informants never got round to explaining the reasons in detail). So local money was resorted to. Then at the same time, goods in short supply were rationed; it was a case of a war economy since Fraga is situated on the road to Saragossa, that is, on what was the Aragon Front. As a result of rationing, serious inequalities were avoided. Each family had a ration book in which were entered the quantities of goods to which they were entitled on the basis of available stocks or supplies.

All goods for local consumption were under the control of the food councillor and distributed by the communal shops, which here too were called cooperatives. Private commerce had disappeared. There was one warehouse for bread, three for groceries, three for butcher's meat and three for pork butcher's meat. The rest were in proportion to consumption or available supplies.

Meat was brought direct from the slaughter houses to the pork and meat butchers' establishments. Consumption was carefully checked. Those responsible for distribution had to render exact returns on sales based on the weights of meat delivered to them. Thus from the raiser to the consumer the whole procedure was perfectly synchronised.

Wheat, both supplies from the individualists as well as from the Collective, was stored in a warehouse for cereals. And in due course controlled supplies would be released to the communal mills which then supplied the flour to the eleven bakeries which produced the golden round loaves which were promptly delivered to the bread warehouse for distribution.

The Communal Council had a system of credits which I did not see applied anywhere else. When a collectivist, or a small proprietor, needed money for a large purchase he approached the organisation for local finance and made his application to them. Two collectivist and two individualist delegates would then work out on the basis of an assessment of what the applicant could earn by his work, barring accidents, in the period during which he needed the loan and also what were his normal outgoings over a period of three months, and on this basis a credit account would be opened for him. Without interest, of course.

This gave more flexibility to the daily lives of the collectivists, and in their case the section of the Collective to which they belonged was also responsible for the credit and guaranteed its repayment.

It would have been surprising had the Health organisation lagged behind. In public institutions, in their clinics or on home visits, two doctors out of three accepted to practise their profession in conjunction with the municipality. Medical care was therefore virtually completely collectivised. The hospital was quickly enlarged from a capacity of 20 beds to 100. The outpatients' department which was in the course of construction was rapidly completed. A service to deal with accidents and minor surgical operations was established. The two pharmacies were also integrated into the new system.

All this was accompanied by a massive increase in public hygiene. As we have already seen, the cowsheds and stables were reorganised on the outskirts of Fraga. One of these, specially built, housed 90 cows. And for the first time ever the hospital was provided with running water and the project in hand was to ensure that all houses were similarly provided, thus reducing the incidence of typhoid.

All this was part of a programme of public works which included the improvement of roads and the planting of trees along them. Thanks to the increased productivity resulting from collective work (which Proudhon pointed to as far back as in 1840 as one of the features of large scale capitalism, but which libertarian socialism can apply and generalize more effectively), there were skilled men available for this kind of work in the Collectives. The municipality under the old regime would never have been able to meet such expenditure.

The advantages of a socialised economy are to be found in many other cases. The scarcity of water in Spain, and the problems arising from its use had resulted in the formation of many *comunidades de regantes* (associations of water users) set up for the irrigation of fields and which share among themselves, more or less equitably, the precious liquid. The problems and individual conflicts which it caused gave rise to the organisation of the famous "Water Tribunal" in Valencia which meets every Thursday to settle amicably without the intervention of the authorities or of official justice, the disputes that are submitted to it.

But such disputes disappear when men no longer have to compete and fight each other to exist, or when the will to acquire wealth for oneself is no longer uppermost. In the region of Fraga fifteen *comunidades de regantes* covering the land in five villages disbanded. The morality of solidarity produced that miracle. The old practice was replaced by a single collectivist administration, which coordinated the distribution of water everywhere, and which was proposing to improve the catchment basin and use of the rivers, especially of the Cinca river, by public works which none of the villages could have carried out individually.

As was the case everywhere, solidarity was extended in all directions. The members of ninety families who for various reasons such as illness, death of the principal breadwinner, etc. were condemned to poverty under the individualist society, were receiving the "credit" established for everybody. The militiamen's families were supported in the same way. A final achievement completes this story of mutual aid in action.

A number of old folk, men and women, abandoned by everybody, sad human flotsam of a society in which misfortune is one of the natural elements had come to Fraga from smaller and poorer villages. It was for these unfortunates that a *Casa de los Ancianos* (Old Folk's Home) was organised and at the time of my visit there were thirty-two of them staying there. They had rooms (or small dormitories), a dining room, a sitting room with a large open fire, the whole place was kept spick and span and reflected the warmth and cordiality of the welcome.

Three women attended them, two of whom were former nuns. I spoke at length with these guests weighed down by their lot. They were sceptical of the future. Whoever has been a lifelong victim of misfortune cannot easily believe in a lasting, relative wellbeing. Perhaps they foresaw that all this would be lost one day, either by the victory of Franco or of the republican government, inspired by the Stalinists, and deep within me I could not be so sure that they were wrong. But I had to make an effort to give them confidence and offered them words of hope. Then I asked them about the way they were being treated. One of them summed up the view of all with the conciseness recommended by the Aragonese writer Baltasar Gracian, *Lo bueno, si breve, dos veces bueno* (the good, if brief, is doubly good) when he said: "We cannot complain neither of the food, nor the wine, nor the beds, nor of the love."

What more could be said?

3. Binefar

By its spirit and its dynamism, Binefar was probably the most important centre for collectivisation in the province of Huesca. Thanks to the high qualities of the local militants it had become the township of a canton of thirty-two villages. Of these, twenty-eight were more or less collectivised. Collectivisation was total in Esplus, and Balcarca (500 inhabitants) as it was for the 2,000 inhabitants in La Almunia. In Alcampel and Peralta de la Sal there were 1,500 collectivists out of a population of 2,000 while in Algayon only nine of its 500 inhabitants remained outside the Collective. In Binefar 700 families out of 800 comprised the new society.

A tenth of the 5,000 inhabitants worked in small industries such as milling, biscuit making, clothing and shoe factories, foundries, machine repair shops, light engineering, shops, etc. . . . and supplied the surrounding villages as well as local requirements. The small numbers engaged in industry did not however prevent there being a social movement of some importance.

The sole syndicate grouping the workers of different trades was founded in 1917. It encountered the kind of difficulties experienced elsewhere too: persecutions, prolonged closures, imprisonment and deportation of militants. Nevertheless during the first two years of the Republic, the membership rose to 600.

Most of them were field workers and, as one can well imagine, their situation was not very bright. The unequal division of the estates was the reason, for nature is fairly clement in Binefar, and irrigation works complete its positive aspects.

The 2,000 hectares of cultivable land available were reserved for intensive cultivation. Animal feed, sugar beet, various vegetables, and olive groves were the main source of revenue. Of these 2,000 hectares 1,200 belonged to the large landowners. The remainder were divided into small parcels one of which was owned by most families. But only about a hundred could make a living out of theirs. The remainder, often husbands and wives, in order to survive had to work for the rich landowners as farmers or employees.

Our forces were still disorganised by recent persecutions when in mid-July the Francoist menace took shape. The municipal authorities belonged to the Popular Front from which the Communists were virtually absent. They did not want fascism, but they were incapable of doing anything. Fortunately, the militants

H

of the C.N.T. and F.A.I. as usual faced up to the danger. And on their initiative a revolutionary *Comité* was set up on July 18 which they joined as a majority alongside two members of the Popular Front.

The Civil Guards, faced by the determination of their adversaries, hesitated. While waiting for reinforcements they entrenched themselves in their barracks accompanied by the principal local reactionaries and fascists. But on July 20, after useless negotiations the barracks were taken by assault, and following an inevitable settlement of accounts our comrades left for other villages where they were needed to help to settle once for all with the defenders of the old regime.

There was no hesitation in Binefar about taking the necessary steps to ensure life for all. Most of the harvest was getting scorched on the large estates whose owners had fled to Huesca. The revolutionary *Comité* took over the abandoned harvest and the mechanical reapers and binders. The wage earners who had worked on the land for the rich decided to continue to work for the benefit of everybody. Teams were made up, just as happened elsewhere, and with delegates to coordinate their efforts, would meet, to start with every night, and when the work was under control once a week.

Once the harvest was gathered, industries were socialised. This was followed by commerce. A general assembly was called of all the local inhabitants, and adopted a Charter the principal articles of which are here reproduced verbatim:

Art. 1—Work will be carried out by groups of ten people, and each group will nominate its delegate. This delegate will have to organise the work and maintain necessary harmony among the workers; where necessary he may apply sanctions voted in the assemblies.

Art. 2—The delegates are expected to present to the Agricultural Commission each day a report on the tasks completed.

Art. 3—The working timetable will be established according to requirements.

Art. 4—A central committee consisting of a member of each production branch will be nominated in the general assembly of the Community of Binefar. The committee will give a progress report at the monthly assembly on consumption and production, as well as reports from the rest of Spain and abroad.

Art. 5—All those who will manage the activities of the Collective will be nominated by the general assembly of collectivists.

Art. 6—Each member will receive an inventory of the goods and chattels he has brought [to the Collective].

Art. 7—All members of the Collective without exception, will have equal rights and duties; they cannot be obliged to belong to one Syndicate rather than to another;[18] it will suffice that they fully accept the resolutions adopted by the Collective.

Art. 8—Any profits may not be shared out. They will be part of the collective wealth, for the benefit of all. Foodstuffs will be rationed and one will have to see to it that food stocks are set up in case of crop failures.

Art. 9—When circumstances demand it, as in the case of urgent agricultural work, the Collective will be able to require women comrades in sufficient numbers to do jobs in keeping with their sex.[19] A strict control will be exercised to ensure that women comrades fulfil this productive effort.

Art. 10—Young people will not start to work before they are 15 years old; and will not engage in heavy work until they are sixteen.

Art. 11—Assemblies will take the necessary decisions so far as the administration of the Collective and the replacement of the administrative commission are concerned.

It is clear that the Collective embraces the whole of social life. For its task extends, as we shall soon see, to education, health and all public services. Practically speaking the Syndicate plays no role at all. It has prepared the new order, but the latter establishes itself and extends beyond the Syndicate.

Neither is there a municipal organisation in the traditional sense, even if we go back to the communes of the Middle Ages. The Syndicate is inadequate and the municipality has been left behind. The Collective is the most typical organ of the Spanish peasant revolution which embraces all aspects of life.

For now it is no longer a case of struggling against the boss, of obtaining or snatching reforms, increases in wages and improved working conditions whilst continuing to be subjected to the wages system, but of ensuring production, of replacing for this purpose yesterday's exploiters and organisers. And this production must be geared to direct local requirements and the

18 The reference is to U.G.T. or C.N.T.
19 By which was obviously meant the lighter manual jobs.

needs for barter. Production and the enjoyment of goods, work and the sharing out of labour, are indivisible. As are the method of sharing out labour, the moral concepts which preside over, direct and influence the orientation of work. Everything is inter-dependent, interlinked. The sections of production are the toothed wheels of a whole mechanism which is available to everyone; for men old and young, fit or otherwise, for women who work or not, for children, the sick, the helpless, etc. This feeling of solidarity was to be found in the relationship between the different parts of the mechanism in general A lack of corporate feeling, of rivalry between trades or in work specialisation. The Collective was a *human* and fraternal whole. Industry and Agriculture represented a common fund. No wage differential between the mechanic and the peasant. The producers' sections helped each other. A specially nominated Commission consisting of a chairman (who coordinated the work to be done), a treasurer, a secretary and two members, kept the general administrative accounts, but took care to separate the accounts of each of the specialised sections so as to be able to correct and adjust them if necessary. Furthermore, two comrades, who were in constant touch with the group delegates, were responsible for the supervision of work and the results achieved.

The specialised sections (metal-workers, builders, etc.) met separately to examine their problems, decide upon the work to be done, actions to be taken, modifications to be made to the inventories of requirements. On the other hand, in some circumstances, the administrative Commission would convoke them or the delegates in order to examine what this had to be.

Binefar followed the general pattern adopted without any previous agreement, a spontaneous achievement as it were almost of a biological nature. The small scattered workshops were centralised. There remained only one factory for the mass production of men's wear, a huge workshop for the manufacture of shoes and so on. As for agriculture, the cultivation of wheat was increased by a third—without sacrificing other cultivations—and, but for the inclement weather that year, the production of sugar beet throughout the canton would have risen from the normal 40,000 tons to 70,000. Within a few months and in the light of experience, the constitution of agricultural groups as well as their organisation was modified. They ended up by establishing seven zones, each of which was a complete unit with its own buildings and with about one hundred workers.

On the other hand, putting as ever the law of solidarity above all else, an appeal would be made when necessary to industrial workers and even to white collar workers who could not refuse their help—since it was agreed by the Assembly—with the harvest. During the harvest of July 1937, even the tailors lent a helping hand.

For such a mobilisation street lists were drawn up with the names of married and single women. The former were not called upon except in exceptional circumstances. It was above all the young women who were called by means of the town crier who the day before would move from the square to the cross roads to read out the list of names of those whose turn it was to help.

Visibly, work was not an irksome task. In mid-summer, for the sowing of beetroot, groups of young girls gathered in the early morning and would go off singing. Obviously some would have preferred to stay in bed, but it was impossible for them to cheat. Only those who had old relatives or young brothers and sisters to look after were excused.

The delegate of each agricultural group or industrial section, would enter daily, in each collectivist's producer's notebook, his attendances at work. Infringements (if and when they occurred) could not be repeated without comment.

The Collective guaranteed free lodgings to all its members as well as bread, oil (the only edible fat available) and pharmaceutical products. Other things had to be bought with local money and on the basis of the family wage.

Consumer and other goods were distributed by communal stores. There were many in Binefar for wine, bread, oil, groceries in general, haberdashery and textiles; in addition there were three communal dairies, three butchers, a hardware shop and a furniture warehouse where all the production of the workshops was stored.

As township, chosen also because of its geographic situation and for its communications, Binefar was entrusted with the exchanges between the 32 villages in the canton. Between October and December 1936 exchanges of goods amounting to 5 million pesetas (in hard currency) had been made with other collectives in Catalonia and Aragon. And they held stocks of sugar worth 800,000 pesetas and oil worth 700,000 as well as less important commodities. The telephone and electricity had been installed throughout the canton.

Still, the foregoing catalogue does not give a full picture of the reality for this includes also negative aspects, which stemmed from the general situation. There was frequently a shortage of meat in Binefar and even of potatoes. The canton was more than generous. On the Aragon Front, militias abandoned by the government were without food supplies just as they were short of arms and ammunition. Binefar gave what it could— what it had. For months it sent from 30 to 40 tons of food a week. The whole canton donated 340 tons in one consignment for Madrid. In one day they donated to the Ascaso, Durruti and Ortiz militia columns 36,000 pesetas worth of oil.

The collectives never stopped showing this solidarity. The following is a typical example:

In June 1937 I attended a plenum to which delegations from all the villages of the canton had come. A serious problem was raised; the harvest was drawing near and there was a shortage of sacks, of binder twine, petrol and other things needed for the job. All this had to be purchased by the cantonal federation and distributed to the different villages according to their requirements. The cost involved many tens of thousands of pesetas to obtain for which it was necessary either to sell or exchange oil and many other foodstuffs which were intended for the front and thereby deprive the militiamen of them.

Well, not a single delegate was in favour of such a solution! Unanimously, without any argument, the assembly declared itself in favour of an alternative solution. In the end it was decided to send a delegation to the Valencia government, a step doomed to certain failure, for the sabotage of the Aragon troops was a major consideration in the minds of a majority in the Cabinet who knew that the food shortages would encourage the militiamen to pillage the Collectives.

I therefore decided to send to *Solidaridad Obrera*, our daily newspaper in Barcelona, an appeal addressed to those militiamen, explaining the situation to them and asking them to give a part of their pay to help the peasants. The money was forthcoming and the harvest saved.

All these facts explain the shortage of certain products that an uninformed journalist would note on his way through Binefar, and without taking account of the fact for instance, that an average of 500 soldiers were permanently billeted there.

The spirit of solidarity which is the outstanding feature of the Collectives, invests them with other qualities. Thus Binefar increased its medical service. One doctor who had been in practice for some time, declared himself for the C.N.T. and at a regional congress of fellow doctors he persuaded a majority of his Aragonese colleagues to follow his lead. Then without delay he put himself at the service of the people. Thus the distribution of pharmaceutical products was followed by the construction, outside the town and in a specially favourable locality, of a cottage hospital as a result of contributions in money and kind from the whole canton.

In April 1937 it was equipped with forty beds. An excellent Catalan surgeon had hastened to join the first doctor. Apparatus was purchased in Barcelona. A few months later, surgical, obstetric and traumatological instruments had been accumulated in sufficient numbers to allow a start to be made. An ultra violet ray machine made it possible to treat sickly infants; a pathological laboratory was set up; a wing was added for general medicine and one for venereal diseases—the front, garrisoned with soldiers, was not far away—another for prophylaxis and yet another for gynaecology.

Until then the birth of babies had been left to the care, more often than not improvised, of midwives lacking the technical means for difficult cases—and there was a lack of hygiene in the peasants' homes. The Catalan surgeon started a campaign among his colleagues in other villages to send women about to give birth to the hospital where they would be better looked after as well as the baby, who would not be the victim of the customary lack of medical care.

A consultation service was organised and patients from all parts attended daily.

Apart from a minority of about 5%, the small landowners, who lived tolerably well before the revolution, retained their way of life and were respected throughout the canton so long as they did not keep more land than they were themselves able to cultivate. The exchanges section provided them with a special cash book in which were entered debits and credits on facing pages. Dates, quality and quantities and value of goods delivered and received by them were entered and thus provided an immediate record for both parties as to their liquidity. Anyway they could not exceed the rations allowed to everybody. Which did not imply a vexatious measure against them, since they had the right to take part in the collectivist assemblies where the quotas were established. They had furthermore, and this was more or less general, the right to make use of technical working materials at the disposal of the Collective.

Among the work carried out for the improvement of sanitation, apart from cowsheds built outside the village, was the draining of a swamp covering some 20 hectares. This swamp, which harboured colonies of mosquitoes and foul gases, belonged to a large number of small proprietors each of whom owned a strip but who did nothing with it, since their lack of technical resources prevented them from undertaking the work of improvement. The Collective drained, levelled, sowed and harvested this former swamp and the yields were higher than average.

One must however recognise that there is not an infallible conscience among all men and women who make up the population of the collectivised villages. From time to time one comes across human weaknesses. I remember a discussion between a woman of about fifty and a much younger comrade who was in charge of supervising work and housing arrangements. She lived with her husband, son, daughter-in-law and their children and wanted to change house: "My daughter has become unbearable," she declared. "I want to live on my own, as we don't get on."

The comrade, whose name was Turmo—with the soul of a child, the courage of a lion, and a voice of thunder—strove like the devil against the artful woman who didn't lose her calm, but had in the end to retreat grumbling. I then asked Turmo why he had not given in. He explained that the proportion of salaries being higher for each person when the families consist of a small number of people, some large families wanted to split up in order to receive more money, even though their calculation was wrong. And it was a fact that there was not enough accommodation available and it would be necessary to wait a long time before more could be built in view of the numbers of conscripts who had been sent to the front which had been stabilised some forty kilometres away.

It was a small matter; there were others, and the organisers of the Collectives had to cope with them calmly or with a sense of humour, and it was impossible not to have admiration for these men so full of self-sacrifice who, as determined constructors, did things so quickly and well. For in Binefar, as in general among the Aragonese Collectives, not one cog in the general organisational wheel failed, neither in the workshops, nor in the distributive system, nor in work in the fields. I travelled many times on the Tamarite-Binefar road. On one occasion, with a doctor who had also come from Barcelona, we passed by car alongside the fields sown with cereals, planted with vines and olive trees, where the market gardens and orchards alternated with the golden crops. I was pointing out all this to my companion. "These kilometres of plantations and cultivations where nothing has been neglected belong to the Collective," I told him with pride. Two days later I pointed out to him in Esplus where I had accompanied him for the organisation of his work, other vast plantations, this time of potatoes, and more vines, and on the way I repeated to him almost with fervour before the miracle of this revolution that had at last been realised: "It's the Collective, the Collective that has done this!"

*

The brigade led by the communist Lister was soon to abandon the front to go and destroy "manu militari" almost all the Aragonese Collectives, including that of Binefar and its canton. Many of their organisers, such as the Blanco brothers, were murdered, or seriously injured. The estates were handed back to the landowners and the hospital was completely ransacked.

4. Andorra (Teruel)

Andorra covered an area of 25,600 hectares. Its 3,337 inhabitants were divided into 909 families. Large landed property was unknown. The richest worked just as did the poorest, and only one proprietor owned four draught animals. The average was two. At the bottom of the social scale, families possessed a donkey and helped each other to work the land and gather the corn.

Once again, in Spain—as in many other countries in the world—the land area is not necessarily a guarantee of wealth. There is hardly any rainfall in the region of Andorra. Therefore extensive cultivation mainly of wheat, grapes[20] and olives. Barley, oats and rye were of secondary importance. The few irrigated

20 In terms of must, the average yield per hectare from the vineyards was 60% less than in France.

areas were irrigated only for short periods. In drought years the springs dry up and no water comes down from the mountains. Add to this the sudden frosts which so often destroy plants and fruit blossom, and hail which in 1937 reduced the olive harvest from an average of 28,000 sacks to 6,000. If the individualist landed proprietors had been in control Andorra would have probably become one more *despoblado* (depopulated area).

These climatic conditions obliged 300 families to live in large run down shanties called farms dotted in the mountains. The remainder of the population spent eight months of the year there. In the event, the village was almost always underpopulated. People would return on Saturday night and go off on Monday morning, pushing forward their donkey which was loaded with bread, wine, oil, beans, chick peas, potatoes, dried cod and pork meat—in other words, the food they had bought for the week.

There was however a social category even more poverty stricken, below the lowest rung in the social ladder; they were the disinherited who worked under lease land belonging to widows, old people, spinsters, the doctor, the chemist, some landowners who were crippled or unable to work their lands. These farmers, who were *medieros*, received only a half of the harvest produced by their work.

Two-thirds of the land was cultivated, but one must bear in mind that at least a half of dry lands in Spain was left fallow. In Andorra, even with chemical fertilisers and the manure produced by the large number of livestock, the land had to rest one year out of two or three.

On the poor pastures which with rocks cover a third of the area, about 13,000 sheep and 2,000 goats were reared. The animals were sold to other regions. The peasants hardly ever ate meat.[21] They would sell their corn to local monopolist buyers who naturally earned much more than them.

Until 1931, the Right wing monarchists were triumphant at the elections. But after the downfall of King Alfonso XIIIth, the Republican Left was on top. In July 1936, its local section boasted as many as 450 supporters. The workers' movement was born painfully and had to feel its way step by step. The C.N.T. and U.G.T. had a small nucleus of sympathisers; in

21 In general in Spain, the herdsmen and shepherds only ate meat when a lamb had been half devoured by the wolves or a sheep had fallen over a precipice and had been killed or badly injured.

1932 both formed a Syndicate. The lack of social experience of the militants and workers resulted in both Syndicates disappearing that same year. On May 1, 1936 a second double attempt was made. And each Syndicate had 15 members when the revolution erupted.

On four occasions fascists who had come from other regions succeeded in being masters of the village. Driven back four times, they finally withdrew altogether—at least they had not returned at the time of my visit. A revolutionary Committee was nominated, for here too the initiative had to come from the village, the State apparatus having broken down and the government having completely lost contact with the inhabitants in general.

The Committee consisted of three members each from the Republican Left, the U.G.T. and C.N.T. This generous treatment of the Syndicates could be explained both by the broadmindedness of the local political faction and by the growing desire of the people for the new revolutionary solutions. The change was such that the Republican Left by May 1937 had only 80 members left whereas the U.G.T. had 340, the young socialists 160, the C.N.T. 220, and the libertarian youth 100.

The local Collective, which at the time of my enquiry included all the village and the whole population, was constituted on November 1, 1936, when on the combined initiative of the three forces mentioned, the revolutionary Committee called a general assembly at which republican socialists and libertarians spoke in favour of the new social organisation. Approval was unanimous. The individualists were allowed freedom of action, but there was not a single one.

At the beginning, the revolutionary Committee was entrusted with the administration of the Collective. Then when the municipal Council had been reorganised by orders of the Valencia government, it was entrusted with the task under eight councillors and a secretary. Shortly afterwards, and to ensure the complete freedom of the Collective, an administrative Commission was constituted of the latter and it was this Commission which assumed the vital responsibilities concerning local activity. It was divided into five sections: chairmanship and treasury, distribution and food supplies, industry and commerce, agricultural production and livestock, and finally public works which included education. Two sections each were in the hands of the U.G.T.

and C.N.T. and one was held by the Republican Left.

For the organisation of agriculture, the territory was divided into four farm groups. In each of these farms lived a group of families and workers who went on going down to the village on the Saturday night and returning to the mountain on the Monday morning.

A perusal of the rules concerning them will allow one to see how these workers organised and directed their activities:

"1. Workers in each farm group will name a delegate and an assistant-delegate with a view to ensuring the smooth running of the work to be done.

"2. The delegate will be entrusted with the organisation of work, naturally in agreement with the comrades on the farms.

"3. The delegate must know at all times where the farm comrades are working and what work they are doing.

"4. He will also be entrusted with the preparation of the equipment and the farm machinery required, always in consultation with the work delegation which will give all necessary instructions in writing.

"5. It will also be the delegate's task to supervise the work being done on the farms, and to enter in the book with which he will be provided all the produce delivered by each farm, and all that the Collective hands over: that is to say the various outgoings and goods received.

"6. When products are supplied to a farm, the delegate of the farm concerned will be expected to call at the work delegation to make a return.

"7. When a farm comrade has to absent himself for personal reasons or because of illness, he must inform the delegate; if the comrade does not give notice of his absence, the delegate will report the fact to the work delegation.

"8. When for health reasons, or for any other reason, a delegate will not be able to carry out his tasks, the workers of the farm groups will choose another, and if they do not succeed, then the work delegation will make the choice for them.

"9. In the event of illness, or unavoidable absence of any kind, the delegate's post will be filled by the assistant-delegate who will take over the supervision of work.

Additional Article—In all matters concerning the grazing of the herds, cultivation for forage, and similar questions, the farm delegate will get together with those who are looking after the animals and with the shepherds who are working in the same area in order to ensure efficient administration and mutual aid.

If for reasons beyond his control a shepherd cannot release his herd, a comrade from the farm will do it for him and the delegate for livestock will look for another shepherd."

One sees that work was the major preoccupation, dominating and imposing its law on everything; there was no place in the rules for the demand for personal freedom or for the autonomy of the individual. Work, production, solidarity are in the forefront. This awareness of responsibilities determined the conduct and activities of everyone.

Every Saturday night the farm delegates met with the general work delegate, and put in their requirements for materials and foodstuffs; the accounts of receipts and outgoings would be checked; thus each farm knew, day by day, the balance of its activities.

More than 200 men were at the front, 53 were working in a lignite mine that had only been operated since the revolution started; another 80 were due to leave for the army. In such conditions it was not surprising that there had not been an increase in cereal sowings in 1937 over the previous year, but the potato planting acreage had shown an increase of 80% and in addition 100,000 lettuces and 20,000 tomato plants were grown as well as many other vegetables in large quantities.

Previously, these cultivations were on a minute scale; the fact is that under the system of private property, the initiative of one person, however good, more often remains just with the one person, whereas in the Collective the new spirit and the new methods encourage everybody very soon to take initiatives. In Andorra the general concept, and methods used in agriculture were rudimentary. The creative spirit of all enriched it and especially since there was no longer the fear of difficulties in disposing of the produce grown.

Efforts were also being made to solve the water problem to develop the market gardening side of their activities. It involved prospecting for it and acquiring the engines and pumps that would be needed to raise the water from the deep land depressions which surround the village. The small proprietor could have never undertaken such a task which was outside his sphere of action and beyond his means and experience.

[125]

Collective work and mentality produce miracles. I saw the first, modest start on water pipe laying being carried out by unemployed tailors—no one was ever idle and as was customary the sections helped each other. In a few years' time, the enthusiastic collectivists told me, Andorra would have enough water to irrigate hundreds of hectares and fill reservoirs which would allow them to deal with the periods of drought: but that if the Collective was destroyed this great work would be impossible, and each peasant would return to the bitter poverty of the past.

The livestock was distributed among the mountain farms by two delegates who directed the distribution of the herds and the steps to be taken according to the quality of the pasture and the supervision the animals required.

Each trade had a single workshop. As in Fraga and Binefar, a collectivist needing anything out of the ordinary, asked the administrative Commission to have it made for him. He would then be given a voucher to take to the delegate of the workshop which undertook to make it. On receipt of the finished article he would pay the administrative Commission for it.

Local currency was printed, and a scale of wages based on the size of families. A single person received 2.25 pesetas a day; two adults received 4.50 pesetas, three adults 6 pesetas, four adults 7 pesetas, five adults 8 and beyond that at the rate of one peseta per person whether the members of the family were able to work or not.

Where there were two producers in a family, 1.50 pesetas was added to the base wage; where there were three they added 3 pesetas and for four producers 4 pesetas. According to these principles the individual claims of each worker demanding "the full product of his labour" (the early slogan of collectivism) and the wage-bargaining drive of traditional syndicalism had disappeared. What was being practised was a "one for all and all for one" in which everybody was interdependent, and each earned, all things considered, enough to live on.

Housing, electric light, hairdressing saloons, medical care, pharmaceutical products which by June 1937 had already cost 16,000 pesetas, were free, as also was bread which was unrationed. Eighteen litres of olive oil were distributed per person per year. Meat which was earmarked for the militia and for consumption by city dwellers was rationed to 100 grammes a day—in spite of the large herds. Austerity was in the make-up of the Spaniard from the Interior. All these consumer goods were distributed in the communal shops. One was reserved for oil, soap and wine; another for bread; another for butcher's meat in the former orphanage (there were no more orphans in Andorra or in any other collectivised village: all children without parents found a family). Seven tailors made clothes for the workers who had until then very rarely bought clothes. When in the past did a shepherd ever possess clothes made to measure?

When one comes to the question of education, need one say that it was not neglected. Until July 1936 the school was installed in a dark and filthy building. Yet, six months earlier a new building had been completed but local politics, as filthy and obscure as the old school building, prevented it being used. The Collective did not lose a day, and started classes there immediately.

Education was made compulsory effectively. The new order would not allow parents to keep children of school age at home. Consequently the number of pupils increased dramatically. Some sixty young shepherds between 12 and 14 years of age who came down to the village two or three times a year, who were born and raised among the sheep, the goats, the dogs and the wolves, were moved into the village and, when I was there, were attending classes at the school and obviously enjoying it. Two new classes were started and many books purchased for them from specialist publishers in Catalonia and the Levante.

The nursery school groups also increased in number. Out of eight men and women teachers the State paid for three, the Collective for five. But it did not limit its contribution to supplying the means. It also supervised the work of the teachers. One of them, stupid though qualified, complained that the heavy hand was no longer tolerated. It was a revelation.

*

I want to mention separately the mine in Andorra. The province of Teruel is fairly rich in lignite. During the first World War it was used to replace the coal imports from Britain, which normally supplied most of the needs of the town of Saragossa. In 1937 with practically the whole of anti-fascist Spain cut off from the Asturias, the main carboniferous zone which was occupied by Franco's armies, there was a shortage of coal. It was natural to think of increasing the production of lignite in the Teruel zone. Equally natural that the government had not thought of it. So, the miners and the peasants continued or undertook the exploitation of the mines.

In November 1936, seven miners who had already worked in the region, began to dig at a spot near Andorra on a hunch that deposits were there. With picks and shovels they dug three workings 50 metres deep. In 1937 when I was there, their numbers had increased to 53 and they were planning for more. No machines apart from a motor pump to remove water that was seeping through everywhere, or sometimes appeared suddenly as a water-spout from old wells that had been dug centuries ago at the time of the Roman or Arab occupations.

With their feet stuck in the mud and their hearts in the clouds, these peasants turned miners continued, in spite of the harmful gases released by the explosions from the dynamite charges (there was no system for ventilation), to extract the lignite from this improvised mine. Working conditions were so bad that there were always seven or eight of them hospitalised. But when they came out, after inadequate treatment, they would resume their work with pick and shovel.

This method of extraction produced only 30 tons of lignite a day. In the Asturian mines, poor compared with those in other countries but rich compared with those of Teruel, the average output per miner per day was of the order of 400-450 kilos. And they had at their disposal infinitely superior technical means.[22] Though here they lacked the equipment and the seams were even poorer, yet the average output was 525 kilos for miners who for the most part were inexperienced. Blessed solidarity! Blessed devotion to duty! "We are only at the preparatory stage, in a short time we will be supplying coal in large quantities"—said the man in charge, as if he had to make excuses.

But what with the water that seeped from the walls and the roof of the working that I visited, and the fact that I knew that they had had to stop work for some weeks to dry out the bottom and remove the danger of landslips, I could not but ask myself with anxiety whether this wonderful optimism would not be destroyed by some horrible tragedy. But our improvised miners were not concerned; they were supplying fuel which kept several factories running in Catalonia, and they were helping the Collective.

22 Nevertheless, the shallowness of the seams did not allow of the use of coal-cutting equipment as used in the Ruhr and in Pennsylvania.

It is true they received extra pay compared with their comrades in other jobs; one kilo of soap a week, a pair of canvas shoes a month, and a pair of overalls . . .!

5. Alcorisa

First of all I want to say something about Jaime Segovia. He deserves it, or rather his memory deserves it for he paid with his life for his support of the finest human ideal, and for his devotion to the cause of the workers, the exploited and the defeated.

For those who know the Spanish language really well and the profound meaning of words, this name and forename have echoes from far off Castilian nobility. In fact my comrade and friend descended from an old aristocratic family. And on his face along with the goodness and intelligence there was also a worn look of the "end of a breed", of human stock in the process of degeneration.

By the age of twenty-one he was a lawyer. Though his ancestral fortune had been broken into and divided from generation to generation, his real estate at the beginning of 1936 was still worth half a million pesetas which represented quite a tidy fortune. With his land he could exploit peasants and profit handsomely from his university qualifications; but he despised even the thought of such an eventuality. Our comrades seemed to him to be people who interpreted life in the most sensible way and were closer to human truth. Rejecting the worldly hypocrisies to support what he felt was most worthy, he moved towards them. And when the revolution exploded he brought to it all his wealth and energy.

Alcorisa, in the province of Teruel, had 4,000 inhabitants. It is the centre of nineteen villages. The land there is not as poor as elsewhere, irrigation was sufficient and economically the people were privileged compared with the rest of the canton. There were few landowners, and there were even fewer farmers. The large *terratenientes* also owned estates elsewhere. Industry— flour and oil mills, soap, lemonade, soda-water factories and sulphur production—employed only 5% of available labour. The badly paid day-labourers dominated numerically.

Our Syndicate was the only one able to establish itself there and it went back to 1917. It suffered setbacks and persecution such as were experienced in many other villages. And as everywhere else our militants persisted in the struggle. Their efforts succeeded.

In the first place Alcorisa fell into the hands of the fascists, but was retaken at the end of a week by a column organised by our comrades in the mountains where they had taken refuge, and which forced the Civil Guard and those it was protecting to withdraw in the direction of Teruel. Instead of disbanding, this column reinforced itself. Combatants from other villages joined them, armed with revolvers and pistols (often quite ancient), old shot guns or with arms taken from the Civil Guard, with bombs hastily and crudely assembled. Then without any kind of military discipline, they set off to the other sectors of the Aragon front to fight the well armed, equipped and disciplined fascist forces.

From the moment Alcorisa was retaken, a local defence *Comité* was organised composed of two each from the C.N.T., the Republican Left, the Republican Alliance and the Anarchist Federation (F.A.I.). And the next day on the same basis a "Central Administrative *Comité*" was nominated.

So far as economic questions were concerned this *Comité* had only one alternative: either to leave things as they were— respect private commerce, allow the politically suspect tradespeople to sabotage the stability of the new order, and the well-to-do to secure for themselves three or four times as much food as could those who were not—or control everything so that nobody lacked anything, and prevent economic chaos resulting in solutions favourable to fascism. The *Comité* chose the latter.

In the first place, it was necessary to establish a control, supervise the movement of foodstuffs and the sale of the normal consumer goods, which could not be done if every tradesman could dispose of goods as he wished. Free trade in the bourgeois sense of the word was therefore abolished. Neither could one leave each family to buy on the sole basis of the means at their disposal. Complete equality started with consumption.

Then the struggle, the departure of 500 men for the front, the solidarity which united the inhabitants in that period of collective exhilaration, created other problems. The crop had to be brought in, but no one was going to harvest with scythes and sickles whilst the mechanical harvesters belonging to the rich were lying idle. Three days after the *Comité* was formed a meeting of all the agricultural workers decided on the organisation of 23 teams each of which named its delegate and shared out the machinery and the tasks. Socialism was born there as elsewhere, very simply, almost without an awareness of the extent and significance of the task being undertaken.

Three weeks after the victory, the 23 improvised sections were definitively constituted, on the basis of a detailed division of the municipal territory. Account was taken of the characteristics of the soil, the kinds of cultivation to be undertaken, the numerical importance of the population, the varieties and numbers of livestock, and the technical means at their disposal. And by taking this course, the tendency, a year later, was to make each of these sections into an economic unit which was as complete as possible, though always based on collective activity duly coordinated.

In due course the Collective was definitively constituted. The following were the main Articles which were more complex, because more erudite, than those of other Collectives which did not have jurists at their head:

"Property in goods—Personal and real estate as well as machinery, tools, money, credits provided by the workers' only Syndicate, by the Municipal Council and by the members of the Collective, will constitute the property in goods.

Usufruct—The Collective will hold in usufruct the assets that will be handed over to it by the Municipal Council and by the defence *Comité* in order to use them to advantage, including those which are provisionally handed over either because, for reasons of age or illness, their owners cannot make use of them, or because they have been abandoned by the owners.

Members of the Collective—All the members of the single Syndicate of workers will be considered as founder members of the Collective; all who join later will be equally accepted as members. They will be admitted by a decision of the Assembly. All requests will have to be accompanied by a statement of the applicant's political antecedents and a list of the applicant's property.

Withdrawal—Any member of the Collective can withdraw of his own accord; but the assembly reserves the right to express its views on the reasons given for withdrawal, and when such reasons do not appear to be valid, the resigner will not be entitled to the return of the goods and property he brought to the Collective. Also anyone expelled from the Collective loses the right to demand the return of what he handed over at the time of joining.

Administration—The administration of the Collective will be entrusted to a commission of five members of whom one will deal with food supplies, another with agriculture, a third with labour, one for public education, and finally a general secretary."

Other Articles followed on the role of the general Assembly, the rights and duties of the Collectivists, the conditions for dissolution, etc.

One feels here the influence of two lawyers—for with Jaime Segovia there was another, an equally good organiser whose name escapes me—who worked with our peasant comrades. In the statutes of other Collectives one finds less juridical language and knowledge, but more practical and human substance.

Successive general assemblies took the decisions on which the Collective in Alcorisa was operating when I visited it. By their decision the 23 agricultural delegates met weekly to organise the work in the fields.

They made original innovations for distribution. Firstly, they had introduced completely free consumption as best reflecting the principles of libertarian communism. All that each family had to do was to appear before the administrative *Comité* and ask for, and receive, a voucher requiring those in charge of foodstores to supply the voucher holder with his/her requirements of oil, potatoes, fresh and dry vegetables, clothing, etc. At the time only meat and wine were rationed but two months later everything had to be rationed.

No formalities were required to go free of charge to the cinema, the cafe (where lemonade was the only drink available), the barber or the hairdresser, or even to receive one's share of the small quantity of tobacco that could be obtained during the war.

But I was told there were abuses and for some articles the demand far exceeded supplies. So for three months they experimented with a local money which was used exclusively for purchasing clothing, shoes, household utensils, coffee and tobacco. A man had a peseta a day, a woman 70 cents and a child over 14 years 40 cents . . . no doubt *"para vicios"* ("to indulge one's weaknesses") as they would say in the North of Aragon.

A list was printed. It stipulated what each individual could receive on the basis of the food situation. The following rations were maintained until November 1936 (bearing in mind that a large proportion of foodstuffs was sent to the front):

Meat 100 grammes a day; bread 500; sugar, rice, dried beans 40; a half-litre of wine; and 1 tin of sardines per week. In addition everyone was entitled to half a kilo of salt, one kilo of soap, two bluebags for the washing, a broom and half a litre of lye per month.

But this solution did not satisfy the libertarians in Alcorisa, nor even the republicans who were libertarians by temperament, and had all joined the C.N.T. after having dissolved the local section of their party. It seemed too rigid, unintentionally vexatious, to oblige people to consume what was imposed on them or leave it.

On the other hand the prime movers of the Collective wanted at all costs to avoid a return to the monetary system, to accursed "money". Many of them including Jaime Segovia racked their brains for days to find a new solution. And what they came up with was a points system which operated in the following manner:

The 500 grammes of bread were worth $4\frac{1}{2}$ points and 100 grammes of meat 5, therefore $66\frac{1}{2}$ points per week. All the remaining items, soap, beans, pasta, wine, etc. were also allocated points. On that basis a man was entitled to 450 points, a single woman to 375 and a married woman to 362, and a child to 167 from birth.

Within these limits each family, each individual, could spend as they thought fit their allocation of points, consuming more meat and less dried beans, more wine and less oil, etc. . . . An excessive consumption is thereby avoided while at the time respecting everybody's freedom of choice.

For footwear, clothing and household goods a separate accounting was maintained. Calculation in money terms had disappeared and was replaced by a special booklet on the first page of which was indicated the points entitlement for each family for goods other than food. Thus 24 points for household utensils per person per year, 60 points for footwear, 120 for clothing, etc. . . .

As well as its general store, Alcorisa had four collectivised grocers, a shop called a textile cooperative, a haberdasher's, four magnificent, clean, butcher's shops for the inhabitants to get their supplies. Everything else was also distributed in specially organised shops where the purchases of each family would be entered in the general register with a view to attempting a detailed study of the trends in consumption, and ensuring an accountancy so detailed that it could be checked over at any time. If a member of the Collective were to lose his card then what he had consumed and what he was still entitled to, could be ascertained without delay.

We have seen that children were entitled to 167 points from birth. And their points cards had an additional ration of soap and lye, 100 grammes of meat and pasta. These substantial foods were obviously not intended for the newly born babies but for the mother, who could also dispose of the points as she wished.

Alcorisa felt the effects of the absence of the 500 men at the front. Nevertheless the cultivated area was increased by 50%. Such a large increase was possible only because some of the fields which normally would have been fallow were ploughed and sowed. The task was facilitated by the purchase of excellent ploughs which had rarely been used in the past. Furthermore, greater use was made that year of chemical fertilisers than previously, with the result that the future for agriculture was bright.

The redoubled efforts by everybody also contributed. Not only by the men who had remained but also by the women, as well as by those militiamen who regularly sent half their pay to the Collective.[23]

Changes were made to some activities. A church was transformed into a cinema, and a convent into a school. Two competing garages were reduced to one which was quite sufficient for the needs, and in the other they set up a well organised hairdressing saloon and a small shoe factory in which all the machinery from all the previously dispersed workshops was assembled. Good shoes, and sandals both for the people of Alcorisa and of neighbouring villages were being produced there. The person in charge had been a reactionary employer, therefore potentially a Franco supporter. But he had only been expropriated. When I spoke with him he told me that he had been convinced of the advantages of socialised production, for working with the old individualist system output was a third of what it now was.

One factory newly set up was supplying the whole region and some of the militiamen on the Teruel front with salt provisions. There was one tailor's workshop, one carpenter's shop and a blacksmith's belonging to the Collective. The building workers who got ready a fine building for the Syndicate also did repair work to houses at no charge to the occupants. The lye, lemonade

23 The Republican government paid militiamen ten pesetas a day which was the equivalent of a good average wage in the towns.

and soda-water were all made in one establishment. A hotel was organised and a stud farm set up where selected horses and donkeys were sent with a view to rapidly improving the non-bovine draught animals in Alcorisa and in the surrounding country. Finally, a fine, clean, healthy herd of cows was housed in a single cowhouse.

As everywhere else there were in Alcorisa classes within the classes, poor amongst the poor, outcasts among the outcasts of fortune. And the income of all the small proprietors had not been the same; and some workers earned less than some favoured peasants, as did a labourer compared with a skilled worker, or a shepherd compared with a labourer. The Collective transformed everything, guaranteeing to everybody the same means of life.

The recalcitrant smallholders in Alcorisa (there were about a hundred in all), as in all other villages living under the new regime, could not trade in their produce. They had to deliver it to the municipal Council, entirely composed of members of the C.N.T., and were paid with money specially created for their use. But so far as consumption was concerned they were subjected to rationing as applied to everybody. After all one was at war.

The villages in the canton of Alcorisa engaged in a system of compensatory mutual aid as was the case in the other regions of Aragon and Spain where Collectives had been established, and actual barter arrangements extended to 118 towns and villages in Aragon, Levante, Catalonia and even in Castile.

In the early days as a result of the vicissitudes of the armed struggle, the teaching arrangements had been insufficient. There were only two schools in July, 1936. Jaime Segovia had to improvise as a teacher while they were waiting for qualified teachers to join them from the towns. The cost of education was borne by the local administration.

This same administration was responsible for providing accommodation and furniture for all new domestic set-ups. Legal marriage had completely disappeared, but unions were officially recorded in a book in the town hall.

Alcorisa was not one of the worst but neither was it a model village in Aragon. The houses there were oldish, and the narrow streets, sometimes encased between boulders, made expansion of the inhabitable area difficult. Our comrades had plans and a start had been made—one could clearly discern Jaime Segovia's spirit of initiative in all this—to create within the municipal boundaries twenty-three units. It was hoped that each unit would have its owns means of existence, with in addition agricultural production, livestock and poultry, all the means for comfort and the cultivation of the mind; electricity, swimming pool, radio, library, games, etc. Already at the time small waterfalls were being used to generate electricity for lighting.

I visited the unit where work was most advanced. The area had been divided into two: one intended for agriculture, the other for stock raising. It covered eight square kilometres. In the former cereals, vegetables, fruit, grapes, hay and lucerne were produced; all that one would normally expect from good land, good husbandry and good irrigation. In the latter, the initial effort had resulted in the construction of a vast concrete piggery with divisions permitting the individual housing of 100 animals which, as in Graus, all had individual access to the open air. Work on expanding the accommodation was about to start and the fact of this specialisation indicated that economic relations, of other kinds too, had to be maintained between the twenty-three libertarian phalansteries.

The rearing of lambs was also increased and large numbers of heifers were purchased here and there and the project was to construct in one of the units a cowhouse to accommodate some hundred cows. As to poultry, rabbits, etc. . . . they were concentrating on increasing rabbit production as there was an abundance of suitable food for them.

When Franco's troops arrived in Alcorisa, Jaime Segovia who would not leave, was arrested, tortured, and at the end of six months, shot.

6. Mas de las Matas

To the north of the province of Teruel, Mas de las Matas is the chief village of the canton bearing its name, and comprises 19 villages. It had 2,300 inhabitants. The most important of the surrounding localities were Aguaviva with 2,000 inhabitants, Mirambel (1,400), La Ginebrosa (1,300). Only six villages were entirely collectivised by May 1937, four were almost completely, and for five others collectivisation was 50%. Three others were about to collectivise and only one village was hesitating. Very soon all the villages were 100% collectivised.

Here the libertarian movement preceded the syndicalist movement. Smallholdings were widespread, and did not favour the emergence of associations of wage earners. And in Mas de las Matas where thanks to irrigation life was relatively comfortable compared with the surrounding villages which were more or less without water and life was hard, libertarian ideas took root from the beginnings of the century. Not so much on class issues as for reasons of human conscience. If groups were started to fight against the exploitation of man by man, for equality and social justice and against subjection by the State, their inspiration was above all humanist. It was the last generation of these men who were at the head of the collectivist organisation of the canton.

Under the monarchy liberal tendencies predominated. The Republic of 1931 brought about some changes, so mild that they disappointed most of the population. The result was that they tended towards the revolutionary Left; in 1932 the first C.N.T. Syndicate was created and on the 8th December of the same year, in an insurrectional coup which covered Aragon and a large part of Catalonia, libertarian communism was proclaimed. The Civil Guard, at the orders of the republic as it had previously been in the service of the monarchy, put down this first attempt in two days, and the Syndicate was closed until the eve of the legislative elections in February, 1936 which gave victory to the Popular Front. The Syndicate was then immediately reconstituted.

Five months later the local fascists were defeated without a struggle and towards mid-September our comrades launched the idea of an agrarian Collective. The initiative was accepted unanimously at a meeting of the Syndicate. But not all the smallholders were members of the Syndicate. It was therefore necessary to set up a separate group. A list of those who had already joined of their own accord was circulated and within a fortnight 200 families had joined. At the time of my visit the number had risen to 550 out of a total of 600 families comprising the population of the village. The remaining 50 families belonged to the socialist U.G.T. and obeyed the instructions issued by their leaders.

Throughout the canton the same principle was applied. One

was free to join the Collective or to carry on cultivating the land
individually. The various stages of socialisation achieved by the
different villages was proof of this freedom of choice.

In none of these villages was there a written list of rules.
Simply each month the assembly of members of each Collective
would indicate to the Commission consisting of five elected
members, the general lines to follow on specific problems that
had been openly discussed.

In spite of that, my recollection of Mas de las Matas is linked,
quite unconsciously, to the happy Icaria to which the utopians,
and especially Etienne Cabet, have often referred. The faces and
the behaviour of the people, the attitude of the women seated
on the thresholds of their homes, or knitting and talking outside
their houses, were peaceful and happy. One guessed that underlying it was a good way of life. Let us seek to discover what
it was.

In Mas de las Matas 32 groups of workers were set up; they
were more or less of the same size, determined by the tasks to
be undertaken, or the extent of the agricultural areas to be
worked which were limited by their capricious encirclement by
the mountains. Each group cultivated some of the irrigated land
and some of the dry lands. Thus the pleasant and less pleasant,
heavy, work was equitably shared by everybody.

The blessings of water made it possible to grow large quantities
of vegetables and fruit. The other, less fortunate, villages could
only grow cereals, mainly corn—9 quintals per hectare, perhaps
less—and olives. In all the Collectives of the canton the groups
of workers chose their delegates, and nominated their administrative
Commissions. And just as the delegates in Mas de las Matas who
always set the example, met weekly to organise the work to be
done, a similar procedure was adopted in the other collectivised
villages. As everywhere, efforts were constantly being coordinated.

At the time of my visit it had not been found possible to
increase the area under cultivation. Full use was already being
made of the irrigated lands. But the dry land which had hitherto
been used only for grazing livestock, were earmarked for growing
cereals and to this end they had started to fold the sheep on the
mountain slopes, now freely available, where there was enough
vegetation to feed them. At the same time a start was made to
get ready the land for sowing corn, oats and rye. It is one
of the many examples of the rational organisation of the economy
which we so frequently encountered. It was in fact thought that

the effort would be intensified once the conscripts returned.

It was an easier matter to increase the herds. The numbers of sheep were increased by 25%; breeding sows doubled from 30 to 60, and milch cows from 18 to 24 (there was no suitable pasture in the area for cattle). A large number of piglets were purchased in Catalonia and were distributed among the population, since there was no time or labour to construct collective piggeries, the work on which, however, was due to start at any moment. Meantime each family raised one or two pigs which would be slaughtered in one large operation and salted and then distributed on the basis of the needs of each household.

But production was not limited to agriculture and livestock. In this chief village of the canton, as in all collectivised chief-villages and villages of any size, small industries sprang up: building, boot and shoe making, the manufacture of clothing and slippers, meat processing, etc. . . . As in Graus and many other places, these specialities constituted a section of what was called the "general Collective" which operated for the general good.

If then the agrarian section needed to purchase certain tools it would apply, through its delegate, to the administrative Commission which would then issue him with a voucher for the delegate of the metal workers to whom their requirements were explained. The order was at the same time entered in the account book of the engineering section. If a family needed furniture they would also get in touch with the administrative section who would hand them an order voucher for the delegate of the cabinet makers, or the carpenters (woodworkers all belonged to a single Syndicate). Such was the mechanism by which the activities of each group of producers was checked as well as the expenditure by each family.

Neither official currency (pesetas) nor local money was used by any Collectives in the canton.

Socialisation of commerce was one of the first stages. But it was not complete. At the time of my visit there were still two recalcitrant grocers whose businesses were in a bad way because of a lack of supplies. But generally speaking municipal stores also replaced the former system of distribution.

Let us look more closely into the functioning of a collectivised village. It is difficult to describe adequately by the written word this large scale movement which comprises agrarian socialisation. In Mas de las Matas as in every collectivised village one was confronted by red and black placards affixed not only to all the workshops, communal stores, hotels and so on but also to the cantonal warehouses for chemical products, cement, raw materials for the various industries, where the collectivists from other cantonal villages came to replenish their stocks in accordance with the norms established by their delegates at fraternal meetings. In the shop of a former well-to-do fascist tradesman who disappeared there were stacks of clothing intended for the inhabitants of the canton. Elsewhere was the section for general supplies where vouchers were supplied to individualists on request and also where requests by each family were entered on a card index.

In the cantonal distillery—a new initiative—they were extracting alcohol and tartaric acid from the residues of grapes sent there from all the villages. And those villages had set up an administrative Commission for the distillery which met periodically. When one visited the factory one would be shown the technical improvements introduced to produce 90° alcohol which was required in medicine and for surgical operations at the front.

In the tailor's workshop, men and women workers were engaged in cutting and making suits to measure for comrades who had ordered them. On the racks, wool or corduroy garments, each with its label bearing the name of the consignee were waiting to be dealt with on the sewing machines.[24]

Women bought their meat in a well appointed, marble lined establishment. Bread which was formerly baked at home by the overworked housewives was being kneaded and baked in the collective bakehouses.

At the café everybody was entitled to have two cups of roasted chicory (that was all there was), two refreshments, or two lemonades, daily.

On a visit to the surroundings one would discover a nursery where vegetable seedlings were being raised, in huge quantities for planting out throughout the canton, by a family who previously had prospered in this business but who had joined the Collective right from the beginning.

In the dressmaking workshop not only were women's clothes made up but, as in many other villages, young women were learning to sew for themselves and their families to be.

24 For a family consisting of mother and father and two children between the ages of 6 and 14, an annual clothes allowance of 280 pesetas was made. This represented twice or three times the amount a peasant family would have spent on clothes previously.

A placard attracts one's attention. It reads: "Popular Bookshop". It is in fact a library. On its shelves were from six to ten copies of different works of sociology, literature, general works on cultural and scientific subjects made available to everybody, including the individualists. There were also to be found in large numbers text books for schools (history, geography, arithmetic), story books, novels, and readers for the young and for adults; then there were exercise books, and excellent printed courses for learning how to draw, with excellent examples to follow based on the most modern teaching techniques.

Here too, though the spirit and practice of general solidarity inspired the conduct and behaviour of each and all, every family was allocated a small plot of land on which to grow vegetables and fruit and to raise rabbits. This supplemented the food supply arrangements which in any case were not rigid; things were so arranged that everybody had a choice. Thus rationing was not synonymous with bureaucratic conformity.

The scale for consumption—foodstuffs, clothing, footwear, etc.— had previously been marked on the family *carnet*. But following the resolution of the Congress in Caspe, it was thought preferable to use the standard booklet produced by the regional Federation of Collectives for all the Collectives, in order to avoid excessive differences depending on the relative prosperity or poverty of the villages and even of the cantons.

When therefore clothing was also rationed it was not because in this part of Aragon the Collectives lacked the necessary resources to buy them. They generally had enough goods, especially corn, to barter for cloth, machines and all that was produced in Catalonia, where manufacturing industries predominated. But things were strained by the war effort. And furthermore the value of the corn, meat, vegetables and oil supplied without payment to support those on the fighting front was enormous. Supplies, without payment, were also sent to Madrid which was besieged by the Francoist armies. It was also a fact that some industrial regions badly socialised or lacking raw materials to produce certain goods, could not honour the barter arrangements made.

Medical care and pharmaceutical products were free. Furthermore, as well as the public library referred to, there was another, operated by the Syndicate and the Libertarian Youth. School attendance was compulsory up to the age of 14. In a group of *masias* (small farmhouses), built on the mountain slopes some distance from the village, a school was opened for older children who had never before sat at a school desk. And in Mas de las Matas two new classes had just been improvised, each to deal with 50 children whose education was entrusted to two young women who had taken a course in advanced studies in Saragossa and Valencia.[25]

Public entertainment was free both for collectivists and individualists.

On the basis of the agreements made throughout Aragon, as well as in Castile and the Levante, no Collective could conduct business on its own account. In this way any possibility of speculation that could arise in that agitated war period was avoided, as well as the kind of competition which so often manifested itself among the collectivised factories in Barcelona, especially in the textile industry.

These measures of a moral nature, ran parallel with the sense of organisation which emerged in most of the socialised villages. Each village Collective communicated to the cantonal *Comité* a list of its surplus goods and of those it needed. Thus each village in the canton of Mas de las Matas had a current account in the books kept in the chief village in which were entered what it supplied and what it received. At the same time the cantonal *Comité* knew exactly what stocks of wine, meat, oil, corn, potatoes, sugar-beet—widely grown in Aragon—were available in each village.

Furthermore if the village which supplied the oil did not need the wine offered, it could ask for other goods. These would be supplied and that village's surpluses would be sent to Mas de las Matas where they would be held in reserve for eventual barter with other Collectives in the canton. It was a kind of clearing-house. Thus through the intermediary of the general Warehouse or the communal depot, barter within and outside the village was possible at all times.

This system of compensation was carried out without the least reticence for the spirit of speculation had disappeared. Any village which was going through particular difficulties and had

25 Fifty children seems a lot. But in view of the backwardness of the Spanish educational organisation, this represented a step forward. What mattered was to teach people to read at any price. The writer (in the 1920s) had 52 pupils from 5 to 15 years of age in the "rationalist" school in Corunna where he had to improvise as schoolteacher. He coped with his task until the time when Primo de Rivera ordered the closure of these establishments.

nothing to barter was not thereby condemned to poverty or to having to raise loans on which the interest charges and repayments would grievously jeopardise its economic situation for years to come.

In the interdependent cantons the problem did not present itself in these terms. Thus for instance in that of Mas de las Matas the main economic resources of Seno and of La Ginebrosa had, that year, been destroyed by hailstorms. Under a capitalist regime it would have resulted in untold privations, even to emigration for several years for some of the men. In a regime of strict justice, loans secured with difficulty could be a permanent millstone round their necks. Under the regime of libertarian solidarity, the difficulty was shared by the effort of the whole canton. Foodstuffs, vegetable plants, seeds, were all supplied in a fraternal manner, without mortgages, and without contracting debts. The revolution had created a new civilisation.

7. Esplus

For its 1,100 inhabitants, Esplus had at its disposal 11,000 hectares of land of which 9,000 were irrigated. But the Duke of Luna had cornered 5,500 and the estates of the monarchist Alvarado, former Finance Minister, who certainly showed more concern for his interests than for those of the nation, accounted for a further 1,100 hectares. Another landowner owned as much and a few others less. There were more who were not as rich, but very comfortably off, each of whom owned from 70 to 100 hectares.

There was not much left over for the people, half of whom were exploited by the wealthy and the very rich, cultivating their estates on the basis of a system called *terraja*, which consisted in clearing and reclaiming land, getting it ready, levelling it and growing crops on it and handing over a quarter of the produce to the landowner. These workers had also to pay an annual rent of six pesetas per hectare, and obliged to use a pair of mules purchased by them to improve each hectare that had been sowed. The fields which had been thus cultivated were then offered to *medieros* who paid in lieu of rent, a half of the harvest.

The history of our movement there was as turbulent as in

Belver de Cinca and elsewhere. A Syndicate of the C.N.T. constituted in 1920 was closed down four years later by the dictatorship of General Primo de Rivera. It re-emerged in 1931, following the proclamation of the Second Republic and had 170 members when, in 1932, the Leftist government of Manuel Azaña, in which Largo Caballero was the Labour Minister (and used his office to wage war against the C.N.T. for the benefit of the U.G.T. of which he was the outstanding leader) closed down the local Syndicate which was reconstituted when the Right-wing Republicans were triumphant at the polls; but the Republic of Alejandro Leroux was no different from that of its predecessor and took the same action. So much so that after the triumph of the "Popular Front" in February 1936 our comrades set about the task of building up the Syndicate for the fourth time, but there were only seventeen of them when the Francoist attack was launched. So much persecution had discouraged the workers and poor peasants.

Nevertheless there took place in a discreet way what we have seen occurring in many other places. Our comrades had joined the local section of the Left Republicans in order to protect themselves from any further reactionary measures, so as not to be once again dragged from their homes and marched off to deportation. It was for this reason that in July 1936 the municipal Council of Esplus consisted of six libertarians posing as Left Republicans and of three Right-wing Republicans, who five years earlier had been monarchists and who were still monarchists at heart.

The general strike declared in reply to the Francoist *coup d'état* lasted a fortnight. A revolutionary Committee was nominated, consisting of a republican majority which had gone over from the Right to the Left, and of a minority of our comrades. But the two tendencies could not agree among themselves. The new Left Republicans went on manoeuvring and very ably founded a reformist workers' syndicate supporting the U.G.T. in order to make use of it to put a brake on the revolution.

They succeeded in gaining time by prolonging the debates and discussions within the revolutionary Committee. So, realising that agreement would never be reached our comrades constituted a local *Comité* which confiscated the large estates and took them over; it was the only way of avoiding the distribution of the land that was being demanded by the political turncoats and some ambitious peasants.

Nevertheless, the monarcho-republican conservatives turned UGTers did not let go, and in the end, forcing some miserable workers to take action, they attacked the local *Comité* and opened fire, protecting themselves with women and children behind whom they sheltered. Our comrades replied by attacking the men; the conservatives were overcome and the Collective was organised.

Eight months later there were only two individualist families whose rights were respected in accordance with the general rule.

The new form of organisation had already been clearly thought out by our comrades when they were engaged in underground propaganda during the Republic, and were preparing the organisation of an agrarian community, purchasing in advance tools, machines and seed.

Agricultural work was taken over by ten teams of land workers. Principal aids were ten pairs of mules per team. Four additional teams dealt with the less heavy work (weeding, seed selection, etc.). Young women helped when necessary. Married women especially those with children were not bound to. But in exceptional circumstances an appeal would be made through the public crier for volunteers. Only the older women would remain at home to look after the young children. But none of the old folk stayed away. They could not conceive of life without work.

There were 110 men at the front. The increase in acreage cultivated was therefore less; the trend was rather to diversify cultivations and above all to increase the number of livestock.

At the beginning of the revolution, three of the former proprietors each owned 200 sheep and ewes. Another had a herd of 50 cattle. And most of the families had a cow or a pig. Pigs were killed once a year, but poor peasants sold the hams to the rich and kept only the carcases for themselves. Nevertheless at the time when I used to visit Esplus, the hams were specially kept. There were 400 reserved for the reapers at the time of the harvest, as their work demanded richer nourishment than usual. Four kilos were allowed per man. When I observed the "guitars" hanging from the rafters of a huge room in anticipation of the feast of the Harvest (religious festivals were beginning to be replaced by new pagan festivities) I understood more vividly the importance of the change that had taken place.

The Collective had constructed four piggeries; one for breeding sows, another for the piglets, one for growing pigs and the fourth for fattening for the butcher. Two hundred pigs had been

K

bought at the beginning and by July 1937 hundreds had already been reared.

The cows were kept in two good houses. Only the poor milkers were slaughtered.[26] As for the sheep, though the meat had been consumed locally as well as being sent to the soldiers at the front, the flocks had increased from 600 to 2,000.

Collective stables had been constructed, but their numbers were still insufficient. Some of the mules were being housed by their former owners; they were not used until after rational planning of the work decided upon by the Collective.

Medical care, pharmaceutical products, housing, lighting, hairdressing saloons were all available without payment. As almost everywhere, each family disposed of a plot of land on which they grew vegetables or flowers and raised a few rabbits or some chickens, according to their preferences. Fresh vegetables were available in any case without payment; but bread, meat, sugar, soap had to be paid for. A single man received 25 pesetas a week, a couple 35 and an additional 4 pesetas per child under the age of 14, and 13 pesetas for those over 14.

The prices of goods, which were so unstable in republican Spain at the time because of the situation upsetting everything, did not increase in Esplus any more than they did in most of the villages which printed their own local money. Money vouchers were guaranteed by production. The mechanism of their circulation was very simple: they were distributed on Saturday afternoon and exchanged for goods at the communal stores, called a co-operative, which on the Saturday would hand them to the local *Comité* which would then put them back into circulation.

People unable to work were paid the same as the others. There were examples of a chronically sick man with four young children, a bedridden man and his daughter, etc.

A hotel was opened for single people, another for some of the many refugees from Aragon territory occupied by Franco's forces. All those who were thus supported enjoyed the same services that were available to the active members of the Collective.

Building operatives were working with enthusiasm. They had started off by applying the eight-hour day, but the peasants pointed out that they worked a twelve-hour day. They therefore yielded to them and carried out all of the necessary repair work to the house in Esplus. A large carpenter's workshop was being built

26 The custom in Spain was to kill cows for butcher's meat.

in which it was intended to instal machinery for mass produced furniture for all the village and, it was hoped, for surrounding villages as well.

Esplus engaged in the barter of goods using Binefar, chief town of the canton, as the go-between. As it is a naturally rich village, it delivered 200,000 pesetas' worth of goods which the cantonal *Comité* distributed either as a contribution to the feeding of the troops at the front or for helping the poorest villages.

This summary gives only a partial picture of what had been done and what was being done. I paid many visits to this village and one evening was there when the flocks were coming down from the mountains, as they did once a week, to be herded into the village sheep-pens. Bleating sheep and lambs, delicate and shy ewes, rams swinging their jingling bells, dogs on guard and watchful shepherds . . . The Collective's flock seemed to be unending. What a fine effort and what good results!

What good results, too, those acres of market gardens where for the first time vegetables of all kinds were being grown on a big scale. The different varieties of plants, and the care lavished on them aroused much admiration. And on one visit I discovered more fields of potatoes about which nobody had said anything. Yet the normal production in the Collective's *huerta* was sufficient for all local needs. This additional effort represented a precautionary measure in favour of the towns, which were much too self-confident, for the soldiers at the fronts, and for any unlucky villages. This surplus actually doubled the normal potato crop.

Before starting the reaping for which they feared a shortage of hands so abundant was the harvest (though in fact reinforcements arrived from other villages), the members of the Collective celebrated the Harvest Festival in which all the inhabitants of Esplus joined. The huge feast, to which I had been invited, took place in a large cornfield that had just been harvested. Women and children enthusiastically helped the men to sample the hams, revolutionary hymns were intoned and I believe some danced Aragonese *jotas*, without, however, for we were in Spain, allowing joyfulness to make them lose their dignity. By which is understood that there was not a single case of drunkenness.

CHAPTER VI

COLLECTIVES IN THE LEVANTE

General Characteristics

The regional Federation of the Levante, an integral part of the
National Confederation of Labour (C.N.T.) comprising that is
workers' and peasants' Syndicates, traditionally organised by the
Spanish Libertarians, served as the basis for the parallel Federation
of Agricultural Collectives of the Levante. It covers five provinces
which are, from North to South, Castellon de la Plana, Valencia,
Alicante, Murcia and Albacete. The development of agriculture
in the first three of these, all Mediterranean, among the richest
in Spain also in terms of population—about 3,300,000 inhabitants
in 1936—resulted in the social achievements that took place
often assuming unsuspected proportions. In my opinion it is in
the Levante, thanks to its natural resources and the forward
looking spirit of our comrades, that the work of libertarian
reconstruction was most widespread as well as more complete. I
was unable to study it in the same detail as for the Aragon
Collectives, but from my own direct observations and much information graciously imparted by the local comrades, as well as
from first hand accounts and original documents, I will attempt
a general picture, completed by a number of monographs which
will bring to life the characteristics and extent of the social
transformation that was achieved.

Of the five provinces in the Levante it was understandable
that the role of Valencia should be outstanding. Firstly for

demographic reasons. It boasted 1,650,000 inhabitants at the time of the Revolution.[1] Murcia was next in importance with 622,000 inhabitants and in which the famous gardens covered only a very small part of the territory which had always been a land of misery and emigration. Alicante which was richer had a population of 472,000, then came Castellon de la Plana with 312,000 and finally Albacete with 238,000 inhabitants.

Anybody knowing however little of the social history of this region is not surprised to learn that the province of Valencia, especially in its achievements in agriculture and horticulture, advanced and developed faster than anywhere else. From 1870 the libertarian movement had always numbered outstanding militants in its ranks, especially in the country; the case of the "martyrs" of Cullera is famous in the annals of the social history of the region. There were others, as we have already mentioned. And whereas in the towns of the Levante republicanism often dominated the opposition at the time of the monarchy, the fighters in the country areas were very often defending anti-statal ideas, a position which was, in any case, widely adopted among the peasantry. Thus in the period 1915-1920, it was to them (often they were smallholders) that libertarian propagandists coming from other regions frequently had to appeal in order to reorganise the movement, the rebirth of which had been encouraged in part by the high hopes aroused by the still little-understood Russian Revolution.

We had, therefore, in many places in these five provinces, militants who were economically and politically free, for whom the revolution was not just a matter of thoughtless agitation or of simple political changes but above all meant expropriation of the land and the organisation of society through libertarian communism.

In 1936 the villages of this province in which our social movement had put its roots were grouped in 22 *comarcas* (cantons) with their respective chief villages in Adamuz, Alborache, Carcagente, Catarroja, Chella, Foyos, Gandia, Jarafuel, Jativa, Moncada, Onteniente, Paterna, Puerto Sagunto, Requeña, Sagunto, Utiel, Villar del Arzobispo, Villamarchante, Alcantara del Jucar,

1 The variations in geographical characteristics as well as of dependent resources were such that in 1936, regions in the same province had a population density in the Mediterranean zone of 450 per sq. kilometre, and in other places only 25 to 30 kilometres from the coast, the density was less than 20.

Titaguas, Lombay and Denia.

The province of Murcia comprised six cantonal federations the chief towns of which were firstly Murcia itself, then Caravaca, Cartagena, Vieza, Lorca, Mazarron, Mula, Pacheo, Elche de la Sierra, Hellin.

Then there was the province of Alicante with nine federations, again cantonal, in Alicante, Alcoy, Almansa, Elda, Elche, La Nucia, Orihuela, Villajoyosa, Villena.

The province of Castellon de la Plana comprised eight organised cantons each of which as usual grouped a greater or lesser number of villages. These were in Castellon, Albocacer, Alcora, Morella, Nulès, Onda, Segorbe and Vinaroz.

And finally the province of Albacete, the least favoured where, furthermore, during the civil war the Collectives had to put up with the presence of the men commanded by the notorious French Communist Marty, nicknamed "the butcher of Albacete" for the cruelties committed in the name of the anti-fascist struggle. In this province we had only four organised cantons: Albacete, Alcarraz, La Roda, and Casa Ibañez.

It should be pointed out that very often the structure of our cantonal organisation had no connection with the traditional cantons of the public or state administration. As in Aragon, they had often been reorganised according to the needs of work, exchanges and other vital interests. More than for political reasons it corresponded to a need for direct union at the base and for that human cohesion which has without any doubt exercised a decisive influence in the constructive task of our creative federalism.

*

The development and numerical growth of Collectives in the Levante surprised even those of us who were the most optimistic as to the possibilities of social reconstruction. For in spite of the many difficulties, in spite of the opposition of our adversaries often in a coalition against us—republicans of different tendencies, Valencian autonomists, socialists and U.G.T-ists, Communists, many elements of the bourgeoisie, etc.—there were 340 Collectives represented at the congress of the Levante Peasants Federation held on 21-23 November, 1937; five months later the number had risen to 500 and by the end of 1938 a figure of 900 had been reached, and that of heads of households had risen to 290,000. Roughly speaking at least 40% of the population belonged to the Collectives.

The significance of these figures can be better appreciated if we make a different calculation. The five provinces of Levante consisted of 1,172 localities from the largest town to the smallest village.[2] It was therefore in 78% of the localities in the richest agricultural region in all Spain that in twenty months these 900 Collectives sprang up.

It is true that as units they did not achieve the high percentage achieved by the Collectives in Aragon. In Aragon the almost total predominance of libertarian forces for a long time prevented State administration, municipal or national police forces, political parties supported by governmental authorities, assault guards and "carabineros", to hamper changes in the social structure. Whereas in Levante—and one should not forget that from November 1936 the Central government had moved to Valencia which had become the capital of legal Spain—all these forces were present and that with the small tradesmen, the liberal bourgeoisie, who were anti-Francoist but also anti-Collectivist, they opposed by every means, including violent ones, this attempt to put libertarian socialism into operation. There were pitched battles when even army tanks were brought up. In such conditions what was achieved savours of the prodigious.

The more so since in the Levante region, and as a consequence of the wealth and the density of the population in certain areas, the localities are often concentrations of from 10 to 20 thousand people in which the social classes and the forces facing each other are more solidly constituted and can more easily coordinate their efforts. Thus when our comrades took the offensive for socialisation the resistance was all the more vigorous. It required all the flexibility, ingenuity, imagination, and the intelligent and useful adaptation to circumstances, and the energy they undoubtedly possessed, for the revolutionary effort to be realised in spite of everything.

It is one of the reasons why the Levante Collectives were created in most cases on the initiative of the peasants' Syndicates in each locality, for they brought at the same time moral integrity, a tradition as organisers, experience in the struggle and numerical strength.

2 The population of Spain is much less dispersed than that of France, for instance, and the number of communes was, even when taking into account the smaller population, considerably lower. The figures for the Levante are no less eloquent.

But in spite of close contact with these Syndicates—often the same men were at the head of the two organisations—the Collectives at first constituted an autonomous organism. The Syndicates of the C.N.T. continued to group most of their members but also "individualists" who though not collectivists neither were they reactionaries, prevented either by a questionable interpretation of the meaning of individual freedom or because their land was isolated. In some cases it was by a more or less justified hesitation based on fear either of governmental reaction after the victory, or of a fascist victory.

The role played by the Syndicates was therefore most useful. They constituted a step forward, an element of attraction. They also had another practical function. It was to them that the individualist trade-unionists would bring their produce which they undertook to barter with the Collectives. Commissions were set up in the Syndicate for dealing with rice, citrus fruits, vegetable seedlings, etc. In each locality the Syndicate had its food store where non-collectivists could get supplies. But the Collective had also its own. It was later thought that such an arrangement required double labour and the decision was taken to telescope the two in favour of the Collective, and with joint administrative representation. The individualist trade-unionists continued to bring their goods and collect their supplies in the same way as the Collectivists.[3]

Then mixed commissions were started for the purchase of machines, seeds, fertilisers, insecticides and veterinary aids. Lorries were shared, solidarity was spreading while avoiding, nevertheless, excessive confusion between the two organisms.

Socialisation rested then on two bases. With that remarkable flexibility which one has often observed among the builders of Spanish libertarianism, it embraces all that can be included, integral achievements as well as partial realisations. The means for inveigling them are complementary.

But very quickly the Collectives tended to unify and rationalise all that could be. Rationing and the family wage were established at cantonal level, the richer villages helping the poorer or less favoured as happened in Aragon and Castile. In every cantonal chief-town a team of specialised technicians was created to include accountants, an agronomist, a veterinary surgeon, an engineer,

---

3 It should be added that a number of socialist peasants or who belonged to the U.G.T. joined the Collectives. This was another good reason for maintaining the autonomy of the Collectives.

an architect, an expert in commercial questions, etc. These teams were at the service of all the villages.

The practice of mutual aid allowed for the equitable distribution and use of the means required for the smooth operation of the Collectives. Most of the engineers and veterinary surgeons throughout the region were members of the C.N.T., those employed by the non-collectivised economy collaborated as well, and generally without material gain, in preparing plans and projects, for the creative spirit of the Revolution carried forward those who wanted to contribute to economic and social progress in general.

Thus agronomists would put forward necessary or possible projects; planning agriculture, moving cultivations to land and climatic conditions which were more favourable but which hitherto, for reasons of private property, and the vested interests of different groups of smallholders, had not been possible. The vet in the Collective put stock rearing on a scientific basis. In the event he consulted the agronomist as to the feeding arrangements that could be made available. And he in his turn discussed this production problem with the peasants' commissions. But the architect and the engineer were also called to the rescue over the construction of stables, piggeries, cowhouses, barns for the Collectives. The tasks were being planned and the activities integrated.

∗

Thanks to the engineers, a large number of *acequias* (irrigation canals) were excavated and wells sunk which made it possible to convert dry lands into irrigated land. By using pumps, water was raised and distributed over large areas. The very porous, sandy nature of the soil and low atmospheric precipitations— 400 mm. on average when at least three times that amount was required—made the extraction and the good use of this precious liquid very difficult, especially as wells had to be sunk to depths of from 50 to 200 metres. This was a feasible proposition only for the large landowners who cultivated or employed people to cultivate profitable crops such as oranges, or for the Collective.

It was perhaps in the regions of Cartagena and Murcia that the greatest efforts were made in this direction. Near Villajoyosa in the province of Alicante the construction of a dam made it possible to irrigate a million almond trees which had previously suffered from permanent drought.

But the architects in the Collectives did not only deal with a habitat for the livestock. They went through the region giving advice about the human environment. Types of houses, location, aspect, materials, plumbing, etc., . . . indispensable considerations which previously had been opposed both by the ignorance of some and the vested interests of others.

The close proximity of the villages to each other helped that active solidarity which puts all resources at the disposal of the whole community. Practical work was often intercommunal. A team would, for instance, be set up to deal with plant diseases, sulphur dusting, pruning, grafting, working the land in a number of localities; another team would be organised to grub up trees and carry out unusual cultivations or improvise new cultivations on the sites of those trees. All this facilitated the coordination of efforts and their synchronisation on a general plan of action which was developed not only on the abstract concepts of technocrats or technicians without experience, but also according to the practical lessons learned from work and from contact with men and realities.

It was a new society, a new world that had been created.

Let us examine more closely some aspects of general organisation. The 900 Collectives were brought together in 54 cantonal federations which grouped themselves and at the same time subdivided into five provincial federations which at the top level ended in the Regional *Comité* of the Levante Federation situated in Valencia and which coordinated the whole.

This *Comité* was nominated directly by the annual congresses answerable to them and to the hundreds of peasant delegates, chosen by their comrades, whom the fine speeches of bureaucrats or domineering agitators would not dazzle, for in their great majority they knew what they wanted and where they were going. It was also on their initiative that the Levante Federation was divided into 26 general sections in accordance with specialisations in work and other activities. Those 26 sections constituted a whole which embraced probably for the first time in history outside the State and governmental structures, the whole of social life. We will assemble them into five main groupings, implying a corresponding administrative organisation:

AGRICULTURE: Cereals (particularly corn, the cultivation of which was often improvised or stimulated as a result of the Francoist occupation of the cereal growing areas); rice growing;

citrus fruits (oranges, lemons, tangerines); fruit growing and its subdivisions (almonds, peaches, apples, etc.); olive groves; vineyards; vegetable growing or market gardening; livestock, especially sheep and goats; pigs and cattle.

FOOD INDUSTRIES: The Federation being essentially of the peasantry, the industries that one encountered were mainly connected with agriculture. The specialised sections were the following: wine production; fruit and vegetable packing houses; distillation of alcohol; fruit juices, various liqueurs; perfumes and by-products.

NON-AGRICULTURAL INDUSTRIES (not derived from agriculture): Building section; various manufactures; carpentry; manufacture of packaging materials for citrus fruits, clothing, etc. . . . One should note here the tendency for the integration of activities, thereby reducing, to a certain extent, the role of the Syndicate which the syndicalist movement had always considered as the sole organiser of industrial production. These problems were resolved on the spot, in a friendly spirit between sister organisations.

COMMERCIAL SECTION: Apart from large scale exports, which will be discussed later, this section covered imports of machinery, road and sea transport facilities, and various products.

PUBLIC HEALTH & EDUCATION: Finally, the section for hygiene and sanitation which coordinated the efforts preserving and improving public health, and that of education which thanks to its schools, its teachers and the contribution by the Collectives, pursued with enthusiasm the duties which fell on them.

All these activities were synchronised on a scale involving 900 Collectives, many of them involving thousands of people. It will be easier now to appreciate how widespread these achievements were and how superior was this form of organisation. Obviously I cannot here describe it in every detail. But I will add precise details to some aspects already outlined.

Rice growing for example. In the province of Valencia alone, 30,000 out of a total national production from 47,000 hectares, were in the hands of the Collectives. The renowned region of La Albufera, which Blasco Ibañez has so exhaustively described, was entirely collectivised.

Half the orange production, that is 4 million quintals, was in the hands of the peasants' Federation, the federated Collectives and the Syndicates; and 70 per cent of the total harvest, that is more than $5\frac{1}{2}$ million quintals, was transported and sold in the European markets thanks to their commercial organisation called FERECALE[4] which at the beginning of 1938 had established in France sales sections in Marseilles, Perpignan, Bordeaux, Sète, Cherbourg and Paris.

It should be noted in passing that the importance of distribution was considerably greater than that of production. With first hand information on the subject we can make the following comparisons: as we have already said, the producers of the Levante Collectives were numerically about 40% of the total population. As a consequence of their superior technical organisation, their production was 50-60% of the total; and for the same reasons the collectivist system was responsible for between 60 and 70% of the total distribution to the advantage of the whole population.

The organisation in general and the extent of the resources that it guaranteed, made other achievements possible, as well as methods of work without which the tasks undertaken would often have failed due to a lack of technical means, and insufficient return or to the excessive cost of the efforts involved.

The spirit of active solidarity, the will to coordination were always and everywhere present. When, for instance, the members of a Collective or a local *Comité* considered it worthwhile to establish a liqueur or fruit juice factory or to process foods for human or animal consumption they informed the industrial section of the regional-federal *Comité* of Valencia of their initiative. The *Comité* would examine the proposal, and if considered necessary would invite a delegation to attend, with which it would study the pros and cons of the project. If on the basis of estimated demand, the availability of raw materials and other foreseeable factors the idea was attractive it would be adopted; if not it would be rejected after explanations and a full examination of

4 FERECALE (the initials for the Regional Federation of Peasants of the Levante) was constituted for the transport and the marketing of citrus fruits. It was made up of the following sections: technical personnel; warehouses; depots; land transport; home market; international exports; general accounts; sea transport. General delegations had been set up in Castellon, Burriana, Gandia, Denia and Alicante.

It owned its fleet of motor vessels of 120-150 tons. The orders which came from abroad were sent to the regional warehousing centre in which the fruit (especially oranges) according to the quality required was stored. The goods were despatched from each centre to its corresponding embarkation section; the invoicing centre then transmitted the registration to the accounts section. Furthermore the control sections established in the ports transmitted by telephone the receipts and outgoings to the headquarters of FERECALE in Valencia; and the depots from which the goods had been removed acted in a similar manner.

the proposals. Another reason for rejection would be availability of existing factories.

But acceptance of the project did not mean that its original promoters would become its owners, even at the level of the local Collective. By employing from the beginning resources supplied by the Collectives as a whole, the Federation became the owner of the new factory and the local Collective was not entitled to sell for its own benefit the goods that were produced there.

Expenses and Income were therefore everybody's concern. It was also the Federation which allocated the raw materials supplied to all the factories and localities according to their kind of production and their needs respectively.[5]

The situation also required great flexibility which was impossible both on the scale of an isolated peasant or tradesman, and in purely corporative organisations where the individualist spirit and attitudes prevailed. Thus, until the Revolution vast quantities of fruit were left to rot on the ground because of a lack of markets at home and abroad. It was the case with sales to Britain which had to compete with supplies coming from Palestine and South Africa, and made it necessary to lower prices and, to some extent, production as well.[6]

But apart from the civil war, the loss of some European markets and of the home market occupied and cut off by Franco's troops, as well as the difficulties subtly put in the way of the libertarian socialist experiment by the government and its allies, made the situation worse. Not only was there a surplus of citrus fruits, but also of potatoes and tomatoes. So, once again, the initiative of the Collectives manifested itself.

An effort was made to put these oranges to better use by manufacturing essences extracted from the peel on a larger scale than before; a new food was manufactured, a kind of dessert called "honey-orange", and "orange wine"; the pulp was used for the preservation of blood from the abattoirs, and this provided a new food for poultry; the canning of vegetables and fruit was increased; the most important factories were located in Murcia, Castellon, Alfafar and Paterna. As the German

5 Of course there were depots with raw materials distributed among the five provinces, for it goes without saying that everything was not concentrated in Valencia.

6 The home market could have expanded. But apart from the cost of transport in this excessively mountainous country, the old system had never taken it up.

peasants had been doing for a long time in their specialised cooperatives, drying plants for potatoes were set up in order to produce potato-flour for human and animal consumption and the same procedure was used for tomatoes.

We have said that the location of the cantonal federation centres was very often determined by their proximity to road junctions or railways, thus facilitating the transport of goods. In most cases food surpluses of the Collectives were stored in these centres. The corresponding sections of the federal *Comité* in Valencia were informed of the quantities of each variety, the quality, the date of production of the goods warehoused, and thus knew exactly what were the available reserves for deliveries, exports, barter, or for redistribution among the cantons or the Collectives.

The intensification of egg production and of chickens and rabbits, was further confirmation of that creative spirit. In July 1937 the Collective of Gandia alone was producing in its hatcheries 1,200 chicks every three weeks. New breeds of rabbits and fowls, unknown to most peasants (who too often were attached to the traditional and uneconomic ones) were introduced, and the Collectives that had taken the first step in this direction helped those who, for various reasons, had not yet started.

Furthermore the efforts at organisation and economic justice were not all that was achieved. The yearning for culture, the intense desire to spread education were one of the mainsprings and one of the major objectives of the Revolution. Thus every Collective created one or two schools as promptly as it set about its first economic initiatives. The family wage and the new ethic made it possible for all children to attend school. In their sphere of influence the Spanish Collectives gave the *coup de grâce* to illiteracy in record time. The magnitude of the achievement can be gauged if one bears in mind that in the Spanish country-side in 1936, 60% of the people were illiterate.

To complete this effort, and with an immediate practical end in view, a school to train secretaries and accountants was opened at the end of 1937. More than a hundred students were immediately sent there by the Collectives.

The last major innovation was the agricultural university of Moncada (province of Valencia). Its purpose was to train agricultural technicians. In the different classes and in the practical courses young people were instructed in the various specialities in land husbandry and zootechny (animal care, methods of selection, characteristics of breeds; horticulture, fruitgrowing, bee-keeping, forestry, etc.). When the university was in full swing it had 300 students and there would have been many more if there had been more accommodation and more teachers. The University of Moncada situated at the foot of hills covered with orange trees was also available to the other regions.

A final example of solidarity in practice. The Collectives of the Levante had also received a large number of refugees, especially women and children from Castile who had fled before the fascist advance. Reception homes were set up in the heart of the country, and camps where the youngsters were well cared for in every way and could forget the war. Long lines of lorries coming from the villages took free supplies of food to Madrid. The Collectives of Benjopa, Oliva, Jeresa, Tabernes de Valldigna, Beirrairo and Simat (all in the canton of Gandia) donated 198 lorry loads of food in the first six months of the war. Shortly after the fall of Malaga a simple phone call produced seven lorry loads of food for Almeria, which was crowded with refugees who were exhausted and hungry.

For, faced with the necessities and responsibilities of life our comrades were not paralysed nor dehumanised by the bureau-cratic spirit and the red-tape of the State. As good libertarians they practised a new humanism among themselves and with others, without cheating, without speculating even on the pro-paganda value of their gestures, with no other reward than the deep joy deriving from practical solidarity.

1. Carcagente

Carcagente, a large country borough rather than a small town, situated in the province of Valencia, had a population of 18,000 at the time of my first visit in November 1936.[7] Though its social history was less traumatic than that of Sueca or Cullera. our movement had long established roots and exerted a great influence. Thus in November 1936, our peasants' Syndicate had 2,750 members, including some hundreds of small proprietors; that of the orange packers numbered 3,325, mostly women; in addition there were 320 buildings workers, 150 railwaymen, 120 engineering workers and 450 workers of various trades and

7 The influx of refugees from Castile had not yet begun.

professions—all members of the Syndicate. In all 41 per cent of the whole population. But if one takes into account the percentage represented by children, then the percentage of workers in the C.N.T. was extremely high.

In the outskirts of Carcagente within the jurisdiction of the town itself, as well as in the surrounding though less important localities, large estates, almost all specialising in the production of citrus fruits, dominated the economy. And a fair number of small proprietors who could not make a living from what their land produced supplemented their insufficient earnings by working for the rich or by all kinds of expedients. A not infrequent situation in Spain and one which must have contributed to tipping the scales in favour of the social revolution when the upheaval caused by the insurrection and fascist threat took place. The logical consequence was the overwhelming influence of our syndical organisation, which without hesitation set about socialising the large estates. The task was made all the easier because the large *terratenientes* had vanished and what had to be avoided was that the productive wealth that had become socially available should not be shared out among new beneficiaries who would only reintroduce, though in a somewhat modified form, the basically identical system of exploitation, chaos and inequality that had just been done away with.

Simultaneously, and following the achievement of libertarian communism for which they had been struggling for so long, our comrades tackled the traditional small proprietors in order to transform as many of the parcels of individually cultivated land, scattered and broken up into huge areas, rationally exploited thanks to the common social property and to the use of techniques, which it had made possible.

I met again in Carcagente comrades I had previously known in Barcelona or in Buenos Aires where they had emigrated during the dictatorship of Primo de Rivera. They told me that to bring about these fundamental transformations they did not use force and especially was this the case in regard to the small growers. Those who joined did so of their own free will, following the example of the militants who set the example by handing over their land, animals and tools. There remained a number of recalcitrants, but our comrades had complete confidence in the superiority of group work, in the practical and moral results, that could be achieved by mutual aid. They *knew* that by example they would succeed in winning over those who still hesitated. They were so convinced that, in many cases—and I and others came across similar examples on many occasions—they did not hesitate, in order to complete collectivised areas in the middle of which were parcels of land belonging to individualists, to offer them better land in exchange for theirs and to help them settle in.

In a few months positive results were apparent. In the first place a local economic crisis had been wiped out. Difficulties created by the civil war and its repercussions had produced economic and commercial stagnation which hampered the disposal of the crops and each small grower, left to his own devices, was faced with disturbing problems. In due course the practice of union and solidarity made it possible to find ways to dispose of their produce, if not in Carcagente itself then in Valencia or in other provinces.

But this only partially remedied the slowing down in activity. The breakdown of the normal channels for exports and the commercial blockade or semi-blockade of Spain made the situation very difficult. And there was no question of solving it by the municipal organisation of public charity. This was the driving force towards a more far reaching social transformation. Thus all the time more peasants were offering their land to the Collective in return for membership. For only the Collective was capable of taking revolutionary action and finding the right solutions by the reorganisation of local life.

When I arrived there I was shown the latest batch of applications for admission that had been received. They gave details of area and the locations of the land, its condition as well as of the numbers in the family, details of livestock and of working tools. In all this no signs of coercion.

Nevertheless, and in view of the gravity of the situation created by the civil war, individual freedom or the autonomy of producers who had remained outside the Collective, did not mean that the latter allowed them to put a brake on or interrupt production. Our comrades understood from the first day that it was necessary to collaborate for victory by redoubling their efforts. And without waiting for the municipal authorities and the political parties to undertake these responsibilities, the land-workers' Syndicate nominated a Commission to supervise the work being done in the countryside and to be on the lookout

[161]

L

that there was no slackening either in the individualists' or the collectivists' passion for their work.

But naturally it was above all the Collective, organised by the peasants' Syndicate and placed under its control, which preached by example. I traversed huge orange groves, one of which covered five villages, and was struck by the tidy and clean cultivations. Every inch had been worked, as if combed, with meticulous care in order to ensure that the trees enjoyed all the natural goodness in the soil. The Valencian peasant was renowned for the love with which he tended his land and the crops he grew on it. And it was clearly visible. There was no need for fertilisers. "Previously,"—said the comrades who were escorting me across the plantations of golden fruits—"all this, that belonged to the capitalists, was worked by wage earners who were somewhat indifferent to the results of their labours. The proprietors bought large quantities of chemical fertilisers or *guano* whereas all that was needed was to look after the land to get good harvests."

And it was with joy and pride that later they showed me grafts that they had made in order to improve the stock and the eventual quality of the fruit.

However in some places I came across crops growing between the rows, and to my enquiry the comrades pointed out that if the war lasted a long time the towns would be short of food. It was for this reason that in this generally gravelly soil, not very suitable for horticulture, they had planted early potatoes. They did more: taking advantage of the four months that elapse between harvesting the rice and the sowings that follow, they had sowed in the Valencian rice-fields, duly cultivated, early wheat.

As it was my first contact with an agrarian Collective I asked for details of the general organisation of work, and discovered that it was both simpler and much more complete than I had imagined. At the base, a public meeting of agricultural workers which included unionists and non-unionists (the latter were not numerous, as is apparent from the figures already given). On the proposal by those present, individualists and collectivists, a *Comité* was nominated by a majority vote if unanimity could not be achieved, which was divided into two sections: the technical section with six members entrusted with the management of production and the problems of disposal on the home and export markets, and the administrative section consisting of five members to deal with accountancy. The technical section included former professional exporters whose abilities were known and recognised. They were carrying out their tasks ably and seemed really integrated into the new social structure.

In Carcagente industrial socialisation started *after* agrarian socialisation. But it was launched in a manner that promised well for the future. Building work was in the hands of the Syndicate of the building industry, and engineering was controlled by the metalworkers' Syndicate; the woodworkers' Syndicate—cabinet-makers, joiners, carpenters—brought together all the small businessmen and craftsmen in one huge workshop where each received a remuneration decided on by all; where no longer did one have to wait for the client or ask oneself how bills were to be met at the end of the month. Other less important trades were grouped in a single Syndicate. Hairdressers shops where lighting, organisation and hygiene often left much to be desired were replaced by a number of collectivised establishments which were clean and comfortable. Yesterday's competitors had become workmates.

As one has already noted the packing of oranges for export employed the greatest number of hands. Several buildings in Carcagente disposing of the equipment required were used for this purpose. Each was directed by a *Comité* nominated by the workers, and consisting of a professional expert in commercial affairs, and a delegate for each of the specific activities: manufacture of wooden boxes, grading, packing, conditioning, etc. In the various operations men and women workers carried out the tasks with enthusiasm, following the rhythm of the mechanical graders alongside which the orange boxes, which offered a kind of artistic *cachet* common to the people of this region, were lined up waiting to be closed and loaded up. The destination of the fruit was Britain, Sweden, France, Holland, etc. . . . And the workers would say to me, "We want them to see abroad that with socialised production we work better than before."

It was also a *Comité* specially appointed by the assembly of workers which managed the building industry. Houses were not being built—not only because of the war (in grave crises building work is always the first to grind to a halt) but also because a large number of residences belonging to the rich and the local fascists were handed over to those who were the most ill-housed. But conversions and repair work were carried out. A number of

[163]

former employers supported the communal effort and worked well; and one of the two architects in Carcagente joined the Syndicate.

The brick works and the parpen factory as well as all other trades were organised along the same principles, and on the same bases for remuneration.

When I returned to Carcagente, at the beginning of February 1937, the orange export trade was the only one that had been socialised. But it was done independently. Firstly the local section of the U.G.T. had supported the new achievements; secondly, it was done in conjunction with the regional *Comité*. When orders came from Valencia, the selectors would move to the areas where they knew they could find the varieties and quantities required. These selectors would also indicate when fruit trees were ready for picking on the basis of the travelling time involved as well as of the climatic conditions of the purchasing countries.

So far as distribution in general was concerned, and in spite of the advice I had given with a view to avoiding a slow, but persistent, increase in prices which counteracted some of the positive results achieved in production, the local shop continued to operate. It constituted a negative factor, and the time had come to ask oneself whether one should not move towards a new stage which would complement the first.

A first step in that direction had been taken in a number of cases above all in the region of the Levante, by the constitution of a food supplies *Comité* which undertook to secure for local consumption essential foodstuffs which were not produced locally. The same *Comité* organised the application of barter on the largest possible scale. My friend Grañén, later executed by a fascist firing squad, was planning the organisation of distribution centres in the various districts, which would give the population control over the price mechanism and the distribution of consumer goods. The idea was taking shape rapidly there as well as in many other localities, and within six weeks half the trade of Carcagente was socialised and Grañén had high hopes for the other half.

At the same time part of the orange groves were grubbed up, as there was no sale for the fruit, and replaced by vegetables. One was moving towards economic integration, which was also noticeable elsewhere.

2. Jativa

I cannot think of Jativa (situated like Carcagente in the province of Valencia) without remembering its style, as Arabic as its name, the beautiful valley in which it had been built long ago, its wonderful climate and the deep blue of its brilliant sky. With some local comrades I went to visit the ruins of a large Moorish castle still standing and steeped in history, along the top of hills flanking the town, where mimosa grew in profusion between the random stones. From that height it was a dream landscape that one saw. In the foreground various cultivations, and then immense orange groves in which the golden fruit hung, as if in bunches along the branches which were bending under their weight and surrounded by the green varnished leaves which gleamed in the sunshine.

The founding of the Collective in Jativa did not take place as quickly as in Carcagente, which is after all not so far away. Yet the social movement there also went back many years, and it always included good militants. Of the 17,000 inhabitants, 3,000 were members of the C.N.T. Agriculture predominated and industry played a very minor role and was above all linked to orange production and the tasks that stemmed therefrom, to rice production, prepared and ground locally, to olive production, used for oil produced in local oil-crushers.

The fascist attack had brought together all the Left factions who, as happened in many other places, converged on the municipal Council. Soon this was composed, on the basis of the numerical strength of the forces represented, of five representatives each from the C.N.T. and U.G.T., one socialist, one Communist, a Left republican and a member of the Valencian autonomists party.

Though industry stemmed from the needs of agriculture, socialisation was initiated by industry. It was not general in all trades and professions, and among the last to do so were the hairdressers who in January 1937 were prepared, with their employers, to collectivise the shops which until then they had only been allowed to control.

In the industrial field the functional structure and operation followed the familiar pattern: technical sections for organisation, administrative sections; the Syndicates managed workshop activities in which workers elected the *Comités* entrusted with management at the place of work itself.

But the agrarian Collective created on the 16th January, 1937, three weeks after my first visit, seems to me to be more important, for it got off to a flying start which was quite remarkable.

There was a fundamental reason for this which explains many similar cases I had occasion to observe: most of the members of the C.N.T. were hard working peasants, accustomed to responsible work, to direct dealings, whereas in the local section of the U.G.T. there was a predominance of administrative employees in the private and public sectors, numbers of tradespeople, and the conservative elements among the small growers whose social-reformist headquarters made the defence of traditional ownership of the land a profession of faith.

This was in direct contradiction with the basic postulates of Marxism and the views of Marx and Engels, but the Marxism of the Spanish socialists was quite as anaemic as that of the French socialists. And Marx and Engels as well as their continuators have said so many contradictory things!

Our comrades did not propose, however, to seize anybody's goods by force—unless they were fascists, *terratenientes*, or caciques; and apart from a few isolated cases which we are prepared to assume took place, one cannot accuse them on this score. On the contrary, one is surprised to see how tolerant they were in general to the "individualists".

The emergence in strength of the agrarian Collective can be explained by other reasons which complement those already given. Before the uprising, the local libertarians exercised a *constructive* influence over a large number of peasants who were members of a local mutual benefit society. It was the active, organising, dynamic nucleus of that mutual aid society which was to constitute the basic elements of the social microcosm in the process of being formed. It is extremely difficult to improvise as an organiser, and very often one finds in the antecedents of this revolution, a practical activity which explains the sureness of the advance and the rapidity of its success.

Furthermore, Jativa offers many other examples of a social conscience. There was the case of the owner of an oil-crusher —worth a fortune in local terms—who gave his working capital and lands to the Collective. Or that of his son, also one of the privileged, who brought all his capital and his wife's to the common cause. Or again that of the secretary[8] who did likewise.

8 This secretary, a very young man, surprised me by his knowledge of the problems of Spanish agriculture. And yet, he was unknown, even in our movement.

One cannot be surprised therefore by the idealistic optimism which could be read into the expressions, the actions, even the bearing of those who were busying themselves to create a new world, always on the move dealing with the many tasks with which they had been entrusted.

This spirit emerges in the Rules produced following many deliberations and published in a small white notebook, a copy of which I have preserved to this day. The following are the most characteristic Articles.

"ART. 1. Collectivisation will be the work of the peasants, *medieros* and smallholders, who join voluntarily and will be accepted by the General Assembly.

ART. 3. When a smallholder's land is located in the middle of collectivised land, constituting thereby an obstacle for the Collective, it will be exchanged for another holding, of better land and with more advantages for the owner who has been displaced.

ART. 5. Widows without other means of life than land can, if they wish, join the Collective.

ART. 10. The defence of our production and the administration of the cultivations will be assured by the following Commissions: (a) Statistics; (b) Irrigation; (c) Fertilisers, seeds and new cultivations; (d) Plant diseases, spraying and fumigations; (e) Steward's office, purchases and selling prices; (f) Livestock, poultry keeping, beekeeping; (g) Tools and machinery; (i) Tests; (j) Animal feed; (k) Means of transport available for the Collective; (l) Production and appropriate technical management; (m) Land workers.

ART. 15. In the event of illness, members of the Collective or their families will receive treatment on behalf of the Collective which will be responsible for all expenses incurred.

ART. 16. Rent for private dwellings occupied by members of the Collective will be paid by the latter, independently of the wage.[9]

ART. 17. Furniture for new households will be paid for by

---

9 This measure was taken for the members of the Collective who did not own their homes. They were, as one can see, a minority. It is also worth mentioning that collectivists lived at home individually. So nothing in common with the views of Etienne Cabet and other reformers, which led to many community experiments during the last century in N. America failing largely because of excessive communizing and at all times, which stifled the personality. This separation was practised in all Spanish Collectives.

the Collective if the beneficiaries have been members for at least six months and if they act as real collectivists.

ART. 21. Children under the age of 14 will not be accepted for work; they will be obliged to attend school from the age of six. Their parents or guardians will be responsible for their attendance at school; the penalty for a child's unjustifiable absence from school will be a deduction of six pesetas from the family's wage.

ART. 22. The Collective will, for the good of Mankind, help the most gifted children to take courses in higher education. The Collective will be financially responsible.

ART. 28. Should the Collective have cause to complain of the behaviour of one of its members, it will call him to order on up to two occasions. On the third occasion he will be expelled from the Collective without any right to indemnification. The general assembly will deal with such cases."

The family wage was established. A single man received 35 pesetas a week while a single woman received exactly a half.[10] Each dependent child entitled the family to an extra seven pesetas a week; and then from 10 to 14 years this was increased to 10.50 pesetas for boys and 8.75 for girls.

Very few essential matters were overlooked, but if experience revealed that one had, there was nothing to prevent the modification and improvement of the existing Statutes. One should add that not only was education compulsory but was given in the Collective's schools which from the beginning had staff and had fitted up three school buildings in which to hold the classes, and in addition a fourth building which was at the disposal of

10 This difference in the means of life, which one finds elsewhere though not always, will come as a shock, and rightly so. It must not be forgotten that Spain has retained some of the consequences of the Arab presence which lasted 800 years, followed by the most backward Catholic Church that has ever existed. That is one explanation. Then, in practice, it is exceptional for a woman to live alone; generally the spinster or the widow lives with her family—family traditions are more respected in Spain than in France or Britain. The problem of the single woman does not present itself in the way that might be supposed when viewed from the point of view of French ways of life. It should be added that at the family table, everyone, men and women, eat their fill. There is no distinction made except in the poorest families, where often if, for instance, their means allowed them to buy only one egg, it would be kept for the head of the family not so much because he was the head as that he was the breadwinner and needed to be nourished to maintain his strength to work.

the children in their leisure hours, during the day, to study or to play.

Projects on such a scale must be based on a solidly established material situation. It was so. In a fortnight nearly 500 families applied to join the Collective, offering to it all their goods. The majority belonged to the C.N.T. with a minority from the U.G.T., for almost everywhere socialists or members of the reformist trade union organisations did not follow the directives issued by their leaders. And the supporters would have been even more numerous had the organisers not thought it necessary to show caution, in order not to risk being overwhelmed, or hampered by collectivists who were still unsure.

On joining, each new member completed a form giving details about himself, his family and dependent relatives; then of his assets or liabilities and debts, in land, money, tools and draught animals.

The total area of collectivised land, including the expropriations from fascists and the large landowners as well as land brought by members, amounted to 5,114 hectares of which 2,421 were irrigated. A fortnight after the official inauguration, the technical *Comité* was managing operations on 446 hectares. Thanks to its initiative and to the enthusiasm of everybody, 75 hectares had been reclaimed and prepared for cultivation, later being sown with corn and potatoes in anticipation of the threatened scarcity of food in the towns.

On the basis of a general plan prepared by the technicians-practitioners, a quarter of the land was to be planted with rice, another quarter as orange groves, and a half for market-garden produce.

It was also decided to introduce stock breeding. Within three weeks 400 sheep and goats (the renowned Murcia goats were conveniently situated) were ordered for breeding purposes. In due course it was hoped to supply the whole town with the meat it required: an urgent matter seeing that the main supply areas (Castile, Estremadura, Galicia) were in the hands of the Francoist forces.

A similar initiative was launched for poultry and egg production. Two incubators were purchased to make a start. Bee-keeping was still under consideration, but the conditions in that area where flowers and fruit trees abounded were favourable for this hitherto unexplored activity. Finally all the part of the Sierra which could not be cultivated by man and which erosion was denuding at an increasing rate was to be planted with pines. The seedlings had already been purchased.

In a very short time, the Collective had also acquired three lorries. It undertook large-scale works to improve and extend irrigation to the dry lands. In one week *acequias* were dug, and others started. The plan adopted consisted in raising the water by means of motorised pumps to a water tower from which it would be distributed to the land which until then had remained fallow because the small owners had neither the initiative nor the required resources for such undertakings.[11]

The Rules refer to the steward's office. Members of the Collective could obtain from it, at cost price, available goods that they required. Everyone could even ask for these goods in large quantities, paying by instalments without interest, so that housewives did not have to shop every other day for soap, lignite, lard, oil, etc.

As in all Collectives, the draught animals—donkeys, horses, mules—were housed in large stables specially fitted up, and were used both for heavy and light work. In the morning, specially trained boys would harness them to the carts and other equipment, saving time for the carters and landworkers. When they returned at night they no longer had to spend a further half hour unharnessing and grooming their horses before going home, for this task was done for them by their comrades. As also when there was much unloading to be done, others would come to help.

Less than two months after its constitution, I received a letter from the secretary of the Collective of Jativa which I feel deserves to be quoted in full.

Jativa, March 8, 1937.

Dear Comrade,

I have waited to reply, in spite of my promise to do so as soon as possible, because I wanted to give you as much information as possible on the progress of the Collective, and as the study I have in mind to write would make me delay too long, I have decided to send you what hard facts are available and leave a more detailed report to a later date.

11 This project was in due course carried out. When the water gushed forth for the first time in the direction of the orange groves, flooding seemed inevitable. A young runner was dispatched post haste to ask them to turn off this wonderful torrent!

The membership of the Collective has reached 408, of whom 82 are members of the U.G.T. while the others are from the C.N.T. Twenty-three applications for membership are waiting for the nominated Commission to decide one way or the other. There are many applications but we want to advance with caution.

The enthusiasm of the collectivists is fantastic, so much so that our members are working twice as much as they did before. For this reason we prefer to backpedal a little on accepting new members so that they shall not be influenced simply by material considerations, and that nothing should intervene to harm the wonderful spirit that exists and which is the guarantee for success.

The total wages for the 408 member families amounts to 22,811 pesetas a week, from which amount we must deduct 1,108.50 pesetas which some collectivists earn outside in other trades and which they hand over to the Collective in accordance with the Rules on this question. Other expenses have to be added such as:
Doctors, operations, dentists, confinements,
   oculist, medicaments   estimate per year 26,600 ptas
Purchases of furniture for new households per year 9,250 ptas
House rents for collectivists   per month 2,632 ptas

All the above represents weekly *outgoings totalling 22,999 pesetas which divided by 453 working persons—we obviously do not include the elderly and the incapacitated—gives a family wage of 50.70 pesetas.*

We have not yet been able to prepare our estimates for the purchase of fertilisers, materials for fumigation, machinery, feed for livestock and other expenses; neither have we estimates of income from the sale of our products; we are too absorbed by the meetings with peasants who have not joined, to decide amicably which land they can cultivate individually and which they can give up to us.

Things are happening all the time so that it is impossible to establish exact estimates until all these matters are settled. Nevertheless the life of the Collective is now and henceforth guaranteed. One can already make the following estimates in round figures:
Value of the crops from 340 hectares of orange
   groves at the minimum price of 3,000 pesetas
   per hectare   ...   .   1,020,000 ptas

ditto from 100 hectares of rice plantings average
    720 quintals at 350 pesetas a quintal ... ...   *252,000 ptas*
ditto 280 hectares of irrigated land at an average
    certainly greater than 6,000 pesetas ... ...   *1,680,000 ptas*
ditto 1,000 hectares of dry lands at 300 pesetas   *300,000 ptas*

                                             3,252,000 ptas

The difference between the outgoings noted and the above estimated gross income is 2,052,752 pesetas which will permit us to improve our working equipment, to purchase fertilisers, feedstuffs for the animals, etc. We have kept our estimates as low as possible in order to improve the living conditions of the members of the Collective as and when our reserves will make this possible. This will encourage the farmers and small-holders who have so far hesitated in joining to make up their minds. The results obtained will then make them join us in a happier frame of mind than if they were to join now.

In the three months since our Collective was founded we have bought three lorries at a cost of 100,000 pesetas; we have also purchased 12 she-mules and 230 goats and are expecting delivery of forty cows. We have organised a poultry farm and bought six incubators. At the moment we are producing 3,000 eggs a month. We have decided to develop this farm as quickly as we can to ensure that eggs and poultry will be available to all members without payment.

The production and monetary return at the moment from all the collectivists amounts to 400,000 pesetas a month.

                               Fraternal greetings . . .
                                         V.G.

The detailed account of the Collective in Jativa ends here, but it is worth underlining once again the different conditions in which the Collectives in Aragon and those in the Levante were born. In Aragon it was possible to obtain from the beginning the support of a large proportion of the population because of the absence of opposition from the republican authorities, and because the traditional political parties had disappeared. Often the Collective merged with the village. In the Levante, in the circumstances, the Collectives were usually only partial—the estimate of 40% of the total population is a fair one in my view. But on the one hand the spread of their action, and on the other the greater demographic density, resulted in there being more numerous, with more members and, as a consequence of the abundance of their resources, their constructive achievement in the economic field was much more important. On the human level Aragon has certainly not been surpassed.

3. Other Methods of Operation

SEGORBE (province of Castellon de la Plana). As well as many libertarians, there were in this small town of 7,000 inhabitants also many militants among the socialists, U.G.T.-ists, Republicans and Communists. In addition there were the farmers who thought they would be able to keep the land which they formerly rented from the *terratenientes*, now dispossessed, and the traditional smallholders, satisfied with their situation, who were not attracted by collectivist organisation. These adverse forces constituted a solid front of resistance to the socialisation proposed by the C.N.T.-ers, even more so since the Minister of Agriculture, the Communist Uribe, made vehement speeches over the Valencia radio inciting the peasants to "resistance" against the Collectives, whilst La Pasionaria,[12] official leader of the Party of Moscow, echoing the arguments formerly circulated by the reactionaries, was declaring over the same radio, to the benefit of the waverers: "Is it not a fact, comrade peasants, that it is painful to work and break one's back throughout the year, only to be deprived of the fruits of your labours by some immoral scoundrels when it is time to gather the harvest." Declarations of war on the supporters of collectivisation followed.

One came near to bloody incidents which the Stalinists were at pains to provoke, and when I went the first time to Segorbe, to address a meeting on the advantages of collectivisation from the social and economic points of view, I was hard pressed afterwards to bring calm among the tense comrades, advising against a violent confrontation with their detractors and for, to begin with, a modest, free community, as had been done elsewhere in order to win over supporters by the power of example.

The canton of Segorbe comprises 42 villages where, as in so many other places, our comrades had entered the municipal

12 Leader and rabid Stalinist militant.

Councils through which they sought to have social reforms accepted, some of them fundamental.

On their initiative, price controls were established in most villages; then trade was socialised, firstly in order to share in the revictualling of the front which was not far off. A new stage was the establishment of a *Comité* which distributed goods to the controlled tradespeople. Then the "municipal cooperatives" were born in complete agreement with the delegates of seven villages who had been elected to constitute the distribution *Comité* for the whole canton. Finally the "Free Commune of Segorbe" was created with an initial nucleus of 42 families. A month later there were ninety. Fenner Brockway the English socialist was in Segorbe at the time and on his return to England referred to the deep impression he had received from that visit.*

JERICA (province of Castellon de la Plana). There too, and not because it was reactionary, the population did not readily accept the collectivisation of the land, not even of the expropriated estates belonging to the rich fascists, because the collectivists spirit was foreign to large numbers of people. And again it would be interesting to know to what extent the fear of a Francoist triumph or of a backward move by the Republic after victory influenced the attitude of those who, as was the case of some villages in Aragon, refused to participate in the new solutions.

Eight months after the 19th July uprising the C.N.T. had only 200 members—incidentally, as many as the U.G.T. but with this difference, so often noted: that support for the U.G.T. by the conservative smallholders, tradesmen and other recent converts to trade unionism was dictated by a desire to counteract the revolutionary enterprises of the C.N.T. and maintain in existence a class society in which everyone seeks to benefit at the expense of somebody else.

Nevertheless a start was made by socialising industry. Then our Syndicate seized five estates, one of 70 hectares, onto which

Translator's footnote: Brockway in an article, "The C.N.T. as I saw it" (*Spain and the World,* July 19, 1937) wrote of Segorbe: "Most of all I enjoyed my visit to the Agricultural Collective of Segorbe. I must not delay to describe it in detail; but the spirit of the peasants, their enthusiasm, the way they had contributed their stock to the common effort, their pride in it—all was an inspiration . . . The anarchists of Spain, through the C.N.T., are doing one of the biggest constructive jobs ever done by the working-class."

70 families belonging to the C.N.T. and 10 to the U.G.T. moved. From these beginnings the number of collectivists rose rapidly.

SONEJA (province of Castellon de la Plana). The libertarian movement there has a long history—which probably goes back to the First International. In 1921 a number of our comrades organised a plasterers cooperative as a way of freeing themselves from the boss class and of doing something constructive. Ten years later almost all the plaster used in the village and its surroundings came from their firm which in 1936 had liquid assets valued at 300,000 pesetas. This was a small fortune in villages where a tradesman's rate was seven pesetas a day.

The resources that were at their disposal made it possible for our comrades to build a small school which they donated to the local Syndicate, and which they maintained at their expense. Then they founded a cultural group and a public library. Thanks to them, there were no illiterate children in Soneja. They were also looked upon as the most idealistic in the region and their moral rectitude, which was proverbial, meant that they were often called in to arbitrate in disputes.

After 19th July, a new municipal council was elected in which they were in a majority. As in Segorbe, industry was socialised first. It was not until the following March that the local general Syndicate undertook to socialise what it could in agriculture, only with the estates abandoned by their fascist owners, land neglected due to lack of initiative or because of physical disability.

Good work was done but it did not achieve the completeness that was noted in other localities, though it went on improving.

SUECA[13] (province of Valencia). On July 19th, as in all localities in the Levante, the anti-fascist forces, C.N.T.-ers, republicans and socialists constituted a defence *Comité*, took the necessary protective measures against the fascists, sought to ensure the means of life for all the inhabitants, and confiscated the large estates.

These estates were in the first place cultivated for the benefit of everybody. Then, surmounting a second stage, the Defence *Comité* took all the cultivable land under its control and proceeded to a new division according to the needs of families and the average yields of the various zones. A system reminiscent of the Russian "mir"; it was the only example of its kind in agrarian solutions,

13 Our movement had deep roots in Sueca, where its history had been at times, dramatic.

even provisional, that I had heard of. But as in the "mir", the land was given in usufruct, not as property legally recognised.

A household would receive two hectares of excellent, irrigated land; an extra hectare for the first child and, following the convention established with family wages, a decreasing amount for each addition to the family. The middle range landowners were reduced to the common share which permitted them to live by their work.

At the same time, and perhaps before, the same Defence *Comité*, inspired by the libertarian elements who were in it, established a control of ricefields, rice being the main crop in that zone. The administrative agricultural commission was especially nominated and given a mandate to sell the crop and take charge of the proceeds. Then it opened accounts in a local bank in the name of each family who could thereby draw on their share of the money each week or month, up to the limits established so as to avoid waste and chaos.

It was at this point that on 10th January, 1937, about six months after the Civil War started, that the peasants' Syndicate, with 2,000 members and affiliated to the C.N.T., started the agrarian Collective of Sueca. 400 families joined, contributing their land and their working tools, so from the start 1,000 hectares of very rich land for general agriculture were available as well as 200 hectares for market gardening and a proportional share of the estates taken from the fascists. Juridically this land belonged to the commune (parish) but the occupiers did what they wished with it.

Shortly afterwards 32 families of members of the U.G.T. and ten of members of the Communist Party in their turn formed a Collective. Example was asserting itself with our adversaries.

BENICARLO (province of Castellon de la Plana). The method of application in Benicarlo reminds one of Segorbe with some variables. None of the fifty-two villages in the canton decided to attempt a partial or complete collectivist experiment at the beginning, nor was it the case of our comrades wanting to impose it by force. Nevertheless the resistance weakened later and some Collectives were set up.

Once again it was the participation of the municipal council and the kind of solutions provided for the problem of food supplies that paved the way. Private business being at a standstill, our comrades met the situation by commandeering lorries and vans and organising a municipal *Comité* entrusted with the task of sales and purchases "for the whole of the fifty-two villages of the canton".

This organism started by buying from the peasants their produce which they despatched to the consumer or to disposal centres or even abroad. Then it centralised supplies of seeds and fertilisers and distributed them with a view to intensifying the production of corn and potatoes, bearing in mind the food shortages to be expected that winter. (The peasants seemed to us to be more farseeing and concerned with the fate of the towns than the governors and citizens whose concern it should have been.) This led to the supervision of the work of the smallholders, to avoid any sabotage or negligence in a period when the general needs had to prevail.

At the same time the cantonal *Comité* of Benicarlo, thanks to the friendly relations which permitted a growing unity between agriculture and industry, brought immediate improvements to the peasants' conditions. Farmers and *medieros* had no longer to pay land rent either in money or kind. They very soon benefited from the free installation of electricity, the result of excellent intersyndical relations on a regional basis, and each village had its telephone. The necessary resources for these enterprises came from the rents on the houses of the people of Benicarlo itself, who were invited to pay them to the municipal Council where our comrades had their headquarters. In return taxes were abolished and the proprietors were never thrown out onto the street.

Then schools were started, kindergartens organised. All this convinced the doubters, and in the end the Collectives made their appearance.

In the case of Benicarlo, initiative came therefore mainly from the centre. It was by beginning at the centre that it was possible first to start and then to extend the "Confederal Communities", thus called because of their affiliation to the C.N.T. Everything concerning the canton went through Benicarlo which was strategically well situated. Every morning an average of 150 carts brought or collected goods of all kinds. The fraternal network was finally established, and later completed.

Carried along by the tide of events, the political parties either accepted the *fait accompli* or collaborated.

M

CHAPTER VII

THE COLLECTIVES OF CASTILE

Circumstances beyond my control interrupted my first-hand study
of the achievements of the Spanish social revolution much too
soon; as a result I was unable to observe on the spot the
Collectives of Castile, or more exactly of the two Castiles: the
Old and the New. Collectivisation in the Centre took place
after Aragon and the Levante and was at the same time a
natural development and a necessity. Yet the Castilian region,
especially the one that a mind historically informed automatically
evokes, did not seem ready for such a venture which was so
contrary to the role that it had played since the suppression of
the "comuneros" at the time of Don Carlos.[1] For since the
triumphant Reconquest at the expense of the Arabs, it was the
home of centralism and of political domination set up by Ferdinand
and Isabella (called, with reason, the "catholic kings") and
maintained by force of arms. The establishment of the Court in
Madrid, understandably engineered by Charles V, succeeded in
infusing among the population, as almost always happens with
the population of capital cities, a power complex, and the most
fanatical Church which the monarchy made into an instrument
of power, added to it the seal of its intransigent fanaticism.

However, political and religious convictions do not necessarily

---

1 Though the suppression took place at the time of Charles V it was
not his doing. Whatever it may cost some Spaniards to admit it,
it was the Spanish aristocracy alone which annihilated the democratic
uprising: the repercussions had far-reaching importance in the social
history of Spain.

always destroy higher human qualities. It is the case of the Castilian peasant, the nobility of whose spirit and soul, whose uprightness, courage and profound honesty are his greatest virtues which inspire the esteem of others, and whose respect for the State has not become a voluntary and servile submission. Every individual being in the first place a man, it is in the first place within himself, from his innermost conscience that he draws the reasons for his behaviour.

On the other hand, municipal and customary right has held out in Castile as in other regions of Spain, and under the authoritarian structures of the central power, it very often maintained, as with the fire under the ash, a spirit and a practice of mutual aid that people like Adolfo Posadas and Joaquín Costa have praised in such works as *El Derecho Consuetudinario* or *El Colectivismo Agrario en España*. For the Castilian peasant, a tradition of mutual aid, of municipal rights, persists, and a word given is worth more than the law. He is hospitable and generous. He is a worker, making the corn which feeds the whole country grow on land which is hard, unproductive, and at an average altitude of 700 metres above sea level, exposed throughout most of the year either to bitter frosts or torrid heat. The continual struggle has developed in him a characteristic austerity and courage.

Yet libertarian ideas had penetrated very little the vast Castilian plateau. Conservatives predominated there, with the centuries-old "caciquism" of the large landowners. Whenever an awakening to new ideas had taken place it was the reformist socialists who had benefited.

But the Civil War changed many things. For from the first moment in a large part of the region it did not develop against fascism. On the other hand, it extended inevitably to the largest landed estates, implicitly or explicitly its allies. The flight of men who immediately went to the regions that had been taken from the Republic, facilitated or provoked the revolutionary seizure of their estates.

And from the first moment, in all the villages which had previously been dominated by a social organisation from another age, the Popular Front nominated administrators who confiscated not only the land but the machines and the draught animals as well.

At the same time, the reformist trade union, the U.G.T., appointed administrative *Comités* for the management of the expropriated estates. And the Communists, who were part of the Popular Front, infiltrated these new organisms as fast as they could.

The manner in which this incongruous bunch of administrators, without any creative initiative, conducted affairs was disastrous from the start. The Republicans, naturally legalists, and who had never thought about such responsibilities, did not know what to do with the means of production. The Communists and socialists, accustomed not to act without receiving instructions from the Party's Central Committee, or from the State institutions, were waiting for orders which never came, or which were too vague when they didn't arrive too late.

Now, work on the land demands constant initiative responding to the diverse circumstances which cannot be foreseen from an office, and nothing is more unbearable to the peasant than to be given orders from a distance by people who know nothing about the job. The militants of the political parties were putting a brake on the tasks needing to be done instead of being the instigators.

As a result yields fell on the large landed estates that had been seized under the auspices of the State which was undertaking, almost by force, an agrarian reform about which there had been talk for years without anything being done on the kind of scale required. Then the workers were blamed for the situation, and that the partial stoppage of work on the land (which was in fact caused by the incapacity of the local authorities, of the management committees to choose between large private property and socialism) had caused a decline in production which was threatening the towns.

The situation therefore became favourable for the organisation of Collectives. Soon there was in addition the departure of the government from Madrid before the advance of the Francoist troops which were being contained with difficulty twelve kilometres to the south of the capital. Relieved of the State machine the spirit of the population began to unwind, to "degovernmentalise" itself, and things were ordered through the freed, or at least much freer, initiative of the population.

A new stage in which the libertarian influence began to make itself felt with unexpected vigour. Until then it was only in the capital that it was developed to a degree which had the potential to attain historic proportions. For some years past, especially since the proclamation of the Second Republic in 1931, the libertarian movement had made progress in Madrid where the royal residence, the presence of the Court, of Parliament and the various organisms of the State, and the absence of industries, imposed and favoured institutions of a parasitic and bureaucratic character and dulled local customs. But during those five years our movement had shot forward, and our daily newspaper *C. N. T.* had increased its circulation to 30,000 copies. The building workers' Syndicate which had cost our militants much effort to organise against the opposition of the existing Syndicate, whose paid organiser was the reformist leader Largo Caballero, had 15,000 members on the eve of the Francoist attack; that of the woodworkers had absorbed a third of the labour force among cabinet makers, joiners and carpenters. The Syndicate of liberal professions included a growing number of journalists, engineers, and writers whose fundamentally anti-State feelings drove them out of the U.G.T. which continued to be managed by State socialists.

During the dictatorship of Primo de Rivera (1924-1931) an *Ateneo* (centre for studies and cultural activities) had been organised, and had begun to spread information on social matters.[2] Once the Republic was proclaimed some thirty *Ateneos* of the same kind though of less ambitious proportions, for which a library was the starting point, were organised in the central area as well as in the districts where there was a chain of them, and which provided not only a reading room used also for lectures and where books were available in quantities, but workers syndicates established their headquarters there; thus the class struggle and the development of the individual went hand in hand. The districts of Tetuan, Cuatro Caminos, La Bombilla, Cerretera Extramadura and many more each had its *Ateneo*. And naturally these *Ateneos* had set up a Federation and a network which covered the city and its suburbs. The high moral level of this activity explains to a large degree the influence of the C.N.T. and the constructive achievements which took place as soon as the situation made it possible to act.

Our Madrid comrades who had already established contacts with peasant groupings intervened slowly, advocating what was

2 This *Ateneo* with a libertarian spirit served to complement, relatively speaking, the *Ateneo* founded under the monarchy by the liberal Madrid intellectuals and whose campaigns and political positions certainly exerted an influence on public life in Spain. On many occasions, libertarian militants, among them Orobon Fernandez, a young man of great merit who died of consumption, were invited.

being done in Aragon and in the Levante. Very soon they got a hearing, the more so as the majority consisted of manual workers and not of bureaucrats, and that those workers could easily put down the hammer and the trowel and take up the pitchfork when it was deemed necessary to do so.

And the Collectives were created, spreading to the north and south of Madrid, across those parts of the two Castiles that had not been conquered by the Francoists: two-thirds of the province of Guadalajara, almost all the province of Madrid, Toledo and Ciudad Real,[3] and the entire province of Cuenca. In a year, there were 230 Collectives with about 100,000 members with their families. Six months later the number of Collectives had risen to 300. No one doubted that the movement would have developed well beyond this had Franco not won the war. The reader may be very surprised to learn that the Federation of Land Workers which was after all affiliated to the U.G.T., itself joined the Collectives.

The Collectives were a success right from the start, the results of solidarity, a community of efforts, and of the use of the most effective techniques. There was no waiting for slogans and for official or semi-official approval before forging ahead. Land clearance, irrigation works, new sowings, tree planting, collective stores ("cooperatives"), poultry yards, economic equality as a result of the establishment of the family wage . . . After all, the workers who supported the U.G.T. more often than not had the same objectives as those who belonged to the C.N.T. Like them, they wanted the expropriation of the large landed proprietors which the mini-reform effected by the government of the Second Republic was carrying out with exasperating slowness. They wanted the establishment of social justice in practice, with the right to a living, to consumer goods, to the satisfaction of material needs for themselves and their families. And they knew full well that this would be impossible so long as the land belonged to a minority of exploiters and parasites. Agreement was therefore easily reached between the two peasant organisations.

In December 1937, the secretariat of the National Federation of Agriculture attached to the C.N.T. was able to declare that the region of the Centre, roughly comprising the two Castiles,

3 Ciudad Real (Royal Town) was renamed during the revolution Ciudad Libre (Free Town).

came second among the regions so far as the results of socialisation were concerned. First came the Levante, and we have already outlined the extent of its achievements, and at the time the Collectives of Aragon were deeply affected by the ravages caused by the brigade led by the Communist Lister which was then showing more courage against the collectivist peasants than against Franco's armed forces.

The achievements in Castile were not only due to the efforts of the libertarian militants of the region[4] and of the socialists who dared to join forces with them. A fact which deserves to be mentioned, and which once again demonstrates the deep solidarity that linked the regions: In July 1937, 1000 members of the Levante Collectives had been sent to Castile to help and to advise their less experienced comrades. As a result of this concentration of complementary activities it would seem that in Castile, with the lessons of Aragon and the Levante to assist them, great strides were made in a minimum of time.

From the administrative point of view, the organic structure of the Castilian Collectives is basically the same as already described for Aragon and the Levante. A Management Commission, nominated by the village or collectivist assembly and responsible to it; groups of producers constituted and organised according to age, suitability for work, their sex and the variety of tasks;[5] delegates from the groups meeting periodically to plan overall and to coordinate efforts.[6]

As in Aragon and the Levante, the administrative Commissions consisted of as many members as there were branches of activity: agriculture, livestock, housing, education, etc. . . . In the small villages or in Collectives with few members, a single delegate would undertake a number of these functions, and generally would go on working at his normal job. For, to quote from a report published at the time: "in a well organised Collective nobody has to give up being a peasant".

The Economic Council for Castile which resided in Madrid

4 Many militants from Madrid who had effectively participated in the propaganda effort in the countryside, contributed to the organisation of the Collectives.
5 It should be remembered that women only worked irregularly—"to harvest the lucerne and to thin out the sugar beet plants" as the Collectivists of Albalate de Cinca put it in their report.
6 What happened in Castile was the opposite of what took place in the Levante. For it was the militants from the towns who went to the countryside to spread the message.

[183]

was itself advised by experts, with and without diplomas, on agricultural problems and stock rearing. At the same time local accountancy, generally entrusted to a professional often coming from the town, recorded everything concerning production, consumption, wages paid, goods in store. Thus everything was controlled by the peasants, who were regularly apprised; on the other hand what was produced at the cantonal level was communicated to the corresponding commission of the cantonal federation which, in turn, informed the Collectives set up in the country districts. They thus practised a decentralisation of administrative functions.

*

From the economic point of view, the Collectives in Castile did not always have the same organic structure that one finds, for instance, in those of Aragon. Often they could only develop in the vast estates which the socialising peasants took possession of. On the other hand, and as in Andalusia, some estates were so large that with the personnel settled on them they literally constituted socio-economic units, so that an isolated Collective could nevertheless be a very important one. But it was also the case that within the jurisdiction of some villages many scattered Collectives were linked together by a coordinating local *Comité*. In other cases practically the whole village was collectivised, or the part of it that was constituted a homogeneous and integrated unity in the multiplicity of the general activities.

For whatever may have been the significance of those realisations, all of them, from the beginning, tended to unify and even, to use a verb dear to Bakunin, to "solidariser"* their action. It explains why each Collective belonging to the cantonal Federation, after covering its expenses (payment of wages or transfers—the word "wages" was repugnant to most people—purchase of fertilisers, seed, machines, school outgoings, sanitation, etc.) would send any cash surplus to the "Cantonal Equalisation Fund". This Fund, the administrators of which were nominated by a general assembly of delegates from the Collectives and responsible to them, had as its main function the distribution of moneys, supplied by the more favoured Collectives, among the less favoured ones.

Thus, as in Aragon, the libertarian communist principle was

* *Translator's note*: "solidariser" = to make common cause with.

applied not only within each Collective, but *between* all the Collectives. No village ravaged by a hailstorm, or drought, or frost and receiving compensation for the damage sustained, was expected to reimburse a penny of what it had received.

But the *federal* Equalisation Fund had also other functions. It was not enough to help the village or isolated Collective which was through no fault of its own constantly in the red. With the help of the specialists from the *Comité* of the federation of the Centre it looked into ways and means for remedying the difficulties by improving yields in agriculture and by organising auxiliary industries.

As in the case of other regions in Spain, all the cantonal funds in the Central region were federated. The headquarters were in Madrid. The region thus constituted a unity the parts of which freely settled local problems, but also, generally speaking, common problems such as those concerned with production. In a year the Madrid *Comité* distributed a million pesetas worth of fertilisers and machines to the poorest Collectives.[7] It had obtained that money from the sale of the surpluses of the wealthiest Collectives. So the general and federal mechanism was well set up. Nothing was left to chance. And the general regional organisation did not limit itself to the functions we have so far enumerated. It gave advice, full time guidance as to the best techniques to adopt, and the most suitable methods of production. Already in November 1937, the peasants' regional Federation[8] had established its laboratories which were consulted on problems such as cultivation depth, suitable fertilisers, recommendations as to cultivations and seeds following chemical analysis of the soil. But it was considered not enough simply to give advice: the section for fertilisers acquired and supplied what had been recommended by the laboratories section. There was always complete synchronisation.

Campo Libre (Freeland), organ of the Federation, published as did the other regional organs of the libertarian Collectives, detailed information on how to cultivate or deal with cereals, vegetables, vines, fruit trees, according to the varieties, climate and soil. It included technical data on dealing with diseases, on storing produce, as well as on suitable stock breeds for each region

---

7 One cannot appreciate the amount involved unless one also knows that at the time a quintal (225 lbs.) of corn was worth 58 pesetas.
8 Which had become the regional Federation of Peasants and for the feeding of the Centre.

and on rational feeding to be adopted, etc. And the technical sections of the Federation published in the organs of the press announcements such as the following:

"We beg our local and cantonal Syndicates and Collectives which need to renew their vines and to improve them with American stock to get in touch with us as soon as possible, indicating the varieties and quantities they require. That is when they know what is best needed. In other cases, will they let us know how many plants they need and send us samples of the soil at different depths for analysis so that we may establish what is the most suitable variety. In this way we will be able to secure in good time the necessary plants to secure the best results from the vineyards."

Other advice and suggestions on all aspects of agricultural production and its by-products contributed to the technical development of the peasantry and all these efforts facilitated the rapid rationalisation of agriculture which was enthusiastically assisted by our agricultural engineers, chemists and other experts.[9]

One found this morality, this solidarity, this responsibility, this collectivist application in all aspects of life. Already towards the end of 1937 when the comrades who had been sent from the Levante or from Catalonia with vans arrived in no matter which collectivised village in Castile looking for corn, they always ran into a refusal. Even if there were available stocks the reply they got was, "Comrade, what we have here does not belong to us; you must get in touch with the secretariat of the regional Federation in Madrid." No offers of money or goods could in any way change this attitude for it was understood that respecting decisions taken ensured the success of the whole enterprise. So that all the prospective buyers could do was to phone Madrid or go there, where the section for barter or commerce accepted to supply the goods asked for if the general interest of the less favoured regions and the ever-present considerations of the demands of the war permitted.

We have said that the regional Federation of peasants of the Centre had become the regional Federation of peasants and of

9 What we know of the Russian Revolution and the press that appeared from the first years of Bolshevik rule, permits us to say that one did not find any advice being given which reflected such a constructive spirit.

food supplies. It was firstly a case of the awareness of the role played by producers, secondly of the organic integration for which precedents existed, though less developed, in Aragon and in the Levante.

On 25 October 1937, on the initiative of the peasant organisation of the region of the Centre, the fusion took place between the 97,843 peasants and the 12,897 workers in the distributive trades who also belonged to the C.N.T. It was yet another step in the coordination of complementary functions. From that moment, production and distribution were one activity. It was the distributors in the producers' Federation who undertook the distribution of products in the cooperatives and stores or public warehouses, which was organised as quickly as possible, both in the villages and in the towns, not forgetting the capital of Spain. Private trading was eliminated or at least kept under control, and thus was eliminated the possibility for a minority of middlemen to speculate on the produce brought by a majority of growers and take over control of the material means of the whole population.[10]

Then, as in Aragon, as well as in the Levante and in Catalonia, and we feel sure in the parts of Andalusia and Estremadura which for some time were in the hands of our comrades, this economic reorganisation was completed by the creation of a large number of schools, children's colonies, important irrigation works and a great number of initiatives for getting waste land into production, even in Madrid, sometimes at the price of superhuman efforts. One must further add the positive measures our comrades succeeded in getting accepted in the municipal Councils where they endeavoured to extend the role of the Commune (parish) and to transform it into an active element of social reorganisation.

Here now are a few examples which give one a fairly clear idea of the achievements of the three hundred Collectives of Castile.

Collective of Miralcampo—It was founded on the vast estate of Count Romanones, the famous leader of the monarchist liberals. In 1936, before the Revolution, wheat had been grown on 1,938 hectares and barley on 323 hectares. After collectivisation

10 Here is some cogent evidence: in Barcelona, and in Catalonia in general, it was not possible to socialise and amalgamate production and distribution. And the meal that cost 12 pesetas in a Barcelona restaurant cost 3 pesetas in a socialised restaurant in Madrid.

the acreage sown was increased to 4,522 hectares for wheat and 1,242 hectares for barley. Wine production increased from 485 to 727 hectolitres as a result of the improved treatment of the vines and the organisation of irrigation (for there had not been the time to replace the plants). The value of melon production rose from 196,000 to 300,000 pesetas and that of lucerne from 80,000 to 250,000 pesetas.[11]

Furthermore the Collective had a splendid rabbit industry, some 100 pigs and a food warehouse at which 800 people got their supplies.[12]

Throughout the canton the constructive achievements of the Collectives of Tielmes, Dos Barrios, Cabañas Yelpe, Cislada, Tomelloso, Almagro compared favourably with those of Miralcampo.

Manzanarés—The collectivists' achievements here were on a much larger scale than in Miralcampo. At the time this town had a population of 25,000 and surprisingly, for it was in Castile, the libertarian movement had put down numerous roots there.[13] Furthermore, collectivisation was undertaken as early as August 1936; from the start our comrades succeeded in carrying along with them the local members of the U.G.T.

In 1937 the Collective had 22,500 hectares of land, and 2,500 hectares of woodlands and forests. Half this wealth came from expropriations, the other half from gifts and voluntary membership. In the archives were kept the particulars of 63 expropriations, 23 voluntary gifts in perpetuity and of the gifts of 500 collectivists

11 At that time prices had not risen more than 10% over 1936 prices.
12 In his book *Historia del Anarco-Sindicalismo español* published in Madrid in 1968, the writer Juan Gomez Casas wrote: "The Collectives organised by the regional Federation of the Centre of Spain on the estates of Count Romanones in Miralcampo and Azuqueca, province of Guadalajara, specially deserve to be mentioned. The peasants completely transformed the whole physiognomy of these regions, they diverted the course of a river in order to irrigate the land, greatly increased the area under cultivation, built farms, a mill, schools, communal refectories, home for the collectivists and enormously increased production."
   Let us add that when he returned to his land at the end of the war, Count Romanones, who was a good sport was so amazed at what he saw that he prevailed on the fascists who were holding the organiser of this constructive achievement in prison and would certainly have shot him, to set him free.
13 Out of the normal population of 18,000, the C.N.T. had an average of 3,000 members; at the beginning of socialisation and as a consequence of recent persecutions there were 2,000. A few months later it had a membership of 6,000.

who had previously been smallholders. The initial nucleus consisted of 1,700 people, men, women and children.

The following year they were producing 87,610 quintals of wheat, 96,840 hectolitres of wine, 630,000 pesetas worth of secondary cereals and fruit and vegetables valued at 900,000 pesetas.

From February 1937, the Collective possessed 700 mules and she-mules, as many carts and ploughs, six tractors, four threshing-machines for the cereals, six hand operated and three motorised blowers, 80 pumps for extracting and distributing water onto the vegetable cultivations. In addition 3,000 sheep, 80 goats and two huge pigeon houses each with 6,000 birds.

That is not all. There were three oil-crushers equipped with hydraulic presses, thirty wine cellars with a capacity of 131,200 hectolitres, an alcohol distillery for medicinal purposes, a printing works, two cartwrights' workshops with modern equipment, a joiner's shop, a workshop for the weaving of esparto grass, a plaster factory, a sulphur factory for the sulphur dusting of the vines, and an engineering workshop.

It is true that almost all these installations already existed but the Collective got them to maximise their production. And being the cantonal headquarters, it assisted the Collectives of Membrilla, La Solana, Alhambra, Villarte, Arenas de la Vega, Daimiel, Villarubia, Almagro and Bolanos with whom it was linked by a community of effort. Such was the confidence it inspired that the Institute for Agrarian Reform, the official organism of the State, granted it a loan of 800,000 pesetas to tide it over the organisational period and which it was able to return without difficulty, even though mobilisation for the war involving a large number of members deprived it of willing hands which would have made it possible to do more.

Alcazar de Cervantes—It was in this town, where the traditional name Alcazar de San Juan had been changed by the Revolution, that Cervantes was born (this is a controversial matter). From October 1936 the local sections of the C.N.T. and of the U.G.T. began the socialisation of agriculture. Of 53,000 hectares within the jurisdiction of the municipal Council, 35,000 hectares passed into the hands of the Collective.

An administrative *Comité* consisting of three members from each of the Syndicates was nominated. The chairman, an old peasant, small proprietor and member of the U.G.T. was not perhaps the best choice for this revolutionary undertaking but his nomination was, so far as our comrades were concerned, a gesture of toleration. And in the event there were no grounds for complaint.

The first task for the Collective was, as always, to intensify agricultural production. Until then the growing of cereals was virtually non-existent. A year later production had reached 19,000 hectolitres of wheat, 15,000 hectolitres of barley. No mean achievement on hard land and under generally unfavourable climatic conditions.

In February 1938 the Collective had 1,800 mules and she-mules and a breeding flock of 400 sheep which though it had not increased in size because it was always being drawn upon in order to contribute to the feeding of Madrid and those at the front, nevertheless had by July 30, 1937 produced after payment of family wages, a net gain of 211,792 pesetas.

The region is most suited to the cultivation of the vine. In 1937 the harvest produced 48,300 quintals of grapes which were delivered to the presses attached to the collective cellars. A thirtieth part of the production was kept for local consumption and the money received from the sale of the balance was used to improve the standard of living and to bring, by the distribution of clothing and furniture and the carrying out of repairs to houses, comforts previously unknown.

Industrial collectivisation appeared only in March 1937, six months after the birth of the agrarian Collective. Presumably the results obtained by the latter acted as an incentive to act for those who had so far hesitated. The members of the C.N.T. started by establishing an engineering workshop in an abandoned house. Some craftsmen and small tradesmen helped them, and shortly afterwards, the workshop boasted 40 engineering workers with a technical manager nominated by them. It had been started with tools which each of them had brought along, but the situation was improved as circumstances allowed.

CHAPTER VIII

COLLECTIVIST BOOK-KEEPING

We have seen that the overwhelming majority of Spanish anarchists had supported libertarian, or anarchist, communism or anarcho-communism, or again, in the period going from 1918 to 1936, anarcho-syndicalism, of which the formula and name made headway as one of the consequences of the Russian Revolution, but added nothing, in fact quite the contrary, to the constructive ideas of anarchism which we can qualify by the generic term social.[1]

We have also seen that the communist anarchist formula, as well as that of libertarian communism and of anarcho-syndicalism, was one of free consumption which seemed to guarantee an equal right for all to the means of life, and to be the practical expression of true social justice. It was for this reason that Kropotkin had simplified it in summing it up in his book *The Conquest of Bread*, by the formula which was too readily believed literally of *"prise au tas"*: each and all would take freely what they needed from the communal stores. But for quite a long time reservations had been expressed among social anarchists. The first among them was undoubtedly Malatesta, whose critical mind was quite frequently aroused, though he was generally unable to offer constructive, valid solutions to those he criticised. He had expressed doubts as to the possibility of putting this principle into practice in complete freedom, and stated that it could not be applied until production of consumer goods had considerably increased; unfortunately he was unaware

---

1 Individualist anarchism never made headway.

of the fact that the increase in needs always follows, assuming it does not precede, the increase in production, and that for this problem there would never be a possibility of free consumption.

But less well known militants, among them the writer of this book, had posed the problem in their own way. Some of them suggested the use of a form of money—which, incidentally, Malatesta had done about 1922 without pursuing the matter. Some also preconised a form of money without explaining its financial mechanism, and to prevent it giving rise to dangerous hoarding, imagined it to be "melting" and losing its value in a short space of time. Other solutions were advanced such as, for instance, that distribution should be organised, with some control, by syndical cooperatives and municipal stores, which would avoid waste and prevent sabotage by counter-revolutionary elements in the form of excessive consumption and waste. Nevertheless by 1936 no valid theoretical solution had yet been found, especially so far as the towns were concerned.

Nothing then had been formulated with sufficient breadth and precision. So once the revolution had started it was imperative to find one or several solutions. The situation demanded it. In the regions where, as in Castile, in Catalonia or in the Levante, the official politico-administrative structures were being upheld and continued by the presence of the republican State, the use of official money was retained and backed by gold.[2] In the regions we have just referred to all that had to be done in order to avoid inequalities was to establish the family wage. The peseta remained as the standard of value and the means of distribution.

But—and this was the case especially in Aragon—where the State did not dominate, many original solutions had to be improvised; and we mean "many", for each village or small locality introduced its own solution.

At the beginning, then, there was no tacit agreement other than for the abolition of money, the expression and symbol of traditional injustice, social inequality, the crushing of the poor by the rich, the opulence of some at the expense of the poverty of others. For centuries, and from as far back as the complaints of the outcasts of fortune had been transmitted from generation to generation, money had appeared as the greatest of all means of exploitation, and the hatred of the common people had built

2 Spain was one of the countries in Europe with the largest gold reserves; it was estimated that the State Bank had about 3,000 m. pesetas (gold).

up against the cursed metal, against the paper money which the revolutionaries had set their minds on abolishing first and foremost.

In Aragon they kept their word. Nevertheless, for all that the principle of the "prise au tas" or in economic terms free consumption, was not applied. Apart from access, without control, to existing goods available in great abundance, and which were not the same in every village (here it was bread and wine, elsewhere vegetables, oil or fruit) some form of order was established from the first days when it was felt to be necessary, just as it was for the prosecution of work and production. For the revolution was considered right from the beginning a very important constructive undertaking. Especially in the countryside, there was no revolutionary orgy. The need to control and to foresee events was understood from the first day.

We have preserved confirmatory testimony of the manner in which the collectivist book-keeping was established. Let us begin with the simplest of all.

We are in the village of Naval situated in the north of the province of Huesca. No money, not even local money, no rationing. Free consumption from the first day, but supervised consumption. Everybody could call at the "Antifascist *Comité*" which is advised, if necessary, by the local libertarian group. A cooperative for general distribution was improvised and it produced a book of coupons numbered 1 to 100, in which were marked from day to day the commodities handed over on demand, and the consumer's name.

On September 15, the day collective life began there, Antonio Ballester—or somebody in his family—received half a kilo of chickpeas and a kilo of soap; José Gambia received a pair of canvas shoes; Serano Bistue, wire netting for a rabbit hutch and some string; Prudencia Lafulla a kilo of rice and a kilo of sugar; Joaquina Bastos a kilo of soap; Antonio Puertolas two kilos of meat; Ramon Sodomillo three litres of wine; José Lafarg a loaf of bread; José Arnal a little girl's dress, a kilo of soap and one of rice;[3] just as Sotero Fuentes who also took a kilo of soap and one of lard; Sesouta, nails for the cabin for the guard; Joaquina Solanona and others each take a kilo of soap, while others take

3 The fact that a man should have gone to collect those articles and that others went on doing so were indications of an instant revolution in customs. What Spanish male would have previously done the shopping at the grocer's and also bought a little girl's dress?

N

sugar, condensed milk, rice. And to end the first day one finds an entry on counterfoil No. 25 an exchange of half a dozen eggs, presumably brought by an individualist in exchange for half a kilo of sugar.

Naval at that time had 800 inhabitants and 176 families. There was not therefore on that first day excess or waste. And the counterfoils on subsequent days showed the same moderation of free consumption; two pairs of canvas shoes for two men, three kilos of soap; a bottle of lye; a kilo of chick peas; a kilo of sugar; 150 grammes of lamb's meat, "for a sick person" is the comment as if to explain the reason for requesting this luxury food; a litre of oil, sewing thread, then two kilos of bread, three litres of wine (special); a kilo of *pasta;* and again more soap, and more lye, and again more soap.[4] Each of these articles was asked for by different people and entered on separate counterfoils.

Such was the most simple procedure for control adopted by Naval and other villages in the early days. But it was further simplified later. For on December 1st of the same year, the book of counterfoils was replaced by a booklet without counterfoils which was distributed to each family. And for the family, whose booklet we picked at random, purchases of groceries and meat amounted to 107.30 pesetas in December, 79.20 pesetas in January, 68.85 pesetas in February, 90.80 pesetas in March, 83.00 pesetas in April. A separate account was kept for haberdashery, clothing and shoes.

But behind that primary control, in all its simplicity, one found a more strict and complicated accountancy. The following details are taken from the notes we made on consulting the account books of the general control and from the documents we have examined or have kept.

Firstly an account book where are entered daily outgoings and incomings, purchases and sales of all products without exceptions. Then the Large Book in which are to be found all the transactions on a daily basis for the respective sections specially established. And another book dealing with the slaughter of animals with the date, details of the animals, number, place of origin, weight, quality, quantity of meat held for the sick and quantity delivered to the butcher.

In a small separate account book is entered what is supplied to the collectivists *"para vicios"* ("for vices") as the writer,

---

4 Soap was, as one can see, one of the articles most in demand. This concern for cleanliness speaks volumes.

who must have been a bit of a puritan, puts it with relish; the "vicios" were tobacco for the men, a few toilet products for the women, sweets for the children . . . The men had two pesetas a week, women one peseta and children fifty cents. This account book had a counterpart in which were entered the accounts of the two village cafés where one could obtain lemonade, a glass of wine—one only—soda water or a "coffee" made from roasted barley.

I was then shown the account book dealing with the two lorries which the Collective had purchased and the account of expenses incurred for them (petrol, tyres, repairs, etc.). There was also an account book for the sale of pottery made locally and sold throughout the region. Then a separate receipt book for sales of salt locally obtained. Finally the Expenses book in which were entered the total expenses incurred by each family.

An accurate accountancy, though improvised by men who had never kept accounts in their lives.

So far as distribution was concerned, whatever the form or method adopted, the organising initiative was appearing all the time. In hundreds of villages, *libretas de consumo* (consumer books) in different sizes and colours were issued. Ration tables were appended, for one had to ration not only in the event of a reduction in the reserves and perhaps in production, but because it was also necessary to send food supplies to the front and the towns, which only too often appeared not to appreciate the gravity of the situation. Here then is a *libreta* issued in Calanda (province of Teruel). It is on green paper and a rather large format (22 cm x 13 cm). It covers the period from March 1, 1937 to February 2, 1938 and each page covers a week. The first column lists the products that the holder or his family may obtain, from meat to lye, including grocery products, preserves (in Aragon this meant generally tomatoes and sardines), dry vegetables, furniture, material and even perfumery. Altogether 27 items. Alongside the list are columns for each day of the week where the value of purchases reckoned in pesetas is entered. The weekly total can be easily obtained and auditing carried out.

The *libreta* for Fraga is smaller (15 cm x 10 cm) and in the first column are printed the days of the month from 1st to 31st, and along the top is a list of fourteen products, with their corresponding columns, that it was thought necessary to ration (on the basis of local production, existing reserves and commitments to the militia or the nearby fronts). The *libreta* for

Ontiñena (in this case called *libreta de credito*) was of the same size as that for Fraga. But there were no specific dates nor a list of available products. The corresponding columns were completed at the time of purchase. The *libreta* for Granollers (in the province of Barcelona), was based on a different concept. Produced by the municipal Council, it had eight thin sheets per week and these were divided into perforated coupons on which were indicated the quantity of wine, eggs, sugar, potatoes, butcher's meat, poultry (boiling fowl or rabbit), salt cod or pork meat which each family was entitled to buy (calculated on the composition of the family) and on which days, which was specially indicated on the basis of the established organisation for food supplies.

Thus there were in Catalonia and especially in Aragon some 250, perhaps more, *libretas* all with a similar concept but of different forms. But there were other forms of food rationing and control. All this varied according to the available resources, existing reserves and the approach to the problems. In the town of Barbastro, the second most important in the province of Huesca a rations table was established without *libreta,* without national or local money.

Bread was not rationed; wine was, sometimes; oil also but on average 30 litres was distributed per person per year. It was, as in many places, the only source of fat used in cooking.

It should be added that children over the age of fourteen counted as adults.

All these examples and others we could quote on this aspect of collectivist book-keeping demonstrate that there was never disorder. On the contrary, one could perhaps reproach the prime movers of the Collectives with having sometimes organised things too much. One has seen how in Naval only a minimal part of the expenditure was reserved for small extras, *"para vicios"* This concern was to be found where rationing had reached a touching degree of austerity. *Hojas de fumadores* (smokers' cards) which at the same time took into account a human weakness and put a brake on excesses, were issued and distributed in many Collectives, as well as *vales* or consumer vouchers entitling the holder to a cup of grilled barley "coffee". In Ontiñena for instance each Collectivist received a card for ten drinks, excluding alcohol, which was punched at each tasting, and if he invited a friend to "have one" he would simply have one "coffee" or lemonade less that week.

Wherever strict rationing and official money were eschewed, a local money replaced them. Villages which did so had vouchers printed with their name and 1, 2, 5 or 10 pesetas, sometimes even with 25 or 50 centimes overprinted, and this fiduciary currency was, locally of course, as sound as the official peseta guaranteed by the Valencia government. It even had the advantage of not losing its value.

Nevertheless, it must also be recognised that it could only be used at a local level. This did not escape the notice of those who took the initiative for social reconstruction. Nor, for that matter of those inhabitants wishing to travel. In such cases the *Comité* of the Collective supplied the necessary pesetas to allow the person to travel to parts where official money was law.[5] But to bring to an end the multitude of local currencies, the congress of the Aragon Collectives, which we summarised in an early chapter, had unanimously agreed to completely abolish their use and to establish an egalitarian rationing system for all the Aragon Collectives.

Consequently they produced a family rations book valid for everybody. This *libreta* which was dated from April 1, 1937 to December 31, by the week, listed 21 articles and groups of articles which, incidentally, give one an idea of the sobriety of the life of a Spanish peasant (and which had been redoubled by the exigencies of the war). They were, in the order in which they were printed: bread, wine, meat, oil, chick peas, beans, rice, pasta, sausages, sausage, blood sausage, fatty pork, various preserves (not specified), sugar, chocolate, tinned tomatoes, potatoes, milk, lentils, olives, lye, soap, hardware, household articles, haberdashery, footwear.

The Communist attack which took place shortly afterwards was to prevent the general application of this project. Having to retire within themselves, greatly reduced in numbers by the destruction they had suffered, the Collectives were, as a result, condemned to a precarious existence.

One can, nevertheless, come to the following conclusions: for the problem of distribution, which from certain points of view was greater than that of production itself, the Collectives demonstrated an innovatory spirit which by the multiplicity of its facets

5 This was and still is practised in the Israeli kibbutzim which otherwise cannot, on many points, be compared with the Spanish Collectives, for one finds in them norms and an organisation almost conventual, which reminds one of the communities advocated by a host of reformers of the 19th Century, and in which individual freedom is altogether overlooked.

and its practical commonsense, compels our admiration. The collective genius of the rank and file militants succeeded in solving problems which a centralised governmental organisation would have neither been able nor known how to solve. If the pragmatic methods to which they had to have recourse may appear to be insufficient, and sometimes unsound in view of some contradictions which one observes here and there, the development tending to eliminate these contradictions was taking place rapidly (in eight months, or less, depending on the cases, structural resolutions had been taken) and progress was being rapidly made towards unifying and decisive improvements. During that time, in the part of the country where the official money ruled, the peseta was continually being devalued because of the inability of the government to hold down prices, and speculation was getting under way and growing.

During my stay in Mas de las Matas I asked the principal organisers of the Collective (youngsters inspired by idealism, intelligence and faith) for exact figures on the livestock which I had been told had increased in the Collective. They supplied the figures which I am transcribing from the original:

GENERAL COLLECTIVE OF MAS DE LAS MATAS

Pigs for slaughter	570
Piglets	99
Sows	61
Milk Cows	24
Rearing Calves	61
Sheep	708
Lambs for slaughter	471
Young ewes for breeding next year	471
Goats	164
Kids	116
Year old goats	270

Consumption of meat during the month of April: 194 lambs, 50 sheep, 16 first quality, and 18 kids.

Mas de las Matas, May 5, 1937.
The Collective *Comité*.

One could not be more precise and I am certain that no mayor in a French or German Commune could provide in so short a time such detailed returns. Well, in the 1,600 or so agrarian or mainly agrarian Collectives (half of which included the whole village) in Spain at that time the same precise book-keeping was maintained day by day. And if there were exceptions unknown to us, they were exceptions that proved the general rule.

We found the same care for good organisation in other aspects of economic life seen on a much larger scale. Thus we asked the local *Comité* of d'Angüés, head village of the canton of the same name, in the province of Huesca, to explain to us the method used for the movement and the control of exchanges in the locality and for the canton with other zones in Aragon as well as in Catalonia. Our curiosity was satisfied with the following document:

CANTON OF ANGUES (PROV. OF HUESCA)

Deliveries made by our cantonal Federation of different products sent as barter to the cantonal Federation of Granollers:

1937		Value in pesetas
3 April	13,300 kilos of grain @ 0.53	7,049.00
10 April	22,050 kilos of grain @ 0.53	11,686.00
14 April	13,300 kilos of grain @ 0.53	7,049.00
17 April	Diff. of 25k on previous delivery	13.25
17 April	2 pigs @ 60 pesetas each	120.00
	Total	25,917.75

Deliveries made by the canton of Granollers to our cantonal Federation:

3 April	192 store pigs @ 60 pesetas	11,520.00
10 April	214 store pigs @ 60 pesetas	12,840.00
10 April	Sum received in pesetas	7,800.00
	Total	31,360.00

SUMMARY

Debit	31,360.00
Credit	25,917.75
Owing to Granollers	5,442,25

CANTON OF ANGUES (PROV. OF HUESCA)

Deliveries made by our cantonal Federation of different products sent as barter to the Municipal Council of Tarrasa:

1937		Value in pesetas
25 March	35 sacks flour @ 70 ptas/100 kg.	2,450.00
25 March	40 sacks flour @ 70 ptas/100 kg.	2,800.00
26 March	35 sacks flour @ 70 ptas/100 kg.	2,450.00
28 March	80 sacks flour @ 70 ptas/100 kg.	5,600.00
30 March	Miscellaneous goods as per invoice no. 31.36	7,762.00
2 April	25 sacks flour @ 70 ptas/100 kg.	2,450.00
14 April	40 sacks flour @ 70 ptas/100 kg.	3,000.00
	Total	26,512.10

Deliveries made by the Municipal Council of Tarrasa to our cantonal Federation:

9 March	Goods as per invoice	2,086.45
24 March	Goods as per 5 invoices	7,789.00
12 April	Goods as per 12 invoices	18,056.70
	Thimbles supplied by Ramon More	2,247.50
	Electrical goods	54.00
	Total	30,234.00

SUMMARY

Debit	30,234.10
Credit	26,512.10
We owe Tarrasa	3,722.00

Such were on those dates the accounts for barter arrangements between the village and canton of Angüés in Aragon and the small towns of Granollers and Tarrasa, both in the province of Barcelona. In separate registers were entered all purchases. We noted many other examples of this book-keeping in other localities. The lorries went to and fro between the regions, carrying goods. Each canton knew the details of the production of other cantons. They were all in touch with each other, allowed each other whatever credits were asked for on the tacit guarantee of the harvests or sales in the near future, and balanced their production by barter.

We asked the administrative *Comité* of the Collective of Albalate de Cinca for as detailed an account as possible on the whole organisation. Our comrades replied as follows:

"Our Collective comprises 113 families and 470 inhabitants of all ages. Three hundred can work. There are eight groups for work on the land and 25 people work in other, non agricultural trades. All the population belongs to the Collective.

"We have 2,900 hectares of irrigated land and 800 of dry land. The last harvest amounted to 696 quintals of wheat, 20 quintals of barley, 30 of oats, 161 quintals of potatoes, 40 hectolitres of broad beans and a similar quantity of maize. We planted 90 hectares of sugar beet and lucerne, which is undoubtedly the most productive crop, gave an average return of 25 quintals a hectare on the 200 cultivated. Increases in production were 15% for wheat, barley and oats, 25% for maize, potatoes and vegetables.

The Collective owns 13 draught oxen, 45 milk cows, 48 heifers, 57 calves, 900 sheep and breeding ewes, 300 lambs, 100 sheep for slaughter, and 200 pigs."

The informants ended with the following:

"Since in Albalate we can harvest large quantities of lucerne and dispose of more meadows, these resources will be put to use to increase the number of farms and production; as to consumption, everyone belongs to the Collective; everyone is free to work as he wishes, individually or in small groups or in the Collective; but all production is taken over by the local *Comité* to meet the exigencies of the war and the Revolution.

"P.S. Included in the 300 people capable of working we have included women who represent half the total and are employed on the harvesting of lucerne and for hoeing the sugar beet."

Let us look a little more closely at what we will call the "solidary book-keeping" at the level of the Federation of Aragon Collectives and of all the Collectives in the other regions. It had been classified at the *plenum* which took place in Caspe on April 25, 1937, three months after the congress where the Regional Federation had been constituted. Among other new resolutions, the delegates rejected the offer made by the Minister of Agriculture of a financial loan which could have helped the Collectives to solve certain difficulties arising from the retention of the peseta, and from the fact that they did not accept barter except with other Collectives or Syndicates belonging to the U.G.T. or the

C.N.T. All relations with private business, "individualists" or the State were absolutely banished.

The application of these principles brought with it the need to know exactly what resources were available so as not only to engage in barter but also for mutual aid on a permanent footing. Thus, shortly after the April *plenum,* on the basis of questionnaires sent out wherever necessary, the following figures were available for a first group of 77 village Collectives or collectivised villages which were producers of wheat. Surplus wheat available amounted to 17,180 quintals; but on the other hand other villages suffered from a shortage amounting to 1,653 quintals, so after making up the deficiencies to these villages a balance of 15,520 quintals remained for disposal.

For oil the calculations referred to the same group of 77 villages which had a production of 4,053 quintals. But elsewhere there would be a deficit of 1,637 quintals because of the vagaries of the climate. So after making good the deficit there remained 2,415 quintals for barter (machinery, clothing, etc.). The villages that benefited from this solidary aid, which was quickly organised no longer simply at cantonal level (as we saw in the case of Mas de las Matas) but at regional level, had their current accounts and paid with other goods, calculated in peseta values, when they could. But this practice of solidarity rapidly went beyond the narrow framework of the canton and took place through the intermediary of cantonal *Comités,* at an entirely regional level.[6]

I would add a detail which demonstrates with what lucid stubbornness the collectivist organisation defended its autonomy and above all its liberty against the non-collectivist organisms. We have pointed out that a Regional Council had been created in Aragon which constituted an independent political organism in order to prevent the government of Valencia from extending its powers over the region (it did so nevertheless by July-August 1937). That Council was headed by a majority of libertarians with a member of the Ascaso family, all of whom were more or less well-known militants, as its chairman. And it happened

---

6 At that time, the Caspe *Comité* had sent a circular to all villages and Collectives in order to carry out a general survey on the number of fruiting trees (pears, apples, nuts, olives, vines, almonds, etc.), on the numbers of head of animals (donkeys, mules, horses, sheep, cattle, pigs, goats) and on the availability of manpower and of the area of suitable land available, proportions of irrigated and dry lands. Thus a general organisation was being prepared at the level of the whole region.

that that semi-governmental organisation wanted to semi-govern, particularly in monopolising foreign commerce, reserving to itself the profits from the operations. But the Federation bluntly refused to accede to this intention, declaring that it was prepared, if necessary, to pay a tax so that the Aragon Council could discharge its responsibilities, but that the economy rested on the Collectives and that it was not prepared to give up its control.

CHAPTER IX

LIBERTARIAN DEMOCRACY

There was, in the organisation set in motion by the Spanish Revolution and by the libertarian movement, which was its mainspring, a structuring from the bottom to the top, which corresponds to a real federation and true democracy. It is true that deviations can occur at the top and at all levels; that authoritarian individuals can transform, or seek to transform, delegation into intangible authoritarian power. And nobody can affirm that this danger will never arise. But the situation was quite different from what it is or would be in a State apparatus. In the State which Marx, when he was seeking to court favour with the Paris Communards who had escaped the slaughter, so as to win them over to his cause, called a "parasitic superstructure" of society men installed in positions of command are inaccessible to the people. They can legislate, take decisions, give orders, make the choice for everybody without consulting those who will have to undergo the consequences of their decisions: they are the masters. The freedom which they apply is *their* freedom to do things in the way *they* want, thanks to the apparatus of law, rules and repression that they control, and at the end of which there are the prisons, penal settlements, concentration camps and executions. The U.S.S.R. and the satellite countries are tragic examples of this.

The non-Statist system does not allow these deviations because the controlling and coordinating *Comités*, clearly indispensable, do not go outside the organisation that has chosen them, *they remain in their midst*, always controllable by and accessible to the members. If any individuals contradict by their actions their mandates, it is possible to call them to order, to reprimand them, to replace them. It is only by and in such a system that the "majority lays down the law".

Since 1870 this system had been adopted by the Spanish libertarians, who, in their determination that the mass of members should pronounce and decide for themselves as often as possible on the problems that arose as well as on the running of activities were following the ideas of Proudhon and Bakunin.

Did this mean that there were no minorities, no individuals exerting an often decisive influence on the assembly, or in the daily life of the Syndicates, Collectives, Federations? To answer in the affirmative would be to lie and would deceive nobody. As everywhere and always, there were in those organisms militants who were better prepared, who were the first to stand in the breach, and to preach by example, risking their own skins, and who, driven by the spirit of devotion and sacrifice, were better informed on the problems, and found solutions to them more readily. The history of mankind concedes a worthy place to the minorities who have assumed the responsibility for the happiness of their contemporaries and the progress of the species. But the libertarian minority assumed that role according to anti-authoritarian principles, and by opposing the domination of man by man.

To emancipate the people it is first of all necessary to teach them, to push them to think and to want. The sizeable and enthusiastic libertarian minority sought therefore, as we have seen, to teach the masses to do without leaders and masters and to that end were always communicating information to them, educating them, accustoming them to understand the problems affecting them either directly or indirectly, to seek and to find satisfactory solutions. The syndical assemblies were the expression and the practice of libertarian democracy, a democracy having nothing in common with the democracy of Athens where the citizens discussed and disputed for days on end on the Agora; where factions, clan rivalries, ambitions, personalities conflicted; where, in view of the social inequalities precious time was lost in interminable wrangles. Here a modern Aristophanes would have had no reason to write the equivalent of *The Clouds*.

Normally those periodic meetings would not last more than a few hours. They dealt with concrete, precise subjects concretely and precisely. And all who had something to say could express themselves. The *Comité* presented the new problems that had arisen since the previous assembly, the results obtained by the application of such and such a resolution on the volume of production, the increase or decrease of any particular speciality, relations with other syndicates, production returns from the various workshops or factories. All this was the subject of reports and discussion. Then the assembly would nominate the commissions; the members of these commissions discussed between themselves what solutions to adopt; if there was disagreement, a majority report and a minority report would be prepared.

This took place in *all* the syndicates *throughout* Spain, in *all* trades and *all* industries, in assemblies which, in Barcelona, from the very beginnings of our movement brought together hundreds or thousands of workers depending on the strength of the organisations. So much so that the awareness of the duties, responsibilities of each spread all the time to a determining and decisive degree.

*

The practice of this democracy also extended to the agricultural regions. We have seen how, from the beginning of the Civil War and of the Revolution the decision to nominate a local management *Comité* for the villages was taken by general meetings of the inhabitants of villages, how the delegates in the different essential tasks which demanded an indispensable coordination of activities were proposed and elected by the whole assembled population. But it is worth adding and underlining that in *all* the collectivised villages and all the partially collectivised villages, in the 400 Collectives in Aragon, in the 900 in the Levante region, in the 300 in the Castilian region, to mention only the large groupings which comprised at least 60% of "republican" Spain's agriculture, the population was called together weekly, fortnightly or monthly and kept fully informed of everything concerning the commonweal.

This writer was present at a number of these assemblies in Aragon, where the reports on the various questions making up the agenda allowed the inhabitants to know, to so understand, and to feel so mentally integrated in society, to so participate in the management of public affairs, in the responsibilities, that the recriminations, the tensions which always occur when the power of decision is entrusted to a few individuals, be they democratically elected without the possibility of objecting, did not happen there. The assemblies were public, the objections, the proposals publicly discussed, everybody being free, as in the syndical assemblies, to participate in the discussions, to criticise, propose, etc. Democracy extended to the whole of social life. In most cases even the individualists could take part in the deliberations. They were given the same hearing as the collectivists.

This principle and practice were extended to the discussions in the municipal Councils in the small towns and even in sizeable ones—such as Villanueva y Geltru, Castellon de la Plana, Gerona, Alicante or Alcoy. We have seen that when, because of the exigencies of war, our comrades had joined these Councils, as a minority, they nevertheless very often exercised an influence far greater than their numerical strength, firstly because they secured the agreement of the other parties, who could not easily refuse, that discussions should be open to the public. Ordinary people with free time made a point of attending them. And often social reforms of immediate value (building of schools, nurseries, children's playgrounds, decent conditions for the old) were snatched from the political majority which would not have been granted if the discussions had taken place behind closed doors.

Both at the individual and local levels, we think these different aspects of libertarian democracy ushered in a new civilisation. To give a more exact idea of what is meant, we will observe the unfolding of a village assembly in Tamarite de Litera, in the province of Huesca, at which the writer was present.

The *pregonero* (public crier) presents himself at the cross roads, in the square and at the busiest corners of the village. He blows three times on his small horn with which he always announces his presence, then in a slow, light tenor voice which, for some reason I do not know, is used by all *pregoneros* in Aragon, he reads, clipping the words and sentences somewhat at random, from a paper on which is written that the members of the Collective are invited by the administrative Commission to attend the general assembly which will take place that same evening at 9 o'clock.

At 9.30 p.m. the local cinema is half full. At 10 p.m. it is packed. There are about 600 people including some 100 women, girls and a few children.

While waiting for the opening of the meeting, everybody is

talking without shouting in spite of the expansive temperament of the inhabitants of that region. In the end the secretary of the Collective mounts the platform alone. Silence falls and the secretary immediately proposes the adoption of necessary arrangements:

"We must," he says, "nominate a secretariat for the meeting."

Immediately one of those present asks to speak "on a point of order".

"There are some individualists in the hall. They are enemies of the Collective. They have no business being here, we must turn them out. What's more, it is imperative that women should remain silent during the discussion, otherwise they will have to be removed as well."

Some of those present seem to be in agreement with the double proposal; others clearly have doubts. The secretary replies that in his opinion the individualists should be allowed to remain and even take part in the discussions. "We have nothing to hide and it is by seeing how we act that they will end by being convinced." As to the talkative women—they are peasant women who had never attended such discussions before and who also have a right to speak—they will surely keep quiet and there will be no need to have recourse to such extreme measures. The assembly approves and the individualists remain.

Then the secretariat is nominated, consisting of comrades who are elected in turn. Then the chairman speaks. He is, naturally, one of the most active militants, and one of the best informed on the problems included in the agenda. He starts by dealing exhaustively with the reason for the Commission calling this extraordinary assembly. Though intelligent, he is no speaker, but makes a great effort to express himself with the utmost clarity, and succeeds.

First question: Four comrades on the Commission must be replaced because they are not carrying out their tasks satisfactorily, not through any bad will on their part, but because they lack the necessary background. Furthermore, there is a certain amount of discontent with the delegate dealing with food supplies. He is very able but has a difficult personality and his manner is too brusque, which results in unpleasant confrontations, particularly in inter-regional relations; it would perhaps be better if in future he dealt with the barter arrangements with more distant regions where individual contacts are not so important. The delegate for industry and commerce could look after distribution at local level, and the relations which this involves with members of the Collective.

The assembly accepts, without unnecessary discussion, the changes recommended and nominates successors. Then the delegate for food supplies has his duties limited in one direction and extended in another.

Another question which is on the agenda: A fairly large group of members of the Collective have just recently withdrawn from it to return to individualist activities. But the Collective which has taken over non-agricultural local production possesses all the bakehouses for breadmaking and the individualists' group claims one.

Faces are serious, concentrated, tense. Women make their comments without raising their voices. A collectivist has the floor:

"We must lend them a bakehouse for a fortnight or a month to give them time to built one for themselves."

"No," replies another, "they should have remained with us. Since they have left us, let them get on with it!"

A third declares that there are already too many bakehouses in the village and one must not build any more. Many other members expressed themselves with that economy of words which is a characteristic of the Aragonese peasants. When nobody else wishes to speak then the chairman expresses his opinion.

In the first place there is the problem of the smooth running of the economy. To construct another bakehouse is to waste material needed for other uses; it will in due course involve an expense for wood and electricity, which must be avoided, for the repercussions of bad management do not rebound only on the individualists but also on the whole national economy. Now, we must show that we can do better than the capitalists. This is why, instead of increasing the number of bakehouses being used we must even reduce them. Let us therefore make the bread for ourselves and for the individualists. But they will supply us with the amount of flour required to make the amount of bread they need and there will be the same quality of bread for all of us. Besides, we must not refuse bread to the individualists for, in spite of their error they must be in a position to eat, and in a situation in which the present roles were to be reversed, we would be happy if our adversaries did not prevent the collectivists from feeding themselves.

The chairman has convinced the assembly, which, following

o

the comments of some collectivists, approves without dissentients.

The next question concerns the pros and cons of rationing bread. The high family wages paid by the Collective allows them to buy large quantities, which encourages some abuse, and even sometimes inequalities which the Revolution cannot permit. Consequently it is necessary to establish a top limit for consumption to ensure that every family can obtain the quantities it needs but without there being waste.

The assembly accepts rationing, but then a juridical problem is posed: who will apply the measures decided upon, the municipal Council or the Collective? The former covers the whole population; the individualists who represent an eighth, and the Collectivists. If the municipal Council takes charge, rationing will have to be established for everybody. If it's the Collective, the individualists will not consider themselves obliged to respect it. Many views are put forward which allow for an assessment of the powers of the two organisations. And it is decided to ask first the municipal Council to undertake the task. If it does not accept, the Collective will—at least within the limits of its possibilities.

But the withdrawal of the individualists has posed another problem. Many of them have left their old parents on the hands of the Collective, while at the same time setting themselves up on the land which formerly belonged to the old folk they have now abandoned. Those dispossessed have been taken care of by the Collective because they are old and unable to work, but the behaviour of those individualists is unacceptable. What action can be taken?

The chairman, who has outlined the dispute, makes it quite clear from the start that there is no question of expelling the old folk. In any event they will be assisted, but their children must take back their parents or forfeit their land. Such is his opinion.

A number of members of the assembly take part in an orderly manner throughout. One suggests that the irresponsible sons should be deprived of half their harvest. Another repeats that it would be a shame to oblige these old folk to leave the Collective: anything must be considered but that. They return to the suggestion made by the chairman: either the individualists take their parents to live with them or they will have no land and solidarity of any kind will be withheld from them. The moral issue is uppermost. The proposal is approved.

Every time a solution is approved and before another is taken up, the assembly comments, giving free expression to its thoughts. Nevertheless the general conversation is not noisy, and barely lasts a minute.

Now the question to be discussed concerns the potteries which in normal times were a source of revenue as they supplied many villages in the region and even some small towns with jugs, porous water coolers and *cantaros* (earthenware pitchers). They also manufactured tiles and bricks there. But as there was a shortage of manpower in the fields because of the mobilisation for the front, the potters were sent there and abandoned the potteries; others too were at the front. Thus production had fallen off sharply. What should be done?

One man suggests that the potters should work a ten hour day instead of eight; another that one should increase the manpower in the potteries; a solution supported by a third speaker who adds that they should try to bring in skilled men from other regions. He also suggests that the tile factory which had been closed as a result of the current situation, should be reopened.

He is given the reply that we are in a war situation and that one can do very well without tiles. Laughter from the assembly, which approves, and as someone asks why cannot the skilled workers produce this year as much as in the previous year, the secretary of the Collective, a former mayor and who is well informed on these matters, explains that before many cantons obtained their supplies from Huesca and since this town is now in Francoist hands, they get their supplies from Tamarite. One must get the potters to return to their craft and in addition we must put an appeal in our Press for skilled workers from other regions to come and live here. Proposal accepted.

They have come to the end of the agenda, and move on to "any other business". One of the members points out that in Tamarite there is an *alpagatero* (a canvas shoe maker) who is good at his job. One could organise a workshop where the women could go and work instead of wasting their time gossiping in the street. The women laugh, but the proposal is accepted. A man of between 50 and 60 points out that the little girls of the village are not serious, since they prefer to go out instead of going to work in the workshop specially set up for them to learn dressmaking. As a solution to the problem he suggests that a good dressmaker be selected with the task of training them, but that classes should be held in a church without windows.

The door would be bolted, and the little girls not allowed out during the working hours. Everybody laughs, the parties concerned more than the others.

Many collectivists express their views in turn, and it is decided that in every workshop a woman delegate shall supervise the apprentices. Those who do not attend on two consecutive occasions without good cause will be dismissed. But the man who would have them kept under lock and key was implacable; he suggests quite seriously, or so it seemed, that to punish them when their work was unsatisfactory the young girls should be made to fast for two or three days. To that there is a general roar of laughter.

New problem: The nomination of a new hospital director (and we learn that the director is a woman, which is fairly unusual). This hospital has been converted into an Old People's Home, but they are now being treated at home by a doctor who joined the Collective and the cantonal hospital is at their disposal for all urgent cases or serious illnesses. This again poses a problem of jurisdiction. It is a general hospital. It is a question of ascertaining whether or not it comes under the municipal Council reconstituted following the publication of the decree emanating from the Valencia government. If it does, the hospital is everybody's responsibility, collectivists and individualists, and the latter must also share in the expenses. So far the Collective have paid everything, and its enemies have take advantage of its bounty. A matter for further study.

Following the examination of questions of less importance the chairman closes the session. The assembly has lasted $2\frac{1}{2}$ hours. Most of those who took part were peasants from the village or its environs, accustomed to rise early, and who at that time of the year had worked twelve or fourteen hours.

Yet no one left before the end of the discussions, not even those who had remained standing as there were not enough seats to go round. No woman or child had gone to sleep Eyes had remained wide open, and faces as wide awake. One read on them, at the end, as much, often amused, interest as one had observed at the beginning. And the chairman, at the same time paternal, fraternal, and the teacher, had to insist to prevent a much longer agenda.

The final resolution adopted concerned the frequency of assemblies which from being held monthly were to take place weekly.

And the collectivists made their different ways home to bed commenting on the discussions and resolutions adopted as they went. Some lived a fair distance away and travelled either on foot or on bicycles.

CHAPTER X

THE CHARTERS

In earlier chapters we have sought to introduce, within our space limitations, as many documents, or the most important sections of rules and Statutes which illustrated the essential principles on which the agrarian Collectives were founded and organised. We now add, separated from those chapters so as to avoid too many repetitions, other texts which, such as those already reproduced partially or in full, confirm the spirit, at the same time constructive and humanist, which guided the Spanish libertarian organisers in their historic task.

In order to study and know about this phase in human history this has for us the same importance as have the charters of the Communes and the towns of the Middle Ages. These texts remain for the future, factors to be appraised, and in which those who will continue the struggle for a more equitable and rational society may find inspiration. Perhaps by examining them under a microscope, a critical mind could put forward some objections of secondary importance. But in spite of any clumsiness in drafting, we are convinced that never, so far, has a revolution shown such a precise constructive spirit, such clear radical concepts, and such a noble social ethic. Considered in their essentials, one can state that the ends pursued, the methods outlined and adopted, constitute a doctrine of socialism which "fits" life and which can lead men to a better future charged with real justice and true brotherhood.

[214]

Statutes of the Workers' Free Collective of Tamarite de Litera

Article 1. With the title of Collective and cooperative, there has been set up in Tamarite on October 1, 1936 a Collective composed of peasants and industrial workers with the aim of exploiting collectively the agricultural properties and industrial enterprises formerly belonging to factious elements who participated directly or indirectly in the fascist uprising in Spain and whose goods thus pass to the Collective. Also included in this action of collective exploitation are the goods of collectivists and of property owners or industrial enterprises which have remained loyal and in agreement with the revolutionary movement, as well as the goods of those who, without being fascists, do not properly farm their land or do not use their own labour, or have stopped cultivating their land.

Art. 2. Our Collective composed of, as we have already said, peasants and industrial workers, will be guided by humane sentiments and the noblest social principles.

Art. 3. The ends aimed at by the constitution of this Collective shall be: the improvement of the social and economic condition of the mass of peasants and industrial workers who have always struggled for the ideas of social recognition both before the fascist uprising and during the revolution.

ASSETS OF THE COLLECTIVE

Art. 4. The assets of the Collective shall consist of all properties, urban, rural as well as of the goods expropriated from fascist elements, and the goods of the Collective itself and of those who, without being fascist, do not properly cultivate their land by their own efforts.

Art. 5. In no case will the assets of the Collective be broken up, whether they come from fascists or from voluntary members. Land will be cultivated in common by a single community which will divide into three or more sections; each section or delineated zone will dispose of all the equipment needed for agricultural work, working animals, tools; each group will nominate its technical delegates to ensure the best use of the expropriated estates.

(a) As already stated, the workers will be divided into three sections, or more, according to individual aptitudes; some to attend to the olive trees and the various fruit trees, others for

harvesting lucerne and cereals, others for land work with spade or hoe, others to handle the mules, others on minor tasks; by this organisation we shall eliminate weak points and shortcomings of which we are only too well aware.

(b) Every collectivist is authorised to belong to whichever section he wishes and will then be able to change domicile with his family; all will have the obligation to carry out the instructions of the responsible delegates who will have decided at preliminary meetings on the work to be done; if anyone does not apply the agreements made in those meetings the administrative Commission will be informed by the responsible delegate who will decide on the expulsion of the comrade or comrades who have adopted that position.

(c) The groups previously constituted will have the right to carry on, according to the already established constitution.

(d) All those who own 3½ hectares of irrigated land as well as of dry land will be free to join the Collective or to be individualists, but they will be allowed to cultivate their land only by their own efforts: however both collectivists and individualists will have to help in the ways asked of them by the community, by bringing their working animals as well as their personal effort. Those possessing less than 3½ hectares will have to join the Collective.

(e) Each group as well as each collectivist will receive from the management commission a book in which will be entered income and outgoings.

Art. 6. With a view to ensuring the best administration possible, an inventory of all the assets of the Collective will be prepared in which all the different parcels of land, other property and goods, etc., will appear with a mention of their fascist origin.

Art. 7. As the products of communal enterprise are harvested they will be stored in places chosen by the Collective, the sharing out or private warehousing not being authorised.

Art. 8. On land which by its situation or where the number of inhabitants provides favourable conditions, large farming units will be set up.

Art. 9. Those who will apply to join the Collective will have to bring to it all their goods, thus ceasing to be individualists and becoming members of, and in solidarity with, the Collective.

Art. 10. In order to know the position of each Collective at all times each section will have to keep a permanent account of production and consumption.

Art. 11. Fascist elements who were to consciously sabotage the work and be a liability on the Collective will have to be expelled —for we well know that if the situation were to change, these elements would become not only our persecutors but even of the members of our families.

RIGHTS AND DUTIES OF THE COLLECTIVE

Art. 12. The Collective puts at the service of collectivists the general consumers' cooperative which deal with all needs: food, drinks, heating, clothing; equally it assures medical and pharmaceutical services and everything concerning collective needs and development; it also disposes of four oil crushers, one flour mill, a soap factory (in conjunction with oil crushers for the production of lower grade oil), a lye factory, three lime kilns, three for ceramics and bricks, and one electricity generator.

Art. 13. Every collectivist has the right to rear pigs, hens, turkeys, geese, rabbits, where he lives, in order to assure a surplus. 10% of the poultry and rabbits will be handed over to the collectivist units, and any surplus eggs will be passed to the cooperative in order to supply those workers engaged in industrial work and all those who may need them until such time as the new collective units can produce them for themselves.

Art. 14. All collectivists working in industry and all those who, not being agricultural workers, cannot cultivate vegetables will receive supplies for themselves and their families free of charge.

Art. 15. The Collective guarantees to the head of each family a weekly wage in local money. The scale of payments in local money is as follows:

A young couple	25.00 pesetas
An old couple	21.00 pesetas
Three adults	33.00 pesetas
For each additional person	1.00 peseta per day
For each minor	0.70 peseta per day
For two single women	20.00 pesetas per week
For a single man	18.00 pesetas per week
For a single woman	14.00 pesetas per week
For those taking their meals at the Collective's canteen	9.00 pesetas

These figures can be modified up or down depending on circumstances, and general examination by the assembly of collectivists.

Art. 16. All members of the Collective, without sex discrimination, will have to work from the age of fourteen to sixty except in cases of physical disability medically confirmed; in such cases work will be voluntary and not obligatory.

Art. 17. Expenses for medical treatment, medicaments, light and shelter are borne by the Collective, as well as supplies of edible oil for the whole year.

Art. 18. When a member of the Collective takes a companion, that is to say, wishes to start a new family, the Collective guarantees her material needs.

Art. 19. When for valid reasons or unavoidable circumstances a collectivist is obliged to go and live elsewhere, the Collective will assume responsibility for the expenses involved in the move.

Art. 20. Every collectivist comrade will have the inalienable right of withdrawing from the Collective whenever he wishes to do so; but 15% of the value of the assets that he brought on joining will be retained.

Art. 21. The administrative Commission will consist of one delegate for each section or zone; the delegates will decide among themselves the position and functions of each. The nomination of the delegates and the tasks of the various sections of the Collective will take place at a general Assembly of Collectivists; the duration of these functions will not be limited; they will end at the request of the delegates themselves, and when the Assembly expresses itself in these terms.

RULES FOR THE COLLECTIVE OF SALAS ALTAS

The undersigned gathered together in general Assembly and after having defined collectivist norms, freely decide to organise a Collective and to join it. And they approve the following bases to ensure its economic development.

1. Every inhabitant in Salas Altas, whatever his condition and without distinction of workers' organisation or party, may belong to the Collective.

2. The members of the Collective will nominate a *Comité* consisting of a chairman, vice-chairman, a secretary, an accountant, a treasurer, and as many members as deemed necessary, according to the tasks to be dealt with.

3. This *Comité* will have a purely administrative character and will explain its activities before the assemblies of collectivists who will be able to approve of them or dismiss them if they have not carried out their mandate satisfactorily.

4. Members will bring all their goods and chattels; land,

cultivating tools, draught animals, money and various means of work.

5. The collectivists will likewise bring their poultry with a view to establishing a large collective poultry unit to increase this valuable asset. This task will be undertaken by those to be chosen by the Assembly.

6. Communal stables will be organised so that all draught animals can be brought together and attended by a competent staff. In this way drivers will work shorter hours than the time required for agricultural jobs or transport.

7. Sheep will be made up into flocks, and the Collective will nominate shepherds to handle them and take them to the pastures. A skilled person will be chosen for slaughtering. He will decide which sheep should be killed.

8. The produce of the land and groceries will be stored in collective warehouses to ensure better supervision.

9. One or more cooperatives will be constituted; these will secure the products that have to be obtained by barter; they will distribute consumer goods on presentation of a producer's book, and on the basis of the scales established by the Assembly.

10. These scales can be modified upwards or downwards depending on the economic situation of the Collective.

11. Nobody shall consume to excess. In exceptional cases such as in the case of the sick, the request will have to be supported by a doctor's certificate.

12. The assembly will decide on the annual holidays which members of the Collective will take.

13. The money available to the Collective will be used only to purchase goods in those regions where money still exists.

14. In all branches of work (agriculture, stock rearing, mines) delegates may be re-elected; their instructions must be respected; where they were not the Collective would take the steps it deemed necessary.

15. Over the age of fifteen all members of the Collective will have to work. The assembly will have to decide what young married women or people who are unfit to work, should do.

16. Collectivists over the age of sixty are exempted from work; nevertheless if such is their wish and their physical condition permits it, they can undertake work that suits their physical condition in order to help the Collective.

17. Anyone who without justification withdraws from the Collective, will have no rights over the collective assets.

18. Resolutions will be passed on a majority vote of the assembly.

19. Every member will receive a receipt for the assets brought by him on joining.

20. The Assembly is sovereign and its agreements are law even if they modify the present Statutes.

Such is the collectivist Statute which we undertake to implement.

Salas Altas, December 7, 1936.

TEXT OF THE COLLECTIVIST RESOLUTION
OF ALBALATE DE CINCA

"In Albalata de Cinca on January 28, 1937, almost all the inhabitants of the locality met in a general assembly under the chairmanship of Isidoro Castro Gil, chairman of the municipal Council. The secretary read the minutes of the previous meeting which were approved unanimously. Then one passed on to examine the Proposal presented by the Council, the text of which reads:

'So long as present circumstances continue the local administration will be represented by the municipal Council, whoever may be the people comprising it.

'As responsible body for local administration the Council proposes to establish family rationing authorising a maximum consumption per person per day. All expenses will be included in this sum except for those of a medical or pharmaceutical nature. Equally it proposes to fix a payment for those who do not produce foodstuffs, such as blacksmiths, joiners, carters, workers in the cooperative, the pharmacy and other activities which are useful to all of us, with the exception of the posts of members of the Council who must work without payment, which also exempts them from paying for what they obtain to live.

'It also proposes that a workers' Centre be opened where coffee and wine will be served. A caretaker will have to be nominated for this.'

"The question of the Cooperative then followed. It was a question of how clothing would be distributed, especially warm clothing. Several comrades declared that those who had not yet paid their debts should not be supplied. Gabriel Sender Castro intervened to propose a satisfactory solution and recommended the distribution of underwear to all the inhabitants whether they had paid their debts or not, and that done one would firmly demand repayment of debts from those who could pay, by threatening them with not supplying warm clothing if they didn't. This tactic was adopted.

"To various questions Tomas Almunia declared that instead of serving coffee, which was not indispensable, it would be better to save the money for three months and to spend it on a cine-projector with sound if possible. The chairman replied that they would immediately do their best to get both things done.

"Felix Galindo proposed the nomination of controllers for the buying and selling operations and this was turned down. And the meeting was closed."

COLLECTIVE OF PINA DE EBRO
(Bases approved by the local Assembly on Jan. 3, 1937)

(After a prologue consisting of sentimental revolutionary references, the text comes to the point):

"In view of what has been said, workers and peasants rising to the demands of the hour, founds its voluntary Collective on the following bases:

1. Membership of the Collective is voluntary for all the inhabitants of the village, whatever may be their economic situation and so long as they accept the Statute now established.

2. All members in agreement with this new social regime will bring all their assets to the Collective: land, implements, working animals, money and tools.

3. As soon as circumstances warrant it, efforts will be made to build collective stables in order to house all animals suitable for working the land; the same will be done for cattle and sheep, and skilled hands will be chosen for the task.

4. Warehousing of all foodstuffs, groceries and agricultural products in collective stores to ensure adequate control; equally, organisation of one or more cooperatives for the distribution of foodstuffs and different implements that will be required by the collectivists.

5. The quantity of products distributed to the collectivists may increase or decrease, depending on the economic situation of the Collective.

6. Work will be carried out by groups at the head of which there will be a responsible delegate. Efforts will be made to organise sections of carters and herdsmen and of workers with

a trade, so that talented comrades can relieve each other in these tasks.

7. All members of both sexes over the age of 15 will have to work for the Collective. Only people over sixty or incapacitated are exempted unless their physical condition allows them to undertake light work for the benefit of the Collective.

8. The Collective withdraws completely from those who would wish to continue to live in an individualist regime; so much so that they will not be able to have recourse to them in any circumstances. They will work their lands themselves; all land that remains uncultivated in their hands will be taken over by the Collective.

9. Any suspicion of exploitation of man by man is abolished; and consequently all forms of tenant farming, sharecropping or paid employment. This measure will be applied to all the inhabitants of the locality whatever their situation.

10. The Assembly is sovereign and operates on a majority basis. It is at the Assemblies that decisions will be taken regarding members who might disturb the smooth running of the Collective."

PART THREE

Industry and Public Services

CHAPTER XI

INDUSTRIAL ACHIEVEMENTS

According to the last census which preceded the Civil War and Revolution, 1.9 million people were employed in industry in Spain out of a total population of 24 million.

At the top of the list we find 300,000 wage earners in the "clothing industry" but one must bear in mind that more women were employed than men.

In second place was the textile industry which exported large quantities of cloth, even to Britain. It also employed 300,000 workers, men and women. But among the latter were included those employed in the manufacture of women's underwear.

The third industry in order of importance was building. 270,000 men were engaged in the most varied trades of this industry. The fourth was the food industry: canning, salting, manufactured groceries, employing 200,000 people. A further 150,000 were engaged in the fishing industry.

It is only then that we come to basic production, the kind which for the advanced industrial nations consists of what are called, with justification, the key-industries: the mining industry on the one hand, employing 100,000 miners, and the steel industry with 120,000 workers.

Though Spanish industry was not important in comparison with the more advanced nations, it cannot be said that it did not exist, the more so since that approximate figure of 1.9 million workers is out of a population of 24 million and not of 40 million, if for example one were making comparisons with France or Britain at the same period. And though by far the greater part of the population was making a living from agriculture, it would be a mistake to gauge the possibilities of revolutionary socialisation from the activities of the peasants alone.

To these basic statistics it should be added that 70% of industry was concentrated in Catalonia where the abundant waterfalls from the Pyrenees had for a long time made possible the harnessing of water power, while proximity to France, and the opening onto the Mediterranean towards Italy, North Africa and even South America via the Straits of Gibraltar, favoured its commercial expansion, the introduction of raw materials and the export of some finished products. Thus the textile industry which attracted the largest capital investment could be developed with the cotton imported from the United States, Brazil and Egypt, while wool came from La Mancha and other Spanish regions where natural agricultural difficulties and the poor production of the steppes which covered part of Spain obliged the peasants to specialise in the rearing of sheep.

We complete this brief list by including the 60,000 workers engaged in the category "means of transport, transmission equipment and electricity enterprises" and finally the 40,000 employed in 4,000 small works producing chemical products the existence of which indicated a tendency towards the modernisation of the general economy.

To sum up then, according to official statistics, industries absorbed from 22% to 23% of the "active population", agriculture 52% and what is called the third sector, which at that time (July 1936) included a large number of domestic servants, about 25%.[1]

As will be readily appreciated, this economic structure influenced the constructive achievements of the Spanish Revolution as did also, at a certain stage, the lack of raw materials, power, the exhaustion of cotton stocks (which did not arrive because of the coastal blockade) or wool which no longer arrived from

1 Naturally these figures have since radically changed. According to the most recent census which is for 1960, the active agricultural population represents 39.7%, the industrial population 33%, the sector defined as "services" 28%. The category of metallurgy and heavy industry employed 230,000 workers in 1961, and light industry 386,000, building and construction 603,000, textiles 335,000. But here too, in order to make comparisons one must bear in mind the increase in population from 24 million in 1936 to 30.5 million at the time of the census (and to 33 million in 1970).

La Mancha, most of which was in Franco's hands or cut off from Catalonia.

Finally—it should suffice to demonstrate the importance of some economic difficulties of which one is too often aware when it is already too late[2]—the building industry which in Barcelona employed some 40,000 workers was paralysed overnight for in all periods of crisis building is the first industry to come to a halt, the employers disappearing or no longer investing their capital either in new building projects or for keeping in good repair what they already have.

*

It was at the congress in Madrid (known as the Congress of La Comedia—the name of the theatre where it was held) in 1919 that the C.N.T. (founded in 1910) had decided to abandon throughout Spain the traditional trade unions (Syndicates) and trades Federations, offspring of the First International recommended by Bakunin and the extension of which he had advocated for the reconstruction of the whole of Europe. This first workers' organisational structure, which is still to be found in a large number of countries, no longer corresponded, in the opinion of the libertarian syndicalist militants to the development of capitalist structures which made necessary greater combative concentrations. But also, for that end had *never* been forgotten and ranked with the class struggle in capitalist society, it was a question of making better preparations for the social organisation of the future. The intercorporative struggles, of which the Middle Ages and the Renaissance provide such lamentable examples, did not correspond to the spirit of our Spanish militants for whom federalism had always been synonymous with association and practical solidarity. Thus from that point of view, in the syndical and working domain, a labourer, a surveyor, a mason, a brick maker, a cement worker, a plasterer, an architect, a plumber, an electrician all collaborated and participated in the construction of a building or of houses. It was therefore logical and necessary

2 But which revolutionaries wanting to bring down existing society and proclaiming the need to build a new one have ever worried about these problems? Marx himself poked fun at the "recipes" for the cooking pots of the future society. Curiously enough only the anarchist or libertarian school has produced some more or less serious anticipations. And the concern for the constructive task to be undertaken has certainly been one of the factors which prepared the militant constructors whose work we are examining.

to have them all united in the same syndicate. Similarly, the printing of a book or a newspaper, from the paper making stage to its emergence from the printing presses or the rotary presses; or the construction of a boiler from the making of the sheet metal to the caulking, requires a series of operations carried out by different trades, all interdependent. The problem was to unite all these trades, converging in the double objective already described.

But that union had not to be established without system or by ignoring the practice of freedom. After all, an industrial syndicate was a federation of trades and of workers of different trades; each of those trades constituted a technical section, and all those sections were interdependent.[3]

In the short term, when one of them was involved in struggle, the others backed it up with solidarity, which made victory certain. The industrial Syndicate at the same time as it increased immeasurably the capacity for workers' organisations to engage in the struggle, succeeded in preparing a better economic framework for a socialised society.

The acceptance of industrial federations, logical complement of the constitution of the industrial Syndicates, just as the trades federations were the complements of trade unions, came up against uncomprehending and demagogic opposition from the "anarchist Left", to which was added the disorganisation created by too many local and general strikes, insurrectional attempts, boycotts, persecutions and also, it must be admitted, a lack of militants technically prepared to carry through this complementary task.[4] Nevertheless the broad outlines had been drawn at the congresses, and one resolution adopted in 1936 incorporated all the activities in production and services throughout the country in seventeen federations: iron and steel, textile industry, chemical industry; oil and its by-products; water, gas and electricity; land and sea

---

3 Solidarity implies interdependence, or it is no more than a word. Here is an example demonstrating all the difference that existed cn the subject between the old French Revolutionary syndicalist militants and the Spanish comrades. At a kind of round table at which the author was explaining to blast furnace delegates that the wages of iron-foundry workers in Barcelona was the same for all the trades, one of these delegates declared that he could not accept that an iron-smith should have any say in what he, a fitter, should be paid. I explained that in Spain they had gone beyond the corporate morality and for them it was human rights that took precedence. The French comrade was not entirely convinced.

4 In *El Proletariado Militante op. cit.* Anselmo Lorenzo demonstrated that already at the time of the First International this absence of militants with technical preparation constituted a serious handicap.

transport; health services; teaching; entertainment (cinema, theatre, etc.); wood industry; tobacco production; health services; agriculture; banking and financial services; building construction; mines; technology in general.

Later, in 1938, the Economic Plenum held in Valencia, introduced some modifications which were determined in part by the war in a situation that was becoming increasingly complicated because of the difficult relations with the political factions. The industrial federations—which frequently overlapped in their activities, were reduced to fifteen.

*

Before describing the constructive achievements in the industrial field, which were the work of the Syndicates, and for that reason we would prefer to call them "Syndicalisations", some further information is called for. What has been referred to as "Collectives" and "collectivisations" in the agricultural regions was, in fact, in various forms, what at other times would have been called socialisation. But genuine socialisation.

As we have demonstrated, Collectives and collectivisations included then the interdependent whole of the inhabitants of each village, of each commune, or each fragmented Collective organised by those who identified themselves with it. In them one did not come across different material standards of life or rewards, no conflicting interests of more or less separated groups. The overriding law was that of equality and fraternity, in fact and for the benefit of all equally.

But in what have been called the industrial collectives, especially in the large towns, matters proceeded differently as a consequence of contradictory factors and of opposition created by the co-existence of social currents emanating from different social classes. Too often in Barcelona and Valencia, workers in each undertaking took over the factory, the works, or the workshop, the machines, raw materials, and taking advantage of the continuation of the money system and normal capitalist commercial relations, organised production on their own account, selling for their own benefit the produce of their labour. The decree of October, 1936 legalising collectivisations did not allow them to do more, and this distorted everything right from the start.

There was not, therefore, true socialisation, but a workers' neo-capitalism, a self-management straddling capitalism and socialism, which we maintain would not have occurred had the

Revolution been able to extend itself fully under the direction of our Syndicates. And while we were engaged in all-out war, with a massive Francoist offensive in Aragon in the direction of Catalonia, in Old Castile in the direction of Madrid, in Andalusia, in the Basque country and against the Asturias, our Syndicates could not join issue with the bourgeois social forces and the anti-fascist parties whose conduct was equivocal, for even with all our united forces we were not powerful enough to contain the enemy armies.

Some of those who today recall this unpleasant situation were, at the time, by their opposition to our enterprises in social transformation, more responsible than we were for these semi-socialisations. And they have no right now to be the accusers.

Meanwhile, in spite of these shortcomings, which the author was exposing in December 1936, the important fact is that the factories went on working, the workshops and works produced without the owners, capitalists, shareholders and without high management executives; and we know of visitors, such as the Belgian sociologist Ernestan, who later expressed to us their amazement at the fact which they had been able to verify on the spot.

Then very quickly reactions set in which were not given the attention they deserved. In the engineering industry which became the most important industry because of war production, matters had had an equally bad start so far as integral libertarian socialisation was concerned.[5] But the Syndicate succeeded in exercising a strict administrative control on the working of the enterprises where the management *Comités* soon accepted a book-keeping discipline which reinforced the spirit and practice of socialisation. The Catalan government called for this control, which however could only be exercised because the Syndicate agreed that it was necessary.

At all times in the engineering Syndicate the desire to do better was ever present among the militants who were often overwhelmed by complex situations which cannot be visualised from a distance or with the passage of time. It was because of this that the *Comité* of that Syndicate instructed the present writer

5 This was certainly hindered for, in the name of the demands of the war, Indalecio Prieto, the right-wing socialist, intervened in the organisation of the engineering industries and, in agreement with the Communists given key positions, prevented the development of syndical socialisation. See chapter on *The Internal Counter-Revolution.*

to prepare a "syndicalisation" plan for engineering production in Barcelona, and which was accepted unanimously by an assembly attended by thousands of members. I was unable to observe what efforts were then made (the problem of the technical preparedness of the workers also came into it) to put this plan into operation.

But other reactions were expressed, such as that of the Syndicate of the wood industry (cabinet makers, joiners, carpenters and allied trades). One will be better informed by reproducing the most important parts of a manifesto published on December 25, 1936 by them which clearly shows that our militants were aware of the situation: [6]

"Instead of a thoroughgoing takeover of the workshops, instead of giving complete satisfaction to the people, the employers are being obliged to pay wages, which are being increased as the working hours are being reduced. And this in the middle of a war!

"Now that the government of the *Generalitat*[7] has secured all the moneyed wealth, it agrees to the payment of imaginary debts,[8] and distributes such huge sums that those who are doing so will regret it later when the time comes to render accounts, when it will be seen how many millions have been spent without producing, and thereby causing great harm to the economy.

"An enormous number of parasitic bureaucrats have been created, which the Wood Syndicate within the sphere of its own activities has sought to reduce in the undertakings.

"We have been opposed to this waste from the beginning, and within the limits of our possibilities have intensified output in industry. We too could have followed the current, and tolerated the milking of the governmental cow, by dragging money out of the *Generalitat* for unprofitable workshops, and by paying hypothetical invoices which will not be reimbursed by insolvent debtors.

"Having reached this point, we seek to demonstrate our capacity as producers by practical achievements, and at the same time

6 Another Manifesto denouncing the deviation of the Collectives and declaring that they were the opposite of libertarian communism was issued at the same time by the F.A.I. The author of these lines had been instructed to draft it.
7 Official name of the Catalan Government.
8 This refers to real or cancelled debts, payment of which was demanded by a number of contractors.

save the economy and eliminate the bourgeoisie with all its mechanism of parasitic intermediaries, its fraudulent book-keeping, and its stipends.

"In the first days of the Revolution, we could not collectivise our industry because we saw and thought, and still think, that many sections of our Syndicate will have to disappear. And also because from the very beginning there had been a misunderstanding between us and the official world which had not wanted to recognise the rights of the Syndicates;[9] but it is quite clear that if one had acted otherwise one could, by spending many millions less, have improved all the industries, for we must make an effort to ensure that in Catalonia and everywhere, our national industry develops; it has the means to do so.

"Technical organisation must be adapted to the needs of the moment, while thinking of the future. Faced with the demands of the hour, the Wood Syndicate has wanted to advance not only along the road of Revolution, but also to orientate this Revolution in the interests of our economy, of the people's economy. To that effect we have grouped all the small insolvent employers without means of existence, we have taken over all the tiny workshops employing an insignificant number of workers, irrespective of their syndical affiliation, seeing in them simply workers whose inactivity was harming the economy.

"And thanks to our resources and the dues of our members we have organised C.N.T. workshops, workshops with 200 and more workers, as have never been seen in Barcelona, and of which there are very few in the rest of Spain.

"We could have, and it would have been much easier for us, collectivised the workshops whose future was assured but instead we let them go on producing for as long as they were able to, and only collectivise those which are having real economic difficulties.

"There is a misunderstanding when it is stated that we do not accept the Collectivisation Decree. On the contrary we accept it, but quite simply we interpret it from our point of view. What, for some, would have been understandable, would have been the organisation of large cooperatives which only the favoured industries could have started. In return they would have left those without resources to their difficulties, which means creating

9 The decree recognising and containing the Collectives was not published by the Catalan Government until October 24, 1936, three months after the events had started and as a result of the growing number of expropriations by the workers.

two classes: the new rich and ever poor poor."

Following the ideas expressed in this Manifesto, general assemblies were called, attended as on other occasions by the workers in their thousands. The situation was examined, and in the end it was decided to take steps to put things right. A fair number of the largest workshops passed over to syndical control, each with its community number. The authority of the Syndicate, that is to say that of the assemblies whose decisions were final, in the end prevailed. Where there was a surplus of manpower, some of the workers were moved to other undertakings producing useful goods in the new situation, such as simple furniture instead of luxury furniture. The use of available techniques was rationalised, and where the situation created by the war permitted, there was a return to the spirit and practice of libertarian syndicalism. New general constructions were being formulated and from these eager attempts to overcome the difficulties of the moment a general setting of things to rights would not have taken long.

In spite of everything, industrial libertarian achievements were not lacking, and these alone, would have justified a Revolution.[10]

Syndicalisations in Alcoy

So far as syndicalisations are concerned, Alcoy seems to us the most conclusive example and the one with the most lessons. The second largest town in the province of Alicante, it had a population of 45,000 in 1936. It was an industrial and commercial centre of some importance. The total number of industrial workers was 20,000, a very high proportion for a country where the active population nationally was from 33% to 35%. Textile production which supplied not only fabrics but also hosiery, and ladies' underwear, was the most advanced, and employed a fairly large complement of women. Paper making came second.

Our movement goes back to the origins of socialism, to the time of the First International. It went through quiet periods, as happened everywhere, as well as suffering bitterly in times of

10 In Valencia things happened along the same lines in the wood industry. In engineering they did not take things farther than Barcelona for reasons already given.

repression. But from 1919, the organisation of industrial syndicates breathed new life into it.

Anarchist groups here were numerous and generally knew how to struggle at syndical level while at the same time carrying on among the workers (after all they themselves were also workers) their work of social education, the results of which were to be seen in July 1936. And it was in Alcoy that the beautifully produced libertarian periodical *Redención* appeared for seven years under Primo de Rivera's dictatorship (1923-1930). At the time, and later, it was undoubtedly the town that had in relation to its population the highest proportion of militant libertarians including many young people.

At the time of my first visit in February 1937 our Syndicates had 17,000 members, men and women. The U.G.T. had 3,000 including functionaries, who were not revolutionaries, and the anti-revolutionary small tradesmen who hoped to find in that organisation the guarantee of their social status.

These same people also counted on the support of the political parties, naturally hostile to what our comrades might undertake. But our comrades were in control of all activities essential to social life. This was thanks to our Syndicates a list of which follows: Food supplies; Printing (paper and cardboard); Building (including architects); Hygiene (medical, sanitary services, pharmacy, hairdressers, laundries, sweepers); Transport; Entertainment; Chemical Industry (laboratories, perfumery, soap, etc.); Light Textiles; Wood Industry; Industrial technicians; Travelling salesmen; Liberal professions (teachers, artists, writers, etc.); Clothing; Engineering; Agriculture (based on the market gardeners in the surrounding districts).

The very clear image of their mission made our comrades act with precision and speed. Alcoy did not pass through the too often prolonged stages experienced elsewhere of control *Comités* feeling their way, of isolated management *Comités* as happened elsewhere. From the first day, and quickly, the Syndicates took over control of the revolutionary initiative which they were encouraging and this happened in *all industries* without exception.

Let us attempt to trace the development of their achievements.

*

On July 18, 1936 rumours of the impending fascist attack which were rife throughout Spain also found an echo in Alcoy. They expected an attack by the military and the conservatives supported by the Civil Guard; our forces mobilised to meet the attack and took up combat positions in the streets. But the attack did not take place. So our forces who, by their initiative had outflanked the local authorities, turned to them and presented certain demands mainly motivated by the unemployment in the textile industry (our Syndicate at the time had 4,500 members, soon to become 6,500). These demands, without breaking the anti-fascist unity, were for assistance for the unemployed and control over industrial enterprises. All the demands were agreed to.

But new difficulties soon loomed. The employers were quite prepared for the workers' control commissions to examine their books where transactions of purchases and sales, profits and losses were presumably correctly entered. But the workers and more especially the Syndicates wanted to go further. They wanted to control the whole capitalist mechanism which absurdly held back production when there were people insufficiently clad, and which created an unemployment which could not be accepted seeing that there was an unsatisfied demand. And very soon they came to the conclusion that they would have to seize control of the factories, and change everything in society.

Furthermore the employers soon declared their inability to pay wages to the unemployed, which in that critical period was probably true. One part of the factories appeared to be insolvent because of the crisis and could not even pay the workers who were at work. So much so that the point was reached in this absurd situation where the employers asked the workers' associations to advance them the cash to pay the unemployed.

So, the Syndicate of the workers in the textile industry, whose history we know best of all, nominated a commission which studied the situation and presented a report in which it concluded that the textile industry of Alcoy found itself in "a situation of systematic paralysis, financial bankruptcy and of absolute deficiency administratively and technically".

This determined the decisive step taken: on the proposal of the Syndicate, control commissions in the textile industry transformed themselves into management *Comités*. And on September 14, 1936 the Syndicate officially took over 41 cloth factories, 10 thread, 8 knitting and hosiery factories, 4 dyeing, 5 finishing, 24 flock factories as well as 11 rag depots. All these establishments constituted the whole textile industry in Alcoy.

Nothing remained outside the control and management of the Syndicate. But one must not imagine hiding behind this name were simply a few higher, bureaucratic *Comités* making decisions in the name of the mass of unionists without consulting them. Here, too, libertarian democracy was practised. As in all the Syndicates of the C.N.T. there was a dual current: on the one hand that at the base by the mass of unionists and the militants who were part of it. On the other, the directing impulse coming from above. From the perimeter to the centre and from the centre to the perimeter, as Proudhon demanded, or from the base upwards above all, as Bakunin demanded. There were five general branches of work and workers. Firstly weaving which employed 2,336 workers; then thread making with 1,158 skilled men and women; knitting and hosiery employed 1,360 and carding another 550.

At the base, the workers in these five specialities chose at their factory meetings the delegate to represent them in integrating the factory *comités*. One then finds these five branches of work, through the intermediary of the delegations, in the management *Comité* of the Syndicate. The general organisation rests therefore on the one hand on the division of labour and on the other on the synthetic industrial structure.

Before expropriation took place, the enterprise *comités* consisted only of representatives of manual workers; later a delegate from the office staff was added and another from the stores and depots for raw materials. The role of these *comités* now consisted in directing production according to instructions received, and emanating from the assemblies, to transmit to the *Comités* and responsible sections of the Syndicate reports on the progress of work, to make known the needs for new technical material and of raw materials. They also had to pass on large invoices and pay the small ones.

But the representatives of these five branches of work constituted only a half of the management *Comité*. The other half consisted of the control Commission nominated by the Syndicate *Comité* and by the representatives of the manufacturing sections.

The technical commission was also divided into five sections: administration, sales, purchases, manufacture, insurance. It was provided with a general secretary to ensure an indispensable coordination. We will cast a rapid glance at the operation of this commission.

Chosen from among those who were considered more suitable to fulfil this role, the general secretary supervised, and if necessary guided the general activity.

A comrade whose ability for this kind of work was recognised was put at the head of the sales section.[11] He supervised work in his section; this section received orders, arranged deliveries of goods to the various warehouses where they were stored and methodically classified. When a warehouse made a delivery it would notify the accounts department for it to deal with securing payment. Furthermore, the sales section communicated to the manufacturing section the kind and quantity of articles sold so that they could be replaced in good time. Thus the state of all the textile reserves in Alcoy could be ascertained daily.

Warehousing was also the business of this Commission. The stores specialised in different articles (knitwear, hosiery, blankets, overcoats, sheets, different cloths, etc.).

When the orders were for cash, the sales chief authorised them to be executed. He could also in the case of credit customers, but if a longer credit was asked for the decision to supply would rest with the Commission.

As with all the others, the buying section had a comrade with special competence, a specialised professional who also joined the Syndicate. His task was to buy wool, cotton, jute, silk, flock, etc., according to the requirements notified to him by the corresponding sections. When necessary other specialised technicians would be sent to different parts of Spain and even abroad, with the agreement of the technical Commission. This Commission kept an up to date account of the reserves of raw materials in the warehouse, recorded the transfer from one depot or factory to another. Not a pound of materials could be moved without it being duly noted.

The manufacturing section being the most important and having more diversified functions, was divided into three sub-sections: 1) Actual manufacture; 2) Technical organisation of the factories and machine maintenance; 3) Control of production and statistics.

The first of these sub-sections distributed work in accordance with the technical possibilities and specialisations of the factories. After receiving the orders from the sales section, and having decided which workshop and factories would have to carry out the work the criterion being that they possessed the most suitable plant—and naturally the most skilled labour—it transmitted the necessary facts to the purchasing Commission for it to obtain

11 One must not forget that one was still a long way from integral socialisation *in the country as a whole*. Business practices persisted as well as a number of aspects of capitalism, which we were unable to get rid of completely.

the raw materials.

The personnel of the whole industry was divided into specialities; manual workers, designers and technicians. Orders were not distributed and the work involved in carrying them out not discussed without first consulting the factory technicians themselves. Decisions were not taken from above, without seeking information from below. If for instance a special cloth had to be manufactured containing more cotton than wool, or vice versa, five of the most able mechanics among them would be called in to consider if, and where, the technical means of production existed, and in what way they could be used. As to the manual workers, they accomplished their task as scrupulously as possible: they participated in the responsibilities at the level of their activities; if necessary they informed the technical sections, through the works *Comité*, of the difficulties which arose in carrying out their part of the work.

Every Monday, in each factory, the designers, technicians, and worker delegates met, examined the books and the accounts of the enterprise, the production figures, quality of work, orders in hand and all that made up the common effort. These meetings did not take decisions but their results were communicated to the corresponding syndical sections.

The machines sub-section had as its objective to deal with the maintenance of the mechanical equipment and the buildings in which they were housed. It ordered the repairs asked for by the works *Comités,* but had to consult the technical Commission when the costs exceeded a fixed ceiling.

The control sub-commission for manufacture and statistics prepared reports on the individual balance sheet of each factory or workshop, on the return from the raw materials, on experiments in new uses of materials, and the special problems created by them in the distribution of work and manpower, the consumption of power involved, and all other connected matters which could orientate production in general. It also recorded the transfer of plant from one factory or workshop to another.

The administrative sub-section was divided into three sections: counting house, accounts, urban and industrial administration.

The counting house dealt with payments connected with the local textile industry in general, on the instructions given by the director of the corresponding sections. But on the other hand he had to have the agreement of the factories he dealt with.

The second section recorded administratively all purchases,

sales, credit, etc., effected. We will explain later its methods of working, which will give one a better insight into the improvements introduced into the book-keeping system introduced in Alcoy by the Revolution.

Finally the sub-section for urban and industrial administration dealt with the payment of contributions and rents and on all insurance matters involving accidents, and with maintaining permanent relations with the Friendly Society of the Levante.[12]

On the fringe of these five sections or sub-sections, two groups were organised to deal with the archives, one provisional the other permanent. Not only were the share certificates of the former owners preserved there as well as the signed renouncement of their titles at the time of the expropriation, but also everything connected with every activity of the textile industry, both under the new system and under the old, including production figures and the state of affairs under the capitalist regime.

*

We think it necessary to deal separately with the way the book-keeping was organised. It was almost entirely the work of a Left republican who joined the C.N.T. and approved of the transformations that took place. This comrade applied a method which was not entirely original for countries with a developed organisation, but new so far as Spain was concerned. Its first advantage was to carry out with a staff of 70 the work which previously required at least one accountant, and often two, for each of the existing establishments (factories, workshops, goods depots, etc., 103 in all). And he provided me with the information to demonstrate this.

Under the old system invariably adopted in Alcoy the entries in the Big Book for any one day occupied some 25 pages, whereas under the new system all the daily operations for the textile industry were contained in a page and a half of the accounts book; only the summaries were entered. The detailed figures were entered in the books of the thirteen different sections (counting house, banks, Bill-cases, etc.).

Each section entered immediately what concerned its speciality, then filed on the spot the relevant documents. Accounts were balanced each day at four o'clock and the summary entered in the Big Book.

12 The *Mutua Levantina* created by the libertarians which will be discussed in the chapter on the "Socialisation of Medicine".

Furthermore each section had its card-index systems which were in the hands of specialised workers. It was possible therefore, at any moment, to go through any account and check every detail. One also knew on the spot what a customer owed, or the balance sheet of a factory, just as easily as the petrol expenses for any one of the representatives.

In this huge coordinated and rationalised organisation the Syndicate was therefore the directing organism which encompassed everything. The general assemblies which every single worker was entitled to attend passed judgement on the activities of the technical Commission and of the sections that sprang from the factory *Comités*. It was the Syndicate which also assumed the juridical and social responsibility both for the expropriation undertaken and the general management. It established the rate of remuneration and coordinated all activities on a higher level in the collective interest.

As we have already pointed out, the other industries in Alcoy were organised and administered in the same way as the textile industry. The whole organisation was in the hands of the Syndicates. And the Syndicate was in the hands of the workers who effectively participated in the organisation of the industry—and not only of the factory—and rose to the collective responsibilities in the individual sense.

They were hard at work in the engineering workshops I visited, and they too were organised on the principles of libertarian democracy and syndicalism. They had even successfully improvised an armaments industry to assist the armed struggle. The improvements favourably surprised some technically qualified visitors, and the government placed orders for the army.

On the other hand, paper making met with difficulties resulting from a decrease in reserves of raw materials. Once again one can see that if this experiment had taken place under more favourable circumstances the results would have been very much more successful than they were.

Nevertheless the solidarity of the libertarian organisations allowed the printing, paper and cardboard Syndicate to meet the difficulties. In fact, the sixteen other Syndicates which composed the local Federation in Alcoy, gave financial assistance (since the money symbol was retained) to industries which were in the red. They had conquered the corporate spirit, even of narrow corporate syndicalism.

*

The organisation of production was technically excellent in Alcoy at the time when I studied it, and as generally happened, it is probable that it went on improving. The weak point was, as in other places, the organisation for distribution. Without the opposition of tradesmen and the political parties, all alarmed by the threat of complete socialisation, who combated this "too revolutionary" programme, it would have been possible to do better. This opposition obliged them to create their own anti-fascist *Comité de control* which had no combative role to play, but under this guise centralised the purchases of agricultural products, paying on the one hand less to the peasants for their products, and on the other holding down prices and the cost of living. It was not an easy matter to assert themselves so as to avoid friction among the anti-Francoist sectors. For the socialist, republican, and communist politicians actively sought to prevent our success, even to restoring the old order or maintaining what was left of it.

Nevertheless in Alcoy 20,000 workers[13] administered production through their Syndicates and proved that industry functions more economically without capitalists or shareholders and without employers fighting among themselves and thereby preventing the rational use of technical plant, just as the chaos in individual agriculture prevented the rational use of the land and the means of agricultural production.

The government could only bow before these achievements and order arms from the syndicalised engineering workshops in Alcoy, just as it ordered cloth from the socialised textile industry to clothe the army, and ankle-boots from the factories in Elda in the same province of Alicante which were also in the hands of the libertarians.

13 The 3,000 belonging to the U.G.T. accepted the majority decisions not without regret.

CHAPTER XII

ACHIEVEMENTS IN THE PUBLIC SECTOR

1. Water, Gas and Electricity in Catalonia

The workers' Syndicate which from the beginning of the Revolution guaranteed the supply or production of drinking water, gas and electricity in Catalonia had been founded in 1927 under, and in spite of, the dictatorship of General Primo de Rivera. Others had been started throughout Spain, and the federation of these industries was set up in the canton of Barcelona. Next appeared the Catalan regional Federation and finally, uniting all the regional federations constituted in Spain, the national Federation, the secretariat of which was set up in Madrid.

No doubt this structure was facilitated, and encouraged by the nature of the production, especially electricity mainly from hydraulic power[1] and based on the exploitation of the heads of water from the Pyrenees or of barrages situated at great distances —sometimes hundreds of kilometres—from the transformer stations and the distribution centres.

On a national scale, most workers joined promptly. In Barcelona the C.N.T. Syndicate had normally between 2,500 and 3,000 members, and 7,000 in the whole of Catalonia. Then after 19

1 Before 1936 the production of electricity for the whole of Spain had for years remained at about 3,000 million k.w., all from hydraulic power sources. A great number of barrages were later constructed but it was realised a little late in the day that they only filled to about a third of their capacity. It therefore became necessary to intensify thermic production.

July, in the new situation created by the Revolution, workers and technicians together numbered 8,000. For its part the U.G.T. had a little less than that number, in Catalonia that is.

The technicians, semi-technicians, and establishment had set up their own Syndicate independent of the two workers' organisations. But the vitality of the solidarity sprung from the Revolution drove them towards closer union with the manual workers, a necessary union for maintaining production. And an assembly resolved, by acclamation, to dissolve the separate Syndicate and to constitute the technical section of the single Syndicate affiliated to the C.N.T. Later ideological preferences came into play and fifty of these technicians left the C.N.T. to form a section with membership of the U.G.T.

The directors of the power stations who earned anything up to 33,000 pesetas a month while the workers earned less than 250, were mostly foreigners. They received orders from their Consulates to return home. Meanwhile, thanks to the efforts of all workers, and in spite of a lack of some technical staff of international origin, water, gas and electricity continued to be supplied right until the end of the Civil War. Only the bombardments caused temporary breaks in supply.

The initiative in the early days did not come only from our Syndicate as the constituted organism. Just as for the tramways and railways, it came from militants knowing how to shoulder responsibilities. The very day of the Francoist uprising, a handful of them were meeting to guarantee the continuation of these public services. Immediately works *Comités* were set up as well as a central liaison *Comité* between the two workers' organisations. Later this *Comité* supervised the general organisation of work and production for the four Catalan provinces of Barcelona, Tarragona, Lerida and Gerona.

The definite take-over did not occur until the end of August 1936. During the transitional period, of about six weeks, they were prepared to continue production with the existing capitalist organisation, without attempting expropriation. Every worker remained at his job as before; major decisions, which involved a taking over of a technical-administrative nature, were taken by syndical assemblies of the two workers' organisations. And the curious thing was, though it happened on other occasions, that not only did the Syndicates take over the organisation of work to be done from the capitalists, but they assumed the responsibilities that the latter had previously undertaken. Thus it was that they

[241]

Q

took over the financial commitments and the debts from their predecessors, and paid all the invoices, undoubtedly in order not to jeopardise workers employed by the suppliers, and who were also inheriting the situation as bequeathed to them by their employers.

The only debts that were cancelled were the obligations to Spanish moneylenders, most of them privileged people—small savings were to all intents and purposes non-existent in Spain. What money people had was used to acquire some of the necessities they badly needed.

At the beginning of 1937, total income had dropped by 20%. Possibly some consumers had omitted to pay their bills, but there was also another explanation. The unit price of electricity had been reduced; some water rates had risen from 0.70 to 0.80 pesetas a cubic metre and in other cases had dropped from 1.50 to a standard tariff of 0.40 pesetas. And there was no longer a meter charge.

Naturally the attitude of workers in the U.G.T. was combated by the politicians who were at the head of the reformist Union. But their stubborn opposition could not breach the resolve of members, and agreement continued to reign among all the workers.

The system of organisation that was put into operation encouraged this good understanding. Its point of departure was at the place of work, at the undertaking, and rose to the Syndicate. We will take a closer look at how things worked.

In the undertaking itself, the first nucleus is the job speciality. Each speciality sets up a section immediately with groupings by factory, workshop or "building" of at least 15 workers. When there are not the numbers to do so, workers from many trades collaborating among themselves, meet and constitute a general section. The sections are more or less numerous and varied, depending on the size of the factories or of the organisations. Each section nominates two delegates which the assemblies choose: one of a technical calibre who will participate in the *Comité* of the undertaking, and another entrusted with the management of work in the section.

The "building *Comité*" (as it is called) comes next. It is nominated by the section Commissions and consists of a technician, a manual worker and an administrator. When deemed necessary a fourth member is nominated so that the two syndical organisations shall have equal representation.

The manual workers' delegate has to solve, or try to solve,

difficulties which might arise between different sections, those arising within a section being settled by the interested parties themselves. He receives suggestions from workers in the different trades for the nomination or the transfer of personnel. And the sections give him daily reports on the progress of work.

He also acts as go between for the rank and file and the general Council for Industry. Periodically he calls the sections to general meetings which take place at the Syndicate, which tightens the links between the workers from the different undertakings. During these meetings proposals and initiatives are studied which are likely to improve productivity and production, as well as the workers' situation, or be of interest to the syndical organisation. A copy of the deliberations is sent to the Council for Industry. It should be noted that the specific activities of the manual workers' delegate do not prevent him from continuing to work at his job alongside his comrades.

The delegate with administrative functions supervises the arrival and warehousing of materials, records requirements, deals with book-keeping for supplies and reserves, and keeps an eye on the state of income and expenditure. He also deals with correspondence and it is his responsibility to see that balance sheets and Reports addressed to the Council for Industry are prepared.

The delegate with technical functions supervises the activities of his section, and uses every endeavour to increase productivity, to lighten the worker's burden by introducing new methods. He checks on production at the power stations, the state of the network, prepares statistics and charts indicating how production is developing.

Let us now examine more closely the workings of the Councils of Industry at the summit of the organisation.

There are of course three: one each for water, gas and electricity. Each is composed of eight delegates: four for the U.G.T. and four for the C.N.T. Half those delegates are nominated by general assemblies of syndicates,[2] the other half by the delegates of the technical sections in agreement with the central *Comité*. This latter measure has as its objective to ensure, in the composition of the Councils for Industry, the nomination of men who are technically and professionally suitable, which I was told

2 Because of the dispersal of the personnel in production units throughout Catalonia the question poses itself as to how the general assemblies nominated these delegates. And we must admit to not having enquired into this point when we were gathering the material for this study.

does not always happen in syndical assemblies where oratorical gifts, ideological or personal affinities can relegate the more necessary considerations to secondary importance. All this is capped by the general Council of the three industries, which is also composed of eight members with, as before, four from each union organisation. This Council coordinates the activities of the three industries, attunes the production and distribution of raw materials from a regional, national and international point of view, modifies prices, organises general administration, indeed takes and uses all initiatives bearing on the producers' production and needs as a whole. Meanwhile, it is obliged at all times to submit its activities to the scrutiny of local and regional syndical assemblies.

Let us now examine the results of this example of workers' management. From a technical point of view some achievements deserve to be underlined, such as that most basic one of all which we constantly come across, of concentration and of coordination.

Not all the stations, by a long chalk, were as important as those of Tremp and Camarasa which are the main generating stations fed by large barrages. Apart from these two giants, most of the 610 units (including the transformers) dotted all over Catalonia had a small or insignificant output; to keep them in operation suited some private interests, but the public interest hardly at all. It was necessary to link them, to eliminate and to reorganise which is what was done. Six months after socialisation had begun 70% of stations representing 90% of output constituted a perfectly homogeneous technical whole; and 30% which represented but 1% of this output were kept apart.

Among other things this represented a saving in labour which was used on improvements and alterations often of importance. For instance 700 workers constructed a barrage near Flix which increased the available electricity by 50,000 k.w.

Gas production was economically less important, and I did not gather statistics on the subject comparable with my researches into electrical power. The more so as the growing lack of coal due to the sea blockade made it impossible to make noteworthy improvements in production.

By contrast water, especially drinking water the supply of which required a large and costly organisation, generally for every tenant in every apartment, was never lacking even in the towns that had suffered bombing raids. In Barcelona the daily supply of 140,000 cubic metres before the Revolution rose rapidly to 150,000 and went on increasing. Nevertheless the increase was not great for it was not easy in a region so broken up, to set about creating new catchment areas, all the sources having long ago been put to use.

2. The Barcelona Tramways

The tramways were the most important means of transport in Barcelona. Sixty routes criss-crossed the city and served the suburbs and the surrounding localities: Pueblo Nuevo, Horta, Sarría, Badalona, Sens, etc. The General Tramways Company was a private company mainly with Belgian capital and employed 7,000 workers, not only as drivers and conductors but also in the eight tram depots and in the repair workshops.

Out of the 7,000, about 6,500 were paid up members of the C.N.T. where they made up the section of the industrial transport Syndicate corresponding to their occupation. The other, much less important, sections were from the underground (two lines), the taxis which in due course created their own Collective, the buses and, finally, the two funicular railways of Montjuich and Tibidabo.[3]

The street battles had brought all traffic to a standstill, obstructed the roadways by barricades that had been set up all over the city and for which buses and trams often were the main materials used. The roads had to be cleared, and public transport so indispensable for this large city had to be got moving again. So the syndical section of the tramways appointed a commission of seven comrades to occupy the administrative offices whilst others inspected the tracks and drew up a plan of clearing work that needed to be done.

In front of the offices of the company the Commission found a picket of civil guards who had been instructed to prevent access. The sergeant in charge declared having received orders to let no one pass. Armed with guns and grenades, and some of them well protected in the armoured car which the company used for transporting money, our comrades adopted a threatening attitude. The sergeant phoned his superiors for authorisation to withdraw and

3 A mountain rising to 580 m. its lower slopes covered with pines, dominates Barcelona.

this was agreed to.

One must stress one small detail which has something quite piquant about it. All the top level personnel had left, and the syndical delegation found in the offices only the lawyer instructed to represent the company and to parley with them. Comrade Sanches, a leading militant, the most active and experienced of them, knew that gentleman only too well for two years before he had sentenced our comrade to 17 years in prison following a strike that had lasted twenty-eight months; the defender of the interests of the company had actually demanded a sentence totalling 105 years in prison.[4] This gentleman received him most cordially, declaring that he accepted the new situation, and even that, as a lawyer, he was putting himself at the service of the workers. Sanchez' comrades wanted to shoot him on the spot but he was opposed to that. He even gave the personage permission to withdraw. It was a Friday and an appointment was made with him for the following Monday. His confidence restored, the man asked to be accompanied to his house as there were rather a lot of armed revolutionaries in the streets . . . He was escorted, but the following Monday did not show up. He was not seen again.

The *Comité* of seven immediately called together the delegates from the different syndical sections: electric power station, cables, repairs, traffic, conductors, stores, accounts, offices and administration, etc. Yet once more the synchronisation of the industrial Syndicate was working perfectly. It was unanimously agreed to get the tramways moving without delay.

The following day a call was made over the radio—as the engineers had already done for their members—calling manual workers and technicians. Most of them responded; known fascists kept away. All the engineers put themselves at the disposal of the Syndicate, including a former colonel whose active sympathy for the workers had resulted in his demotion from head of the traffic section and director of the Metro to a job in the archives section.

Five days after fighting had stopped seven hundred tramcars instead of the usual six hundred, all painted in the colours of the C.N.T.-F.A.I., in red and black diagonally across the sides, were operating in Barcelona. The number had been increased in order to do away with the trailer-cars which were the cause of many accidents. To do this work had gone on night and day repairing

4 Sanchez had come out of prison with thousands of other comrades as a result of the amnesty granted after the elections of February 1936.

and putting back into service a hundred tramcars which had been discarded as being beyond repair.

*

Naturally, things could be organised so quickly and well because the men involved were themselves well organised. One finds here therefore an *ensemble* of sections constituted by trades and put on an industrial base, according to the organisation of the work to be done, of the enterprise of the Syndicate. Drivers, conductors, repairers, joiners, etc., as many complementary groupings going beyond the simple traditional professional cadre, and brought together in a single organisation.

Each section had at its head an engineer nominated by agreement with the Syndicates, and a representative of the workers and this was how the work and the workers were dealt with. At the top the assembled delegates constituted the local general *Comité*. The sections met separately when it was a question of their specific activities which could be considered independently; when it was a question of general problems, all the workers of all the trades held a general assembly. From the bottom to the top the organisation was federalist, and in this way they maintained not only a permanent material solidarity but also a moral solidarity which linked everyone to the general task, with a nobler vision of things.

Agreement was therefore also permanent between engineers and workers. No engineer could take an important decision without consulting the local *Comité*, not only because he agreed that responsibility should be shared but also because often, where practical problems are involved, manual workers have the experience which technicians lack. This was understood by both parties, and thereafter, very often when the *Comité* of the Syndicate or a delegate thought up an interesting idea, the specialist engineer would be called in for consultations; on other occasions it was the engineer who proposed the examination of a new idea and in that case manual workers were called in. There was complete collaboration.

It was not enough to put the tramcars, even in larger numbers back onto the tracks, nor just to repaint them in the colours of the Revolution. The different corporations decided to carry out this additional work without any overtime pay. The creative drive dominated all. In the sheds there were always twenty or thirty tramcars being checked and done up.

The technical organisation and the traffic operation was improved; the importance of the improvements achieved was remarkable. To start with, 3,000 metal poles holding up the electric cables supplying the current were eliminated as they were interfering with the traffic and causing many accidents and were replaced by a system of aerial suspension. Then a new safety and signalling system was introduced consisting of electric points and automatic discs. Furthermore the company for *Agua, Luz y Fuerza* (water, light and power) had installed in many places and right in the middle of the routes taken by the tramcars, transformer cabins or power distributors, which made all kinds of detours and bifurcations necessary, sometimes very sharp (very often a single line), and resulted in accidents. This had gone on from when the services had first been laid, and were determined by the whims of financial or political interests. The comrades of *Agua, Luz y Fuerza* moved these cabins to where they would be in nobody's way, thus making it possible to straighten out once for all the tramway lines.

Sections of track that had been damaged during the fighting were reconstructed, such as the double track for Route 60 which was completely relaid. In other cases the roadway was asphalted.

These improvements took some time to complete as did some modifications of the general infrastructure. From the beginning the organisers, without for all that forgetting the interests of the workers in the vast enterprise, sought to perfect the tools being used. In less than a year a number of notable acquisitions were made; first of all there was the purchase in France of an automatic American lathe, the only one in Spain, and costing £20,000, which was able to produce seven identical parts at the same time.

Two ultra modern milling machines, and electric warning machines allowing one to be notified of breakdowns and broken cables; new cables replaced the old. And an electric furnace was bought for melting down bearings. Much more technical equipment was thus purchased, including Belgian electrode welding sets for use on the tracks which cost the then high price of £25,000.

Thus tooled it was possible to make appreciable strides forward, and a start was even made on building tramcars, including two new models of funicular cars for the Rebasada line which climbed the Tibidabo and for the one in Montjuich.[5] The new cars

5 A hill in Barcelona dominated by a fortress where Francisco Ferrer was executed in 1909.

weighed 21 tons compared with 35 tons for the old type which also carried fewer passengers.

Before that the whole system of power supply had been reorganised and the dynamos repaired.

*

Let us take a brief look at the financial results of the new organisation. Some figures were supplied to us by the principal organisers of this revolutionary creation; we have obtained other, official, figures published in the workers' press at the time. They go from September 1936 when the accountancy was taken in hand and the figures can be relied on.

TOTAL MONTHLY INCOME

	1935	1936
	pesetas	*pesetas*
September	2,277,774	2,600,226
October	2,425,272	2,700,688
November	2,311,745	2,543,665
December	2,356,670	2,653,930

The monthly increase in receipts varied between 12% and 15%, and it might be thought that the increase was the result of an increase in fares. Not so, for steps were actually taken to lower fares in general. Formerly they were based on distance and varied from 0.10 to 0.40 peseta. In September a uniform charge of 0.20 peseta was made which mainly benefited workers who lived on the outskirts and had been paying the higher rate, and especially those who had to pay the night rates.[6]

Such reductions in fares would have resulted in losses under the previous administration, but the suppression of capitalist profit and of high salaries for the administrative executives and technicians actually made it possible to show an operating surplus.

*

The balance sheet of services rendered is equally positive. During the year 1936 the number of passengers carried was 183,543,516. The following year it had gone up by 50 million to 233,557,506 passengers. This is not all, for the kilometres

6 The first increases took place twenty months after the beginning of the Revolution. This was the result of the increase in the prices of raw materials and the cost of living, which involved wage increases.

covered also increased from 21.7 million to 23.3 million, an increase of 1.6 million kilometres.

It must be recognised of course that these figures can in part be explained by the growing shortage of petrol for motor vehicles as a result of the blockade of the Spanish coasts. Nevertheless the fact is that the new organisation was able to provide an answer, and more, to the growing needs of the public.

To get there they did not have to be satisfied with continuing along capitalist lines; much more had to be done. They did so, even more so than would appear from the brief outline given here. For before the Revolution the workshops of the Tramways Company of Barcelona manufactured only 2% of the material used, and generally speaking were set up to deal only with urgent repairs. The tramways sections of the workers' Syndicate for communications and transport of Barcelona, in its eagerness to work, reorganised and improved the workshops which at the end of the year were producing 98% of the materials used. *In a year* the proportion had been reversed, in spite of an increase of 150% in the price of raw materials which were getting more and more scarce, or coming from abroad at exorbitant prices.

And not only did the tramway workers of Barcelona not live on the reserves of capitalism, as the detractors of collectivisations, or syndicalisations, maintain or imply, but had to deal with financial difficulties they inherited from capitalism, as did the Syndicate in the textile industry of Alcoy, and the shoe factory in Elda. On July 20, while the battle still raged, the tramworkers' wages, amounting to 295,535 pesetas, had to be paid (they were paid every ten days). Shortly afterwards bills totalling 1,272,528 pesetas for materials previously purchased by the company had to be paid. And up to the end of 1936 general operational expenses amounting to 2,056,206 pesetas were paid, a further 100,000 pesetas for medical services and accident benefits, 72,168 pesetas in bonuses for economies made in power and materials —a scheme operated by the old company; finally 20,445 pesetas in insurance payments for staff.[7]

7 To these sums must be added taxes which other socialised undertakings also paid. The Valencia central government demanded 3% on the gross receipts; but the Catalan Government, with its seat in Barcelona, demanded what it had been previously receiving from the foreign capitalist company: no less than 14 different taxes which made a total of 4 million pesetas. The Syndicate requested a meeting with the government and after minor discussions agreement was reached with a lump sum payment of 1½ million pesetas.

Nothing was overlooked. It is true that we are not yet at the stage of the complete and completely humanist socialisation of the agricultural Collectives, with the application of the principle "to each according to his needs". But we cannot repeat too often that in the towns the republican regime with State institutions had not been, and could not be abolished; that a fair proportion of the bourgeoisie and the traditional political currents still existed, that it had not been possible to socialise commerce. It was inevitable that even the most daring achievements should feel the effects of this. Nevertheless what was done by syndical socialisations was in itself far reaching.

For the spirit of the workers of Barcelona and other cities such as Valencia was probably the most likely in the whole world to bring about economic equality and the application of mutual aid. It was thus that both in order to help them to meet temporary difficulties and to contribute to their development, the tramways section of Barcelona financially assisted other sections of urban transport. The buses received 865,212 pesetas, the funicular lines of Tibidabo and Montjuich 75,000, Barcelona port transport 100,000, and the Metro undertaking 400,000. And on December 31, 1936 the Barcelona tramways had 3.3 million pesetas in hand.

An odd fact: not only did the Spanish libertarian workers agree to settle with suppliers all debts contracted by the company, but they also wanted to deal with the shareholders. There must have been quite a number of them, the capital consisting of 250,000 shares each of 500 pesetas, but they probably all lived abroad. Our comrades by means of posters and press announcements invited shareholders to a general assembly. Only one, a middle-aged woman, who owned 250 shares turned up. Quite unalarmed by events, she declared herself satisfied to entrust the management of her small capital to the workers' Syndicate with whom she would henceforth maintain relations of trust. I do not know the end of this story but if this woman had no other resources I would be surprised to learn that she had been deprived of all her means of support. Such inhumanity was not common among our comrades.

It now remains to see what part of the profits went to the tramway workers. At the time of the uprising the *peones* (labourers)

earned between 8 and 9 pesetas a day, traffic controllers received 10, lorry drivers and skilled engineering workers (lathe operators, fitters, etc.) 12. All wages were readjusted so that labourers received 15 pesetas and skilled workers 16. One was approaching a state of basic equality.

But other improvements in working conditions deserve to be mentioned. Firstly washbasins were installed in the sheds and workshops, which had never been done before. Showers were installed (and one should bear in mind that this was 1936) in all undertakings employing numbers of workers. Tramcars were disinfected weekly. Then a medical service was organised from which we can draw some lessons.

This service was based on the division of Barcelona and its surrounding districts into thirty sectors. A doctor was in charge of each sector and was paid by the Tramways Syndicate of Barcelona. These doctors did not only treat tramway workers but their families as well. A home help service was also set up, the members of which looked after the sick and brought them human warmth, advice, moral support, all those things which often are more needed than medical treatment itself. At the same time, it was used for checking up on possible malingerers—one had not yet attained human perfection. When it did happen— and it was not often for the outlook was not what it was under capitalism—the Syndicate took steps which could go as far as withholding a week's money. Normally a sick person received his full wage.[8]

To this organisation of home helps was added the use of a fine clinic which until then had been available only to the rich. Apart from being comfortably appointed in contrast with the traditional hospitals in Barcelona, the walls were repainted, decorations provided, radios installed, specialised treatment was provided by a gynaecologist, a specialist in the digestive tracts, and a specialist in general surgery. All three were working in the service of the Syndicate.

8 Work discipline about which the new social order was, generally speaking, more strict because there was a concern not to fail, but to prove a greater administrative ability and greater production, was to be found also in the tramways syndicate, whose decisions in the cases of drunkenness, very rare and deeply repugnant to Spaniards, were always taken in general assemblies. The steps taken would consist in suspension from work and the man's pay would be handed to his wife, for several weeks, thus giving her the possibility to exercise her rights to deal with the household budget.

Spontaneous discipline, workers' morality, were recognised by all. There was support of, and participation in, the common task, and efforts were constantly made to sharpen the imagination to find technical improvements and new methods of work. In the different workshops "ideas boxes" were put up so that anybody with an idea could submit it in writing.

This participation went even beyond the framework of the undertaking and of the Syndicate. As they were well tooled the workshops produced rockets and howitzers for the Aragon front. The workers worked overtime without pay and even came in on Sundays to do their share for the common struggle, without pay.

To conclude this aspect of things, it is worth underlining that honesty was general. Not that there were no cases of unscrupulous actions but in three years they amounted to six cases of larceny which would not even deserve to be mentioned but for the fact that we do not wish to appear to gloss over the negative aspects. The most serious case was that of a worker who from time to time took away small quantities of copper which he would sell when he had made up a kilo's worth. He was dismissed, but as his wife came to tell the undertaking's *comité* that she had a child which would suffer the consequences, she was given three or four weeks' wages and her husband was moved into another workshop.

3. The Means of Transport

During the Spanish Revolution, an attempt was made, particularly in Catalonia, to coordinate the means of transport by land and sea which the growing difficulties created by the war, itself absorbing a growing volume of human energy and mechanical and thermal power, undoubtedly prevented from being brought to a successful issue. But what was done deserves to be recounted. We shall see it in the description of the organisation of the railway network of Madrid-Saragossa-Alicante (M.S.A.) which I had the opportunity to study at first hand, and which will assist the reader to understand how the railways as a whole operated in anti-Francoist Spain when the workers were responsible for their operation.

There were two large railwaymen's associations in Spain: the

[253]

National Syndicate of Railways which was a part of the U.G.T. and the National Federation of Railway Industries was part of the C.N.T. In July 1936 the first of these two organisations grouped, on a national level, a majority of members, but the difference in the months following was no longer very large as our Federation watched its numbers steadily growing. In Catalonia the C.N.T. was in a majority.

Once the militaro-fascist forces had been defeated in the streets of Barcelona, and obliged to withdraw to the barracks and allow themselves to be disarmed, our railway workers did not lose their time dancing in the streets to celebrate the victory. On July 20 they summoned the top management in order to dispense with their services. On the 21st those who took on the responsibility of getting the trains moving, which was a matter of urgency if contact with the other regions was to be maintained, and replenishing food stocks in the city and transporting the improvised militias to the Aragon front, started organising without waiting for the tracks to be repaired. And the same day, the first trainload of militiamen made its first run under revolutionary control.

The discarded technicians were replaced by militant workers who though they obviously lacked the specialised training of the men they were replacing, would with the support of the rank and file who had nominated them, manage to do their work adequately. That was all that mattered.

The network that has been expropriated comprised 123 large and small stations grouped in nine sectors. The administrative personnel remained at their posts and continued to work. The railwaymen likewise. Agreement was complete and expropriation accepted with a high degree of responsibility. In a few days services were back to normal.

All this had been achieved on the sole initiative of the Syndicate and militants of the C.N.T. Those of the U.G.T. in which the administrative personnel predominated had remained passive, never having found themselves in such a situation. Accustomed to carrying out orders coming from above, they waited. When neither orders nor counter-orders came, and our comrades forged ahead, they simply followed the powerful tide which carried most of them along with it.

Thus five days after the triumph of the Revolution, four days after the seizure of the railways by the members of the C.N.T. Syndicate, a U.G.T. delegation came to ask to be a part of

the central revolutionary *Comité* consisting of six of our militants.
The *Comité* was therefore reorganised with eight members. Though
fewer in number, and of no worth from a revolutionary point of
view, the reformist section was, on sufferance and by a desire
for brotherhood, given equal representation so that there were
four delegates from each side.

But that number was clearly insufficient. With the technical
sections organising themselves, it was realised that ten and a
chairman and a director general, a total of twelve delegates, six
from each syndical movement, were needed. In this way they
expected to deal with the various activities; the Operational
division, then the commercial division, electrical services, accounts
and treasury, traction services, various supply depots, sanitary
organisation, tracks and works, matters in dispute, finally control
and statistics.

From the beginning, the control of these divisions did not
operate from above downwards, as in a statist and centralised
system. The revolutionary *Comité* had not such powers. The
restructuring was carried out from the bottom to the top; in
each section and subsection an organising *Comité*, entrusted with
the responsibility of work, had been formed. It disappeared fairly
quickly, for it was necessary to mobilise many people to assume
these functions; there only remained therefore in each section
and subsection one delegate chosen by the meeting of workers
from the stations in the small towns, villages or in the large
towns.

Norms for organisation, initiative and control were established.
All the workers of each locality would meet twice a month to
examine all that pertained to the work to be done. Parallel with
it, the militant prime-movers met once a week. Then the local
general assembly named a *Comité* which managed the general
activity in each station and its annexes. At the periodic meetings,
the management of this *Comité*, whose members worked, after
hearing reports and answering questions proceedings at which
those present could take part, would be subjected to the approval
or disapproval of the workers.

The impulse retained its clearly federalist character. One cannot say that the direction was determined by the central revolutionary *Comité* of Barcelona. Quite simply work went on everywhere, as before July 19. The members of the Barcelona *Comité*
being content to supervise general activity and to coordinate that
of the different routes that made up the network. They slowly

[255]

drew together the different parts of the organism and prepared a better management for the morrow.

It is important that as in the factories and works, even still imperfectly socialised, without shareholders, without engineers, without the usual hierarchy, the trains continued to move, the stations were manned, passengers and goods were transported, the regions that had been supplied before went on being supplied.

They even went further for the sake of a revolutionary pride, by increasing the number of train services which was, as one will see, a mistake they were to appreciate later.

From July 19 onwards they operated 292 trains a day on the network. In October of the same year the number was 213, the drop being partly due to a reduction in freight tonnage and passengers, as a result of the severing of links with Aragon and beyond Aragon with that part of Castile occupied by the fascists, and along which train convoys to and from Madrid had been operating. In October 1935 there were 28,801 wagons recorded; in October 1936 as a result of the events which had upset everything there were only 17.740; but by December the total had risen to 21,470. The difference would have been much smaller if Spain had not been cut in two.

In spite of everything such figures make one realise the importance of the train movements of just the one network we have examined. Even so they give only an incomplete picture. For instance the ten specialised administrative sections which we have already listed, were subdivided in their turn into technical sub-sections. For instance the operational service included control of train timings, general movements of trains, distribution of railway materials, goods traffic and services at all the stations. General organisation therefore was much more complex than one might suppose at first sight.

We said that it was a mistake to want to immediately increase the number of services operated. Firstly because there was a need to economise on coal that came from Asturias, surrounded and besieged by Franco, and from Britain which, because our ports were blockaded by the enemy's fleet, would not risk its ships. Another technical weakness was soon to be revealed: 25% of the boilers on the locomotives were out of service at the time of the takeover; and tubular boilers were built in the Basque country which was also besieged by the Francoist forces, and where every man was mobilised for the armed struggle. Rationing of transport was as essential as of consumer goods. It was only realised rather late in the day.

The problem of remuneration for the workers came up for wages varied from 2.50 pesetas a day for women employed as level crossing gate keepers, 5 pesetas a day for unskilled railway workers to the princely salaries paid to the chief engineers. The average wage was 6.50 pesetas and at the time, depending on the regions, one kilo of mutton cutlets cost from 4 to 6 pesetas. A basic wage of 300 pesetas a month was established for all workers without exception. Those who received more than 500 pesetas—such as the recently engaged engineers—were the exception and a lack of qualified technicians had made this compromise necessary, and my comrades told me in February 1937 that five engineers had joined the management and their demands had to be satisfied by paying them 750 pesetas a month. That is more than twice as much as the general run of railway workers.[9] Nevertheless much ground had been covered in relation to the injustices that existed under the capitalist regime.

*

But somewhat unexpected difficulties, though not altogether surprising, arose from the U.G.T. side, where higher officials, who from Madrid must have moved on to Valencia, after having accepted syndical socialisation in principle (presumably in order not to be left out of the railway brotherhood) changed their minds and replaced the authorised representatives of their Union who were part of the railway *Comité* of Barcelona. In their stead they appointed delegates of their own choice who, being more manageable, would oppose the socialisation that had been undertaken, or at least slow it down. And this was done without consulting their members.

Yet our comrades had, at the beginning, sought a middle of the road solution, which could have been widely applied. In the Centre and South of Spain, faced with the departure of the executives, administrators or foreign engineers who managed the other railway networks, the State, unable to do anything by itself, had to call in the syndical organisations. An "Operational Committee" was organised; it was composed of three members each from the C.N.T., the U.G.T., and three from the government whose members left the task of getting things moving again and of supervision to the syndical delegates. But with the

9 In U.S.S.R. the ratio was and is in the order of 18 to 1.

R

growing success of the railwaymen's efforts—that is in the South-East and Centre—the State as is its custom increased its control and wanted to take over everything. Official bureaucracy was asserting itself on the workers' achievements, and the Syndicates resisted.

In Catalonia the same offensive had been launched due to the bias of the U.G.T. in which were to be found more and more socialists with a bureaucratic-statist mentality, and Communists who, to camouflage their game, called themselves the Catalan United Socialists (P.S.U.C.). Thus our comrades, who were, after all, in a majority, and who distrusted State intervention, even under the pretext of innocent statistical information, did not allow their administration of the Madrid-Saragossa-Alicante network to be supervised.

It certainly was not the case that they could not present their accounts, for they opened their books to this writer from the start. But before attempting to summarise them we should note the modifications introduced into the operations of the Catalan network which, as a result of the reduction in traffic and the traditional imbalance between receipts and operation costs,[10] were showing a deficit. It should be borne in mind that the M.S.A. network gave financial aid to the Northern network, which also always showed a deficit. The fact is that operation costs in Spain were three times as high as in France because it is an extremely mountainous country, with relatively little traffic due to the low density population and the low tonnage of freight carried. To all these causes must be added the cost of constructing 30 km. of tracks in a very badly serviced area in the Republican zone of Aragon.

Let us now cast a quick glance at the accounts of the M.S.A. network. On July 19, 1936, the Company had 1,811,986 pesetas in cash and 2,322,401 in the bank: a total of 4,134,381 pesetas. The directors at the central office in Madrid withdrew 1.5 million pesetas from the bank, leaving 2,634,787 pesetas at the end of July. Furthermore the company owed current creditors one million pesetas. Also the staff had to be paid. The expropriating workers, who also accepted the company's debts, found themselves when all was said and done with a deficit of 502,660 pesetas. What is more all transport in the direction of that part of Aragon which was under our control, that is towards the East-West front, was carried out without payment. To all this had to be added the increase

10 For this reason the Spanish government guaranteed payment of a fixed interest on foreign capital invested in the Spanish railways.

in the cost of the small amount of coal from the Asturias that arrived with difficulty at the Mediterranean ports and the price of which rose from 45 pesetas a ton in July 1936 to 67 and by February 1937 was costing 150 pesetas a ton; the difficulties of coastal transport had become overwhelming, and were getting worse.[11]

In spite of all these difficulties, and a general falling off in traffic which resulted in average daily receipts dropping from 236,363 to 192,437 pesetas in the second half of January 1937; and though aid to the railways of the Northern network amounted to 26-27% of total receipts;[12] and in spite of aid to branch lines and an increase in wages, fares had still not been increased in March 1937, that is in nine months since the Revolution had begun. And there was no question of increasing them. To deal with the difficulties plans were being laid for a general reorganisation of the means of transport.

*

It needed the libertarian revolution in Spain to ventilate the idea of coordinating production in almost all the industries and services throughout the country. Naturally the initiative came from militants of the C.N.T. In the case under discussion they started by considering a technical reorganisation of the railways as a whole, and a financial and economic synchronisation.

Just as for the land cultivation, or the running of workshops and factories, the dispersal of forces represented an enormous loss of energy, an irrational use of human labour, machinery and raw materials, a useless duplication of efforts. It was what Proudhon in the first place and then Marx, who had thoroughly read his Proudhon, had pointed out demonstrating the advantages of the large enterprise which uses collective labour and benefits therefrom, compared with the small enterprise. Our comrades had not read Marx and knew nothing of the Proudhonian

11 In the first two or three months of the war the Republicans were masters of the seas thanks to the superior power of the cruiser *Jaime I* which was in their hands. This allowed them to maintain coastal shipping which was of importance seeing that most of the principal cities were on the coast. But when the Francoists reversed the situation with the cruiser *Canarias,* coastal shipping suffered and eventually supplies of coal to the Mediterranean region completely dried up.

12 The coordination of the activities of the two networks through a liaison *Comité* located in Barcelona was, it should be noted, a permanent arrangement.

theories, but commonsense was their guide. They therefore developed a project for reorganising the Catalan railways. I possess a copy of that project—or to be more precise the plan, for it had been accepted and was in the course of being applied. Firstly it brought together in a single federation of railway operation the Catalan network of M.S.A., the North network and Catalan system of secondary lines. Each of these networks constituted a sector and all these sectors were locally and regionally linked by liaison *Comités*.

"We constitute,"—we read in the first line of the plan—"the regional central *Comité* which regroups all the railways of Catalonia." Then come the outlines of the revolutionary reorganisation.

There are three main divisions: traffic, technical services, administration (here they are following the model of the M.S.A. network).

The section for research and purchases aims to improve the railway services, by the introduction of new methods and suitable materials, which will make it possible to prove "all the time a high sense of the constructive capacity of the new organisation of rail transport".

It has to purchase raw materials, tools, fuel, construction and manufacturing materials, etc. . . . It provides all the local sections with these supplies to get the work done and centralises all the statistics on the general activities of the network.

The traffic division is spread over three sections: operation, control and statistics, commercial and complaints.

The first section deals with everything affecting the personnel in stations and depots, the organisation of trains, timetables and loading and unloading operations, freight transport and deliveries, the distribution and movement of wagons, etc. Thanks to the commercial section it studies the traffic requirements for passengers and freight, prepares the timetables, organises the depots, hotels, transfers, and so on.

The control and statistical section supervises the general movement, undertakes all payments, deals with the distribution and sale of tickets, settles the accounts for the networks according to their category on the information provided by the stations.

The commercial and complaints section settles the different rates, whilst seeking to simplify them; it avoids the competitiveness of the capitalist system, organises combined services in which all the means of surface, sea and air transport will be coordinated.

It still has to study foreign legislation, revise Spanish legislation, modify certain agreements, maintain friendly relations with companies in other countries, apply all the new official decisions, especially fiscal ones—taxes have to be paid to the State—deal above all with changes of a syndical nature, and finally with complaints tending to continually improve the services.

The technical services consist of three sections: rolling stock and transport, power, permanent way and construction.

The first deals with the maintenance of rolling stock, depots, locomotives, wagon supplies, workshops. The second with everything connected with electricity and coal over the networks, the stations, traction power, telephones, signalling. The third with construction and maintenance of the permanent way, bridges, tunnels, stores, minor stations, etc.

The auxiliary administrative division is also subdivided into three sections: sanitation, accountancy and treasury, provisioning.

The first ensures hygiene in the means of transport, deals with sick and injured employees, and first aid posts set up in the stations.

The second, where all the financial resources of the railways converge, receives daily the receipts from all the stations; it constitutes the centre for all the various sources of income and closely observes the returns from each service.

The provisioning section has to supply employees, at cost price, with food and refreshments.

The divisions must have at their head a representative from each network. The sections will have the technicians needed, who will be answerable to the central *Comité* of which they could belong as advisers. The divisional secretaries will take part in the deliberations of the central *Comité*, so that no decisions can be taken by the latter without knowing the opinions of the different branches, lines and networks.

In the general organisation the personnel will not belong definitively to one section or division in particular but will have to agree to transfers in accordance with the demands of their work.

All the divisional *Comités* are constituted by an equal number of comrades of the C.N.T. and of the U.G.T. In the general organisation of traffic the demarcation zones will be defined by a special *Comité* whose members, representing each service, will be at work like their comrades—except in unusual circumstances recognised as such—and will meet after their day's work to

[261]

examine the results obtained. Nominated directly by their comrades in the zones or by the central *Comité* with the agreement of the respective zones, they will have to control the general activities and submit to the divisional *Comités* their observations and their initiatives. Each demarcation *Comité* will choose someone to be responsible for the administrative functions of the office.

In each office, station, workshop or gang, workers will freely elect a delegate responsible for the management and coordination of the services. When it is deemed necessary by the sections. they will form control *comités*. In localities where there will be many sections of different networks or lines, a liaison *comité* will be set up.

Each service, or division, will have mobile technicians whose task will be to continually go on improving the smooth running of the railways.

Finally, technical schools will be organised to further technical and administrative knowledge for workers so that they do not continue to be, as has been the case hitherto, simple mindless cogs in a machine, the life and functioning of which escapes them.

*

The idea of the coordination of all the means of transport came almost immediately after the seizure of the railways by the workers. We have evidence of it in a circular dated September 5, 1936—a month and a half after the Revolution started—the gist of which was:

"The profound socio-economic transformation which has taken place in our country obliges us to open new and wide horizons for the exploitation of the railways. We must therefore multiply new activities and to that end gather, in all the rail zones, informed assessments which will make it possible to study the process of production and that of consumption, so intimately linked to the railways. The results will be in the public interest.

"We therefore ask all our comrades to reply as soon as possible to the following questions:

1. What localities are covered by your station?
2. Which is the zone of influence of the railways in your region?
3. What are the means of transport between the station and the villages situated on the perimeter of this zone of influence?
4. What is the industrial and agricultural production and to what places are surpluses sent?
5. What are the means of transport most used?

6. If this transport is not by rail what are the reasons and what can be done about them?

7. Is there a coordination of services between rail and road?

8. If there is not, how can it be established and what hope of a solution?"

This questionnaire was followed by a second one which was more complete and with a surprising amount of detail. To facilitate its distribution they succeeded not without difficulty in arranging for its distribution by the Statistical and Transport Service of the government of Catalonia.

In this document no fewer than fifty-seven questions were asked concerning the geo-physical surroundings, the means of communication, dispatch and reception of goods, the importance and location of schools, the number, quality, of taxis, buses, lorries, cars, boats in the case of maritime localities, and the degree of collectivisation of each branch of transport. Finally information was requested on the syndical aspect of the problem.

A great number of replies were received. They were classified in two card index files, one dealing exclusively with the municipal life of each locality in which the station was situated; the other at the periphery of economic influence and on the means of transport.

In the archives of the administration of the M.S.A. railway network there were detailed reports from 200 towns and villages and others were expected to arrive.

More information was obtained by these methodical means, such as the exact number of lorry, bus, coastal shipping services for the whole of Catalonia. The total number of undertakings was ascertained as well as the number of owners, passengers and tonnage of goods transported. Everything was recorded, classified and marked on special charts which at the same time served to prepare the new order of things as well as to demonstrate the absurdity of the capitalist system.

Indeed, alongside a railway line shown in black, 8, 10, 12 red lines represented that number of companies and road transport services which were competing with the railways and among themselves. It was a useless duplication which was to be found especially on the Mediterranean littoral, in the densely populated and prosperous province of Barcelona.

By contrast, on the chart showing means of transport for the province of Lerida, in the interior of Catalonia, there were great expanses, whole cantons without regular communications.

Huge areas which, because they were impoverished, were condemned to stagnate in isolation, ignorance and poverty—though an improvement in the means of transport could, as often happens, favour some aspect of development of production. And my comrades, who always put social interest, viewed in its global aspect, above corporative self-interest, or of narrow syndicalist outlook, decided that some of the lorries and buses in overabundance in the province of Barcelona should be sent to the province of Lerida. At the beginning, at least, the services would be run at a loss, but profitable services in the Barcelona area would more than compensate for these losses. What was required was to ensure to all the inhabitants of Catalonia then, and later for all the people of Spain, the same chances of well being and happiness. Did not the Collectives in Aragon, the Levante and Castile act in this way?

The general reorganisation extended to the merchant fleet. Not all was done, nor could be done at the time in view of the Francoist naval supremacy. But a start was made. Once again maps were produced. On one of them two parallel lines in red, one of which hugs the coast; it is a coastal shipping service Barcelona-Tarragona; the other red line followed the same coastline but on land. It was a railway line. The coastal service was withdrawn. But what they were dreaming of doing in the future was to coordinate rail, road and sea transport: ever Coordination!

4. The Socialisation of Medicine

By 1937 the National Federation for Public Health, a section of the C.N.T., had 40,000 members and it goes without saying that such large numbers could not have been assembled so quickly had not the way been shown by others over the years.

Some precedents explain, only partly, the creative drive that was to take place. A number of doctors were among the best Spanish libertarian militants. There was Dr. Pedro Vallina, a courageous fighter[13] who played such an important role in the social struggles in Andalusia; Dr. Isaac Puente, by far his junior, was one of the most outstanding personalities in the libertarian movement during the years following the establishment of the second Republic; Dr. Amparo Poch y Gascon, was the most cultured woman in

13 Who died recently in exile in Mexico.

that movement; Dr. Roberto Remartinez's knowledge was encyclopaedic, and Felix Martí Ibañez, was a brilliant representative of the young generation of sociologist-doctors, a humanist and specialist in sexual and psychoanalytical problems. Along with these doctors, best known because of their writings and activities, there was a large number of others who supported the constructive concepts of the libertarian ideal of a new civilization, a more rational and just organisation of society. At the local level, these men, often in contact with the workers' Syndicates, performed wonders of human solidarity. In the chapters on agrarian Collectives we have given examples of mutual aid societies founded or administered by the libertarians in the villages or small provincial towns. The disinterested collaboration of one or two or more doctors was secured by them. Sometimes it would even go much further. Thus, in Valencia, then the third largest city in Spain, was the headquarters of a *Mutua levantina* or Mutual Aid Society of the Levante, founded by libertarians whom this writer got to know in his youth, and who brought together many doctors with different specialities, professional people with experience in the different fields of public health. More than a simple society for mutual aid, it was, basically, an association of practitioners of medicine which extended over the whole region of the Levante and in which the spirit of mutual aid dominated in its most human implications.[14]

When the Civil War broke out, there was no doctors' Syndicate specially organised in Barcelona, but a "Syndicate of the Liberal Professions" with various sections: journalists, writers, teachers, lawyers, doctors. How many of the latter? We do not know, but their number must have been fairly large to judge by the speed with which initiatives sprung up when the time was ripe.

There are two reasons for this. In the first place, the sanitary problems; questions of social hygiene; infant mortality; the struggle against tuberculosis, venereal diseases and others, were subjects openly discussed in our press, particularly in the libertarian review *Estudios* which as we have already mentioned had a circulation of up to 75,000 copies (in a country of 24 million inhabitants of whom 40% were illiterate). The minds of many militants were therefore aware of these problems.[15] Then the

14 In 1970 that Society continued to exist in spite of Francoism.
15 We should also mention that many lectures had been given over the years by sympathetic doctors in the *Centros Obreros* (workers' centres), the equivalent of the *Bourses de Travail* in France, and though the architecture was less imposing the spirit was more militant.

disorganisation of the sanitary services, administered by a religious personnel which, after July 19, disappeared overnight from the hospitals the dispensaries and other charitable institutions, made it necessary to improvise new methods of organisation and to set up new establishments not only to continue to succour the sick, the blind, the infirm, but also to operate, to tend and treat the wounded from the Civil War who were being brought in all the time.

Individual and collective initiatives were encouraged; stately homes were requisitioned and the rooms were furnished, and beds set up all in good order. Then the importance of the sanitary question loomed large, so large that the Federation for corresponding services soon appeared among the sixteen large organic divisions in which the whole life of the country had been divided on the basis of a national plan which was perhaps excessively organising.

It was thus that in Barcelona the Syndicate for Sanitary Services came into being in September 1936.

*

But before proceeding further we must in the name of objectivity mention the emergence at the same time of a new element in this vast improvisation. In that month of September 1936, faced with the public's demand for a unification of the anti-Francoist forces, the C.N.T. decided to join the Catalan government and, shortly afterwards, the national government led by the socialist Largo Caballero. Among the three Catalan "councillors" it nominated, one of them, Garcia Birlan, the best known contributor to the Spanish libertarian press (using the pseudonym *Dionisios*) was appointed Minister of Health. He chose his collaborators from among his ideological comrades, and it was thus that Dr. Felix Martí Ibañez was nominated director general of sanitary services and of social assistance in Catalonia.

A study in depth would reveal that in many similar situations the government used libertarians to carry out practical programmes for their ministries. Thus in Catalonia, the work of the Ministry of Public Education was performed, so far as practical achievements were concerned (and some were most laudable), by pedagogues who were militants of the C.N.T. Thus in the Asturias the control of activities connected with the fishing industry, one of the most important economic factors at the time, was given to a specially constituted governmental organism which in its turn entrusted militants and the syndicates of the C.N.T. with the practical task of getting the job done.

One of the reasons which explain this official attitude towards the official sanitary services was that the C.N.T. could, thanks to its contact with the working masses, and its constructive and organising spirit, be a valuable and even necessary aid, though the government, or whatever was in its place, held the advantage of disposing of the financial resources which those on the revolutionary side lacked.

The result of the situation created in Catalonia was that the existence of these two forms of activity, at the same time divergent and convergent, were to provoke a fraternal and inevitable rivalry. Dr. Martí Ibañez in his book *Obra* (Work) published in November 1937 bears witness to this. In it the author, who was obliged to give up his post as a result of Stalinist manoeuvres, describes what he and his collaborators had achieved. His Ministry did more in ten months than other Catalan ministries had done in the five years of the Republic. It is true of course that the revolutionary situation, and the participation of C.N.T. militants, made it possible to speed up the rhythm of achievement.

We are only too anxious to establish a parallel between the action of the governmental organism and that of the syndical organism, both in the hands of the libertarians. On this subject Dr. Martí Ibañez starts by paying a tribute to the creative drive of members of the C.N.T. to which he belonged. From the first day of the struggle, he writes, "We, the doctors of the C.N.T., constituted, thanks to the workers' sanitary organisation, the first sanitary control which was also the first effort at organic cohesion of the sanitary services in Catalonia. When the time is ripe we will describe those hectic days during which the sanitary control by the C.N.T. improvised, at high speed, solutions which the innumerable problems that arose continuously demanded."

This "hectic" activity of our independent movement continued, and it explains the powerful take-off by the Syndicate that was constituted as a result. And that the balance sheet of the two forms of organisation was all in favour of the direct creation according to the principles of the C.N.T. For, right at the beginning, as we have seen, it was from the syndical movement, from the syndicalist militants, even though the specific sanitary organisation had not yet been constituted, that everything stemmed; in fact Garcia Birlan and Felix Martí Ibañez simply transferred to the Ministry of Health what was already living in the

[267]

thoughts, in the souls of the utopians, impatient to convert utopia into reality.

Apart from the financial advantages that a Ministry could enjoy, and the aid that it received from the syndical organisation (thanks to fraternal action shown by the militants who knew each other) and from the industries providing the necessary technical elements, we note that the new hospitals placed under a kind of governmental aegis, were only the old establishments with a change of name, whereas those, much more numerous, taken over by the Syndicate were, with considerably less means, created all of a piece.

We are not underlining these facts for petty reasons but in order that the importance of the achievements of our syndical organisation should be better understood.

∗

The Syndicate for Sanitary Services, as we have already said, was constituted in Barcelona in September 1936.[16] Five months later it included 1,020 doctors with different specialities; 3,206 male nurses; 330 midwives; 633 dentists; 71 specialists in diathermy; 10 unspecified specialists; 153 pharmacists; 663 assistant pharmacists; 335 preparers of dressings, an unspecified number of masseurs, and 220 veterinary surgeons. In all more than 7,000 people organised according to the libertarian and industrial norms of the Syndicates of the C.N.T. so as to integrate all the activities contributing to a global task and to harmonise its different aspects.[17] The significance of these numbers can be appreciated when one takes into account that the population of Catalonia was then 2.5 millions.

Once again the moral principle of human solidarity and that of technical coordination aiming at the greatest efficiency amalgamated. Which is even more understandable since it was a question of at the same time confronting a grave temporary situation and of fundamentally reorganising, inspired by a great social ideal, the whole practice of medicine and of Public Health Services. A very necessary task in Spain where out of 24 million inhabitants 80,000 children less than a year old died annually from causes

16 Similar organisms certainly arose at the same time in other towns in Spain: the figures given at the Valencia Congress make it possible to assume this. But the author was unable to carry his enquiry further.
17 As well as the number of direct supporters one must add the support given by numbers of doctors, nurses, etc., who did not think it worth joining the Syndicate.

mainly social; where, for instance in the 5th District of Barcelona which was entirely working class, infantile mortality was more than double that recorded for the 4th District which was specifically a bourgeois area.[18] Demographic statistics at the time indicated that for the whole population the death rate reached 18-19 per 1,000, one of the highest percentages in Europe in spite of the salubrious climate.

Thus our comrades laid the bases, from the beginning, for a general restructuring of sanitary services. I was unable to learn in detail, bearing in mind the all-absorbing activities of the prime-movers, how this groundwork was achieved and what was its real extent. I can only therefore summarise it imperfectly, indicate some of the results obtained, summarise the plans established for the future at the time when I was able to undertake this research, and note what palpable facts I was able to collect.

*

In Catalonia the region was first of all divided into nine large sectors: Barcelona, Tarragona, Lerida, Gerona,[19] Tortosa, Reus, Bergueda, Ripoll and the Pyrenean zone to a certain extent lost in the mountains. Then, around these nine centres 26 secondary centres were constituted according to the population density and the demands of public health. In all, 35 centres of greater or lesser importance, covering the whole of the four provinces in such a way that no village or hamlet, no isolated farm or *mas*, no man, woman or child was without sanitary protection or medical care.

Parallel and complementary each large sector included a technical medical centre, a syndical centre the cantonal *Comité* of which controlled and to an extent directed the services.

In their turn, the cantonal *Comités* on the federal principle, had ramifications in Barcelona which had greater technical facilities and specialised establishments, and where patients requiring urgent or special treatment were taken by ambulance or taxi.

The sections constituted on the basis of specialities were autonomous so far as their method of organisation within the Syndicate was concerned, but their autonomy did not imply an absolute independence, and even less isolation or indifference

18 These differences were not limited to Spain, but were more pronounced in Spain than in other countries, and put greater pressure on the need for change.
19 These towns were the capitals of the four Catalan provinces.

of Barcelona, which the plenary assembly would periodically reappoint—or modify if the case arose—met with the delegates of the first nine zones. Technically and geographically the spirit of togetherness was always present, and their federalism was always constructive.

Very soon the population felt the benefits of this vast undertaking. In a year, in Barcelona alone six new hospitals had been created, including two military hospitals for war casualties. At the same time nine sanatoria had sprung up in different parts of Catalonia. They were generally established in properties that had been taken over and which were situated in open mountainous sites, in the middle of pine forests, the heights of which dominated the countryside or the sea.

The internal equipment of the hospitals was less easy. New appointments had to be improvised which would serve the sanitary demands and needs immediately.

Nevertheless, to summarise: there were in Barcelona at the time (June 1937) 18 hospitals managed by the Medical Syndicate (of which 6 were created by it), 17 sanatoria, 22 clinics, 6 psychiatric establishments, 3 nurseries, one maternity hospital as well as 2 annexes to the General Hospital, one for bone tuberculosis and another for orthopaedic treatment. "That," some of my comrades told me with pride, "will make this hospital into one of the best in the world."

Out-patients departments were set up in all the principal localities in Catalonia, to which the smaller localities were attached. They had the services of medical specialists and were provided with sanitary equipment which made it possible to prevent the crowding of patients and the injured in a few large centres.

Just as with other workers, doctors were sent where the need for them was being most felt. In the past the rich areas were over-doctored but this had changed. When the inhabitants of a locality requested the Syndicate for a doctor, it would first check up on local needs and then select from its list of available members the practitioner whose qualifications were most suited to the sanitary conditions of the place. And he would have to give good reasons for refusing the post. For it was considered that medicine was at the service of the community, and not the other way round. Social duty was in the forefront.

The Syndicate lacked money and so financial resources for the hospitals were supplied in part by the Catalan government and partly by the municipalities. The funds for the out-patients departments in the small towns and villages came from contributions by local municipalities and the Syndicates as a whole who also supported and administered the dental clinics.

Such were the first achievements in the socialisation of medicine.

*

Nevertheless at the end of a year it had still not been possible to eliminate private practices, and perhaps in the interests of the patients it was probably not altogether desirable. But already the Syndicate had got rid of the abuses which had previously been so frequent. It had fixed the fees for consultations and operations and it exercised a strict control by the method which we have observed in practice by other services in Castellon de la Plana, in Alicante and Fraga. Patients who had recourse to the services of a doctor or a surgeon privately, paid for services rendered through the intermediary of the Syndicate which maintained a close check on fees charged.

In the new clinics, operations were carried out free of charge as also was treatment in psychiatric hospitals.

What was the attitude of doctors to this upheaval? Different answers can be given, indeed contradictory ones. But as my comrades explained to me, there are essentially two groups: that of the "old ones" who constituted the privileged class—a part of whom left Catalonia and crossed over to France—and for whom medicine was above all a source of considerable material gain; that group, as was to be expected, was not at all satisfied with the changes that took place. The other group which had not yet "arrived" offered no resistance and even collaborated with good grace in this general series of changes.

By contrast the young joined with enthusiasm. For many of them the future was problematical. After having qualified they had to work virtually unpaid in the hospitals and the sanatoria. In the clinics the official doctor, handsomely remunerated, hardly ever showed up; a younger doctor would stand in for him, waiting for the "boss" to die so as to step into his shoes. Alongside him, a younger doctor still acted as secretary, waiting for a shake-up in the hierarchy to move up in his turn.

Under the new system, all hospital doctors received 500 pesetas a month for three hours work a day.[20] They had in addition their

20 A means of comparison: in Barcelona at that time (July 1937) a good worker earned an average of 350 to 400 pesetas a month for an eight hour day.

private patients who paid along the lines already indicated. We know only too well that this was not yet economic equality but within the limits of what was possible, a great step had been taken. There were no longer "señores doctores" receiving huge fees while other doctors lived virtually in conditions of poverty. In the hospitals, clinics, etc., no one could receive two salaries. More than half the practitioners collaborated voluntarily in activities in their competence, in their own time.

And they did it with pleasure, in agreement with the Syndicate even when they were not members, and without the need for the use of authority. The secretary of the doctors' section, an enthusiastic and indefatigable Basque, told me that

"what is so encouraging is the moral revolution that has taken place in the profession. Everybody is doing his work honestly. The eminent doctor who is being sent once a week to work without a fee in a district dispensary never fails to go. The important personage who in the old days would go through the wards in the hospital followed by a retinue of some half a dozen less qualified colleagues, with one carrying a wash-hand basin, another a hand towel, a third the stethoscope, the fourth opening the door, the fifth closing it and all of them prostrating themselves before an authority who was not always scientific—that personage has disappeared. Today there are only equals who esteem and respect each other."

*

Having seen what was done just for medicine and related activities, let us observe the projects that were developed in the Syndicates and in the Commissions specially nominated by them. One of the steps taken deals with the general organisation of everything to do with pharmaceutical products. At the end of 1937 a plan had been drawn up which divided the related activities into four groups: laboratory and research centre; manufacture; large scale distribution; distribution to the consumer.[21]

The four sectors in the process of organisation were represented in a study Commission which assumed complete responsibility for the undertakings designed to satisfy public needs. Efforts were made to get the U.G.T. to join in these efforts for many of the

21 One finds here what is perhaps rather more a human tendency and moral philosophy than a rational organisational principle for the coordination and continual harmonisation of efforts.

pharmacist-shopkeepers joined the rival organisation which officially opposed socialisation. The role of each of these sectors had been defined as follows:

The research laboratory must be the axis around which the general initiatives will develop. It will coordinate the studies as a whole and dispose of the technical means the use of which will be centred on it.

In disposing of the necessary means, the manufacturing section will group the laboratories and the factories manufacturing pharmaceutical products, coordinating and planning their activities.

The general warehouse will be used to control the centres for bulk supplies; it must also centralise the whole administration.

Finally, the distributive section will see to the setting up of local sales points in accordance with the needs of the people, and of course by arrangement with the first-hand distributors.

But new initiatives were being taken all the time. Improvements in the treatment given for injuries suffered at work according to the nature of the injuries; in large factories and works full-time medical services were organised which would make it more possible to reduce the powers of the insurance companies. Permanent injuries and deaths would be dealt with by the national Insurance Fund which was in the hands of the State.[22]

∗

So far we have seen what had been done in Catalonia with, as the driving force, the Barcelona Syndicate which grouped more than 7,000 professionals in many fields of medicine and allied activities. There is no doubt that more was done later which the writer was not in a position to study on the spot. Nevertheless a noteworthy fact of great importance allows one to see further. The Spain that was struggling against Francoism had then about half the Spanish population, that is 12 million

22 That the libertarians should have thought of such a solution which implies the recognition of the existence of the State (but the recognition of a fact does not imply approval of it) may surprise and shock the theoreticians who ignore the practical facts. But firstly neither this Syndicate nor any Syndicate possessed the funds accumulated by the State services thanks to special legislation, and which must have involved vast sums. Then as we have repeated many times, we were in a mixed and most complicated situation in which the State, the government and the political parties, remnants of private capital and individual property persisted, in which even the socialised economy paid taxes, etc. In this situation, many activities escaped our control.

S

inhabitants from which number one had to deduct, if we do not accept the demagogy of the time, those who had voted for the Rightists[23] and who were, more or less, pro-fascists. Now in February 1937 a congress was held in Valencia by the Federation of the Health Syndicates. These Syndicates, spread throughout the different towns of "Republican" Spain, about 40 in all grouped 40,000 members, representing a variety of functions similar to those we found in the example of Barcelona. This makes it possible to guess at the number of tasks and initiatives that were undertaken in that period of creative effervescence.

But even if I could not go from town to town, from hospital to hospital, and from clinic to clinic, to produce a bulky volume, information and original documents reached me, the contents of which prove once again that without the initiative of C.N.T. syndicates in taking over the medical and sanitary services, not only would the private and public organisation of the hospital and sanitary services not have developed, but the existing organisation would have for the most part been in jeopardy.

For in this connection official initiative was virtually nil. It was the Syndicates and their members who undertook, often with the responsible military personnel, to organise field hospitals behind the various fronts. It was they who obliged recalcitrant crypto-fascist or fascist pharmacists, to open their shops, or who seized the shops when the owners had disappeared. It was the sanitary Syndicates of the C.N.T. who organised, again often with the aid of the corresponding military services, the evacuation of large numbers of old folk, women and children from the threatened war zones; it was they who organised the anti-gas brigades and very often, with the help of the municipalities, street shelters; and it was they who took part in building bomb shelters.

And though we lack detailed information on the subject, it is certainly true that it was also thanks to them that a fair number of hospitals, dispensaries, clinics, rest homes, sprang up in the Levante, Castile, in Asturias, etc. The State in these matters revealed its incapacity and the Health Minister, unsuited

23 We have not at hand the figures of votes cast for the Right wing parties at the February elections of 1936 in the provinces which constituted "Republican" Spain in the period 1936-39 but it is clear that there were quite a large number. Furthermore, anti-Francoists living in the provinces occupied by Franco were reduced to silence. If one recognises that at the end of the first year Franco dominated a half of the Spanish population, the numerical advantage was already on his side, unlike what was being affirmed by demagogues who were stupid enough to actually believe what they were saying.

and inept, spent most of his time making demagogic speeches instead of fulfilling the task entrusted to him. There would be many anecdotes to retail on the subject.[24]

*

It was under the inspiration of this effervescence that the February 1937 congress was held, exactly *seven months* after the unleashing of the Francoist attack.

Let us see what were the main resolutions adopted by this congress. The first paragraph of the motion which was presented by the sanitary federations of Catalonia, the Centre and the Levante on the *General and Specific Functions of the Unitary Syndicates of Public Health*[25] reads:

"The unitary Syndicates of Public Health have as their principal mission the putting into practice of a Sanitary and Social Assistance Plan in their respective regions so that, in the whole organisation, the cantonal and local federations constitute the links of a general chain. On such bases the national plan will be constituted and put into effect taking into account the initiatives approved by the local, cantonal and regional federations, all combining to form the superior organism."

One cannot say more in so few words. And we do not believe that any regime, of free enterprise or of the State, has ever enunciated such precise aims, nor specified a plan as general, as concrete, as well as how to achieve it.

The resolution then went on to insist on the social ends aimed at and on the principles of organisation adopted, as well as on the problems posed by the general structuring of the sanitary services and the defence of public health. But in extending the one and the other

24 Here is just one which we recount without pleasure, but which speaks volumes on the moral corruption that the exercise of power brings with it. Two libertarian nurses had organised at great cost in time and ingenuity, a cottage hospital in the small Andalusian town of Ronda, in the province of Malaga. As they lacked financial resources to purchase some of the equipment they decided to go to Valencia to see the Health Minister who belonged to the same movement. They called at her residence but only found the chauffeur, who took them in the minister's car to her office. The minister's only reaction was to inveigh against the chauffeur for having taken the two women in her car and without her permission. Then our two Andalusians let fly, and the minister winced. But the two nurses left empty handed.

25 And signed respectively by José Ibuzquiza (the Basque earlier referred to), Candido Penã and F. Tadeo Campuzano.

"It is on the whole a question of establishing services having as their objective to protect or restore health, on the one hand by encouraging economic prosperity and by increasing well-being, while on the other by eliminating what is prejudicial to public health; to this end the unitary Syndicates of Public Health propose the union of workers, technicians and intellectuals, an indispensable union for public health and for the national economy."

A sociological concept of medicine; it embraces all that is connected with medicine, all that depends on it and on which it depends. Solidarity of all aspects of social life is present here. And the resolution, which leaves out nothing, tackles other factors which influence the achievement of the aims being pursued: it asks for the "reorganisation of technical teaching", "in order to raise the intellectual level of workers in Public Health", the organisation of classes, schools and workshops for "professional training"; "the sanitary education of the people and the spread of information for first aid"; the formation of "specialists for the abnormal, for the blind, etc." Finally it recommends "the organisation of an Economic Council in the sanitary Syndicates" and of "*Comités* for technical and administrative control of clinics, sanatoria and other related institutions, having statistical sections, taking adequate measures to stimulate collective organ-isation, and organising work centres to encourage the development of different sections and services."

The tasks of the Syndicate were divided into four principal groups:

a) General medical care.

b) Social hygiene and health, in relation to the general organisation of society as a whole.

c) Sanitary inspection.

d) Social assistance.

The different aspects of the tasks of medical care as a whole were enumerated under twenty-one headings of which we cite: domiciliary visits by doctor and consultations in surgeries, surgical clinics, in pediatric, psychiatric, gynaecological and dermatological-venereal clinics. The clinics would be organised on local, cantonal, regional levels as would also be the case for maternity hospitals, sanatoriums, Roentgen Institutes, convalescent homes, etc. These specialised establishments as a whole should constitute a network through which everything would be rationally coordinated.

The resolution adopted on the second point of the Agenda

envisaged also a sanitary organisation at the different geographical levels; the creation of institutes of hygiene; the generalisation of physical education with stadiums, swimming pools, gymnasia, etc., a campaign against rodents and harmful insects—all things which had been partially achieved in other countries but not in Spain, and above all not realisable without a social plan that was not feasible in an individualist economic regime, or in which bureaucracy dominates almost everything.

This vision of the whole and of the different complementary aspects of the problems explains why the treatment of animals and the methods of feeding them should have been considered as one of the tasks of public health, forming part of the social responsibilities of the Federation. Once again we are coming out of the corporative framework, and if some correlations may shock, they seem to be justified with regard to the general interest.

At that same congress projects and plans were presented for dealing with certain diseases, especially with contagious diseases, the most important of which was tuberculosis. The Catalan delegation, through the intermediary of its Basque secretary, presented a project which after careful examination was to serve as a model for other regions. A reading of it allows us to gauge the intensity and scope of the effort which would have been realised had fascism not triumphed.

Following an exposé illustrated with telling statistics on the gravity of the disease, the forms and social causes of contagion, the proposers outlined the different aspects of the struggle for its prevention: examination of mothers-to-be, general progress in hygiene, greater use of "the pick and shovel" to knock down more insalubrious houses and slum quarters, veritable breeding grounds, and to rebuild on bases dictated by hygienic considerations; transformation of school sites, preferably outside the town centres. There followed the enumeration of the means of direct struggle against the evil.

So far as the towns, large and small, were concerned the basic ingredient accepted was that of antitubercular dispensaries strategically situated, always according to a general plan corresponding at the same time with the number of homes affected, and the density and way of life of the inhabitants. Thanks to the specialist doctors at their disposal, these dispensaries would engage in a systematic tracking down of the disease in the Collectives, especially among the young (schools, institutes, universities, workshops, barracks).[26] The doctors thus detailed would maintain a necessary and obligatory contact, preparing reports and card indexes which would be carefully classified and utilised.

The towns would be the seat of the central dispensaries which would coordinate the activities of those established in less important localities in order to follow methodically the results obtained and to modify or improve the methods of acting on the strength of the lessons learned from experience. Each district in Barcelona would have to have at least one dispensary and it was also proposed to establish one in some 24 Catalan towns including the provincial capitals.

All these centres would have to be in organic contact with the epidemiological control set up in the Catalan capital, in order to follow the progress of the struggle being waged throughout the region.

So far as the immediate tasks were concerned there was a precise statistic of numbers of tuberculous patients admitted to the hospitals of Catalonia, the number of beds available and the number to be installed urgently. It had been possible to collect and coordinate this information as a result of the work done by the Syndicates and at the Federation which encompassed the whole enterprise.

Much research still remained to be done and these initiatives had to be implemented in the other regions of Spain. We do not know when this would have been done. But if the new society had been established, such an organisation would not have been long in emerging everywhere. For the socialisation of medicine was not just an initiative of militant libertarian doctors. Wherever we were able to make a study of villages and small towns transformed by the Revolution, medicine and existing hospitals had been municipalised, expanded, placed under the aegis of the Collective. When there were none, they were improvised. The socialisation of medicine was becoming everybody's concern, for the benefit of all. It constituted one of the most remarkable achievements of the Spanish Revolution.

26 We had not yet come to the end of the civil war.

PART FOUR

Towns and Isolated Achievements

CHAPTER XIII

TOWN COLLECTIVISATIONS

In the variety of forms of social reconstruction the organisation which we shall call municipalist, which we could also call communalist, and which has its roots in Spanish traditions that have remained living, deserves a place to itself. It is characterised by the leading role of the town, the commune, the municipality, that is, to the predominance of the local organisation which embraces the city as a whole. The other institutions even the most modern and which, because they are the most modern, are not as deeply rooted: Syndicates, cooperatives, even communities, are a part of the whole, except for some Collectives, especially those in Aragon, but are not the whole, do not embody the collective soul. It is what one finds in a small industrial town such as Granollers in Catalonia with 18,000 inhabitants, in an important village such as Binefar in Aragon or in provincial capitals with bigger populations but relatively less industrialisation, such as Castellon de la Plana, or Alicante in the Levante. Even when the Syndicate exists and plays an important role it does not direct the whole of social life, contrary to the concepts of the theoreticians of syndicalism.

In some cases, as in Fraga, and in Rubi, the direct organisation by the city, embracing the whole, merges with that of the producing Collective, and one could say that the two structures interpenetrate.

[279]

Locally, self-determination of the whole asserted itself, and the organisation of the town was confirmed, which reinforced its personality vis-à-vis the State as well as the freedoms and the practice of independence so far as social life was concerned.

1. Elda and the S.I.C.E.P.

Situated in the province of Alicante, Elda is a small town with a population of 25,000. It is at the same time the centre of an agricultural area and of industrial production, being well situated for transport and on a river which is harnessed for hydraulic power.

As so often was the case in the Levante region, our movement was solidly established there for more than three quarters of a century. Elda was the scene of social conflicts, historic strikes as dramatic as any in Spain. Combats marked by an extraordinary grandeur were waged, such as the one lasting for three months by the workers in the shoe-making industry to demand that a militant blacklisted by the employers should be re-engaged. One should never forget that moral reasons have at least as much as material reasons, inspired and supported the activities of the Syndicates founded and activated by the Spanish libertarians.

With such antecedents and experience of the struggle it is obvious that once the fascist menace had been strangled, at least at local level, and our comrades being, as were the republicans and socialists, convinced that Franco would soon be defeated,[1] they undertook the social transformation for which they had struggled for so long. Nevertheless the political situation in Elda was not the same as in Alcoy, not far distant, and furthermore our comrades had maintained a residue of the communalist spirit which is to be found, alongside more modern concepts, in the historic work of the libertarian sociologists. These reasons and the desire so widespread among the population to maintain the united anti-Francoist front so long as the struggle lasted at a national level, resulted in the libertarians of Elda accepting to enter the municipal Council renewed under the pressure of circumstances.

1 The republican governments engaged in demagogy which completely deceived the masses, and greatly contributed to the final defeat.

The representatives of the different movements and parties were appointed. The U.G.T. and the C.N.T. each had five delegates though the latter was numerically stronger. The Left Republicans, whose leader was Manuel Azaña, the cantankerous President of the Republic, had two as did the Socialist Party; the Communist Party only had one and was by far the weakest of the political parties.

In this sharing out the socialist current was somewhat at an advantage, for the members of the U.G.T. would normally act in concert with the Socialist Party. But on the other hand the situation often tended to make the reformist syndicates of the U.G.T. follow the revolutionaries (though one can also cite many cases, and this book is full of such cases, in which these same reformists were the active opponents of socialism).

It was not the case here. Nevertheless, from the first day, the initiative for the new social structure came naturally from our comrades. It was undoubtedly due to the fact that as in Granollers, Gerona, Hospitalet and Valencia to name a few, the mayor was a libertarian.

The new councillors began to transform the structure of the municipal organism from the bottom to the top. Until then it had been above all a haven for an inert petty bureaucracy without initiative, and unorganised. The mayor had two deputies and a councillor who had to advise him in his activities, but that small world slept the sleep of small provincial monarchist or republican towns. Traditions were therefore turned upside down, and the council structured more or less in the same way as in the collectivised villages, by large active groupings. First a defence section was set up, then one for public education, one for work based on the socio-economic situation of the locality, one for agriculture, one for health and social assistance.

Up to then public education had been more than neglected, and many children did not go to school. The municipal section concerned tackled this problem without considerations of cost, appealed to the building workers' Syndicate and within five months two new schools were ready, one for 400 and the other for 70 children. More would have been done if it had not been necessary to requisition the club where previously those of "higher" social circles in Elda used to meet, in order to billet militiamen in training before going to the front. Then it was necessary at the same time to organise reception centres for youngsters from Madrid, who were among the 1,500 refugees who had been evacuated to relieve the congestion in the besieged city. The libertarian *Ateneo* and the local federation of syndicates had to put their premises at the disposal of these unexpected guests.

All these difficulties did not prevent the section for health and hygiene from making changes in the organisation of the hospital, the services of which had been quite inadequate. Three new doctors were engaged as well as two auxiliaries and two mid-wives whose services were free, which was an innovation. In the early months of 1937 a project was on foot for the installation of sanatoria and clinics. In a word, they marched boldly towards the municipal socialisation of medicine.

But Elda, as we have pointed out, was an industrial centre. Around this centre which was known for the important shoe industry that developed there, for its tanneries, and leather industry, gravitated four other localities of less importance, engaged in the same industry, a number of whose workers were employed at the factories in Elda. The small town of Petrel alone had 3,500 shoe workers of both sexes while Monovar, Novelda and Sax 2,000; 7,500 were employed in Elda of whom 4,500 were members of the C.N.T. But the important social achievements could not be realised everywhere equally.

These achievements appear in two different forms. In Elda there was a group of a dozen factories entirely socialised which employed 2,800 workers. Their organisation reminds one of what one observed in other cases so far as the characteristics of the work are concerned. Each factory had at its head a *comité* consisting of five *technical* delegates (our comrades insisted on the adjective, which they thought removed any authoritarian connotation from the delegation) representing the five main operations in the manufacture of shoes. To these five delegates a sixth was added, representing the work and the workers engaged in the stores.

The twelve socialised factories were, then, managed by these twelve *comités* controlled by the ordinary and extraordinary workers' assemblies. At the same time these twelve *comités* acted in concert with the Syndicate which coordinated the work, centralising the statistics of production and reserves. Thus whatever autonomy was possible in the organisation of activities was allied to solidarity in the collective effort.

Naturally, the factories did not trade on their own account. All the sales operations were carried out under the auspices of the Syndicate.

It was in the socialised factories of Alcoy that I encountered a new kind of delegation: the *moral* delegation. In each undertaking two workers, one from the U.G.T., the other from the C.N.T., elected by their comrades, were instructed to maintain good relations, encourage enthusiasm, and a spirit of harmony, and stimulate if need be a sense of responsibility. (And yet the precaution was probably not necessary. As my comrades pointed out, "There was no need to impose any kind of discipline for from the first hour there was the kind of self-discipline which comes from the conviction that one is working for the community.")

Apart from some details, which have their importance, the form of organisation that we have briefly described was no different from the kind we have observed elsewhere. But what was most original in the achievements at Elda was the creation of the S.I.C.E.P. (initials for "Syndicate of the Footwear Industry in Elda and Petrel").

This Syndicate was more like a consortium of a new kind. It was founded in August 1936, *only a month after the events that shook Spain*. The shoe industry which was already working at only 60% of its productive capacity, was threatened with a complete stoppage. And with it, the whole economic life tottered, as well as the new order which had to be supported at all costs to prevent Francoism from making inroads. It was then that, through the initiative of the C.N.T. and with the agreement of the U.G.T., it was decided that all available means had to be brought together to prevent a collapse which would have grave repercussions. And thanks to the guarantees offered by the two Unions, they persuaded the employers to raise loans from the local banks on their properties and assets, with which to deal with the situation. The Syndicates undertook to be co-guarantors. In addition the Ministry for Industry granted a credit of 7 million pesetas. 575,000 pesetas a week was needed, of which 300,000 for wages. Only then could production be resumed, and maintained. But all this required coordination in the economic and financial efforts as well as in the management of work.

The S.I.C.E.P. was therefore set up, and covered *eighty establishments*, large and small, dotted all over the region and to the four localities mentioned and involving 12,500 workers, men and women.

Constituted by the factories which were at the control stage (the employers still remained, but served mainly to provide the funds taken out of their bank accounts), the S.I.C.E.P., the effective management of which was in the hands of the workers' delegates, centralised and coordinated the whole of production. It purchased and distributed raw materials according to the needs and specialisations of the different undertakings, it made payments and settled debts. It handled income from sales, giving nothing to the employers that could be described as profits. Anyway, profits were not possible in the situation as it was, for the non socialised factories were closed several days a week and S.I.C.E.P. helped them, thanks to help from the socialised industries, by sharing out the orders for army boots received from the government.

S.I.C.E.P. worked hard to find new buyers. Having asked the the factories to produce new shoe models, it received 900 and they managed through a marketing organisation which extended from the coasts of the Cantabrian sea, and the North Atlantic to North Africa, to dispose of quite large quantities. But not in sufficient quantities to escape the difficulties resulting from the war. The warehouses owned by the S.I.C.E.P. in Elda, Valencia and Barcelona, as well as the factory warehouses, were full of unsold goods, valued at some 10 million pesetas.

2. Granollers

Situated a little to the north of Barcelona, Granollers which had a population of 18,000 in 1936, was at the same time a cantonal chief town, an important commercial and industrial centre, as were many others in this part of Catalonia. Our movement went back to the beginnings of socialism in Spain, that is to about 1870. As almost everywhere, union activity predominated, with bitter struggles, determined efforts at organisation, repressions, empty periods and magnificent revivals. Our effective strength depended on circumstances.

But for a very long time, the number of workers belonging to the C.N.T. averaged 3,000. It was less during the dictatorship of Primo de Rivera, and also, after a passing reawakening under the Second Republic, the first government of which was socialist and republican, the second openly Rightist, and acted with the kind of brutality which reminded one of the worst days of the monarchy. So much so, that in July 1936, in spite of the amnesty that had meant the release of 30,000 libertarians from the prisons, there were not more than 2,000 members in the Syndicates of Granollers.

With the unleashing of the Civil War and the Revolution, soon the Syndicates of the C.N.T. had 6,000 workers from the factories, workshops, building trades, transport, etc. The remainder—technicians who considered themselves a class apart, Council employees, civil servants and bureaucrats—totalling 1,000, joined the U.G.T.

Our militants, enlightened workers who were inspired by the ideal, had always given proof of their organising capacities. But the war made first demands and most of them left immediately for the Aragon front. Only some six or seven of those who played a leading role in the syndicates at local and regional level were left.

Nevertheless, a libertarian spirit was manifesting itself among a section of the population, with a very clear conception of our goals of human emancipation. Thus, two days after the end of the struggle in Barcelona, that is on July 22, 1936, the building workers decided—and historically it was one of the first initiatives of its kind—to socialise their work. They called an assembly to which they invited the employers, mostly small contractors, and proposed to them to "collectivise" syndically all building trades. And what may appear surprising is that the employers accepted straight away. Thus was public spirit inspired by the ideas of social transformation in some regions of Spain.

Then, the same situation occurred immediately afterwards in the printing trade. It was followed by shoe retail shops; and it spread as if by a miracle in all branches of work and human activities where until then the social classes had opposed each other.

Granollers socialised but in its own way, and the way it did so deserves looking at more closely.

The general pattern was that from the beginning the Syndicates were both the initiators and managers of the new creations. Hence the term "syndicalisation" which we have used purposely in order to avoid the kind of confusion caused by the different methods adopted or followed, especially in Catalonia. But this syndicalising conception was accompanied by communalism which often took first place. This explains why our comrades in Granollers made up their minds to carry out a communal structural plan, as proposed by our comrade Dr. Isaac Puente,[2] a talented propagandist who had elaborated a project for the town of the future in a series of articles published by the magazine

2 Shot by the Francoists.

Estudios, and in which he advocated a reorganisation of society on the basis of federated communes. These articles had been gathered into a booklet of some 60 pages with the title *Comunismo Libertario,* and the clear and attractive text, completed with diagrams and graphs, had been absorbed by many libertarians.

In reality, in spite of very positive indications at local level, these proposals were insufficient if one approached the economy with the mentality of an economist, bearing in mind existing organic solidarity at a national level; and furthermore, the existence of the federations of industry which in fact leaned in the direction of that organisation in terms of the whole of Spain, was also in contradiction with that limited vision of things.

But because Isaac Puente's concepts were communalist, they were better understood and more easily accepted when our comrades in Granollers suggested to the other anti-fascist sectors to put them into operation. And when the writer went to study the organisation and the functioning of the new social organisation on the spot, he noted on the one hand that the exploitation of man by man had disappeared, that there were no more employers or employees, and on the other that all the anti-fascists including our movement had come together fraternally in the municipal Council, which had supreme control over local life as a whole.

The general administration of Granollers was managed by eleven departments, taking in all social activities, established at the municipal Council, and which consisted of twenty-two delegates; six from Azana's Left Republicans, six from the C.N.T., four from the U.G.T., two from the share-croppers union (Catalan *rabassaires,* whose only desire was to become the owners of the land they cultivated) and two from the P.O.U.M. (the Marxist party with Trotskyist leanings).

Of the eleven departments, five were entrusted to the C.N.T. which shows clearly its importance, more economic than political. In addition this organisation, ever enterprising, had established independently an Economic Council consisting of a delegate from each Syndicate, for the Syndicates were the driving force of all local industries.

This Council met every week with the representative of the corresponding municipal department. Thus municipal section and Council coordinated their efforts; but in fact the initiative mostly came from our comrades and from the general assembly of the local Federation of C.N.T. Syndicates which was the best informed on matters concerning production and the organisation of work.

The economic section of the commune set up a "technical bureau" consisting of three experts, and which in agreement with the syndical Economic Council, steered the work of the industrial undertakings. Graphs and charts referring to each industry, were constantly in the hands of the experts, so that if one enquired about any industry, coloured charts, one colour for each industry, would be produced showing where each undertaking was located, thus building up a network of coordinated activities.

Managed in this way, all the undertakings, factories and workshops passed into the hands of the workers but at the same time belonged to the municipality. And the major policy decisions were not the result of syndical initiative only, for over and above the latter are interests which, let us face it, direct the whole. But one should recognise that the mutual toleration met with there was quite exceptional.

*

The Syndicate was at all times a prime-mover. All kinds of initiatives tending to improve the operation and structure of the local economy could be attributed to it. Thus in a very short time, seven collectivised hairdressing salons were set up through its efforts, replacing an unknown number of shabby establishments. All the workshops and mini-factories on shoe production were replaced by one large factory in which only the best machines were used, and where necessary sanitary provisions for the health of the workers were made. Similar improvements were made in the engineering industry where numerous small, dark and stifling foundries were replaced by a few large working units in which air and sun were free to penetrate. The joiners and cabinet makers' shops underwent the same changes. Socialisation went hand in hand with rationalisation.

This industrial reorganisation did not prevent changes dictated by circumstances in the machinery of distribution. They were considered necessary from the beginning by the corresponding section of the municipal Council on the grounds of social justice. If one agreed to build a more just social order, it was imperative that every inhabitant of Granollers should have the same possibilities of securing nourishment. The members of the Economic Office of the Municipality set up five communal distributive warehouses located in the different quarters according to their population density, replacing the all too numerous small shops. They had started with a fundamental measure which was also taken in other places; from the beginning the agricultural coun-cillor purchased from the peasants in the neighbouring areas—who were very individualistic and very suspicious, and did not organise themselves collectively—the produce of their toil. The rapacious middleman, the tout and the speculative buyer disap-peared altogether. But they also wanted him to disappear in the relations between producer and consumer. Force of circumstances offered the opportunity and the justification for new measures to be taken: the rationing of foodstuffs as a result of the war, fortunately made it necessary to take steps in time to prevent serious food shortages.[3] A food office was therefore set up which started by controlling produce received and sold by the trades-people. Then a card index file was prepared, in which was entered the number and age of the members of each family. The quantity and type of foodstuffs to which everyone was entitled was stipulated in agreement with the doctors. And on these bases every family received each week a booklet in which their entitlement to bread, oil, dried beans, groceries, etc., was marked. In this way the daily and weekly consumption of different foodstuffs could be obtained for the whole town and arrangements made for securing the necessary supplies in advance.

A similar control was maintained on quantities of foodstuffs coming into the communal warehouses.

It was also by this means that that part of socialisation which was acceptable to the peasants, came to the countryside, for the peasants welcomed the elimination of the middlemen. In most of the 42 cantonal villages traditional commerce disappeared.

The profits from the sale of various commodities provided the municipal Council with the resources needed for other communal tasks. Nobody was condemned to isolation or distress. Trades-people obliged to close up shop by competition or municipal action[4] found themselves being given more useful jobs—even if it were only in the distribution centres. Nobody remained without work, and unemployment, which was widespread before July 19, had completely disappeared. All workers, whether they worked the stipulated numbers of hours or not, had their material existence

3 It should be borne in mind that Catalonia was mainly industrial, and even a large part of the Levante produced neither corn nor meat, nor the dried vegetables which they consumed. It was to weigh heavily on the situation in due course.

4 One of the means used was to stop supplying them and to reserve the goods that could be obtained for the communal warehouses.

assured thanks to the principle of equality of remuneration.

The comrades of Granollers had given thought to public education. The schools were few and old, insanitary and ill-lit. On the other hand there were three comfortable, well built convents whose occupants had evaporated into thin air. They were converted into three fine schools which accommodated all the town's children. Indeed there was enough room for new pupils.

The classrooms I visited were spacious, light, and sunny. Modern equipment was introduced and I was touched at the sight of the small, square and movable tables for the very young, and the small chairs made to match. The interior galleries, the shower room, the courtyards, the lavatories, central heating, all this was installed, or purchased, in a matter of a few months.

The initial expenditure amounting to 300,000 pesetas and more had been set aside.

[Postscript. Later on Granollers was razed to the ground by the Francoist air force.]

3. Hospitalet del Llobregat

Situated to the south of Barcelona, Hospitalet was divided into three quite distinct districts with a population of 50,000. 13,000 out of the 14,000 registered wage earners were employed in industry. A thousand more were engaged in intensive horticulture which contributed to feeding the large neighbouring city.

The spinning mills absorbed most of the labour forces. But engineering had also developed. There were two blast-furnaces, foundries, engineering workshops. Cabinet making, building and chemical industries completed the general picture of its productive activities.

Hospitalet had developed only recently. The social movement only went back to World War I. But even before the revolution the C.N.T. and the F.A.I. were engaged there in social activity on an intensive scale. By July 18 the C.N.T. had 8,000 members; eight months later membership had risen to 12,000. The U.G.T. in spite of the desperate efforts of the official socialists and the communists on its behalf, had only 1,000 members.

The local struggle and the state of alert which followed the

Francoist attack, mobilised the population for five or six days at the end of which the C.N.T. as in the other Catalan towns, gave the order for a return to work. To prolong the general strike would have been to the detriment of the workers themselves, who were assuming the responsibility for their own future. Thus the responsibility for the economic and social life passed from the hands of the employers and of the government into those of the workers.

But while work was being resumed, and workshops, factories and works once more being set in motion, the popular forces continued to mount guard at the barricades, keeping a watch on two roads leading to Barcelona in order to prevent any enemy concentration, and to wipe out any offensive advance in the large centres.

It was in the midst of this state of affairs that the constructive revolution began.

It started with agriculture, which was in the hands of a great number of small proprietors who employed skilled labour (thus nothing in common with the *latifundia* in Aragon, Castile, Andalusia or Estremadura). And just as the owners of workshops and factories abandoned production in face of expropriation which they were expecting, so the landed proprietors gave up their cultivations which were being shrivelled up by the sun and the lack of irrigation, or which were being invaded by weeds.

On the other hand a quarter of the landworkers were unemployed and others worked only a three day week. Unemployed and employed called an assembly to which the small proprietors were also invited and where all agreed to socialise immediately work on the land.

And the "Peasants' Collective" was born; former employers and employees joined as equals, and it affiliated to the C.N.T. whose militants were, once again, the best organisers.

Work techniques changed immediately. Large scale cultivation based on a general plan replaced the strips worked by the individual owners, often with poor equipment, or by the day worker engaged two or three times a week.

But money subsisted in Catalonia, and was an indispensable instrument for obtaining machinery, tools, working animals, or for securing the means of existence in-between harvests. All resources were requisitioned, including those at the disposal of the former proprietors, and realising that exceptional efforts were needed, for a social revolution is not a musical festival, they rejected, as did the workers of Barcelona, the 15% increase in wages and the establishment of the six hour day demagogically decreed by the Catalan government, which demonstrated by this attempt to win over the workers its political skill and its ignorance of the most important problems.

After that the workers of the agrarian Collective were organised in *brigadas* as in Tarragona and Tortosa, and perfected their organisation. The *brigadas* would leave in the morning, each to its task, according to what were considered to be the most urgent jobs. The area cultivated was increased by a third. It consisted of 1,470 hectares divided into 38 zones, 35 of which were irrigated.

✳

Local industries went through stages almost universally adopted in that revolution. First came the control of the undertakings, large and small, by the *Comité* nominated by the workers on the spot. That was for the more prosperous factories; those where the employees had only part time employment—and there were many—were immediately collectivised, and their owners put on the same footing as the producers.

Simultaneously the C.N.T. and F.A.I. were creating the Councils for the intensification of production, which obliged the supervised employers to engage the unemployed. But this measure could not produce lasting results, for the lack of raw materials in the textile industry and the lack of outlets for the manufactured cloth inevitably produced a reduction in output and sales at the expense of the general economy.

Furthermore, again through the initiative of the C.N.T., popular Commissions for food supplies were started and organised by the Municipality, which our comrades had joined. These Commissions had as their task to provide food for the unemployed; they were kept going later, for the arrival of large numbers of refugees from those parts of Aragon overrun by the Francoist army created a new kind of unemployment.

We have seen that the collectivised enterprises had at their head in the first instance *Comités* nominated by the workers employed in them. Production and sales continued in each one. But very soon it was clear that this situation gave rise to competition between the factories, or a lack of solidarity, creating rivalries which were incompatible with the socialist and libertarian outlook. So the C.N.T. launched the watchword: "All industries must be ramified in the Syndicates, completely socialised, and the regime of solidarity which we have always advocated be established once for all."

The idea won support immediately. The first to start were the hairdressers, then workers in the entertainments industry, whatever their trade, and the woodworkers (cabinet makers, joiners, carpenters), building workers, food workers and urban transport. In January 1937 the metal workers joined the movement. The chemical industry soon followed.

In such complex circumstances unexpected problems arose and made themselves felt. In Hospitalet as elsewhere economic upheaval made some industries more prosperous while others were working at a loss. Some workers and their families were better paid than others. To right this injustice it was decided to apply a uniform wage for everybody.

Now this would have been impossible to achieve without the solidarity of the different industries. And the problem was to start a common fund which would ensure that all workers, whether they were in a job or not, would receive the same remuneration.

As a first step, financial solidarity was established between industries with the setting up of a general Economic Council on which they each had two representatives. Industries making a profit would inform the administrative Commission of the Council, which closely scrutinised the accounts of the different enterprises. The resources thus made available were used to assist the loss-making industries which would receive the money required to purchase raw materials and equipment needed for production.

When such amounts were large, all the delegates from the different industries would examine the financial and technical state of the industry requiring aid and after hearing observations, opinions, advice, and criticism when there was reason for it, the funds were provided.

This solidarity was soon to be completed by the introduction of the family wage. A detailed census was made on this subject, the results of which were in the hands of the Municipality.

At the time of my visit, they were also examining the question of the restructuring of industries. A general inventory had been drawn up, not only to establish the needs of the population and its resources, but also as to which industries should be retained and which eliminated.

As happened everywhere, our comrades in Hospitalet also dealt immediately with the problem of public education. Out of 8,000 children of school age, only 4,000 attended school regularly. The others could not due to a shortage of school places, clothing, footwear and books. The C.N.T. and F.A.I. did not want to solve such a grave problem with their means only. They decided to join their efforts to those of other anti-fascist bodies from whom they expected a favourable response. At a meeting to which invitations were sent to the militants of the U.G.T. and the Left Republicans, our comrades presented their plan for reforming public education, which was accepted. And nobly united, the three factions set about the renovation of schooling.

In six months, in spite of the difficult general situation, they achieved wonders. Buildings were constructed, others transformed or adapted, and 2,500 new pupils were able to sit in new classes, roomier, brighter, better ventilated than anything that had been seen before. The men and women teachers overtaken by the revolution that was being extended by events even in the field of pedagogy were replaced by elementary schoolteachers of both sexes who were more in sympathy with the spirit of the new times, and who held weekly meetings to discuss their respective experiences.

The care shown for children did not end there. The municipality organised a large crèche where parents could leave their babes while they went about their business. In the factories where women worked, children's nurseries were set up; the first was inaugurated in the workers' Collective T. Sala.[5] They also succeeded in fitting out a maternity home where working women, who until then had had their children under deplorable insanitary conditions, received the treatment prescribed by their condition. A gynaecologist inspired the architect who carried out the necessary alterations.

And every Thursday free cinema shows for children were given in all the halls, to instruct, and amuse depending on the programmes intelligently selected.

Supplementary details regarding health: immediately after their victory the revolutionaries decided that the people of Hospitalet should have clinics, dispensaries, hospitals, doctors, all the attention to which they were entitled. It was rapidly put into effect, and as widely as means allowed, that is to say to a lesser degree than had been desired, for in Hospitalet doctors continued to live on what they received from their parents. In July 1937,

5 See at the end of this chapter the leaflet that was distributed on the subject.

socialisation of medicine had not yet been fully achieved. Never-theless, besides the maternity hospital a large cantonal hospital had been built which conformed to modern concepts of medicine.

From all that has been said, it is clear that to syndical activity was added communal activity, and that both often advanced together, for the communalist spirit was strong among our com-rades in Hospitalet (José Xena, the mayor, was an anarchist). They could have taken over the local Council had they wished. Their honesty, their feeling for anti-fascist solidarity, and because they did not want to provoke too hostile reactions from the other anti-fascist sectors, prevented them from doing so. They invited the U.G.T. and the Republican Left to join them in setting up the Municipal Council which would consist of twenty-four members. They replied with a refusal. As a result there were only eight councillors, ours, who dealt with the essential aspects of local life: health and social assistance; public education, the economy; defence; work and agriculture; public services; food supplies and public works.

Nevertheless, collaboration continued to a certain extent. At the time of our enquiry the situation was that each of the three sectors nominated special Commissions which submitted to the councillor entrusted with these matters initiatives which they considered useful; he decided when the issues were not of importance; when they were it was the Municipal Council which decided. The C.N.T. called popular assemblies, either in the largest hall in the centre of the town, or in the outlying districts, where it informed the people, who freely attended, what had been done and what it was proposed to do. The audience was free to ask questions and express any objections.

There was no question therefore of party politics, of decisions taken in secret, of sleight of hand by *comités* sitting behind closed doors and acting against the will of the people. Close contact with the people was maintained for they remained among the people, and applied as best they could the libertarian solutions which they had always advocated.

In brief, the libertarians of Hospitalet acted according to a municipalist concept which corresponded to their preferences and which imposed itself. They defined the functions of the commune, and of the Syndicate. From them the functions of the latter were integrated with those of the former, as the part is to the whole. And just as the isolated syndicate no longer existed, each one of them having to consult the others before launching itself on a new enterprise, so neither did the Syndicates and their federation impose themselves when the matters discussed concerned all the inhabitants. Thus, education, transport, public works, health, social assistance, planning, concerned everybody. Therefore all the population was invited to decide.

To conclude, the following is the text of a leaflet which the T. Sala Collective distributed in the town and which was addressed to mothers with families.

"*Comrade*: We offer you the Children's House so that your child can receive there, up to the age of five, the best attention during working days when in the past and until now, he was turned out onto the street; and even when you could leave him with someone he was not receiving the education and attention needed to make eventually a physically healthy and balanced person.

"The aim of the Children's House is not only that of providing him with every attention, and to relieve you of some of your chores. It goes much further. The conditions in which you have lived have prevented you from getting the information you need in order to bring up your child sensibly. For this reason we have organised, as well as we can, all the necessary conveniences, and to ensure pleasant surroundings for your child, we have made sure that he lacks nothing in the way of hygiene, education, food, and medical supervision. All will be in the hands of skilled personnel.

"The Children's House will be organised in two main sections: one for the youngest from birth up to 2 years of age; the other for children between 2 and 5 years. At each stage he will receive all that he needs so far as diet, recreation and development of his aptitudes are concerned. And it will be a good thing if mothers take account of the guidance offered by the personnel so that the work of the Children's House is continued within the home.

"For all these reasons, you will understand that it is in the interests of the child that we are today offering you the Children's House."

One certainly finds stylistic clumsiness in the text, but there is nothing clumsy about the feelings behind this initiative.

4. Rubi

This small Catalan town had 10,000 inhabitants in July 1936. Half the workers were engaged in various employments, the most important of which was the textile industry. The only syndical organisation that had established roots was the C.N.T. which in normal times had from 1,500-2,000 members. But to the activities involving the class struggle and direct action which belong to that fighting organisation—which were completed by a libertarian force organised in the F.A.I.—there was a practical spirit and achievements too often overlooked. Since 1893 Rubi boasted a cooperative, organised by our comrades, with an average membership of 400 which was doubled during the Revolution. Furthermore in 1920 members of the C.N.T. had bought a piece of land on which to build a rationalist school to further the work of Ferrer. For this purpose every member contributed a minimum of 10 centimes a month and when the Civil War broke out, not one but two such schools were open and functioning.

Let us add, in order to appreciate more fully the balanced outlook of our comrades, that from the end of the last century, a number of them, for propaganda reasons, belonged to the republican Centre, thus indicating a spirit of tolerance which could only augur positive results.

All around Rubi agriculture was of some importance. The large estates, though not as large as in other regions, dominated it, were generally farmed by the owners who, besides, leased some of their land in return for a quarter, a third or a half of the harvest. This ruthlessness was confirmed by a detail which reminds one, though it was worse, of a similar case mentioned in the chapter on Graus in Aragon: the drinking water that was consumed in Rubi had its source on the land of one of the proprietors, and he charged for it . . .

In Rubi the Revolution was the counter-attack to the Francoist attack, for without it our forces, important as they were, could not have achieved their objectives. It clearly underlines the failure of insurrectional attempts before 1936, to which we have already referred.

But faced with the attack, all enemies of fascism found themselves side by side. From the bourgeois Catalanists to the anarchists, unity had been established. And as was the case almost everywhere, our comrades more resolute, more prepared for the struggle, were soon masters of the streets. Once the danger had passed, men were sent (or men went) to the Aragon front which was being established in the course of the fighting, at the same time as reinforcements were on their way to Barcelona to consolidate the situation. And to consolidate it further, collectivisations were started.

To guarantee food supplies, basic foodstuffs were the first concern. In Rubi there were a dozen bakeries on which bread supplies depended. The C.N.T. decided to deal with the matter and concentrated the whole production in its premises where most of the employers and all the workers agreed to work with a sense of responsibility that brooked no failures.

Next in importance were the means of transport. On the initiative of the Syndicate a professional Collective was created. The small employers joined, bringing with them some 200 lorries, a number of buses, and some 15 motor cars. The administration of this Collective was established at the headquarters of the Syndicate.[6]

Almost simultaneously the building industry was integrated with the social transformation that was taking place. There were some 100 masons and about 150 labourers in Rubi. As in Granollers and Alicante, these small contractors joined and brought with them their tools and equipment. A detailed list was made of these. The member with the highest professional experience was nominated as the technical councillor, with the task of supervising and guiding all the work on the various sites. And accountancy was put in the hands of the specialist deemed the most able.

In Barcelona the building industry was paralysed by the departure of the employers, who had no intention of building blocks of flats, or carrying out repairs to rented premises when the lot would be taken away from them if the Revolution triumphed. But in Rubi there was plenty of work, for what was being done was urgently needed by the inhabitants in general, and the Municipality had the funds to guarantee payment. For instance two bridges were being built to span a wide ravine, a project which had until then remained a wild dream in spite of the need for it. Work was also proceeding under the aegis of the Municipality on a group of school buildings which would provide hundreds of children with places and for which incidentally the Catalan government of the *Generalitat* was contributing to the cost, though it should not be overlooked that public education

6 It should be noted that in this case the professional Collective was not independent of the Syndicate. Indeed it emanated from it.

was in the hands of the libertarians.[7] A length of the road which crossed the town was widened to make it easier for the buses; a great number of houses were repaired; a 1,500 metre channel was constructed to carry water to the land being worked by the peasants and in this connection abandoned and filled-in wells were reinstated and water raised by electric pumps specially installed to irrigate the cultivations.

All this work was managed by a technical Commission of five or six members nominated by the assembly of the Collective. Of this personnel the only ones paid in their capacity as professionals were the director and two secretaries.

In order to be assisted in these many tasks, the builders' Collective asked for and obtained the help of factory workers on these contracts for two hours every Sunday.

The cabinet-makers and joiners also created their Collective which established itself in a huge workshop equipped with modern tools and providing hygienic working conditions previously unknown. Never had they produced so much furniture in Rubi, I was to be reminded by one of the prime-movers in recollecting this worthwhile initiative.

The agricultural Collective was constituted with the farms seized from the large proprietors. That represented three-quarters of the cultivable area. 250 agricultural workers joined this extensive productive undertaking. There were six organised zones; each concerned with a speciality: market gardening, forestry, viticulture, pasture, cereals, fruit. The managing Commission was nominated by the general Assembly, and it in its turn nominated the delegate for each section.

As we have seen, and it was generally the case where Collectives were concerned, the corporative spirit had disappeared. Workers moved from one section to another when necessary. And they admitted measures which went against their own production speciality. Among the initiatives taken under pressure from immediate necessities, was the grubbing of vines in order to plant wheat. And though the land was not the most suitable for the purpose, in Rubi they would have almost succeeded in growing sufficient wheat to satisfy the needs of all the inhabitants if the economic difficulties which extended throughout the region

7 We must honestly recognise that the government of the Generalitat sometimes helped useful enterprises with finance; and while regretting that all too often it dispensed funds indiscriminately, creating stagnation, which as we shall see later, could do untold damage.

had not had severe repercussions on this small town.

There remained a few "individualists" outside these revolutionary transformations; but the majority advanced with the new order. So much so that a number of young men and women had left their families in order to join. Bachelor quarters had to be organised for them. One of the prime-movers assured me that "nothing immoral ever took place" between these youngsters, who anyway were housed in segregated quarters.

The cooperative did not rest on its laurels. Apart from doubling its membership, the part it played in the distribution of goods consequently expanded and nine new depots or sales points were set up. This did not prevent the continuation of private trading, obviously under some control. The retailers were supported by the food supplies section of the Catalan government.

Rubi offers a very characteristic example of development so far as the general organisational structure of society is concerned. When the events of July 1936 took place the majority of the municipal Council consisted of Left Catalanists whose leader, Luis Companys was president of the Catalan government; on August 6, that is three weeks after the Revolution started, faced with the predominance of our forces and the social upheavals which took place through their efforts, this majority resigned. Its situation was made even more difficult because the farmers—the *rabassaires*—supported the upheaval, as did also the P.O.U.M.

But because our comrades did not wish to misuse the victory; because the urgency of the war demanded that they remain united to prevent Spain from being handed over to Franco; because the Left Republicans supported the social reforms,[8] the new Municipal Council that was then set up consisted of six members of the C.N.T. and six representatives of the Catalanist *avant-garde*. But the new law of February 1937 having ordained that all the political parties should be represented (this was one of the first counter-revolutionary manoeuvres) the definitive Council consisted of seven members of the C.N.T., seven Left Catalans, two U.G.T.-ers (the local section of which was then set up by the efforts of the Communists who sounded the alarm for the small reactionary proprietors in order to scotch collectivisation), and two members of the *Acció Catalana* party. So many different tendencies coexisting against their wills in the Council chamber,

8 One can logically assume that the relations, often cordial, that had been established over many years between the libertarians and republicans made mutual understanding possible.

could only give rise to friction and confrontations, for clearly those who were opposed to the establishment of libertarian socialism considered that the C.N.T. was going much too far. For their part our comrades were opposed to the Council's traditional way of operating which was essentially political, and in which the sterile party games, frequently conducted over the telephone by the Committees established in the large cities, would end by reviving the old order of things. But, strengthened by the support of the Syndicates, the various Collectives and even the Cooperative, they did not give in.

So the parties decided not to collaborate any longer in the practical tasks of a municipal nature, or within the jurisdiction of the Council. Our comrades had therefore to take over the most important duties: food supplies, public works, industry and agriculture. They were so successful that the organisers with whom I discussed these achievements fifteen years later had tears in their eyes in recalling that lost paradise.

5. Castellon de la Plana

Castellon de la Plana, chief town of the province bearing its name, had a population of 50,000 when the revolution exploded. Our movement there was not important. There is a twofold explanation for this weakness: on the one hand industry was not very advanced, and this had not given much scope for a powerful syndical force; on the other, if in the surrounding countryside one frequently came across proprietors with a libertarian outlook, the great majority did not go beyond republicanism.

Now, in Castellon and its environs, republicanism *was* popular, and as the Republic was only five years old its supporters had not had time to be swallowed up in the morass created by the new regime. Which explains why on July 19, 1936; the fascist were defeated at local level, and why the population accepted without too much difficulty the local task of transformation undertaken by our comrades. It is worthwhile adding that a majority of republicans who were union men chose the C.N.T. for they feared the danger of statism and state control which they foresaw in a traditional socialist future, and in the party claiming to lead it. This was, in fact, not unusual in Spain.[9]

9 See Libertarians and Republicans in Part V of this volume.

The U.G.T. had more members than its rival the C.N.T., but they were workers whose socialist aspirations had remained intact. These circumstances resulted in the following situation: that at our meetings more than a half of the audience though not libertarians, applauded our speakers.

Circumstances made the task of our comrades easier without, for all that, sweeping away the obstacles. The professional politicians were helpless in this new situation in which for them everything had been turned upside down. Furthermore many employers and landowners were fascists or crypto-fascists; others were not but all the same belonged to the Right parties and hoped for a victory of the insurgent generals. Our comrades knew beforehand what they wanted in a situation such as the one that presented itself. They started therefore by organising control *Comités* in the undertakings. These *Comités* had already been accepted three years earlier when Largo Caballero was Labour Minister and in order to calm the revolutionary passions of the workers and to limit their demands, had legalised the creation of these new organisations.

There was now therefore no reason for legally opposing their extension, and the political parties were obliged to allow them to be created and developed.

And new positions were rapidly captured; the employers were not concerned to maintain production at its normal level, even less to construct armoured cars and to manufacture combat weapons. So the workers, guided by the C.N.T., took their places and started managing the work.

Thus it was that on October 20, 1936 the metal workers' Syndicate decided to take over some workshops. To that end they nominated a *Comité* for expropriation, technical administration and economy which took on the spot the following measures:

1) *Proceed to a detailed inventory of all the workshops and local garages.*

2) *Prepare statistics of wage earners and employers of those garages and workshops.*

Then it organised five sections to be in charge of work; engineering, foundry, metal work, tinplating, garages. Soon the building workers and woodworkers organised themselves similarly. And almost all, if not all, industrial production was socialised under the aegis of libertarian Syndicates.

We will take the organisation of the metal workers and the garages that had joined them, as the model for all the industries.

One reason for such a choice is that it was the most important branch of production.

To start with the syndical *Comité*, which included in the first place a technical Commission concerned with general management of work in all establishments; this Commission was elected by the general assembly, and replaced the specialised employers and the technicians who had defected.

It was also entrusted with allocating labour in the workshops and garages according to possibilities of production equipment, organisation and importance. Indeed one proceeded as more or less elsewhere to a regrouping which eliminated the installations that were too small to be economic, and constituted or enlarged other production units, making them more modern and better equipped for the work to be done and for the workers.

In every workshop or garage the workers' assembly nominated a non-bureaucratic management committee. All the commissions were in contact with the syndical technical Commission, and those in charge met every evening with it to direct general activities.

The administrative Commission specially concerned itself with the handling of money, which continued to exist for, let us repeat it unceasingly, we were in a mixed society, the political pattern of which was predominantly republican and where the petty bourgeoisie, even without always being really hostile, constituted an important local element. It was this Commission which paid workers in accordance with the categories established by the syndical assemblies: technicians, commercial agents, skilled workers, semi-skilled workers, apprentices. It was furthermore divided into five sections corresponding to the work categories. The most important sections had one employee nominated by the syndical council.

The workshops and garages carried out the work (repairs, replacement of parts, etc.) required by the customers living in Castellon and its environs, or even by passing customers. If for example the owner or driver of a car wanted repairs to be done to it, he would go to a garage and ask for an estimate. The responsible delegate would tell him how much it cost and the customer would pay not the workers doing the work but to the Syndicate and given a receipt for payment which he would then take to the garage or workshop where the work was to be carried out.

Thus all accounting was centralised, and all garages, engineering workshops and foundries had a common treasury. But each operation was scrupulously recorded, so as to be in a position to follow in detail the economic life of each work unit. Which did not prevent sections enjoying surpluses from giving support to those working at a loss when the case arose.[10]

Every month the technical and administrative council presented the general assembly of the Syndicate with a report which was examined and discussed if necessary, and finally approved or turned down by a majority. Modifications were introduced when this majority thought it of use. Thus all the activities were known and controlled by all the workers. We find here a practical example of libertarian democracy.

Such were the norms adopted in all trades, and all locally socialised industries. But let us go deeper in our analysis.

As one can well imagine, former employers were not admitted into the Syndicate; nevertheless they were accepted as producers in the workshops. Those who for physical or mental reasons could not work and were without means of subsistence received a wage similar to that of the workers.

From the professional point of view workers wishing to advance to a higher category could do so, but were required to undergo an examination in theory and practice before the central council of the Syndicate and the workshop delegates.

Finally, when the case arose, the Syndicate applied—on the acceptance by the general assembly—disciplinary measures. This is the only case that we have met and noted but cannot affirm that there were not others. In the first months of the Revolution, and believing that the disappearance of the employer justified unusual negligence, some workers displayed excessive laxity (this also occurred among building workers in Alicante). In consequence, at the assembly held on December 30 a resolution was adopted —we do not know whether by a majority or unanimously—the text of which was printed on posters which were displayed in all the workshops.

TO COMRADES AND WORKSHOP DELEGATES

Comrades,

1) The workshop delegates are nominated in accordance with the rule made by you and by the *Comité*.

2) In accordance with Article 5 of the regulations, these

10 For instance the garage workshops established along the road from Barcelona to Valencia had more work than those dotted about the town.

delegates are responsible for technical and administrative questions in the workshops.

3) In agreement with the general assembly of December 30, 1936, a vote of confidence was given to these Delegates, in cases of indiscipline or failure to carry out their duties by the comrades comprising the workshop personnel, disciplinary measures considered necessary should be taken to ensure the smooth running and satisfactory progress of the work in the Syndicate's workshops.

4) These delegates will not be able to apply severe sanctions, such as the dismissal of a comrade from a workshop, without the agreement of the *Comité* and of the management Commission of the Syndicate.

5) Any comrade having cause to complain of the delegate either for union matters or in connection with the work should, in order not to create confusion, abstain from direct and personal criticism; but will refer to the comrades of the administrative Council who will take the necessary decisions.

6) All current matters concerning the work or union matters which will arise among comrades in the workshops will have to be dealt with through the respective delegates.

All of which we communicate to delegates and comrades for their information.

Castellon, January 1, 1937.

Once again we observe that the seriousness with which everything is dealt with to ensure the success of the workers' achievements, implies a discipline freely accepted, and considered as a guarantee for success. And undoubtedly, all said and done, it is better that there should be excessive demands so far as responsibility is concerned than an irresponsibility which would lead to a melting away and failure.

But the activity of our comrades was not limited to the organising of industries. They were integrated in the municipal Council, where, incidentally, they were in a minority. They were not good talkers or brilliant orators, but intelligent, their practical or human sense was not deformed by a politician's mentality, and they knew how to defend with conviction the constructive initiatives which flowed from their ideas and from the new situation. Among the proposed reforms was the family wage and the socialisation of medicine by the municipality. The other councillors, republicans and socialists (supporters of Largo Caballero) who advocated many reforms when they were in opposition, turned them down, invoking the republican constitution, existing laws and economic difficulties.

But unfortunately for the politicians, the Council sittings were public, and the workers as well as their womenfolk attended these meetings with interest. The result was that many U.G.T. members, disappointed by the antisocialist behaviour of their socialist leaders, went over to the C.N.T. and throughout the province the membership of the C.N.T. rose at an unexpected rate. It was the internal development of a society in a period of revolutionary transformation.

The membership of the U.G.T. did not correspondingly fall, for the small artisan-employers, opposed to socialisation, caretakers, generally the defenders of the established order, office employees with the souls of bureaucrats, tradesmen, enemies of cooperatives, and smallholders who believed that we intended to leave them without the means of subsistence and deprive them of their harvest when the time came, joined *en masse* the reformist organisation U.G.T. in which the communists were spreading their influence. Right wingers also infiltrated it in order to make it into a fortress, or at least a defensive bastion for their privileges, whilst waiting to recover what they had lost.

In spite of everything our comrades succeeded in obtaining basic reforms. Most of the doctors who were unwilling to be under the control of the State bureaucracy, but to work inspired by their professional duty and the social problems which they were able to see for themselves, joined our movement and supported the social solutions it propounded.

In the communal field our comrades succeeded in introducing the socialisation of housing. Rents for lodgings were no longer paid to the landlord—so much the worse for the Constitution and Roman Law!—but to the Municipality which had abolished almost all local taxes; and workers' families could enjoy a sanitary and comfortable home, for the building repairs and necessary building were undertaken as soon as the need for them was realised. It should be pointed out that just as the dispossessed landlord not able to work would receive a normal wage, the small proprietor was allowed to occupy the house which he had built by his own efforts. This socialisation of housing was not uncommon.

The example of Castellon de la Plana appears to us to have

had special characteristics. It proves the possibility of achieving very bold reforms in a society which has not entirely emerged from its original political framework. It demonstrates that the struggle against the exploitation of man by man can, if conducted intelligently, with practical ability, tact, and nobility of spirit, loses much of its harshness and gain in effectiveness. In any case it opens up new horizons, as it did in those localities where only some industries were socialised because they were the only ones with sufficiently strong revolutionary cadres, whereas the others had none at their disposal. The twelve million members of consumers cooperatives in Britain do not prevent the existence of private commerce. For the partisans of the creation of a new society, many steps could be taken without the shedding of blood.

6. Socialisation in Alicante

With Elda, Jativa and Castellon, Alicante, capital of the province in which these towns are located, had a social movement with a libertarian outlook of long standing which kept going come hell or high water throughout the social history of that region. And in the events which opened the road to the social revolution, the traditional solidarity existing between those towns, their syndicates and their federated libertarian groupings made possible the achievement of what each isolated town would undoubtedly have been unable even to undertake.

For the armed forces of the C.N.T., the anti-fascist combat groups set up by our comrades or with their participation, prevented, here too, the reactionary elements from taking, indeed of even attempting to take, by assault the republican institutions. Peace was not therefore seriously upset, and the Civil Guard allowed itself to be disarmed.

To realise their ideal our comrades had behind them our Syndicates: firstly the metallurgists', numerically the most important one, grouping all metal workers. Then the building Syndicate, with an industrial structure and including masons, quarrymen, plasterers, joiners, carpenters, painters, roofers, etc. Then the clothing Syndicate with tailors, dressmakers, hosiery and lingerie specialists; then, in order of importance came the Food Syndicate, the chemical industry, and finally the land and maritime transport Syndicate.

Nevertheless it should be noted that the U.G.T. also had a Building Syndicate, a Fishing Industry Syndicate (a branch of the Food Syndicate) and another in the chemical industry. This did not in fact constitute an insurmountable obstacle for forging ahead. Alicante is one of the examples where socialist rank and file workers, though members of the U.G.T., refused to obey the anti-revolutionary directives of their leaders.

The facts we are reproducing were not obtained on the spot. They are based on the testimony of militants who took part in this constructive task and who explained it to the author in discussions he had with them after Franco's triumph. We reproduce what seems to us to be most important, and in a certain sense, original, aspects for they corresponded to a particular social and local situation as well as, it must be said, to the outlook of the people concerned.

Socialisation of Building—The building industry was in the hands of small contractors. At an assembly specially called, the Syndicate of the C.N.T. building workers decided to take possession of building plant and equipment and to socialise its use. This was done. In each case, an inventory was drawn up of all the tools and raw materials controlled by each of the dispossessed employers, for the purpose of compensation. An unusual procedure and contrary to the basic principle of the libertarian movement, but it should not be forgotten that the contractors were small employers, and as was very often the case, they often worked harder than their employees. We will soon be seeing the consequences of this.

For, in the first place, in the system which made the Syndicate into the coordinator and director of work as a whole, it was necessary to select on each site someone to be responsible to his comrades and to the syndical coordinating committee. This person, inevitably, had to be capable of running the site, that is someone having technical experience. Now, in general, the employers in the building industry were better tradesmen than the wage earners. And as they did not wish to run the risk of failure with serious, immediate consequences, it was from among the employers that the site managers were selected.

On the other hand, in practice it transpired that these ex-small-contractors who accepted the new situation without too much difficulty, had a greater sense of duty than that of the average worker, accustomed to being given orders and not to taking responsibilities. And that they paid more attention to the quality of the work than their new comrades. In this case, as in others, it was not possible to put into operation at one stroke the absolute equality of wages, for in the middle of a revolution it was unwise to provoke conflicts which would only hamper production. For all these reasons the Syndicates felt obliged to establish a difference in remuneration. Workers without technical responsibilities received 10 pesetas a day and those with received 14.

This was in all probability facilitated by the relative importance of the numbers of members of the U.G.T. who had supported the syndicalisation and were upsetting our comrades. But once again what was essential was the smooth running, and quality, of the work; one could not risk having new constructions or repaired buildings needing attention after only a few months. That would have been a justification for a return to the capitalist system.

It should be pointed out, anyway, that wages were fixed by the general assembly of the Syndicate, consequently with at least the approval of the majority of workers who bowed to these facts of life.

The building Syndicate therefore exercised control over the sites as a whole, of the former undertakings transformed into sections or cells, in a regime the framework of which had remained republican. A situation reminiscent of the situation in Castellon de la Plana. An important part of social life still conformed to the established juridical principles; social classes still existed as did parasitic or privileged strata—though the importance of the latter had considerably diminished and was going on decreasing—finance capital, with very reduced powers, middlemen in distribution continued to exploit the population but were tending to be reduced to straitened circumstances by growing cooperatives; but also operating along parallel lines were trades, industries, services and production activities, often among the most important, which were in the hands of the workers, previously wage earners subjected to the employing class, who had now become masters of their own destiny.

The building Syndicate consisted of 500 masons, 85 painters in addition to the roofers, the locksmiths, architects, etc. The units of work were duly organised and repair work on buildings and repointing brickwork on houses was started and chargeable to the proprietors. Contact was made with the municipality for public works, and construction work which depended on its goodwill and financial resources. Such work included repairs to schools and hospitals. New buildings sprang up, and as air raids were expected, shelters for the civil population constructed.

The administrative mechanism demonstrates once again the tendency already noted in many places to get everybody to take on general responsibilities[11] or to participate in the management of the life of the community.

But as well as having a technical representative in charge of the work on each site, there was also a union delegate chosen by the workers. Between them they prepared estimates for projects. There was close and constant collaboration. Every effort was made to encourage enthusiasm, moral support, and to appeal to the individual conscience. And when a contract was completed and the balance sheet showed a profit the Syndicate congratulated the workers on the site, just as it expressed disapproval when a loss was made.

One may well ask why the profits were not shared among the workers whose efforts produced them. Simply because any profits were kept for acts of solidarity. Thus, the disappearance of the estate owners or the postponement of building contracts, created a certain amount of temporary unemployment, but for all that there were no real unemployed. Thanks to the funds held by the Syndicate it was possible to allow groups of masons, painters, etc., to take a rest in turn. Unemployment was thereby converted into holidays or leisure days.

The Canning Industry—This industry was concerned above all with fruits and vegetables, which were produced in large quantities in this region of the Levante. But following the concept or principle of organisation being interdependent with related industries it included also the workers dealing with the manufacture, preparation, packing—and not only wooden packing boxes for dispatch but also tin cans. The structure and operation of the general organisation was as follows:

The undertakings generally employed a large number of hands, and the assemblies where women were in a majority, named at their places of work a delegate, man or woman, responsible for 20 workers. In their turn the responsible delegates met to nominate a person to be responsible for the whole enterprise. There was also a delegate from the Syndicate for each section, to supervise workers' working conditions in the offices, workshops, warehouses, depots, etc. Naturally the delegates were themselves workers in

11 To assist this general enterprise and the collaboration between the Syndicates and the Municipality, the latter waived all taxes on the Building Syndicate for three months.

the undertakings.

Fruit and vegetables were supplied by the agrarian Collectives
The fraternal coordination between workers on the land and in
industry and between their respective organisms was therefore
being extended and completed. If one adds to it the collaboration
existing between the Syndicates and the Municipalities one can
see the constitution of a social organism the different parts of
which harmonised and completed, instead of opposing, each other.

The preserves were warehoused and put at the disposal of
the Food Syndicate, which sold them to the municipal Councils
of the region and to the provincial commissions for food supplies;
the Quartermaster-General's department itself was among the
buyers.

Bread making—Between them the U.G.T. and C.N.T. Syndicates
socialised the bakeries. The *hornos* (the bakehouses) became
bakery No. 1, No. 2, No. 3 and so on. Flour supplies were
equitably shared among them, and finances were held in common.
As described in other cases, the personnel of each undertaking
elected a responsible delegate who was supervised by the Syndicate
which in its turn was responsible to them.

Clothing—Most of the factory and workshop owners retired
from the undertakings where they no longer gave the orders, and
of which they were no longer the owners. The undertaking
delegate selected by assemblies of the enterprise, and responsible
to the Syndicate which coordinated the whole, constituted the
axle of the organisational mechanism.

A customer requiring a suit or an overcoat would select the
workshop of his choice, where he would be provided with a list
of prices according to the quality of materials required. In
exchange for the money paid out he would be given a receipt
from a triplicate receipt book and the whole procedure was as
already described.[12]

Cutters and other workers replaced employers in managing
the work. Wages were 10 pesetas a day for men and women
Some of the best tailors would be paid 12 pesetas. These
hangovers of inequality can be explained for the same reasons
as advanced for the building workers. But this inequality was
very small compared with what it had been when there was an
employer. Nevertheless, these are problems which a movement
of change should study.

12 See chapters on Fraga and Castellon de la Plana.

The Metallurgical Industry—In the somewhat summary classifications inspired by the desire for unification, metallurgy in Alicante encompassed everything from the jewellery trade to the iron boiler works. But naturally the jewellery trade played no part in the general organisation of syndical production.

On the other hand the U.G.T. and C.N.T. were in agreement and worked together. They constituted the I.M.S.A. (the Socialised Metallurgical Industries of Alicante). This complex was organised in sections which included a general Council integrated by a work Commission, a technical Commission, a purchases and sales Commission, an administrative Commission, etc. The workers nominated on the spot their delegates who acted in agreement with the union Council.

The two syndical organisations were in contact with the delegates on the Council of I.M.S.A. The workshops like the bakehouses, were identified by numbers. They were parts of a large interdependent whole.

CHAPTER XIV

ISOLATED ACHIEVEMENTS

The Revolution did not always manage to socialise all the workshops, works, and factories of the established industries in a locality or in a region. The resistance of the political forces allied to what remained of the bourgeoisie itself, made it impossible to go beyond certain limits. On the other hand some undertakings were frequently cut off somewhere in the province. Or again the workers had not been won over quickly enough by the organisation of industrial federations on a national scale. And according to the circumstances, some establishments which had remained outside were collectivised, or organised themselves through acting on their own initiative—or by imitating what was being done elsewhere.

Such was also the case with agrarian Collectives in Catalonia. Achievements of this kind were fairly rare in the Catalan country-side, the peasant there being more inclined towards individual smallholdings than towards the social community. The Catalan agrarian Collectives resulted therefore in groupings which cannot be compared with the Federation of Aragon, the Levante and the Centre.

Nevertheless these achievements were numerous and deserve to be listed and studied in depth. And even though it is not possible to include their history in the general structure—local, regional, national—they are of considerable interest. In many cases each would deserve a monograph to itself. If just one of them had been realised today it would arouse the interest of reformers on an international scale. Here are some examples, one agrarian, the remainder of an industrial nature, which surely serve to further illustrate the multiplicity of creative initiatives about which one cannot ever say enough.

1. The Boot and Shoemakers of Lerida

A few days after the Francoist uprising, and under the influence of the hopes that the Civil War had aroused, some shoemakers in Lerida (capital of the province of the same name) who were members of the libertarian movement met not only to see in what way they could participate in the struggle but how to organise a new way of life. The Republican authorities had virtually disappeared so nothing prevented them from making the experiment.

With them at that meeting was a small employer and his son. Soon other workers attached themselves to the original groups; other small employers did likewise. And they organised themselves on a collectivist basis.

This transformation brought with it a revolution in methods of work. It was no longer the case to sew the leather with awl and needle. A few machines were available and these were put to full use, for the orders were increasing and included a growing demand from the authorities for laced boots for the militiamen. More workers joined and in the end there were about fifty collectivists. More machines were bought and soon there were 23 at work.

The responsible management *Comité* consisted of six workers, three from the C.N.T. and three from the F.A.I.; an assembly of collectivists elected replacements on the *Comité*.

Production increased and, at the time of the bombing of Lerida in December 1937, as well as satisfying local needs the community of shoemakers were producing 1,500 pairs of shoes a day.

The Catalan government increased its orders for the militiamen. Shortage of money (according to the communist Comorera who was then Minister of Industry) was the reason given for defaulting on payments for goods received. And when the fascist advance started the said minister owed the Lerida shoemakers' Community some millions. Fortunately the members managed by shoe repairs, by making shoes to measure, as well as by growing some of their own food, to maintain themselves and their families.

2. The Valencia Flour Mills

The upheaval caused in the political domain by the Francoist attack naturally had repercussions in the economic field too. A more or less intensive disorganisation took place in those sectors of vital importance to the population. The authorities were incapable of taking any action of the slightest usefulness, and it was left to the workers, mainly those who thanks to the syndical organisation had an understanding of what needed to be done, to undertake to replace the largely inefficient private capitalism.

For instance one saw this in the case of flour supplies for Valencia, where the central government had set itself up with all its bureaucracy. Some delegates of the U.G.T. and C.N.T. who worked in the food industry, had to meet to deal with the grave shortages which very soon appeared, and constituted one of the factors leading to disorganisation which the fascists would have sought to exploit. And on October 1, 1936 an organism with the name "Socialised Flour Mills" started to operate under the management of a workers' council of members of the two workers' unions: U.G.T. and C.N.T.

In normal times Valencia received and consumed 1,000 sacks of flour daily. But the situation had become more complicated as a result of the Civil War, and more bread was needed to make up for shortages of other foodstuffs. From the French frontier to Gibraltar, Eastern Spain was not a producer of wheat; the great corn belts, as we have pointed out, were in Castile and Andalusia, which fell to Franco in the early days. Furthermore the Levante had the additional burden of an ever growing number of refugees.

In such circumstances, where there was no time to lose, since the daily bread had to be assured, the fairly modern mills quickly passed into the hands of the workers. But the supplies of wheat required were soon under the thumb of the Minister of Agriculture, the communist Uribe, who was certainly obliged to economise and plan his stocks, but who on the other hand took good care not to seek to establish agreement with the "Socialised Flour Mills" grouping. Kill the revolution that they cannot control: such has always been the attitude of the communists from Marx onwards.

That grouping operated just the same. The general organisation was divided into two sections. One, the purchasing section whose agents scoured the countryside and even went into some regions occupied by the Francoists, for supplies of wheat. The other, the sales section, which undertook the distribution of the flour to the Valencia bakers. A third, complementary section of an administrative nature, was concerned with statistics, correspondence, archives, accounts.

From the beginning the organising *Comité,* consisting entirely of comrades of the U.G.T. and C.N.T., presented the Minister of Agriculture with their conclusions based on the gravity of the situation:

1)—All corn stocks in the national territory to be requisitioned.
2)—Distribution to the provinces on the basis of their respective needs.
3)—Freeze the price at not more than 45 pesetas per 100 kilos.
4)—Import immediately supplies from Russia and Argentina.

Their demands were ignored. The precious cereal was soon to be in short supply, which came as no surprise to anyone ever so slightly conversant with the Spanish economy. But so long as there was wheat and flour they were distributed thanks to the "Socialised Flour Mills" of the Valencian region.

3. The Chocolate Cooperative of Torrente

In the province of Valencia, Torrente was renowned for its production of confectionery, especially chocolate. The industry was in the hands of some 45 small working owners who, depending on their means, might each employ one or two workers.

But driven by the desire to modernise production and safeguard the health of workers, members of the C.N.T. called a meeting which took place on September 1, 1936. The employers were invited as well as the wage earners. And as happened on many other occasions, employers and workers were in agreement to go forward.

Thus it was that they unanimously agreed to organise the "Cooperative of the Chocolate Workers of Torrente". Work was started immediately on the construction of a large building sited near the railway, in order to facilitate the unloading of raw materials and the dispatch of the finished articles.

The whole consisted of five sections, each 50 metres long by 30 wide. The first, used for manufacture, soon had 45 machines all at work; some had been provided by their owners while the others had to be specially acquired.

[315]

The second section of the building was used for lesser operations which consisted in giving the articles their characteristic shape. The third was for storing raw materials; the fourth for the process of torrefaction or of preparation; finally, the fifth was the well equipped cold store.

Never before had one seen in Spain a chocolate and confectionery factory as well organised or as large. The hundreds of men and women workers who were employed in the undertaking gave proof of a touching support for the enterprise. When from the beginning there was a question of paying them a higher wage than the employers had paid in the past they refused to accept, deciding to wait until the cooperative had made its first profits. It was also largely due to their initiative that the production of a local "turron" (nougat) was undertaken as well as of a number of articles of a similar kind.

The cooperative—which in fact was more like a community than a cooperative—was managed by a workers' council consisting of six workers from the establishment, each equally responsible for the smooth running of the factory and of the quality of the product.

4. The Agrarian Groups in Tarrasa

Tarrasa was essentially a manufacturing centre situated 30 km. from Barcelona. For a long time the principle industry there was the manufacture of woollen cloth from raw materials provided principally by the sheep from La Mancha, rich in windmills and poor pastures and thistles. The workers' movement here goes back a long way, and the syndical tradition was taken to heart by the town's 30,000 inhabitants. But at the moment of the Revolution the workers' organisations of Tarrasa were, like those of many other towns, far from having acquired the technical preparation needed to undertake the reorganisation of society. That and the opposition of the political parties with whom we co-existed, explains in part why long after the workers had seized the factories and workshops, the Syndicates had still not taken over their management.

With the exception of the building industry which truly had been socialised, the other industries were still, after six months, at the stage of control or management Comités; that is to say at the stage of absorbing the employer when he was on the scene—but the large factories often belonged to anonymous shareholders—and with the management and administration of the undertaking by the workers employed there.[1]

I visited the most important of these factories, where I had worked as a labourer some twenty years previously. It was managed by a "technical *Comité*" divided into seven parts; technical, syndical, work, administrative, commercial, propaganda, insurance.

1,300 men and women worked there. Nothing indicated any slowing up of their efforts. In all their tasks these workers showed the same diligence as under the previous regime. No employers, or foremen as in the past; but one could read on the faces the joy that came from the satisfaction of working for and by oneself.

But what was being done on the land around Tarrasa went much further than what went on in the factories.

*

The Syndicate of landworkers which directs and supervises them was founded after July 19. Before that there had in fact not been any agricultural union organisation except for a peasant section of the local general Syndicate. But with the triumph over the Francoists and, consequently, over the reactionary and conservative Rightists, most landowners disappeared. Some were Barcelona gentlemen, who had had second residences built and surrounded by lawns and where they went to relax for two or three months a year. The others were unenterprising semi-agriculturists who abandoned their estates to the brambles and wild rabbits.

Our comrades knew this and set to work at once. The Peasants' Syndicate immediately took over this new source of wealth. Its members were reinforced by industrial workers sufficiently discerning to see how much could be done.

At the end of six months, sixteen collective farms had been organised. The terrain was too uneven for large scale cultivation to be possible; but here again a general trend in the whole constructive effort in libertarian Spain was manifest. The lands of neighbouring farms and estates were brought together in agricultural units. Thus six properties became one community with a single management *Comité* in order the better to coordinate the general activities.

1 In present-day (1973) terms we could speak of self-management.

To manage the overall work the Syndicate was divided into two main sections: one agricultural, the other for forestry. The first section dealt with everything connected with agriculture and livestock, the forestry section with arbriculture. The Syndicate prepared records from data supplied by the farm managing *Comités* of the local area of each and the different cultivations. In this way the future yields could be estimated.

The Syndicate's role was limited to this and to the creation of new communities when it could secure more land. The communities were organised on the spot; their management *Comité* consisted of a delegate for agriculture, one for livestock, one for working tools and equipment; one for the means of transport. The workers who nominated them, just as the delegates themselves, worked from sunrise to sunset in accordance with decisions taken at their meetings.

Some hundred workers were engaged in forestry, based on the same zone and also managed by a technical *Comité* consisting of representatives of different sections. There too the members of the *Comité* worked alongside their comrades.

The agrarian communities of Tarrasa were not content with securing as much from the seized lands as they could. They had greater ambitions. More and more land was being cleared of thistles, brambles and ploughed ready for cultivation. And on the hillsides and the heights which they also cleared of weeds they sowed.

One typical example was that of the community *Sol y Vida* (Sun and Life). The owner had normally employed six workers. There were now forty who were kept busy all the time, intensive cultivation having replaced arable farming.

But not only was most of the cultivable land not cultivated, or left as poor pasture, there were also whole areas of forest with dense undergrowth which were not producing a worthwhile return. The tractor and men's efforts produced miracles. In a short time 140 hectares were brought under cultivation. Wheat, potatoes, fruit trees, vegetables, were sown or planted on the hillsides, and in the valleys. And work was proceeding with 150 willing helpers, to transform the wide bed of a former river-torrent into a sheltered apple, pear and peach orchard.

Meanwhile they had to live in between sowing and harvesting. That was where solidarity came into the picture. The forestry section which sold its products without difficulty (coal was no longer arriving from the Asturias and logs for fires and charcoal were welcome) helped the agrarian Collectives. Comrades from the town also made their contribution. Some would come on Sundays to work on the land, and help on repairs to the land-workers' homes, all without payment. Among these recruits there were some who had voluntarily given up a 90 pesetas a week wage in the factories to come and join in this creation of a new life, for 60 pesetas.

After visiting almost all the communities I went to inspect one of the finest accomplishments in this region. As most of the masons were unemployed their Syndicate made arrangements with the Peasants' Syndicate, and sent 150 men to clear and clean land, in the mountainous parts, which served only to shelter rodents and other creatures who were playing havoc with the crops. I saw these comrades fell trees, remove tree roots, chop and saw branches, stack logs and faggots, prepare the ovens and raw materials for making charcoal. Each team accomplished a precise part of the task and they left behind them land ready for cultivation.

On the basis of guidance coming from the landworkers' Syndicate some communities specialised in keeping pigs, others cows. The work was rationalised on the basis of available land and climatic conditions. Many comrades were sent to the Agricultural School in Arenys-de-Mar nearby, to study the best agricultural techniques.

The area cultivated by the 16 communities was 700 hectares and they were proposing to double the area by clearing some of the level land from the 4,000 hectares of forest lands.

PART FIVE

Parties and Government

CHAPTER XV

POLITICAL COLLABORATION

Though the aim of this book is as accurate a description as possible of the socio-economic achievements of the Spanish libertarian revolution during the years 1936-1939, the author considers it essential to present a picture, however brief, of the political conditions in which these experiments were undertaken and carried out, so that certain facts may be understood more clearly. This was done in the chapter on *Materials for a Revolution* but we need to add, especially for readers acquainted with libertarian ideas and doctrines, some necessary details.

We have seen that the outbreak of this revolution was part of the reply of the extreme Left to the Francoist attack. That extreme Left, which in the circumstances was the C.N.T. and the F.A.I., had and has always made intransigent anti-governmentalism and anti-statism a profession of faith. Now, for the first time in history we saw the most powerful libertarian organisation in the world, which had always proclaimed the superiority of its well founded choice of direct action; which, consequently, would have rejected as a joke in bad taste the thought of one day entering a ministry, send four ministers to the government: Juan Peiró (Minister for Industry), Juan García Oliver (Minister of Justice), Juan Lopez (Minister of Foreign Commerce) and Federica Montseny, extremist anarchist and intransigent demagogue if ever there was one (Minister of Health). Before that three ministers—modestly referred to as "Councillors" in Catalan—had entered the Barcelona government, modestly called *Generalitat*.

The author was not in Spain at the time and therefore did not incur either direct or indirect responsibility in that extraordinary

[321]

v

volte face, and when he did arrive in Spain the new ministers were already in office. He is no less uneasy in trying to offer an explanation which he feels necessary, for ministerial collaboration and participation for the first time in the Municipal Councils, exerted different influences, both negative—especially in the former —and positive—especially in the latter—but often decisive so far as the attitude of the libertarian movement was concerned.

Let us say straight out that what drove the anarchists in the first place to enter the Spanish government was the war, the Francoist attack and the fear of seeing the implantation of a fascism in Spain the catastrophic consequences of which were easy to foresee.

In fact, in spite of the bragging and the inept outbidding engaged in by the republican governments, the orators, the journalists who addressed themselves to the masses—and, alas, also libertarian agitators—the uncertainty of ultimate victory affected many even before the Francoist forces had in the south reached the gates of Madrid or had gained ground and taken or surrounded some towns in the northern region. Furthermore, the great majority of the population living in the part of Spain still called republican, was above all dominated by the fear of a Francoist victory and did not understand that the political and social forces organised in parties and anti-fascist sectors did not constitute a united front. Not being the prisoners of politico-philosophic principles, the people wanted the C.N.T. and even the considerably less important F.A.I. to enter the government in order to guarantee a coordination which they deemed indispensable.

The leaders of the C.N.T. behind whom were to be found those of the F.A.I. (and it was not always possible to differentiate between them), first of all did what they could in order not to give in. They were undoubtedly inspired by their traditional attitude of opposition to all governmentalism and therefore to all governmental parties. But in fact in the face of the growing danger, the greatest unification possible was needed. They thought up a revolutionary solution: the government would be replaced by a Defence Council composed of five members from the C.N.T., five from the U.G.T. and four from the republican parties. In this way they sought to make clear the supremacy of the workers' Syndical organisations over the political parties, and so kill two birds with one stone.

Based on the numerical strength of the respective organisms

this representation could appear to be justified. But the truth is also that the political parties had behind them a current of opinion consisting of the electorate. The C.N.T. and U.G.T. still had, in a Spain which was half occupied by the Francoist forces, about 1,200,000 members each—perhaps the U.G.T. had slightly fewer but its members were, by an overwhelming majority, under socialist influence; their structure was socialist just as that of the C.N.T. was libertarian. The majority of members would not therefore have accepted this take-in which would have deceived no one.

No more anyway than the statesmen, politicians and professional leaders in the different parties whose influence was a very real one for the majority of the population, and it needed a minimum of commonsense to realise this.

And yet, the idea of the constitution of a unified bloc was gaining ground with many people, even among the libertarians. One of them, Horacio Prieto, the then secretary of the C.N.T., undertook to convince his comrades of the necessity of crossing the Rubicon by entering a coalition government. To that end he had been in touch with Largo Caballero who had become President of the Council, an old political campaigner of the wire-pulling kind,[1] who having played the Leftist role within the socialist party during the period preceding the Francoist uprising, thought that the C.N.T. ministers-to-be would support him against his political opponents of the moment, especially the Communists whose influence was growing rapidly. There was agreement in principle between the two men. All that remained was to convince those most qualified to take the perilous leap.

Juan Lopez and Juan Peiró who were more syndicalist and revolutionary than anarchist, accepted. Then the F.A.I. leaders, Federica Montseny and Garcia Oliver, the bolstering of their egos overcoming the intransigence of principles. It is true that they already had the precedent of the Catalan government, where, there too, pure anarchists very easily abandoned their theoretical virginity.

Nevertheless, whoever examines the facts completely objectively, with a sincere desire at understanding, must admit that the situation

1 Largo Caballero had been a counsellor to the dictator Primo de Rivera; he resigned when the latter was in his decline as was the monarchy. Labour Minister in the Republic and professional leader of the U.G.T., he was a systematic opponent of the C.N.T. though later he got closer to them when it suited his political ends.

was not an easy one. The only way of escaping from the dilemma (ministerial collaboration or the weakening of the resistance to the fascist attack) would have been the organisation, to a certain extent autonomous, of the struggle loyally carried out by us alongside the official armies thanks to a combative force seeking its inspiration in the methods of the *guerilleros*. But let us admit it: the imagination for such a policy was lacking. Back in 1931 the author in his book *Problemas Economicos de la Revolucion Española*, had devoted a chapter to the question of the armed struggle in which, without playing at being the strategist or tactician, he drew attention to the form of combat employed by the "caudillos" such as El Empecinado and other heroes of the war against Napoleon where Masséna and other "enfants chéries de la victoire" had been defeated by the ill-armed peasants. It warned against the error of bowing to modern military methods, instead of having recourse to the tactics of revolutionary war, invented long before Mao Tse-tung defined it in his own way.

Those who improvised as leaders and military commanders had no ideas at all on the subject. Neither Durruti about whom one hears so much nor Garcia Oliver who had placed himself at the head of the Catalan militias and had drawn up war plans which immobilised Durruti at the gates of Saragossa, then hastily abandoned his post to become, of all people, Minister of Justice. The initiative failed: the enemy was given the time to reinforce his armament, the time to choose his terrain and the most favourable moment to launch his offensives. The tactical genius that Makhno had given proof of in the Ukraine, when he obliged General Denikin to halt his advance on Moscow, was completely lacking.

And our eminent personages, or who very quickly considered themselves such, were no more equal to the task at the political level than they were at the military level. Their role within the government was simply pitiful. After they had been ousted from it, they complained that the Stalinists, socialists and republicans had blocked all their initiatives, and they were right. Unfortunately they lent themselves to this game in which they were always the dupes and the losers.

When one draws up the balance sheet of this collaboration, the conclusion one comes to is that from every point of view this excursion in the corridors of power was negative. One can admit in extraordinary circumstances—and they were—that if, over and above his loyalty to his principles a man is faced with the dilemma of personally contaminating himself to serve a cause which is greater than him, he has the right, and even the duty, to prefer contamination. History, and as it happens, that of revolutions, offers such cases. But there was deviation and ridicule, in playing the adversary's game, and in saving nothing at all.

The only constructive, valid, important achievement during the Civil War was in fact that of the Revolution, on the fringe of power. The industrial collectivisations, the socialisation of agriculture, the syndicalisations of social services, all that, which made it possible to hold out for nearly three years and without which Franco would have triumphed in a matter of weeks, was the achievement of those who created, organised without concerning themselves with ministries and ministers. From the point of view of the conduct of the war and resistance to Franco, our ministers were unable to secure anything that was useful. We have even seen them echoing the slanders made by Caballero against the defenders of Malaga, accused of having handed over the town to Franco, whereas the way they had been systematically deserted by the government could not but lead to the town falling into the enemy's hands.[2] The Aragon front which opened the way either for the Francoists to Catalonia or for the antifascist troops towards the heart of Old Castile, was systematically sabotaged, deprived of weapons, aircraft and anti-aircraft guns. During the first year of the war it would have been possible to break through that front which the fascists were holding with a few thousand mobile troops provided with fast means of transport which could quickly move in wherever an offensive was launched by our forces. It was not done, due to a lack of shells and ammunition, and this made it impossible to relieve the Madrid front, and resulted in the massacre of tens of thousands of combatants to no purpose. Instead they preferred to systematically send arms to the Central front, which was the least vulnerable, on the fascist side, but where the Stalinists were in control. The Russian generals conducted the operations on the Andalusian and Estremadura fronts in such a way that it was impossible to win. And often our forces, made to launch an offensive, found themselves faced by much larger forces and were obliged to

2 Largo Caballero, after he had become head of government, told a delegation who had come to ask for arms to defend Malaga: "For Malaga not a cartridge, not a rifle!" The fact was that in the Defence *Comité* in that town, as the author was able to see for himself, the Caballero-ites were in a minority.

retreat at bayonet point to avoid annihilation, leaving behind large numbers of casualties. It was as if the Stalinist and fascist generals were agreed about the massacre of our men. It is true that Stalin was capable of such things and worse; many accounts of the war justify such an hypothesis.

Another aspect of the sabotage which contributed to the rout was the refusal by the Valencia government to give financial aid to the Barcelona *Generalitat* to purchase arms or the raw materials with which to make them.

Against all this our ministers did nothing, either because they could not or would not. Their protests fell on deaf ears, but they did not denounce that sabotage "because we were collaborating in the government and should not air our differences in public". Men like the Stalinist Jesus Hernandez, who on orders from Moscow engineered Caballero's overthrow, have recounted how the policy of the government was conducted on orders from the representatives of the Comintern, and one can say that the best allies Franco had were these master manoeuverers who were quite unconcerned with the disagreements and protests of the "anarchist" ministers.

We therefore repeat that in face of these great national and international political problems, in face of these difficulties for which they were not cut out, even for the major economic problems at *national level* the militants who played leading roles were not equal to the situation. In a situation of unilateral domination and by the use of dictatorship which silences the malcontents and discontentment, and the use of force to which the Bolsheviks had recourse, it is possible to make mistakes and remain in power. It was not a question of that.

But I also wish to put on record that one of the lessons to retain from that collaborationist indiscretion was the harm resulting from the poison of power. In general, the rank and file of the C.N.T. remained sound, remarkably sound, as were the libertarian militants we met in the Collectives or at the head of syndicalisations. Eager to construct, with an enthusiastic effort of will, determined to realise that ideal, they let the ministers, the governors, the police chiefs, ministry officials, state officials and babbling nonentities gesticulate. But the great majority of libertarians who had strayed from their own milieu were intoxicated by governmentalism with a rapidity that was heartbreaking. Some would have started a new political party but for the opposition of the rank and file.

CHAPTER XVI

LIBERTARIANS AND REPUBLICANS

Historically, the contact between libertarians and republicans first appears in the form of a common struggle against the monarchy, but there are also other explanations. From the second half of the 19th Century some Republican factions felt an active sympathy for "the workers". And certain affinities of thought were soon to emerge. We have already said that it was Pi y Margall the great leader, thinker and theoretician of federalist republicanism who was the first to translate the works of Proudhon. And it was as a result of these translations that an-archist thought was born in Spain. From another quarter the centralist republican Joaquin Costa wrote one, among his many books, with the title *El Colectivismo Agrario en España*, gathering together systematically all the examples of mutual aid that existed throughout the country. This book could well have borne Kropotkin's name, and would be a suitable sequel to *Mutual Aid*. Among Spanish anarchists he is still held in well deserved esteem; and he also helps one to understand why the libertarian revolution was possible in the countryside.

Furthermore, at the time of the dissolution of the First International, in 1872, the great republican jurist Nicolas Salmeron, an eminent personality universally admired, eloquently defended in the Parliament this workers' revolutionary organisation's right to exist.

But above all, it is in the local contacts, in many provincial towns and numerous villages that the esteem and support of the republicans for the libertarians was manifested. Especially with the federalist republicans. In the periods of repression when the C.N.T. Syndicates were made illegal as well as the C.N.T. itself, their premises were always open to us and we met there freely, welcomed with a friendship which was unfailing.

Besides, a quarter of the members of the C.N.T. were republicans. The reason was that having to choose between that organisation which was essentially libertarian, and the U.G.T. which was state socialist they preferred ours, whose principles were the greater guarantee of human freedom, whereas Marxism, which the U.G.T. leaders favoured, seemed to them a threat for the future ("the danger of a new Middle Ages for humanity" some of them told me).

One will therefore not be surprised that not only some lawyers, mostly republican federalists, such as Francisco Layret, assassinated by the employers' gunmen in 1921, and Eduardo Barriobero, a jurist and talented writer, shot by the Francoists, and many others whose names now escape me, were always at our disposal.

At the time of our Revolution in 1936 the Second Republic had been in existence for only five years. In such a short time only the politicians—among them Alejandro Lerroux, for a long time a rightist and conservative—had had time to be corrupted. Many rank and file forces had remained sound and for these men republicanism embodied the social question. Thus when the agrarian Collectives emerged, many of them accepted administrative posts especially in accountancy. Belonging mainly to the middle classes they had received a technical training and education which made them efficient collaborators. Libertarian ideas had thus penetrated many republican minds. At the beginning of 1937 this writer was one of the speakers at a large meeting organised by the C.N.T. in Castellon de la Plana. Half the audience, of some 5,000, were republicans who had remained honest. It also explains how it was possible to introduce libertarian social reforms in that town in the conditions which we have described elsewhere.

CHAPTER XVII

THE INTERNAL COUNTER-REVOLUTION

A complete account of the behaviour of the government authorities to the diverse achievements of socialisation undertaken and realised by the Spanish libertarians during the period 1936-1939 would show contradictory attitudes which could be commented on in different ways. That the Ministry of Industry, which in the early months was in the hands of a C.N.T. militant, Juan Peiró, did in some cases help undertakings by financial contributions, such as was the case of the S.I.C.E.P. in Elda, there can be no question. But in general, that aid had as its objective not so much to help socialisation, which was not approved of, but to save the political situation by supporting war industries. This did not prevent the Stalinists, when they were laying down the law inside the government, to sabotage even the manufacture of goods needed for the struggle against the Francoist armies.

But at the same time, the government authorities as well as the Stalinist Communist Party, on many occasions waged war on the social achievements we have been describing. It will not come amiss to enumerate some of the more notorious with which we were acquainted.

These events were sometimes accompanied by incredible violence. The first of these armed confrontations between the builders of the Collectives and the government forces occurred in the region of the Levante. In view of the growing strength of the Collectives they represented as it were the alternative power to the central government (by then installed in Valencia) in the event of military victory over Franco's forces. The government reacted to this threat by launching an offensive against the Collectives. Duly militarised, the "carabineros", a branch of the Civil Guard, and the Assault Guards, another police corps, created by the Republic, were chosen for this offensive the first of which took place in the Levante in March 1937. The attackers came from Alicante and Murcia. Their forces included an artillery section with large numbers of machine guns and tanks which could have been better employed at the front where they were short of them. (Eighteen were counted in the Gandia region and thirteen in the Alfara del Patriarca region.)

Our peasant comrades, who were expecting the attack, had got ready to resist, and fought with rifles, revolvers and two anti-tank guns. The government forces planned to converge on Cullera and on Alfara, strategic points for eventual operations. But almost the whole region rose in arms, and in response to the alarm bells which were widely used, people joined them from the neighbouring villages armed with shotguns, to give assistance to the localities under attack. Hand grenades were widely used and two battalions of the Iron Column followed by two more of the Confederal Column (of the C.N.T.) came all the way from the Teruel front to Segorbe. The cantonal federations of Jativa, Carcagente, Gandia, Sueca having gathered their forces, established the "Gandia Front" while those from Catarroja, Liria, Moncada, Paterna and Burriana established the "Villanesa Front".

In Cullera and its environs the struggle lasted four days at the end of which the official troops, being unable to advance, changed their plans and moved in the direction of Silla. Finally the intervention of the leaders of the C.N.T. brought the struggle to an end. Prisoners and captured arms were exchanged, but in spite of everything some of our people, especially members of the libertarian youth, were imprisoned and only released later. There were dead and wounded, but the Collectives were not destroyed; indeed the number increased at an even faster rate.

It would appear that the whole operation had been mounted by the War Minister, the right wing socialist Indalecio Prieto, in agreement on this occasion with the Communists, whom he hated but with whom he was reconciled for this venture.

*

In Catalonia too the military forces in the rearguard had been organised more quickly than the forces who were languishing without arms along the Aragon front. And when Companys, president of the *Generalitat*, implicitly or tacitly with the other political parties, thought the time had come he approved of what has been called the "May Days" 1937 which ended in the eviction of our ministers and of our comrades in high official posts, and in the Communist take-over in record time of the police corps, the administrative responsibilities and the already infiltrated army. From that moment the persecutions started against our forces and we lost ground everywhere except in production.

One of the most striking examples of hostility was the embittered struggle against the collectivisation of urban transport in Barcelona.

We have seen how the central government had only asked that 3% of its receipts should be paid in taxes to the Finance ministry; and the Catalan government presumably to demonstrate the superiority of federalism and decentralisation demanded payment of 14 different taxes. But both governments were very careful not to upset the new socialised organisation, knowing only too well that it could not replace it, and that to paralyse the means of transport in a city like Barcelona and in the suburbs would cause the kind of chaos which would play into the hands of fascism.

The Stalinists who had no such scruples received the order to sabotage and as is their wont, carried it out conscientiously. Having been removed from the management committee in which by rights they should never have been because they represented an insignificant minority and never missed an opportunity to put a brake on the enthusiasm that existed by diverse and machiavellian manoeuvres, they did not however stop raising obstacles and creating difficulties.

They went about the task in many ways. For instance they had succeeded in becoming a majority in an engineering workshop where 24 workers made spare parts—to be exact, bearings —without which the tramcars would grind to a standstill. They did not refuse to work; indeed they formally undertook to supply what was asked of them. But a month after the delivery date established the bearings had still not been made. When eventually they were made they were the wrong size. It was partly as a means of defending itself against such forms of sabotage that the Syndicate purchased an ultra modern electric furnace.

Another manoeuvre consisted in fomenting disagreements and disputes between the different branches of the transport network. The Stalinists had managed to become the majority in the management of one of the two large bus companies. The tramway workers bought a ticket when they used the buses but schooled by their committee the bus company's employees did not pay when they travelled on the trams. This caused friction, which is what they wanted. An end was put to this situation by threatening to have recourse to strong action.

Again in Catalonia, the forms of sabotage were perfected by adapting oneself to changes in the situation. Three new elements were taken into account:

a) The growing need felt by the population to give the struggle against fascism top priority—a view with which our comrades concurred, but a return to management along capitalist lines of the tramways and other enterprises would, on the contrary, strengthen the possibilities of defeat.

b) The entry of official Communists into the War and Industry Ministry after the May Days of 1937.

c) The rights possessed by that Ministry to requisition, through its agents cunningly placed, the technical means needed for the production of arms and ammunition.

These agents, or ministerial representatives, started by demanding delivery of the chemical products used for welding the rails, with the pretext of using them for the manufacture of explosives. Our comrades complied in order not to be accused of hampering the struggle against Franco but then sent technically qualified men to France to buy equipment based on electrodes (as already described) and the manoeuvre was neutralised. As to the requisitioned chemical products, they were left to go bad in some warehouses where they had been dumped by the Stalinists.

Some weeks later several officers specially instructed, with a written order from the War Ministry in Valencia, presented themselves to requisition the latest model American lathe, though the Ministry could have easily purchased several in France, Belgium or elsewhere.[1] Our comrades offered resistance to this confiscation, and as the excuses constantly advanced were the needs of war,

---

1 Some people might argue that the non-intervention pact signed by Leon Blum prevented them from obtaining the equipment for manufacturing arms. In fact there has been a lot of exaggeration on this question. The Franco-Spanish land frontiers remained at least half-open for delivery of arms, ammunition, tools and even aircraft. Under the pressure of circumstances Blum appeared to subscribe to the blockade of Spain but in reality he saw to it that as much as possible was delivered, and many were the lorries which crossed at Puigcerda, Bourg-Madame, or at La Jonquera, carrying useful loads for the anti-Francoist struggle.

to which they contributed without remuneration, offered to work even more hours without payment in order to satisfy the needs that they invoked. The offer was refused. They wanted the machine in order to disorganise the Barcelona transport services.

In an attempt at conciliation, our comrades suggested exchanging two milling machines of the most recent design, and which the War Ministry could have bought abroad, for two other, older models. This exchange led to an unexpected discovery.

A technician delegated by the Syndicate to go and choose the two machines offered in exchange for theirs found them in a secret depot to which he was taken. It was situated in a place called Sarria, near Barcelona, and our astounded comrade saw there 80 other milling machines, some 40 rectifiers and some hundred lathes.

What were these machines doing there when they were so badly needed by the arms factories and when there were none at all in other regions? Perhaps they were waiting to bring them out when they would be in power at national level. This not having happened the machines remained where they were. They were left to the Francoists to use.

*

The Stalinists went further. In the Aragon countryside where the villages were more scattered, less densely populated and less organised for struggle behind the fronts than were those in the Levante, they succeeded in almost completely destroying the Collectives. The method used was the following.

In June 1937 after the decisive May Days in Barcelona, the Stalinist Uribe, the new Minister of Agriculture, published a decree by which he legalised the agrarian Collectives throughout the Spanish territory, whatever the circumstances in which they had been formed. For anyone who knew what a vigorous campaign this man had waged against the social creations of the peasant revolutionaries, this about turn was surprising. For months he had been delivering radio speeches advising peasants not to join the Collectives, urging the smallholders to oppose them and combat them by every means, and he was speaking in his capacity as a minister, so much so that the conservatives and reactionaries who remained in the countryside felt they were being given official support, while those who hesitated about joining concluded that if the establishment was expressing itself against these new social structures, they would not last very long after the victory over Franco; so better not to risk taking the plunge.

Not satisfied with this campaign, Uribe organised the Peasant Federation of the Levante, which the defenders of private property in the land joined *en masse*. Stalinists and fascists rubbed shoulders cordially. The anti-revolutionary united front was thus on the march.

It was for this reason that the tardy legislation had caused so much surprise, the more so since groups of Young Communists were organised to spread themselves in Catalonia and the Levante, ostensibly with the intention of helping the peasants to harvest and gather the crops. The Stalinist press published whole columns of communiqués, reports and slogans praising this wholehearted collaboration of the "shock brigades".

Those who knew the traditional tactics of these implacable enemies of the collectivisations could have no illusions about the aims of the campaign. It was a case of infiltration of the agrarian organisations, following a traditional method, of using them or of destroying them from within.

But in that month of June the offensive in Aragon was launched on a scale and using methods so far not experienced. The time for harvesting was drawing near, which explains a lot. In the countryside the *carabineros*, often led by men of the Communist Party who had known how to secure posts of command, started to hold up at pistol point food lorries going from one province to another, and taking them to their barracks. A little later the same *carabineros* traversed the Collectives, and in the name of the General Staff with headquarters in Barbastro, demanded large quantities of corn.

The Aragon Collectives could not be accused of meanness, especially towards the fighting forces which without their supplies would have quickly disintegrated (we have given elsewhere many proofs of this). But they were waiting for the harvest to obtain by barter the goods they themselves needed, in some cases urgently. And to hand over large quantities of corn at the beginning of the harvest without compensation, for some cantons such as Binefar which had given everything—cereals, potatoes, oil, meat —this provoked among some of the population a discontent which was exploited by them. For nothing was demanded from the small landowners; and the same policy was later adopted in the Levante.[2]

This demand was immediately followed by another. Always on orders from the General Staff in Barbastro, which in turn was covered by the authority of the Minister of War in Valencia, Indalecio Prieto, they started requisitioning *manu militari* all transport though at that moment it was vital for moving the harvested crops. We have already observed that the Collectives had almost always procured their transport by barter, often depriving themselves of food and other essentials. The lorries were among the acquisitions of which they were justly proud. The *carabineros* took everything, or almost, brutally on the pretext if its being needed for war transport.

At the same time more conscripts were called up with the pretext of an imminent offensive. At the time of the harvest some 50 youths left Esplus, a village which had already provided so many volunteers for the fronts. The other villages were likewise deprived of their young men. But the young people of the same age group who were doing nothing in Catalonia were not called up until later.

Still in Aragon at the same period troops from the front line were withdrawn and billeted in houses in villages carefully selected for their strategic positions. These forces came from other regions; they lived a carefree, parasitical existence, eating, lounging, playing pelota all day long. They were to be used when the time was ripe. At the same time the peasants who had achieved the miracle of cultivating and sowing more land than before, saw the corn fall from the ears in the fields due to a lack of hands to gather it.

Simultaneously the press campaign continued. Playing as usual a double game, the Communist Party could prove to some that it supported the Collectives, by producing the text of the Uribe decree,[3] and evidence of the dispatch of youth brigades to work in the fields, whereas in fact it was destroying, in order to break up a revolution that it did not control, economic resources vital to Republican Spain.

2 In that year the Communists organised a United Levante Council for the export of citrus fruit (C.L.U.E.) to compete against, and if possible ruin the FERECALE, created by the Federation of Collectives of the Levante.

3 To this day (1969) the C.P. states to those who have recently joined and do not know what happened, and leads them to believe that it was thanks to the Uribe decree that the Collectives were organised.

Then one day at the end of July, the brutal attack was launched by a mobile brigade led by the commanding officer Lister whose troops were, in the following month, at the beginning of the offensive on Belchite, to retreat with such alacrity before the fascists that they stopped only when they were fifty kilometres from the front.

The final outcome of the anti-revolutionary offensive was that 30% of the Collectives were completely destroyed. In Alcolea de Cinca, the municipal Council which managed the Collective were arrested, the residents of the Old People's House were driven out. There were arrests in Mas de las Matas, in Monzon, in Barbastro and elsewhere. Pillaging also occurred in most places. Cooperative warehouses, municipal food depots were ransacked, furniture broken up. The governor of Aragon, who represented the central government following the dissolution of the Council of Aragon—which seemed to be the signal for the general offensive—tried to oppose this plundering. He was sent packing.

At the peasants' national plenum which was held in Valencia on 22 October, 1937, the delegation of the regional *Comité* of Aragon presented a report which is summed up as follows:

"More than six hundred organisers of the Collectives have been put in prison. The government has nominated management commissions which have seized the food warehouses and have distributed supplies haphazardly. The land, draught animals and agricultural implements have been returned to the members of fascist families or to fascists who had been left unmolested by the Revolution.

"The harvest has been distributed similarly, as well as the animals raised by the Collective. A large number of Collective piggeries, stables, stockyards, barns have been destroyed. In some villages, such as Bordon and Calaceite, even their seed stocks have been taken away from the peasants, thereby preventing them from sowing the fields that had been prepared."

Such exactions naturally bore their fruits. Almost all the Collectives were re-formed but they were far from attaining to their earlier heights. The "individualists" and the conservatives gained the upper hand, the more so since a number of those who had joined this vast movement of socialisation and who would have belonged to it again had they been free to choose, no longer dared to start again.

Then the Francoists followed the Communists, and nothing

remained of the constructive work of the Aragon Collectives other than some of the technical improvements.

*

Much remains to be written about the manoeuvres adopted by the non-fascist opponents of libertarian socialisation during the Spanish Revolution. We will limit ourselves to two more examples of the methods used by them. One, which the Syndicate of the wood industry had exposed at the time, consisted in keeping tens of thousands of unemployed in idleness rather than give the Syndicates the money distributed among them, in order to create new industries or to keep going those which were essential but were in difficulties. The wasteful spending was preferred to the strengthening of the new social structure.

And when, in Catalonia, the Communist leader Comorera became Minister of Finance after the May Days, the means of struggle he adopted were original. It was clear that it was quite impossible to destroy the outstanding influence of the Syndicates of the C.N.T. To attempt to do so would have paralysed production overnight. So, Comorera had recourse to two complementary procedures; on the one hand he deprived the factories of raw materials or deliveries did not arrive on time, thus resulting in production delays which were knowingly criticised; on the other hand they paid for the deliveries of cloth, clothing, arms, etc., with a delay which affected the workers own budgets. As the wages were distributed under the supervision of the Syndicates, it was against the delegates of the C.N.T. and against the organism of which they were the representatives that the discontent of one section of the workers was directed.

This sabotage, this art of turning the responsibility for the clever manoeuvres against those who suffered its consequences, reminds one of what happened during the first eighteen months on the Aragon front.

We had no arms, for what was being manufactured in Barcelona was virtually nil; and this prevented us from launching offensives which would have relieved the Madrid front, and even perhaps made possible an advance beyond Saragossa. The many desperate attempts which took place were paid for in huge losses of life. As we have already mentioned, the unsuccessful attempts to capture Huesca, a town with a normal population of 18,000, cost us 20,000 lives.

By contrast the Madrid front was largely supplied, thanks to Russian arms supplies (paid for *in advance,* in gold)[4] but with which it was not possible to penetrate the solid defences, backed by the Sierras, of our opponents. Our militias on the Aragon front were raging within at being condemned to impotence and at being uselessly massacred. And the Stalinist press in Madrid published cartoons such as the one in which a militiaman is portrayed spending his time quietly fishing on the banks of the Ebro instead of fighting to relieve the capital which was defending itself with difficulty.

One can imagine the repercussions that this way of presenting the facts had on the minds of uninformed readers and on public opinion.

4 And not reimbursed if the arms ship was sunk in the Mediterranean.

PART SIX
Epilogue

CHAPTER XVIII

FINAL REFLECTIONS

We have so many times said, for it is important to bear this in mind that the Spanish libertarian revolution was set in motion as a consequence of the Francoist attack which made it possible to put into action revolutionary forces which without it were condemned to new and sterile failures. And when we say "sterile failures" we are referring to the attempts made in January 1932, January and December 1933 (revolutionary and insurrectional attempts organised and manned by the C.N.T.-F.A.I.) to which one must add the Asturian miners' insurrection in October 1934 in which socialist, U.G.T. and C.N.T. workers (in spite of the stupid opposition of the national *Comité* of the C.N.T.) and even Communists took part.[1] All these attempts were crushed by the more powerful forces of the State, supported by the non-revolutionary political parties which, for all that, were not fascist.

This last point needs elaborating. The tactical concepts of anarchist communism (and before it anarchist collectivism) implied, according to a tradition going back to the First International, the attack by, and the victory of, the people. Therefore the armed struggles which took place under the Second Spanish Republic corresponded to a doctrine of action theoretically established. This doctrine, which coincided with the teachings of Kropotkin and taken up by his disciples including the present writer, considered that local uprisings, the attempts, even sporadic, and so numerous before the French Revolution, constituted a training,

1 It was on this occasion that the U.H.P. *Union Hermanos Proletarios* (Union of Proletarian Brothers) was constituted.

a revolutionary exercise in which the people learned to fight, and would end by winning the last hand. A little like Peter the Great's celebrated remark in face of the continued defeats inflicted on him by the Swedes: "By going on fighting they will teach us how to beat them."

Unfortunately there was no proletarian Poltava and what we have just recalled provides an explanation that should be borne in mind. If we return to all the factors that intervened in this chapter of history we are obliged to conclude that the defeat of the Spanish libertarian revolution was inevitable. For every social revolution provokes the cohesion of the threatened forces drawn together for exceptional reasons, and in spite of those which normally divide them. It is the lesson that we learn not only from the final defeat of the Spanish Revolution but of history when studied with a concern for the truth.

Apart from some contemporary exceptions which have anyway led to new forms of oppression,[2] generally speaking it is the *political* revolutions that have triumphed, but the same men or the same parties who were fighting amongst themselves for a change in the power structure became reconciled when they were faced with a popular movement which threatened their positions or their privileges. Thus in France, the revolution of February 1848 was simple: liberal bourgeois and workers joined forces to overthrow the monarchy of Louis Philippe. But everything was changed four months later when the workers wanted to introduce socialism. Then the liberal bourgeois allied themselves with the monarchists and Cavaignac, the republican general, struggled with all his might against the insurgent workers.

Other social revolutions, or those which had a definite social content, whether it was the Commune of Paris, or the Peasant War in Germany in which Luther was allied to the nobility in provoking them to the wholesale massacre of the serfs in revolt, or again the Hussite movement in Bohemia, and all the peasant risings in the Middle Ages, are all a repetition of the

2 Such is the case of the Russian Revolution which might not have been crushed in view of the immensity of the country, itself the cause of Napoleon's defeat. As to the Cuban revolution, if its sycophants observed things more closely instead of being tricked by the magic of words, they would see that it has implanted a new form of totalitarianism by setting up a regime which is only socialist in name and which deflected it from the promising road—we are not saying of integral socialism—that it had taken on the morrow of Batista's overthrow.

same facts. One must go back to Egypt in 2200-2000 B.C. to find a victorious social revolution. And even then, two centuries later—probably even before that—a new dynasty had been enthroned and the castes re-established.

Bakunin himself wrote eighteen months before his death, thereby confirming what Elisée Reclus had written to him: "You are right, the day of revolutions is past, we have entered that of evolution." And he explained his opinion by recalling not only the terrible defeats suffered by European revolutionaries in the course of nearly half a century of heroic struggles, but in face of the scientifically organised military power of modern states, and the lack of revolutionary spirit, or desire for emancipation among the masses.

To be sure this latter consideration did not apply to the Spanish people, or at least to that large, dynamic section which made history. But facts oblige us to recognise that the Kropotkinian thesis, to some extent in opposition to the posthumous theses of Bakunin, Elisée Reclus and even of Proudhon,[3] has not been borne out by experience. For fascist totalitarianism, which in Italy after World War I was answering back at a long period of disturbances which did not end in revolution, made its historical appearance. And fascism is the "preventive counter-revolution" of those who are threatened by subversion, even when it is incapable of changing the social order. The people themselves end by preferring the suppression of political and civic liberty to permanent disorder which, let us face it, is also an attack on freedom if only of living a normal life.

There is therefore the danger in pursuing these revolutionary exercises, with an unending series of partial strikes, continuous general strikes and insurrectional attempts, of harming the stability of society.

This is probably what happened in Spain before the unleashing of the fascist attack. Certainly it is not a question of condemning outbursts caused by hunger, impatience, despair, anger a hundred times justified in those who saw their babies dying from lack of treatment, or who had spent most of the year looking in vain for work, and having to send their children barefoot to school—when a school was available. But those who set themselves up as leaders of the C.N.T. and the F.A.I.—the latter organisation

3 Proudhon also rejected the armed revolution and wrote to Marx, "Our proletarians are so thirsting for science that we would be badly received by them if all we could offer them to drink was blood."

embodied a revolutionary passion rather than intellectual worth —needed a strategic vision which they lacked. Here too they were not equal to the situation. The greatness of the libertarian movement was its almost exclusively proletarian character, but it was also its weakness. And this weakness permitted the demagogues, and we had our share of them, to play a role for which they were not cut out.

*

But even more responsible were the socialist and republican leaders who had neither the inspired initiative, the intelligence nor the courage to undertake, with the proclamation of the Republic, daring social reforms which might have satisfied the hunger of some and tempered the impatience of others. They have a greater share of the responsibility because they were better educated and had greater means for action. What was the reason for their indifference? Undoubtedly power had made them faint-hearted, had dulled their imagination as so often happens to the happy beneficiaries of new political regimes. We are not saying this in a partisan spirit. About 1935 an enquiry had shown that the largest percentage of *enchufistas* (people who hold more than one official employment) were to be found among the Socialists and the Left Catalanists. Social reforms interested them much less than the enjoyment of newly acquired privileges. In such an *ensemble* of conditions, the revolutionary fact had to occur.

On the other hand, one of the consequences of the continuous social conflicts was to drive people of the Centre parties towards the Right, and to swell the conservative, reactionary, and fascist forces. The figures at the February 1936 elections prove this, and here one can speak of the responsibility of the revolutionaries. But if the socialists and left republicans had given land to the starving peasants[4] and had undertaken daring social reforms which were clearly exceptional in a situation which was itself exceptional, the tumultuous social struggles would not have been of such a grave nature and perhaps the fascist reaction would not have resulted. But they preferred to limit themselves to copying the constitution of the Weimar Republic.

*

4 Their agrarian reform was like giving a few grains of millet to a starving eagle.

We have said and repeated that the fascist attack created a favourable situation for the libertarian sector to take over an important part of the general situation and of almost the whole economy. Nevertheless the repercussions were only favourable, for negative and positive consequences were about equally balanced. On the one hand many militants, often the best, were, because of the war, mobilised and many died at the front. It was also the best who were missing from the Syndicates, in the Collectives, in the villages where they exercised a salutary influence. And on the other hand, the number of those who became a part of the government bureaucracy were also numerous enough for their absence to be felt.

*

One of the dominant characteristics which impresses whoever studies the Spanish Revolution is its many sidedness. This revolution was guided by certain very clear and very definite principles, which involved the general expropriation of the holders of social wealth, the seizure by the workers of the organisational structures of production and distribution, the direct administration of public services, the establishment of the libertarian communist principle. But the uniformity of these principles did not prevent a diversity in the methods for their application, so much so that one can talk of "diversity within unity" and of a surprisingly diversified federalism.

In a very short time, in the agrarian regions and especially in Aragon, a new organism appeared: the Collective. Nobody had spoken about it before. The three instruments of social reconstruction foreseen among those libertarians who had expressed themselves on a possible future were firstly the Syndicate, then the Cooperative, which did not win many supporters, and finally, on a rather large scale, the commune, or communal organisation. Some foreshadowed—and this writer was among them—that a new and complementary organism could and should appear, especially in the countryside, seeing that the Syndicate had not assumed the importance it had in the towns, and the kind of life, of work and production, did not fit into an organic monolithic structure which was contrary to the multiformity of daily life.

We have seen how that Collective was born with characteristics of its own. It is not the Syndicate, for it encompasses all those who wish to join it whether they are producers in the classic economic sense or not. Then it brings them together at the complete

[343]

human individual level and not just at a craft level. Within it, from the first moment, the rights and duties are the same for everybody; there are no longer professional categories in mutual opposition making the producers into privileged consumers compared with those, such as housewives, who are not producers in the classical definition of the word.

Neither is the Collective the municipal Council or what is called the Commune, the municipality. For it parts company with the political party traditions on which the commune is normally based. It encompasses at the same time the Syndicate and municipal functions. It is all-embracing. Each of its activities is organised within its organism, and the whole population takes part in its management, whether it is a question of a policy for agriculture, for the creation of new industries, for social solidarity, medical service or public education. In this general activity the Collective brings each and everybody to an awareness of life in the round, and everyone to the practical necessity of mutual understanding.

Compared with the Collective the Syndicate has simply a secondary or subordinate role. It is striking to observe how in the agricultural districts, it was more often than not spontaneously relegated, almost forgotten, in spite of the efforts that the libertarian-syndicalists and the anarcho-syndicalists had previously made. The Collective replaced them. The word itself was born spontaneously and spread into all the regions of Spain where the agrarian revolution had been brought about. And the word "collectivist" was adopted just as quickly and spread with the same spontaneity.

One could advance the hypothesis that these two words—collective and collectivism—better expressed the people's moral, human, fraternal feelings than did the terms Syndicates and syndicalism. A question of euphony perhaps, and of a breadth of views, of humanism: man as something more than the producer. The need for syndicates no longer exists when there are no more employers.

If we pass from Aragon to the Levante we see Collectives emerging there too but not as such a spontaneous, one might almost say instant, creation. It was the agricultural and sometimes the non-agricultural, syndicates which were there at the beginning, not to found other Syndicates, and this is most significant, but *to found Collectives*. And those who joined these Collectives, often without belonging to the Syndicates, were also collectivists and acted and behaved as well as anybody else. Let us hasten to add that the groups of organisers often consisted of men who had until then been active in the Syndicates or even in libertarian groups.

But there were some cases where the Commune fulfilled the role of the Collective. Among the examples we have given one especially recalls Granollers, Hospitalet, Fraga, Binefar, and many places in Castile. We also find municipalities which had been reconstructed to conform with governmental decisions (January 1937) and had, as a result, played a more or less important, more or less subordinate, role; and in the Levante the Syndicate and the Collective in the end linked their activities. But in that region the role of the Syndicate was often to become more important, both through direct participation and as inspirer and guide, which it was not in Aragon.

Finally we see in Castile, the Collectives being started in large numbers under the impulse of militant workers and even intellectuals who left Madrid and spread out into the countryside.

This plasticity, this variety of ways of acting allowed for the creation of true socialism, in each place according to the situation, circumstances of time and place, and for the resolution of a great number of problems which an authoritarian concept, too rigid, too bureaucratic would have only made more complicated with, in the end, a dictatorship reducing everything to a uniform pattern. The variety of methods used reflected the variety of the facets of life. Often in the same region, villages with similar forms of production, with a somewhat similar social history, would start by socialising the local industries and end with agriculture, while others would start with the socialisation of agriculture and end with that of local industries. In some cases, in the Levante for instance, we have seen it start with distribution then proceed towards socialisation of production, which was the opposite procedure to most other places.

But it is remarkable that this diversity of organisational structures did not prevent membership of the same regional federations nor, through them, national coordination, practical solidarity, whether it concerned our Collectives, mixed Syndical Collectives or communities at different stages of municipalisation.

*

The general law was universal solidarity. We have underlined, in passing, that the Charters or Statutes in which the principles were defined and from which stemmed the practical attitude of each and all, made no mention of the rights and liberty of the individual. Not that the Collectives had ignored these rights, but simply because the respect of these rights went without saying, and that they were already recognized by the standard of life guaranteed to everybody, in their access to consumer goods, to wellbeing and culture, to the attention, consideration and *human responsibilities* of which each one, as a member of the Collective, was assured. It was known, so why mention it? In return, for this to be possible, everyone had to carry out his duty, do his work like the other comrades, show solidarity according to the ethic of a universal mutual aid.

One was the guarantee of the other. It is for this reason we so often read that same sentence in the Charters though there had been no previous discussion between Collectives hundreds of kilometres apart: "Anyone not having any work in his trade will help comrades in other activities who might need his help." This was supra-professional solidarity in practice.

Going deeply into these matters it could perhaps be said that they were developing a new concept of liberty. In the village Collectives in their natural state, and in the small towns where everybody knew one another and were interdependent, liberty did not consist in being a parasite, and not interesting oneself in anything. Liberty only existed as a function of practical activity. *To be is to do*, Bakunin wrote. To be is to *realise*, voluntarily. Liberty is secured not only when one demands the rights of the "self" against others, but when it is a natural consequence of solidarity. Men who are interdependent feel free among themselves and naturally respect each other's liberty. Furthermore so far as collective life is concerned, the freedom of each is the right to participate spontaneously with one's thought, one's heart, one's will, one's initiative to the full extent of one's capacities. A negative liberty is not liberty: it is nothingness.

This concept of liberty gave rise to a new morality—unless it was this new ethic that gave rise to another concept of liberty. It explains why when the author sought information about changes, and improvements introduced in the lives of everyone, they did not speak of "liberty" though they were libertarians, but, and they did so with deep joy, of the results of their work, experiments, and research on which they were engaged; on the increase in production. No, they were no longer thinking of liberty in the way workers in capitalist factories or day workers on the land of the owner-employer think.

*

On this subject we would like to make an observation to which we attach great philosophical and practical importance. The theoreticians and partisans of the liberal economy affirm that competition stimulates initiative and, consequently, the creative spirit and invention without which it remains dormant. Numerous observations made by the writer in the Collectives, factories and socialised workshops permit him to take quite the opposite view. For in a Collective, in a grouping where each individual is stimulated by the wish to be of service to his fellow beings, research, the desire for technical perfection and so on are also stimulated.[5] But they also have as a consequence that other individuals join those who were the first to get together. Furthermore when, in present society, an individualist inventor discovers something, it is used only by the capitalist or the individual employing him, whereas in the case of an inventor living in a community not only is his discovery taken up and developed by others, but is immediately applied for the common good. I am convinced that this superiority would very soon manifest itself in a socialised society.

*

Lenin, in his report on the Russian situation to the 11th Congress of the Communist Party held in March 1922, declared: "The idea of constructing a communist society with only the help of the communists, is nonsense, pure nonsense. Building the economy must be left to others, to the bourgeoisie which is much more educated, or to intellectuals in the bourgeois camp. We ourselves are not yet sufficiently educated for that."

It is true that Lenin spoke in this way then[6] to justify the N.E.P. (New Economic Policy) which consisted in allowing free enterprise to the bourgeois and technicians of the bourgeoisie still remaining in Russia, in order to get production, which had virtually come to a standstill as a result of the destructive and paralysing action of the State, back on its feet. From 1920, rather than allow the workers and their organisations (the development of which would become an embarrassment to the communist governments) to participate actively in a renewal of the economy,

5 We would remind the reader of the 900 new models of shoes in Elda, the new funicular design in Barcelona, the new transport lines, etc. . . .
6 He had expressed similar views in 1920.

Lenin preferred to make use of his class enemies.[7] But such was the situation that at the end of four and a half years, he was obliged to have recourse to this . . . heroic remedy!

Furthermore if we analyse certain aspects of the present Russian economy, at least at what is more or less verifiable, we note for example, an extraordinary backwardness in agriculture. More than 25 years ago, Stalin was promising, and his successors continue to promise the people "free bread" a slogan with which the French, Italian and Spanish communists hoax their supporters. But free bread (the consumption of which, in the capitalist countries is decreasing anyway and would not represent such an extraordinary conquest) is still only *the bait which hides the hook.*

Another more convincing and important fact is that 45% of the population is actively engaged in the countryside in Russia. In the United States it is 6% and in France 20%. This demonstrates the technical deficiencies of the Russian Communist agrarian organisation, a deficiency which has to be made up by human labour, in spite of the technical progress that has been proclaimed *urbi et orbi* for the past 40 years.

And this is not the most important fact. We are now further from communism than we were in 1917. For communism implies economic equality. But whereas we have seen this equality being established *from the beginning of the constitution of the Spanish Libertarian Collectives,* it is not even any longer a hopeful promise for the men and women land workers grouped in the *Kolkhozes* and *Sovkhozes,* the collective organisations born of the regime referred to—derisively—as communist.

For there are fundamental differences between these organisations and the agrarian Collectives in Spain. The *Kolkhozes* and *Sovkhozes* were created by the State, by State bureaucracy. Producers and ordinary inhabitants live there under the orders of a class of functionaries and technicians who plan, decide, dictate orders as to what must be done or not done according to instructions received from the various ministries. This class, in turn, is controlled by the Communist cell, which at the same time controls all the members of the community including the tractor drivers, the employees of the machine depots, nurses and

---

7 The party faction called "Workers' Opposition" of which Alexandra Kollontai and Chlapnikof were the leaders demanded in vain the participation of workers' syndicates in the building of the economy. She was persecuted.

teachers. Most women have to do the heaviest work (driving tractors and machinery, road maintenance work, etc.). So much so that the women in the *Kolkhoz*, deformed in the course of a life of hard labour, give the visitor the impression of a rough. coarse creature who has lost all traces of femininity.

Piecework was widespread in the *Kolkhozes* and *Sovkhozes* (we do not believe it has been abolished in the recent past) and the wage categories, as well as the "norms" to achieve, were arbitrarily fixed by the leaders of each production cell. And let us not forget that all this exists after 50 years of a regime said to be communist.

Now, nothing similar occurred in the Spanish Collectives where everybody took part in the assemblies. could say what they liked to anyone without fear of reprisals.

In Russia the privileged classes seem to be irremediably established, for they are encrusted in the State, they *are* the State, and castes of the State created by the State. Proofs abound

Thus the Moscow review *Partiinaia Jizn* (The Life of the Party) gave the following figures for 1964: 37.3% of the Russian Communist Party's members were workers; 16.5% were peasants (bear in mind that the latter represent 45% of the population) Out of 11,758,169 members, 5,408,000 were technocrats, bureaucrats, and other members of the "intelligentsia", the latter category constituting, thanks to its superior education, the "new privileged class" with their cars, their "dachas" (country houses), their domestics, their military orderlies, their fine apartments and pleasant holidays on the shores of the Black Sea.

The contrast between the regime founded by so-called State Communism, which was no other than State capitalism, and that founded by the Spanish Revolution was absolute, and it was one of the reasons why the Spanish Communists and their masters combated—and both continue to do so implacably—our constructive achievement.

Furthermore in Spain industrial production was maintained at a high degree of productivity so long as there was no shortage of raw materials and power. Whereas in the U.S.S.R. where these (iron, coal, oil, cotton, wool) could be produced in the country itself, especially in the south, they were in short supply even in the areas where they were produced, due to disorganisation caused by the regime itself, and this continued even when the Civil War ended in 1921.

Kruschev's skilful propaganda put the blame for the non-development of Russian industry onto the Tsarist regime, and for their setbacks on the consequences of the international and civil war. Well, that was not the reason! Even if one takes account of the ravages of war in all its manifestations, in the last analysis it was the regime that sprang from the Bolshevik Revolution that itself undertook to transform the partial paralysis into a general paralysis. "At the time of the census of 28 August, 1920, there were 37,226 industrial enterprises belonging to the State and employing almost two million workers," wrote the economist Serge Procopovicz in his monumental *Economic History of the U.S.S.R.* He continued by pointing out that "on the 1st September of the same year, that is two months after the census was taken, only 6,508 undertakings employing 1,300,000 workers, were shown in the records of the Superior Council of the National Economy."

What do these figures mean? That actuated by its domineering will, the State was causing the disappearance of a great number of undertakings at a giddy rate, by a systematic centralisation, or by the cutting off, of supplies of raw materials or power. It was not the only reason, The seizure of the management of work by the functionaries spread like a cancer, or a swelling of cancers.[8] On the eve of the Revolution there were in Russia 65 blast-furnaces which produced in 1912 5,200,000 tons of steel (France produced in the same year 4,207,000). At the time of the Revolution half the blast-furnaces were still operating. But in 1922, the year when Lenin uttered the words we have quoted, steel production had dropped to 255,000 tons.

Once again the explanation for this vertical drop is in the first place due to statism pushed to its limits by the Bolshevik government, which eliminated the able employers (there were some, there are some everywhere) and the technicians who had to be replaced by bringing in others from Germany and the United States at the time of the world economic crisis.

Another cause of this extraordinary setback was the resistance shown by the personnel in the factories who, from 1918, that is nine months after the Bolsheviks had seized power, began to protest against the introduction of police methods by the

8 At the time of our stay in Moscow in 1921 Kamanev declared at a meeting of the Pan-Russian Railway Committee: "There were 250,000 state employers under Tsarism for the whole of Russia. Today there are 240,000 in Moscow alone."

party in power, which most of the workers opposed,[9] and against the stifling of workers' freedom in the factories. The apologists would say that these workers were worked on by the Mensheviks and counter-revolutionaries. Well, read what Kirov, one of the outstanding members of the Communist Party, wrote at the beginning of 1919:

"All the work of organising the economic life of the country has been done, so far, with the direct participation of the Unions and the representatives of the working masses. The Unions and factory workers delegate conferences in certain industrial branches have been the principal and only laboratories in which the economic organisational services of Russia were formed, and are still formed."

A situation comparable to that in Spain. But whereas in Spain the prime-movers of the Revolution enlarged and perfected this workers' management which gave the kind of results we have seen (bearing in mind the difficulties due to a growing shortage of raw materials and power, opposition by the political parties, food shortages at a certain stage due to the occupation of food growing areas by Franco's armies), in Russia Lenin, who rectified and changed his opinions at each congress, decided that the management of production had to be taken over by the bourgeoisie in order to remedy the paralysis he criticised yet which he continually strengthened. Stalin's monstrous dictatorship, which was the blossoming of that set up by Lenin, was needed to incorporate into this system, at the price of millions of lives, an economy which would have built itself without dictatorship if state worship had not annihilated everything.

If we seek to establish the difference between the Russo-Bolshevik revolution and the Spanish Revolution, we can summarize it, so far as production and economic life as a whole are concerned, as follows:

In Russia after the seizure of power by the Bolsheviks who imposed their dictatorship and set about governing through the State, everything continued to crumble for years both in agriculture and industry as well as in the public services, to the point of dragging from Lenin's lips the admission we have

9 This discontent came from the fact that at the time of the elections for the Constituent Assembly (in January 1918) the Communist Party had only obtained 25% of the votes, that is 10 million; and the revolutionary socialists 50% or 20 million; seeing which the Bolsheviks closed down the Assembly and started to persecute all those who did not accept their dictatorship.

quoted and obliging him to drop socialism completely and have recourse to the N.E.P. as a result of which the economy was on the road to recovery until the years 1926-27. Stalin continued along those lines after eliminating those to whom Lenin had had recourse.

In Spain except in those cases where raw materials were soon in short supply, agrarian and industrial production did not suffer interruptions, apart from the few days following the euphoria of the successes of July 19, but even that was not general. Factories, workshops, transport, public services were rapidly set in motion, except for the building industry in Barcelona, the financial mechanism of which is always unusual.[10]

There is no doubt that had Franco been defeated the economy would have passed more or less entirely into the hands of the workers, and that our Syndicates would have developed it rapidly with technicians of all kinds, engineers and architects already in their organisation or who had recently joined in sufficiently large numbers. Thanks also to the organising contribution of tens of thousands of libertarian militants[11] who not only had a working knowledge of the problems of labour, production, the various operations of the different trades in a workshop, factory, railway network, but also how the different wheels of the economy in general were geared up and operated.

On the other hand this preparation was completely lacking so far as the majority of the 240,000 members of the Bolshevik Party[12] were concerned and with whom Lenin thought (in September 1917, in a pamphlet reserved for his intimates) he could seize power and maintain it. In general, his professional revolutionaries were not labour professionals. This equally applied to the overwhelming majority of bureaucrats who belonged to the left wing social democrats, who had become communists, and who were completely ignorant of the workings of a factory, or of a workshop, of production and its multidirectional relations, coordination between industrial sectors, geographically scattered or concentrated.

Lenin wanted top men who would manage production under instruction from the Party and the resolutions of the Party

10 The Catalan government paid the wages as the Syndicate had no money. It resulted in stagnation in the building industry.
11 We should recall that at the beginning of 1936 we had 30,000 comrades in prison.
12 Figures given by Lenin, which cannot be checked.

congresses. Politics first, even in the name of the materialist or economic interpretation of history. In that policy were included instructions for the conduct of work and of the workers. Socialism was above all a question of authority. And it remained so. For us it was a question of the organisation of work by the workers, manual and intellectual, and it remained so.

*

While praising and proclaiming the constructive achievements of the Spanish libertarian revolution, this writer recognises that it was not without its failures nor was it perfect. We have stated the objective reasons: the war which largely dominated events as a whole; the inevitable survival of the political parties and social classes attached to a society with traditional classes, and the many-sided hostility of Spanish and international Stalinism directed by Moscow.

But there were also subjective reasons. In the first place if the constructive apparatus was, so far as its technical preparation was concerned, superior by far to what it had been in all previous revolutions, it was also, in our view, insufficiently developed. The reason, and still from a subjective point of view, was two-fold: on the one hand the struggles waged for sixty-six years (which we have sketched in the chapter "The Men and the Struggles") because they were so time consuming absorbing forces and energies, prevented the organisation from moving further forward. For this would have required much more thought, which our rank and file militants, who were also struggling against poverty and hunger, and often lacked a sufficient intellectual preparation, could not undertake. On the other hand, demagogic elements in our movement who exercised a negative, anti-syndicalist and anti-organisational influence which had to be combated, contributed, as we have already pointed out to slowing down the constitution of the federations of industry, the existence of which would have made it possible to syndicalise production more quickly and more completely, and above all, the organisation of distribution.

It is true that no social—nor even political—revolution has ever been prepared beforehand in every detail so far as the positive achievements are concerned and we can in the circumstances feel proud of the bases that were established before 1936. Nevertheless we have the right and even the duty to judge our-

Y

selves with severity, and to recognise our weaknesses, our errors or failings. We would have been more successful if our movement had done more towards that economic and technical preparation. That the others did much less or nothing at all and still do not in this age when so many intellectuals, lacking intelligence and with utter irresponsibility, publicly lay claim to a revolution about which they haven't the slightest constructive thought, does nothing to help. Proudhon, Bakunin and Kropotkin, the greatest theoreticians of libertarian socialism, always recommended, especially Proudhon and Bakunin, that this preparation of revolutionary construction should be as advanced as possible. This was in violent contrast to the inexplicable Marxist incomprehension, as evidenced not only in the writings of Marx[12] but also of Kautsky and even Rosa Luxemburg, which always, in the name of so-called "scientific" socialism, combated all anticipation concerning the post-revolutionary society. One can now see where it has led those countries euphemistically called "popular democracies".

Without organic preparation no social and truly socialist revolution is possible. The chances of success depend on the extent of the pre-existing constructive capacity. But this does not mean that the preparation should be only intellectual and technical. It must be, above all, moral, for the degree of specialised intellectuality and technicality achieved depends on the degree of consciousness which creates the sense of duty, imposing the acquisition of the required disciplines. It is above all this awareness of their responsibilities that predominated among the Spanish anarchists, influenced their struggles, their individual behaviour, their propaganda among, and organisation of, the workers in the countryside and in the towns, and their invincible persistence in the struggle waged for a better world and a happier mankind. Without these qualities all the intelligence and techniques in the world would not have been of much use.

Our constructive revolutionary achievement was destroyed by the Francoist victory and by the sabotage and betrayal of Stalin and his agents. But it remains in history as an example and a proof that it is possible to avoid the dictatorial stages when the capacity to organise the new society quickly is present; and

13 Marx wittily poked fun at "the recipes for the casseroles of the future society" and his international disciples naturally fell into step.

dispense with the so-called dictatorship of the proletariat, or more exactly the revolutionary party usurping the representation or delegation of the proletariat which those drunk with power —their power to which the people must bow—persist in wanting to impose on us under pain of massacring us as counter-revolutionaries. Just as in their time Marx and Blanqui, and more recently Lenin and his henchmen and all dictatorial maniacs, they have not the faintest idea of how to reorganise social life after capitalism. But just as Lenin did, they would very quickly organise a police force, a censorship, and in due course concentration camps.

A new way has been indicated, an achievement which emerges as a beacon light of which all revolutionaries who seek mankind's emancipation and not its subjection to a new slavery will have to follow. If they do, yesterday's defeat will be largely compensated for by tomorrow's victories.

BIBLIOGRAPHICAL NOTES

The original French edition contained no bibliography and I do not propose to include an exhaustive one in this edition. There are already three excellent ones which between them cover the period from the First International in Spain up to 1969 and which can be readily consulted, and supplemented for information on the growing number of Spanish and other publications that are now appearing, by the journal of the C.I.R.A.

Gerald Brenan's *Spanish Labyrinth* (Cambridge 1943) covers all the historic period of the revolutionary and socialist movements up to 1936. Frank Mintz's *l'Autogestion dans l'Espagne Révolutionnaire* (Paris 1970) has a 25-page Bibliographical Essay of considerable importance since it includes references to pamphlets, Manifestos, Conference Reports, etc., issued during the events of 1936-39 with special reference to the agricultural and industrial Collectives. And then there is Burnett Bolloten's *The Grand Camouflage* (London 1961) which contains a vast bibliography covering the political aspects of the Civil War in general. However it is the bibliographical references in the footnotes to at least two chapters that are of most value so far as the Collectives are concerned. Chapter 3 on *The Revolution* and Chapter 5 on *The Revolution in the Countryside* are a mine of references to reports from, and accounts of, collectivisations which if followed up would certainly provide material for a full scale work.

REPORTAJES DE «SOLIDARIDAD OBRERA»

Las Juventudes Libertarias crean la moderna Universidad Popular

por JOAQUIN CIERVO

TIERRA Y LIBERTAD

LABOR CULTURAL

Conviene que todas las iniciativas favorables a la cultura tengan una base funcional más que una base orgánica, porque la función crea el órgano

Cultura y solidaridad

por J A. Menéris

A DEEP CONCERN FOR EDUCATION WAS ALWAYS IN THE FOREFRONT OF ANARCHIST PROPAGANDA BOTH BEFORE AND DURING THE REVOLUTION.

(Top) "The Libertarian Youth have created the Popular University" (*Solidaridad Obrera*—CNT daily 27/8/36). *Tierra y Libertad*, the FAI weekly (Sept. 5, 1936) stresses that all initiatives dealing with culture should emphasise a "functional" rather than an "organic basis", for "function creates the organ". "Culture and Solidarity" is the subject of an article in *Soli* (29/10/36); "Culture & Pedagogy" was the weekly organ of the Provincial Teaching Syndicate of Jaen. *(Bottom)* The "Bulletin of the Building, Woodworkers and Decorators Syndicate" (Barcelona) has its cultural feature on the back page dealing with "Art through the Ages—and in present day construction".

And to supplement these, is the Bulletin of C.I.R.A. (International Centre for Anarchist Research) which appears twice a year (Geneva).

＊

In the *Preamble* to this volume Leval deals admirably and succinctly with revolutionary history, geography and economics, the relevance of which may not have been apparent to some readers until they were plunged into the material, physical and political problems that faced the collectives.

On the subject of the pioneering work of the libertarian movement Max Nettlau's *La Première Internationale en Espagne (1868-1888)* (Dordrecht Holland 1969) painstakingly edited and annotated by Renée Lamberet is a monument to them and to the great Austrian anarchist historian himself. But being a source work it is beyond most of us and needs to be digested by interpreters we can trust. Though this volume was not available when Gerald Brenan's *Spanish Labyrinth* was written his is still the only valuable and readable history in English.

Of the more recent history (1900-1936) of the revolutionary libertarian movement, the non-academic historians—José Peirats in *Los Anarquistas en la Crisis Politica Española* (Buenos Aires. 1964) and Ildefonso Gonzales in *Il Movimento Libertario Spagnuolo* (Napoli, 1953)—are to be preferred to the academic historian Cesar M. Lorenzo in *Les Anarchistes Espagnols et le Pouvoir 1868-1969* (Paris, 1969), though the latter is the more widely quoted in academic circles (e.g. J. Romero Maura on *The Spanish Case* (Government & Opposition, Vol. 5, No. 4, London, 1970) refers to it as "one of the best works on Spanish anarchism in the '30s").

In translating Chapter III on *Materials for a Revolution* as well as when dealing with contemporary statistical material quoted by Leval I needed to check the actual figures he gives to avoid repeating any misprints in the original, and found Ramón Tamames' *Estructura Economica de España* (Madrid, 1960. Revised and enlarged 1964) an 800-page readable vade-mecum which besides confirming Leval's statistics had a lot more space for the author to answer every statistical question that one could think of asking as well as being positively critical of the economic performance and programme of the Franco regime to date.

＊

Página 4   SOLIDARIDAD OBRERA   Domingo, 1 Noviembre 1936

REPORTAJES DE «SOLIDARIDAD OBRERA»

Las grandes transformaciones sociales que ha traído la lucha antifascista

Los importantes Almacenes El Aguila, de la antigua razón social Bosch Labrús Hermanos, S. en C., convertidos en Sociedad Obrera C. N. T.
Diez sucursales en España controladas por los trabajadores

Página 2   SOLIDARIDAD·OBRERA   Miércoles, 27 Enero 1937

REPORTAJES DE «SOLIDARIDAD OBRERA»

El espíritu constructivo de la C. N. T.

La industria, en manos de sus obreros

(CONCLUSION)

Jueves 10 de Febrero de 1938   Fragua Social

LABOR CONSTRUCTIVA DE LA C. N. T.

La Colectividad Confederal de Amposta.
Unos resultados - que acreditan la magnífica capacidad creadora del proletariado

CRONICAS MURCIANAS

LA FABRICA COLECTIVIZADA DE «LA ARBOLEDA»

UNA MAGNIFICA OBRA SOCIAL DE LA U. G. T. Y LA C. N. T. UNIDAS
Por T. Cano Ruiz

THE SOCIAL REVOLUTION IN DAY BY DAY REPORTS IN THE LIBERTARIAN PRESS IN SPAIN.

(Top) "The Great Social Transformations brought about by the anti-fascist struggle. The important department stores El Aguila . . . converted into a C.N.T. workers' Society. Ten branches in Spain controlled by the workers" (*S.O.* 1/11/36). "The Constructive Spirit of the CNT. Industry in the hands of its workers" (*S.O.* 27/1/37). "The Confederal Collective of Amposta. Results which do credit to the magnificent creative capacity of the workers." (*Fragua Social* CNT daily, Valencia 10/2/38.) *(Bottom)* "The collectivised factory of La Arboleda in Lorqui [near Murcia]. A magnificent social effort by the united U.G.T. and C.N.T." (*Soli* no date).

[360]

The importance of Parts 2, 3 and 4 as source material cannot be overestimated when one considers what first hand material on the Collectives is available, apart from the articles and pamphlets published at the time (some of which are listed in Bolloten & Mintz). There are two slender volumes: Alardo Prats' *Vanguardia y retraguardia de Aragon* (Buenos Aires, n.d.) and Augustin Souchy's *Entre Los campesinos de Aragon. El comunismo libertario en las comarcas liberadas* (Barcelona, 1937). However works are now being published in Spain on the collectives and Albert Perez-Baro's *30 meses de collectivisme a Catalunya* (Barcelona, 1970), for instance, is important because it is by a militant of the CNT from pre-1936 years who was closely connected with the legislation on collectivisation in Catalonia. There are, however, a number of works on the Civil War which contain material on the collectives derived from the sources already referred to. Souchy and Polgare in *Colectivizaciones. La obra constructiva de la revolucion española, ensayos, documentos, reportajes* (Barcelona, 1937) contains some original material as well as using published sources and documents; José Peirats in *La C.N.T. en la Revolución Española* (Toulouse, 1951, Reprinted Paris, 1971) Volume 1 devotes a 90-page chapter to the Collectives, of interest for the many documents that are reproduced.

In English *Spain & the World* (a fortnightly journal published by FREEDOM PRESS from 1936-39) carried a number of articles on the collectives, some originals such as on *Albalate del Cinca* (No. 7) and on the Collectivised Milk Industry (No. 47) both by Emma Goldman; and Robert Louzon's exhaustive study of the Collectivised town of Puigcerda (Nos. 17-19); *A village in Aragon* written by an English militiaman (No. 35) and two posthumous little pieces by Camillo Berneri on the Catalan villages of *Pobla and Sadurni de Noya* (No. 17)—as well as translations from the Spanish originals on a wide range of topics: from the *Collectivisation of Properties in Badalona* (No. 3) and the *Socialisation of the Wood Industry* (No. 28) [which employed no less than 12,000 workers], to *The Collectivisation of Transport in Barcelona* (No. 29) and the *Victualling Industry* (No. 37). In addition there were reports on a number of Collectives including *Graus* (20), *Balsareny* (27), *Hospitalet* (34), *Prat de Llobregat* (38), *Segorbe* (42), *Liria* (43) and on *The Workers Statute in Palancia* (42).

More recently *The Anarchist Collectives* edited by Sam Dolgoff (New York, 1974) attempts to bridge the gap of silence on the

"NOSOTROS PROPUGNAMOS LA COLECTIVIZACION INMEDIATA DE LOS GRANDES LATIFUNDIOS, PERO RESPETAMOS LA PEQUE-ÑA PROPIEDAD Y LA INICIATIVA PRIVADA" - dice el Comité Regional de la C. N. T. a los pequeños propietarios campesinos de Cataluña.

¡¡¡Trabajadores campesinos de Cataluña!!!

Es deber insoslayable en esta hora histórica el de cooperar activamente en las tareas de reconstrucción social que hemos iniciado.

Deber cuya responsabilidad no puede rehuir nadie. Todos los sectores sociales productores de Cataluña, hemos de compartir ese deber sagrado aceptando la responsabilidad que nos corresponda.

Cataluña está hoy dando ejemplo al mundo de su capacidad constructiva. Es el espejo en que se mira el resto del proletariado peninsular, por sus anhelos creadores Cataluña es la meca del sentido social ibérico, donde se presta a los poblemas económicos la atención e interés máximos, siempre desde un ángulo de visión de vanguardia.

Campesinos y obreros industriales de Cataluña somos los llamados a colaborar al unísono y con gran empeño en esta tarea. Más para que la colaboración sea eficaz es imprescindible laborar en un plano de confianza mutua, de recíproco respeto; en un plano de solidaridad fraterna y de sinceridad y nobleza comunes.

El deber primordial de unos y otros es el de impulsar el ritmo de la producción agrícola los primeros, y de acelerar la producción industrial los segundos, adaptándola a lo que las circunstancias aconsejan.

Los campesinos deben prepararse a la sementera, realizando las labores normales. Deben sembrar las tierras sin temor alguno. Sólo agentes provocadores pueden propalar por las comarcas especies canallescas destinadas a producir confusionismo y desorientación entre los camaradas campesinos. Quien esto haga, no puede ser considerado si no como fascista y adversario de la grandeza de Cataluña.

La CONFEDERACION NACIONAL DEL TRABAJO sale hoy al paso de tan malévolas especies que sólo buscan la ruina de esta tierra ejemplar. Sale hoy al paso de esas especies falsas cien por cien, y dice a los trabajadores del agro catalán:

· Camaradas: Los elementos reaccionarios han tenido como base de su predominio clasista el fomento de una distancia espiritual entre vosotros y el obrero industrial, hermano vuestro. Esta distancia ha desaparecido para siempre. Hoy marchamos todos estrechamente unidos en esta lucha heróica contra la reacción. Unidos como camaradas, como hermanos.

No presteis atención a los que susurran a vuestro oído especies de terror; son sujetos indeseables a los que se debe aplicar su merecido inmediatamente en pago a su labor desorientadora. No deis oídos a los que os invitan a dejar las tierras en baldío; son anticatalanes indignos de pisar nuestro suelo fecundo y fértil. Debeis realizar las labores agrícolas normales sin temor de ninguna especie. Nadie piensa en despojaros del fruto de vuestro sudor, ni la CONFEDERACION NACIONAL DEL TRABAJO lo consentiría; es nuestra tónica dominante la justicia social y por nada del mundo toleraríamos el menor vejámen de que se pretendiese haceros objeto.

No debeis temer, pequeños propietarios campesinos, el afán colectivista de la hora presente. Nosotros propugnamos la colectivización inmediata de los grandes latifundios; pero respetamos la pequeña propiedad, fruto del esfuerzo continuo, y la iniciativa privada. Tal fué el sentir del reciente y magno Congreso Regional de Campesinos de Cataluña; y tal es el sentir nacional de la C. N. T.

La CONFEDERACION NACIONAL DEL TRABAJO, trabajadores del campo catalán, quiere que la confianza renazca en vosotros y reemprendais con entusiasmo las faenas de laboreo y abono de las tierras que señala la estación. No se os va a hacer víctimas de ninguna clase de despojo. de nosotros no podeis esperar más que apoyo y solidaridad en todo momento y en cualquier trance. Entre unos y otros no puede haber diferencias; somos hermanos en el trabajo y en los anhelos de edificar una vida nueva, donde la laboriosidad, la justicia y el apoyo mutuo sean la base.

Que desaparezca de vosotros el recelo y la suspicacia, engendrados por elementos enemigos de la causa antifascista. El sudor de vuestro trabajo es la cosa más sagrada y digna de respeto que pueda existir, y nosotros os ayudaremos a hacerla respetar de quien voluntariamente no sepa rendir tributo al trabajo, fuente de toda vida.

Proseguid, campesinos de Cataluña, fomentando la cria del ganado vacuno y del porcino, filón respetable de ingresos para la economía catalana. Proseguid prestando atención a la avicultura y demás derivados agrícolas. El ruido de las fábricas y la vida de vértigo de la ciudad, no nos han hecho olvidar que la agricultura es la base fundamental de la economía ibérica. Sabemos apreciar en todo su valor vuestro esfuerzo precioso, vuestro trabajo intenso, y sólo queremos que depositeis en nosotros la misma confianza que os brindamos, que nos hableis con la misma franqueza, con el mismo tono de sinceridad, que tengais en nosotros la misma fe que en vosotros tenemos.

No queremos, sino ayudaros. Ayudaros a salir de la esclavitud económica en que vivis, como nosotros. No ignoramos que un pequeño propietario no es un capitalista, sino un trabajador cubierto de necesidades insatisfechas. Y no ignorando esto. mal puede pensar nadie que alimentamos animosidad alguna contra quien es un trabajador como nosotros.

¡¡Trabajadores campesinos de Cataluña!!

En esta hora decisiva y preciosa, no cabe más que un fraternal consejo:

¡¡A trabajar!!

¡¡A trabajar por el triunfo definitivo de la causa antifascista y renovadora!!

¡¡A trabajar por Cataluña!!

¡¡Viva la C. N. T.!!

EL COMITE REGIONAL

A leaflet issued by the Regional Committee of the CNT in Barcelona in 1936 and addressed to the peasant smallholders in Catalonia in which they declare "We advocate the immediate collectivisation of the large estates but respect small property and individual initiative" This was intended as a counterblast to the accusations made by the Stalinists that the CNT were aiming at forced collectivisation in the Catalan countryside.

collectives by condensing Leval, Souchy, Peirats and others, as well as including a running commentary by the editor all into 180 pages.

*

Though a growing number of books are now appearing on the political, and politico-revolutionary aspects of the Civil War very little has been done either to present material on the Collectives or to seek to draw more than superficial conclusions from them. Because the "politicians" in the CNT-FAI were busy trying to be statesmen they virtually played no part in the collectivist movement, which may explain their indifference, and even hostility, to it. It is not surprising that there should have been no great love between "anarchist" Ministers seeking "to make the revolution from above" and workers and peasants actu-ally making the revolution in the occupied factories and fields. Quite recently one such ex-Minister, Federica Montseny, writing in the Italian anarchist weekly *Umanità Nova* (Sept. 8, 1973) in defence of the political manoeuvres in which she and the other leading lights were engaged, considered that "the flight of most employers and landowners induced the workers to take over industrial and agricultural production and to proceed to the collectivisation of the land, and the communal exploitation of production. This was relatively straightforward and easy" com-pared with the political problems at government level. As if collectivisation was simply an economic question without its own political or social implications!

Fortunately Gaston Leval has continued over the years to keep the subject alive, and has published much additional source material as well as drawing conclusions from it in various anarchist publications, but especially in his own monthly journal *Cahiers de l'Humanisme Libertaire* (Paris) which is in its 20th year and of which more than 200 issues have so far appeared. Whether or not one shares Leval's libertarian humanism, or his inter-pretations of economics and politics, or even his three loves. Proudhon, Bakunin and Kropotkin, it must be admitted that he is publishing one of the few intelligent, stimulating journals of ideas, to be found today, combining factual notes on con-temporary economics, interpretation of the anarchist classics. and controversy obviously meant to shake the complacent sloganisers in the revolutionary movement. The achievement is the greater bearing in mind that he has celebrated his 80th birthday!

The one serious attempt to analyse the whole collectivist experiment is undoubtedly Frank Mintz's *l'Autogestion dans l'Espagne Révolutionnaire* (Paris, 1970). Its importance is enhanced by the fact that the writer is an anarchist and therefore seeks to answer the kind of questions non-anarchist historians could well consider to be of secondary importance, and vice versa. For instance Hugh Thomas in his essay on "Agrarian Collectives in the Spanish Civil War" in *The Republic and the Civil War in Spain*. Edited by Raymond Carr (London, 1971) lists his conclusions under five headings: the first four are mainly economic considerations. In the fifth he muses that "whatever the economics of the collectives, there is a good deal of evidence for thinking that they were a considerable social success. . . . From the accounts of most of the collectives, even if they are written by anarchist sympathisers, there does radiate a considerable spirit of generous cooperation without many complaints at breach of privacy and at local tyrannies . . .".

Mintz is less concerned with the economic profitability of collectives compared with the old system, and much more with questions of freedom and equality and thus asks Why? and How? did Collectivisation take place. Were they spontaneous or forcibly created? And when he assesses the "Results of Collectivisation" it is to see, for instance, how far they were successful in departing from the old economic and financial system; how successful were they in breaking down the centralised bureaucratic machine, etc.

My only criticism of this important work is that it is too concentrated: some sentences should have been paragraphs and some paragraphs, chapters. (One appreciates the fact that this work was originally conceived for a university thesis, and though revised in 1970 for publication, still conformed to the imposed limitations on length, language and style.) For instance the whole question of the extent of collectivisation is contained in one paragraph which does not explain how the figures are arrived at nor does he interpret his figures which show that whereas in July 1937 there were in the countryside "without a doubt at least 400,000 collectivists and not less than 802 collectives", by the end of 1938 the corresponding figures were 230,000 and 1,015. (Mintz's figures for the number of collectivists are so low that one is tempted to assume that he is referring to the number of heads of families only.) Some explanation was called for over the fall in the number of collectivists in spite of an increase in the number of collectives for as it stands it gives the impression that in the 18 month period many people left existing collectives while others were forming new ones. Whereas the explanation is that in the period in question Franco's forces completed their occupation of Aragon as well as of Castellon de la Plana, one of the five provinces of the Levante, thus sweeping out of existence 400 or more collectives. In other words the two sets of figures given by Mintz have no real bearing on each other though the way they have been presented by the author makes the reader feel that they have and that he should draw conclusions from them. It is a case where brevity creates confusion. Nevertheless it is the only attempt at analysing the collectivist movement published to date and is a pioneering work on the subject.

V.R.

COMPAÑERO CAMPESINO, ESCUCHA:

QUIENES SOMOS

La Confederación Nacional del Trabajo y la Federación Anarquista Ibérica te dirigen la palabra.

Las dos están compuestas por trabajadores de la ciudad y del campo, por obreros y campesinos que, como tú, trabajan para comer mal, y desean vivir mejor.

Por trabajadores, y nada más. No hay, entre nosotros, gente que viva del esfuerzo de los demás, propietarios, capitalistas, rentistas o burgueses que se apropien del fruto del sudor ajeno. Tú y nosotros, nosotros y tú, formamos parte de la misma familia de los que producen todos los medios de vida, y han visto siempre, hasta ahora, a quienes nada hacían, vivir lujosamente, despilfarrar todo mientras carecíamos de lo necesario.

Ha llegado la hora de que esto termine. Escucha, compañero, lo que nosotros, campesinos y obreros de la C.N.T. y de la F.A.I. te decimos.

TU VIDA

Tus padres, tus abuelos, tus antepasados trabajaron la tierra, la hicieron buena para el cultivo. ¿Los recuerdas aún trabajando, azada u horquilla en mano? Tú trabajas también, como ellos hicieron. Tus hijos trabajarán como tú.

¿Quién se benefició de ese trabajo de tus antepasados, de tus abuelos, de tus padres? ¿Quién se beneficia del tuyo? ¿Quién se beneficiará mañana del de tus hijos si las cosas no cambian?

Es el amo, el dueño de la tierra, el propietario.

Es el Estado y toda su burocracia que nos abruman de contribuciones e impuestos.

Es el intermediario que comercia con los frutos de tu trabajo.

Pagas un treinta, un cuarenta por ciento de las cosechas al dueño de la tierra.

Pagas impuestos muy pesados al recaudador.

El intermediario vende por cien pesetas lo que te pagó cincuenta.

Es verdad que en estos momentos, gracias a la revolución que hicieron la C.N.T. y la F.A.I., esto ha disminuido o cesado en parte. Pero ha cesado sólo de momento, si no te decides a venir con nosotros para que terratenientes, recaudadores de impuestos e intermediarios no puedan imponerse de nuevo.

Cuando hay una buena cosecha de trigo, de arroz, de patatas, de naranjas, de uva o de cualquier otro producto, en lugar de salir beneficiado, como debería ser, sales perjudicado, pues bajo el pretexto de que hay exceso te pagan tan barato que no te recompensan, ni te dan medios de vida.

Cuando hay una mala cosecha, tienes poco que vender y cobras poco.

Todo resulta malo, todo se vuelve contra ti del modo que están organizadas las cosas. Pero el terrateniente sigue viviendo bien, el Estado cobra sus impuestos, el intermediario trafica siempre.

¿Te parece justo esto?

¿Verdad que no?

LO QUE NOSOTROS QUEREMOS

Nosotros, la C.N.T. y la F.A.I., queremos que desaparezcan estas injusticias.

Queremos impedir que otros sean dueños de la tierra que tú trabajas. Queremos impedir que otros vivan de tu esfuerzo, quitándote el veinte, el treinta, el cuarenta por ciento de las cosechas.

Queremos impedir que haya tantos ricos, que no hacen nada, al lado de tantos pobres que trabajan.

Fíjate en una cosa que conoces. Se produce, por ejemplo, una

helada, o una sequía, que destruye una cosecha. Esto, como bien lo sabes, ocurre a menudo. Los campesinos que lo han sufrido quedan sin recursos, pasan un año de miseria, de hambre o escasez.

¿Es lógico? ¿Tienen ellos la culpa? ¿Tienes tú la culpa si ha dejado de llover, si el frío ha llegado inesperadamente, matando los brotes en los árboles, si una plaga destruye tus cereales?

¿Verdad que no? Y si es así, ¿por qué has de ser privado, tú y tu familia, de los medios de existencia que hay en otras partes, cuando a veces se los tira, haciéndote falta a ti?

Nosotros queremos que todo esto termine. Queremos que si un año no puedes ofrecer, por causas de la naturaleza, tantos productos como en los años anteriores, no dejes de recibir lo que precises, siempre, naturalmente, que lo haya en otras partes.

Sabemos que en tales condiciones tú estarías dispuesto también a mandar tus productos a otros campesinos, que fuesen víctimas de la helada, de la sequía o de la plaga.

Por lo tanto, además de suprimir a los que explotan el trabajo ajeno, a los que se enriquecen con él, queremos establecer una sociedad en la cual todos los hombres sean solidarios, donde ninguno pase hambre, donde cada uno esté dispuesto a ayudar al que necesite su ayuda, y ha de recibirla también cuando la necesite.

Tal es lo que defienden la C.N.T. y la F.A.I.

¿COMO ORGANIZAR ESTO?

Vamos a explicarte ahora cómo pensamos organizar esto.

Queremos hacerlo sin políticos, sin burocracia, sin parlamentos. El mundo ha de ser de los trabajadores. Trabajamos, tú y nosotros, en el campo, en la fábrica, en la mina. Debemos organizarnos nosotros mismos, por nuestra cuenta, en nuestros sindicatos y nuestras comunas.

Sólo sirven las asociaciones de trabajadores. Lo demás es nido de vividores.

Producen unos campesinos oliva y uva. Otros producen arroz, o trigo, o naranjas. Los productores de oliva y uva constituyen una aso-

ciación, constituyen otra los productores de arroz, de hortalizas, de trigo, de naranjas. Con los otros campesinos unidos en tu federación, envías a los demás los productos tuyos. Ellos te envían los suyos. Envías tus productos a las ciudades. Los obreros de las ciudades te envían a su vez ropas, zapatos, muebles, herramientas, máquinas, aparatos de radio, etcétera.

¿Es esto difícil? Ciertamente no. Basta tener voluntad de realizarlo, basta asociarte con nosotros, y acompañarnos en esta obra de emancipación para que se realice en muy poco tiempo.

LA PEQUEÑA PROPIEDAD

Los que quieren mantenerte en la miseria, para vivir de ella, afirman que pretendemos arrancar su tierra al pequeño propietario del campo.

Es una artimaña para que no vayas con los que te enseñan el camino recto.

Nosotros queremos quitar la tierra al que no la trabaja. Queremos quitarla al que tiene más de lo que puede cultivar.

Sabemos que la mayor parte de los pequeños propietarios del campo vivirían mucho mejor si la sociedad fuera más justa. Comprendemos su amor a la tierra, que le suministra los medios de existencia.

Por estas razones, no pensamos atacar al pequeño propietario.

Pero sabemos que el trabajo da mucho más resultado cuando la tierra se cultiva en común.

Si diez pequeños propietarios suprimen las divisiones entre sus campos, podrán servirse de las máquinas modernas, que disminuirán su esfuerzo. En cambio, el pequeño propietario, aislado, no puede comprar estas máquinas, y debe trabajar terriblemente para obtener las cosechas. Además, su aislamiento le deja indefenso en los años malos.

Si se trata de un trabajo que no requiere, como el trigo y otros cereales, la maquinaria agrícola; si se trata, por ejemplo, del cultivo de plantas hortícolas, la producción en común da también excelentes resultados.

Alrededor de las grandes ciudades europeas se hacen tres o cuatro cosechas al año, gracias a esta forma de cultivo. Pero para obtenerlas se necesitan instalaciones especiales de cañerías, calefacción, estufas, invernaderos; se necesita emplear elementos químicos especiales, lo que resulta demasiado caro para el campesino aislado. Sólo pueden emplearlo los que trabajan en las colectivizaciones, o los propietarios que explotan ocho, diez o más obreros.

Para disminuir vuestro esfuerzo, o para conseguir lo menos el doble de productos, necesitáis, compañeros campesinos, trabajar la tierra en común.

Esto no significa que pretendamos imponéroslo por la fuerza. Quien os lo dice, miente. Sabemos que, con el tiempo, al ver los mejores resultados obtenidos, los que no se convenzan en seguida irán convenciéndose después.

Pero queremos ponerte en guardia, camarada, contra los que procuran aumentar las pequeñas propiedades existentes, y te dicen que la pequeña propiedad es necesaria.

Lo hacen para ponerte contra nosotros, para que la división entre los trabajadores del campo y los de la ciudad no les permita volverse, juntos, contra los que los mantienen en la miseria.

No queremos arrancar a la fuerza su tierra al pequeño propietario, pero le decimos: «La pequeña propiedad no permite comprar las máquinas agrícolas, o pagarlas si se compran; no permite mejorar el cultivo de la tierra como es debido. Mantiene, por lo tanto, y mantendrá siempre al campesino que la posea en la miseria.

«La propiedad pone al campesino a merced del rico, que le compra su tierra por nada en los años de malas cosechas. Le hace víctima del intermediario, que le paga por nada sus productos.

»Quien la defiende engaña miserablemente al campesino.

»Debes rechazarlo por embustero, hipócrita y traidor.»

TODOS JUNTOS, CAMARADA

Todos juntos, camarada, vamos a construir el mundo de los trabajadores.

El... de los trabajadores verdaderos, de los que empuñan la azada o el martillo, la lima o la hoz, el pico o la pala, de los que manejan el arado y la locomotora.

Todos juntos, camarada, vamos a suprimir la miseria, para que nuestros hijos no conozcan la falta de alimento, de ropa, de cuidados, de instrucción.

Todos juntos, camarada, vamos a impedir que vuelva el terrateniente, el propietario de la tierra que trabajas, el recaudador de impuestos inútiles, el intermediario ladrón.

Obreros y campesinos, unidos, en la C.N.T. y en la F.A.I., vamos a libertarnos para siempre, vamos a hacer triunfar la justicia, la igualdad, la felicidad, en un mundo redimido y organizado por nuestra cuenta y para nuestras necesidades.

Si esta obra te parece bien, camarada, ven a nuestras filas.

Te esperamos.

THE COMPLETE TEXT OF A PAMPHLET ISSUED BY THE F.A.I. REGIONAL COMMITTEE OF ANARCHIST GROUPS IN DECEMBER 1936 OR JANUARY 1937, AND DIRECTED TO WORKERS ON THE LAND. IT WAS THE FIRST OF A SERIES OF POLICY PAMPHLETS DECIDED UPON AT THE REGIONAL PLENUM ON DECEMBER 6, 1936.

It is an excellent example of simple, clear, meaningful propaganda. It is human in approach without any histrionics, factual without obscuring the message. "Comrade Peasant, Listen" begins by answering the question "Who are we?" and "we" are workers and peasants like yourselves. Next in a few telling sentences "Your Life" is outlined. Who has been exploiting generations of workers if not the landowner, the State, the middleman? When the harvest is good they pay you less on the pretext that the market is glutted and when it's bad you get less because you have less to sell. "Do you think this right? You don't, do you?" "What we want" outlines the CNT-FAI's programme to abolish these injustices and to encourage mutual aid among producers and "How to organise this" without politicians and bureaucrats is by learning to organise ourselves in our syndicates and in the communes. Direct exchange will be encouraged. "Small Property" is no problem. "We only want to seize the land of those who don't work it or who have more than they can work themselves." We respect the smallholder but know that we can work the land more effectively by joining together. Ten smallholders removing their boundary fences will then be able to use modern machinery and reduce human effort. The isolated worker cannot afford such machinery anyway, and feels his isolation especially in the lean years. "All united, comrade" we will build a world of productive workers. All united we will prevent the return of the landowner, the tax collector and the thieving middleman. . . . If this task seems worthwhile to you come and join us. We are expecting you."

Is this the tone of authoritarians, ready to collectivise the small farmers by force of arms?

ABOUT THE AUTHORS

Gaston Leval (born Pierre Robert Piller, 1895–1978) was the son of a French Communard. He escaped to Spain in 1915 during the First World War, where he met the young firebrand and writer Victor Serge and joined the Confederación Nacional del Trabajo (CNT) anarcho-syndicalist trade union organisation. Travelling in 1921 to Moscow as a CNT delegate to one of the most important organisations of the international communist movement, Leval wrote an influential report and a series of skeptical articles based on his experiences of the Bolshevik regime and attempted to spearhead action on behalf of imprisoned anarchists and socialists. After living in Argentina for much of the 1920s and '30s, Leval returned to Spain and became a militant fighter while documenting the revolution and both urban and rural anarchist collectives.

Across seven decades, **Vernon Richards** maintained an anarchist presence in British publishing. His chosen instrument was Freedom Press, the oldest existing anarchist publishing house in the English-speaking world. He edited the anarchist paper *Freedom*—and its prewar and wartime variations—into the 1960s. Earlier, he had been imprisoned in 1945, translated the Italian anarchist Errico Malatesta, and photographed George Orwell.

Pedro García-Guirao currently teaches Spanish language, politics, and history at the University of Southampton (UK). He is among a new generation of scholars who are venturing into the critical study of taboo and uncomfortable subjects previously absent from the history of Spanish anarchism through the Spanish Civil War, the Franco regime, and the democratic transition.

Stuart Christie is a Scottish anarchist writer and publisher. He served over three years of a twenty-year sentence for "banditry and terrorism" imposed by a Spanish court for his part in an attempt to assassinate General Franco in 1964. Five years later he was arrested and imprisoned in London for eighteen months for alleged involvement with Britain's Angry Brigade before being acquitted.

INDEX

"Passim" (literally "scattered") indicates intermittent discussion of a topic over a cluster of pages.

ABOUT PM PRESS

PM Press was founded at the end of 2007 by a small collection of folks with decades of publishing, media, and organizing experience. PM Press co-conspirators have published and distributed hundreds of books, pamphlets, CDs, and DVDs. Members of PM have founded enduring book fairs, spearheaded victorious tenant organizing campaigns, and worked closely with bookstores, academic conferences, and even rock bands to deliver political and challenging ideas to all walks of life. We're old enough to know what we're doing and young enough to know what's at stake.

We seek to create radical and stimulating fiction and non-fiction books, pamphlets, T-shirts, visual and audio materials to entertain, educate, and inspire you. We aim to distribute these through every available channel with every available technology—whether that means you are seeing anarchist classics at our bookfair stalls, reading our latest vegan cookbook at the café, downloading geeky fiction e-books, or digging new music and timely videos from our website.

PM Press is always on the lookout for talented and skilled volunteers, artists, activists, and writers to work with. If you have a great idea for a project or can contribute in some way, please get in touch.

PM Press
PO Box 23912
Oakland, CA 94623
www.pmpress.org

PM Press in Europe
europe@pmpress.org
www.pmpress.org.uk

FRIENDS OF PM PRESS

These are indisputably momentous times—the financial system is melting down globally and the Empire is stumbling. Now more than ever there is a vital need for radical ideas.

In the years since its founding—and on a mere shoestring—PM Press has risen to the formidable challenge of publishing and distributing knowledge and entertainment for the struggles ahead. With over 300 releases to date, we have published an impressive and stimulating array of literature, art, music, politics, and culture. Using every available medium, we've succeeded in connecting those hungry for ideas and information to those putting them into practice.

Friends of PM allows you to directly help impact, amplify, and revitalize the discourse and actions of radical writers, filmmakers, and artists. It provides us with a stable foundation from which we can build upon our early successes and provides a much-needed subsidy for the materials that can't necessarily pay their own way. You can help make that happen—and receive every new title automatically delivered to your door once a month—by joining as a Friend of PM Press. And, we'll throw in a free T-shirt when you sign up.

Here are your options:

- **$30 a month** Get all books and pamphlets plus 50% discount on all webstore purchases

- **$40 a month** Get all PM Press releases (including CDs and DVDs) plus 50% discount on all webstore purchases

- **$100 a month** Superstar—Everything plus PM merchandise, free downloads, and 50% discount on all webstore purchases

For those who can't afford $30 or more a month, we have **Sustainer Rates** at $15, $10 and $5. Sustainers get a free PM Press T-shirt and a 50% discount on all purchases from our website.

Your Visa or Mastercard will be billed once a month, until you tell us to stop. Or until our efforts succeed in bringing the revolution around. Or the financial meltdown of Capital makes plastic redundant. Whichever comes first.

JUR🅐 BOOKS

Jura Books has contributed to the publication of this important book—Leval's *Collectives in the Spanish Revolution*—as part of our 40th anniversary. For all that time we have been a voluntary, non-profit anarchist project that's collectively run. The Jura Books shop has run continuously since it first opened in Newtown in 1977, and in our current location for more than 20 years. This is an incredible achievement if we do say so ourselves—especially for a radical, anti-capitalist project which is 100% powered by volunteers and donations.

JURA BOOKS
BOOKSHOP · INFOSHOP
SOCIAL CENTRE · LIBRARY
ORGANISING SPACE

WWW.JURA.ORG.AU
PH. 9550 9931
440 PARRAMATTA RD, PETERSHAM

For four decades, Jura has been spreading anarchist ideas in Sydney and more broadly. We've sold tens of thousands of books, pamphlets and posters. We've hosted thousands of events—from political talks and reading groups to films, gigs and poetry nights. We've lent support to uncountable campaigns and activist groups as best we could. And in our functioning and structures (notably decision-making), we've demonstrated a real-world example of self-managed, organised anarchism.

For all this time, Jura has only been possible and worthwhile because thousands of community supporters have volunteered their time, donated their cash, read our newsletters, and worked together with us to build radical alternatives.

Jura Books
440 Parramatta Rd, Petersham, Sydney, New South Wales, Australia

www.jura.org.au

ABOUT FREEDOM PRESS

The oldest anarchist publishing house in the English-speaking world, Freedom Press was founded in London by a group of volunteers including Charlotte Wilson and Peter Kropotkin in 1886.

The Press has repeatedly been the target of state repression, from crackdowns in the 1890s to raids during World War I and most famously, at the end of World War II. The 1945 free speech case, which saw four editors of its journal *War Commentary* arrested for causing "disaffection in the armed forces," prompted support from many famous names including Herbert Read, George Orwell, Benjamin Britten, and E.M. Forster. Three were jailed.

Despite this and many other threats, from fascists to organised crime, for over a century Freedom has regularly published works on the philosophy and activities of anarchists, and produced its *Freedom Newspaper* for the best part of a century. Freedom now maintains an anarchist-focused news site, www.freedomnews.org.uk, and publishes a biannual free journal.

Freedom runs Britain's largest anarchist bookshop at its home of more than 50 years in Whitechapel, in the heart of London. The upper floors of the Freedom building are home to a number of anarchist organisations, and the venue regularly hosts talks, meetings, and events for the wider movement.

About the Freedom Press Library Series

Freedom Press has partnered with PM Press to republish titles from Freedom's back catalogue, bringing important works back into circulation with new introductions and additional commentary. *Collectives in the Spanish Revolution* is part of this series.

Freedom Press
84b Whitechapel High St
London, E1 7QX

www.freedompress.org.uk
www.freedomnews.org.uk

The CNT in the Spanish Revolution Vols. 1–3

José Peirats
with an introduction by Chris Ealham

Vol. 1 **ISBN: 978-1-60486-207-2**
     $28.00   432 pages

Vol. 2 **ISBN: 978-1-60486-208-9**
     $22.95   312 pages

Vol. 3 **ISBN: 978-1-60486-209-6**
     $22.95   296 pages

The CNT in the Spanish Revolution is the history of one of the most original and audacious, and arguably also the most far-reaching, of all the twentieth-century revolutions. It is the history of the giddy years of political change and hope in 1930s Spain, when the so-called 'Generation of '36', Peirats' own generation, rose up against the oppressive structures of Spanish society. It is also a history of a revolution that failed, crushed in the jaws of its enemies on both the reformist left and the reactionary right. José Peirats' account is effectively the official CNT history of the war, passionate, partisan but, above all, intelligent. Its huge sweeping canvas covers all areas of the anarchist experience—the spontaneous militias, the revolutionary collectives, the moral dilemmas occasioned by the clash of revolutionary ideals and the stark reality of the war effort against Franco and his German Nazi and Italian Fascist allies.

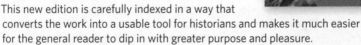

This new edition is carefully indexed in a way that converts the work into a usable tool for historians and makes it much easier for the general reader to dip in with greater purpose and pleasure.

"José Peirats' The CNT in the Spanish Revolution *is a landmark in the historiography of the Spanish Civil War. . . . Originally published in Toulouse in the early 1950s, it was a rarity anxiously searched for by historians and others who gleefully pillaged its wealth of documentation. Even its republication in Paris in 1971 by the exiled Spanish publishing house, Ruedo Ibérico, though welcome, still left the book in the territory of specialists. For that reason alone, the present project to publish the entire work in English is to be applauded."*
—Professor Paul Preston, London School of Economics

Life and Ideas: The Anarchist Writings of Errico Malatesta

Errico Malatesta
Edited by Vernon Richards
with a Foreword by Carl Levy

ISBN: 978-1-62963-032-8
$21.95   320 pages

With the timely reprinting of this selection of Malatesta's writings, first published in 1965 by Freedom Press, the full range of this great anarchist activist's ideas are once again in circulation. *Life and Ideas* gathers excerpts from Malatesta's writings over a lifetime of revolutionary activity.

The editor, Vernon Richards, has translated hundreds of articles by Malatesta, taken from the journals Malatesta either edited himself or contributed to, from the earliest, *L'En Dehors* of 1892, through to *Pensiero e Volontà*, which was forced to close by Mussolini's fascists in 1926, and the bilingual *Il Risveglio/Le Réveil*, which published most of his writings after that date. These articles have been pruned down to their essentials and collected under subheadings ranging from "Ends and Means" to "Anarchist Propaganda." Through the selections Malatesta's classical anarchism emerges: a revolutionary, nonpacifist, nonreformist vision informed by decades of engagement in struggle and study. In addition there is a short biographical piece and an essay by the editor.

"The first thing that strikes the reader about Malatesta is his lucidity and straightforwardness. For him anarchism was not a philosophy for a future utopia which would come about one day as if by magic, or simply through the destruction of the state without any prior preparation. On the contrary, Malatesta was, throughout his life, concerned with a practical idea. His anarchism was something concrete, to be fought for and put into practice, not in some distant future but now. It is in this aspect of practical anarchism that gives him a special place amongst anarchist theorists and propagandists."
—Cienfuegos Press Anarchist Review

Pistoleros! The Chronicles of Farquhar McHarg – I: 1918

ISBN: 978-1-60486-401-4
$18.95   264 pages

Barcelona, 1976: Hired gunmen brutally murder
a lifelong friend and fellow anarchist, forcing
Farquhar McHarg into a race to document an
epic history before he too can be silenced. The
first volume of his memoirs finds him a Glasgow
boy, dropped by chance into Barcelona's
revolutionary underworld at the tail end of the
great imperialist war of 1914–1918, recruited by Spanish anarchists to act as
a go-between with Britain's Secret Service Bureau. McHarg tells of a corrupt
and brutal Spanish regime, bent on bringing a rebellious working class back
under its heel, and the generous and recklessly idealistic men and women
who struggled to transform it after rejecting traditional party politics.

Pistoleros! is a thrilling tale of intrigue and romance, and a sweeping inside
view of the saboteurs and spies, the capitalists and bold insurrectionaries of
Spain's bloody past.

*"A young boy casts his fate with the wretched of the earth, leaps onto the back of
the mad bull that will become the Twentieth Century, and holds on for dear life!"*
—Bill Ayers

*"A rare plunge into the dark whirlpool of politics, passion and intrigue that swirled
around the docks, bars and tenements of Barcelona in 1918 . . . Pistoleros! is a
crack shot that rings out to remind us of times that were less bland."*
—Pauline Melville, actress and author of *Shape-Shifter* and *The Ventriloquist's
Tale*

*"Written with tremendous brio, this is a passionate and gripping tale of an
idealist's coming of age. McHarg's gripping narrative convincingly taps the rich
historical seams of intrigue, protest and conflict of an age in which many of the
streets of Barcelona became stained with blood."*
—Chris Ealham, author of *Class, Culture and Conflict in Barcelona 1898-1937*

The Floodgates of Anarchy

Stuart Christie and Albert Meltzer

ISBN: 978-1-60486-105-1
$15.95   144 pages

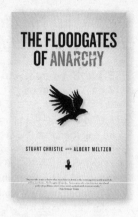

The floodgates holding back anarchy are constantly under strain. The liberal would ease the pressure by diverting some of the water; the conservative would shore up the dykes, the totalitarian would construct a stronger dam.

But is anarchy a destructive force? The absence of government may alarm the authoritarian, but is a liberated people really its own worst enemy—or is the true enemy of mankind, as the anarchists claim, the means by which he is governed? Without government the world could manage to end exploitation and war. Anarchy should not be confused with weak, divided or manifold government. As Christie and Meltzer point out, only with the total abolition of government can society develop in freedom.

"Anyone who wants to know what anarchism is about in the contemporary world would do well to start here. The Floodgates of Anarchy forces us to take a hard look at moral and political problems which other more sophisticated doctrines evade."
—*The Sunday Times*

"A lucid exposition of revolutionary anarchist theory."
—*Peace News*

"Coming from a position of uncompromising class struggle and a tradition that includes many of our exemplary anarchist militants, The Floodgates of Anarchy has a power and directness sadly missing from some contemporary anarchist writing. It is exciting to see it back in print, ready for a new generation to read."
—Barry Pateman, associate editor, The Emma Goldman Papers, University of California at Berkeley

Anarchy, Geography, Modernity: Selected Writings of Elisée Reclus

Edited by John P. Clark and
Camille Martin

ISBN: 978-1-60486-429-8
$22.95   304 pages

Anarchy, Geography, Modernity is the first
comprehensive introduction to the thought of
Elisée Reclus, the great anarchist geographer
and political theorist. It shows him to be an
extraordinary figure for his age. Not only an
anarchist but also a radical feminist, anti-racist, ecologist, animal rights
advocate, cultural radical, nudist, and vegetarian. Not only a major social
thinker but also a dedicated revolutionary.

The work analyzes Reclus' greatest achievement, a sweeping historical
and theoretical synthesis recounting the story of the earth and humanity
as an epochal struggle between freedom and domination. It presents his
groundbreaking critique of all forms of domination: not only capitalism, the
state, and authoritarian religion, but also patriarchy, racism, technological
domination, and the domination of nature. His crucial insights on the
interrelation between personal and small-group transformation, broader
cultural change, and large-scale social organization are explored. Reclus'
ideas are presented both through detailed exposition and analysis, and in
extensive translations of key texts, most appearing in English for the first
time.

*"For far too long Elisée Reclus has stood in the shadow of Godwin, Proudhon,
Bakunin, Kropotkin, and Emma Goldman. Now John Clark has pulled Reclus
forward to stand shoulder to shoulder with Anarchism's cynosures. Reclus' light
brought into anarchism's compass not only a focus on ecology, but a struggle
against both patriarchy and racism, contributions which can now be fully
appreciated thanks to John Clark's exegesis and [his and Camille Martin's]
translations of works previously unavailable in English. No serious reader can
afford to neglect this book."*
—Dana Ward, Pitzer College

*"Finally! A century after his death, the great French geographer and anarchist
Elisée Reclus has been honored by a vibrant selection of his writings expertly
translated into English."*
—Kent Mathewson, Louisiana State University

Kropotkin: The Politics of Community

Brian Morris

ISBN: 978-1-62963-505-7
$24.95   320 pages

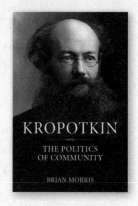

The nineteenth century witnessed the growth of anarchist literature, which advocated a society based on voluntary cooperation without government authority. Although his classical writings on mutual aid and the philosophy of anarchism are still published today, Peter Kropotkin remains a neglected figure. A talented geographer and a revolutionary socialist, Kropotkin was one of the most important theoreticians of the anarchist movement.

In *Kropotkin: The Politics of Community*, Brian Morris reaffirms with an attitude of critical sympathy the contemporary relevance of Kropotkin as a political and moral philosopher and as a pioneering social ecologist. Well-researched and wide-ranging, this volume not only presents an important contribution to the history of anarchism, both as a political tradition and as a social movement, but also offers insightful reflections on contemporary debates in political theory and ecological thought. After a short biographical note, the book analyzes in four parts Kropotkin's writings on anarchist communism, agrarian socialism, and integral education; modern science and evolutionary theory; the French Revolution and the modern state; and possessive individualism, terror, and war.

Standing as a comprehensive and engaging introduction to anarchism, social ecology, and the philosophy of evolutionary holism, *Kropotkin* is written in a straightforward manner that will appeal to those interested in social anarchism and in alternatives to neoliberal doctrines.

"Peter Kropotkin has been largely ignored as a utopian crackpot, but Brian Morris demonstrates in this wide-ranging and detailed analysis that Kropotkin addressed significantly and perceptively the major issues of the present day."
—Harold B. Barclay, author of *People without Government: An Anthropology of Anarchy*

Anarchy and the Sex Question: Essays on Women and Emancipation, 1896–1926

Emma Goldman
Edited by Shawn P. Wilbur

ISBN: 978-1-62963-144-8
$14.95   160 pages

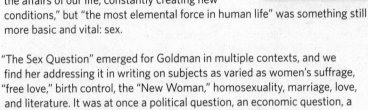

For Emma Goldman, the "High Priestess of
Anarchy," anarchism was "a living force in
the affairs of our life, constantly creating new
conditions," but "the most elemental force in human life" was something still
more basic and vital: sex.

"The Sex Question" emerged for Goldman in multiple contexts, and we
find her addressing it in writing on subjects as varied as women's suffrage,
"free love," birth control, the "New Woman," homosexuality, marriage, love,
and literature. It was at once a political question, an economic question, a
question of morality, and a question of social relations.

But her analysis of that most elemental force remained fragmentary,
scattered across numerous published (and unpublished) works and
conditioned by numerous contexts. *Anarchy and the Sex Question* draws
together the most important of those scattered sources, uniting both familiar
essays and archival material, in an attempt to recreate the great work on sex
that Emma Goldman might have given us. In the process, it sheds light on
Goldman's place in the history of feminism.

*"Emma Goldman left a profound legacy of wisdom, insight, and passionate
commitment to life. Shawn Wilbur has carefully selected her best writings on
that most profound, pleasurable, and challenging of topics: sex. This collection is
a great service to anarchist, feminist, and queer communities around the world."*
—Jamie Heckert, coeditor of *Anarchism & Sexuality: Ethics, Relationships and
Power*

*"Shawn Wilbur has done a great job assembling and introducing Emma
Goldman's writings on women, feminism, and sexuality. As he notes, Goldman's
essays continue to provoke and inspire. The collection artfully documents the
evolution of Goldman's views on freedom, sex, and human liberation."*
—Robert Graham, editor of *Anarchism: A Documentary History of Libertarian
Ideas*

Revolution and Other Writings:
A Political Reader

Gustav Landauer
Edited and translated by Gabriel Kuhn
ISBN: 978-1-60486-054-2
$26.95   360 pages

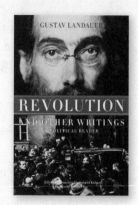

"Landauer is the most important agitator of the radical and revolutionary movement in the entire country." This is how Gustav Landauer is described in a German police file from 1893. Twenty-six years later, Landauer would die at the hands of reactionary soldiers who overthrew the Bavarian Council Republic, a three-week attempt to realize libertarian socialism amidst the turmoil of post-World War I Germany. It was the last chapter in the life of an activist, writer, and mystic who Paul Avrich calls "the most influential German anarchist intellectual of the twentieth century."

This is the first comprehensive collection of Landauer writings in English. It includes one of his major works, *Revolution*, thirty additional essays and articles, and a selection of correspondence. The texts cover Landauer's entire political biography, from his early anarchism of the 1890s to his philosophical reflections at the turn of the century, the subsequent establishment of the Socialist Bund, his tireless agitation against the war, and the final days among the revolutionaries in Munich. Additional chapters collect Landauer's articles on radical politics in the US and Mexico, and illustrate the scope of his writing with texts on corporate capital, language, education, and Judaism. The book includes an extensive introduction, commentary, and bibliographical information, compiled by the editor and translator Gabriel Kuhn as well as a preface by Richard Day.

"If there were any justice in this world—at least as far as historical memory goes—then Gustav Landauer would be remembered, right along with Bakunin and Kropotkin, as one of anarchism's most brilliant and original theorists. Instead, history has abetted the crime of his murderers, burying his work in silence. With this anthology, Gabriel Kuhn has single-handedly redressed one of the cruelest gaps in Anglo-American anarchist literature: the absence of almost any English translations of Landauer."
—Jesse Cohn, author of *Anarchism and the Crisis of Representation: Hermeneutics, Aesthetics, Politics*

Liberating Society from the State and Other Writings: A Political Reader

Erich Mühsam
Edited by Gabriel Kuhn

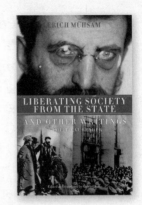

ISBN: 978-1-60486-055-9
$26.95   320 pages

Erich Mühsam (1878–1934), poet, bohemian, revolutionary, is one of Germany's most renowned and influential anarchists. Born into a middle-class Jewish family, he challenged the conventions of bourgeois society at the turn of the century, engaged in heated debates on the rights of women and homosexuals, and traveled Europe in search of radical communes and artist colonies. He was a primary instigator of the ill-fated Bavarian Council Republic in 1919 and held the libertarian banner high during a Weimar Republic that came under increasing threat by right-wing forces. In 1933, four weeks after Hitler's ascension to power, Mühsam was arrested in his Berlin home. He spent the last sixteen months of his life in detention and died in the Oranienburg Concentration Camp in July 1934.

Mühsam wrote poetry, plays, essays, articles, and diaries. His work unites a burning desire for individual liberation with anarcho-communist convictions, and bohemian strains with syndicalist tendencies. The body of his writings is immense, yet hardly any English translations have been available before now. This collection presents not only *Liberating Society from the State: What Is Communist Anarchism?*, Mühsam's main political pamphlet and one of the key texts in the history of German anarchism, but also some of his best-known poems, unbending defenses of political prisoners, passionate calls for solidarity with the lumpenproletariat, recollections of the utopian community of Monte Verità, debates on the rights of homosexuals and women, excerpts from his journals, and essays contemplating German politics and anarchist theory as much as Jewish identity and the role of intellectuals in the class struggle.

An appendix documents the fate of Zenzl Mühsam, who, after her husband's death, escaped to the Soviet Union where she spent twenty years in Gulag camps.

"We need new ideas. How about studying the ideal for which Erich Mühsam lived, worked, and died?"
—Augustin Souchy, author of *Beware Anarchist: A Life for Freedom*

All Power to the Councils!
A Documentary History of the
German Revolution of 1918–1919

Edited and translated by Gabriel Kuhn

ISBN: 978-1-60486-111-2
$26.95   352 pages

The German Revolution erupted out of the ashes of World War I, triggered by mutinying sailors refusing to be sacrificed in the final carnage of the war. While the Social Democrats grabbed power, radicals across the country rallied to establish a communist society under the slogan "All Power to the Councils!" The Spartacus League launched an uprising in Berlin, council republics were proclaimed in Bremen and Bavaria, and workers' revolts shook numerous German towns. Yet in an act that would tragically shape the course of history, the Social Democratic government crushed the rebellions with the help of right-wing militias, paving the way for the ill-fated Weimar Republic—and ultimately the ascension of the Nazis.

This definitive documentary history collects manifestos, speeches, articles, and letters from the German Revolution—Rosa Luxemburg, the Revolutionary Stewards, and Gustav Landauer amongst others—introduced and annotated by the editor. Many documents, such as the anarchist Erich Mühsam's comprehensive account of the Bavarian Council Republic, are presented here in English for the first time. The volume also includes materials from the Red Ruhr Army that repelled the reactionary Kapp Putsch in 1920 and the communist bandits that roamed Eastern Germany until 1921. *All Power to the Councils!* provides a dynamic and vivid picture of a time of great hope and devastating betrayal.

"Gabriel Kuhn's excellent volume illuminates a profound global revolutionary moment, in which brilliant ideas and debates lit the sky."
—Marcus Rediker, author of *Villains of All Nations* and *The Slave Ship*

"This remarkable collection, skillfully edited by Gabriel Kuhn, brings to life that most pivotal of revolutions, crackling with the acrid odor of street fighting, insurgent hopes, and ultimately defeat… In an era brimming with anticapitalist aspirations, these pages ring with that still unmet revolutionary promise of a better world: I was, I am, I shall be."
—Sasha Lilley, author of *Capital and Its Discontents* and coauthor of *Catastrophism*